MW00808711

Designing and Analyzing Language Tests

Also published in
Oxford Handbooks for Language Teachers

Designing and Analyzing Language Tests

Nathan T. Carr

OXFORD
UNIVERSITY PRESS

OXFORD
UNIVERSITY PRESS

Great Clarendon Street, Oxford OX2 6DP

Oxford University Press is a department of the University of Oxford.
It furthers the University's objective of excellence in research, scholarship,
and education by publishing worldwide in

Oxford New York

Auckland Cape Town Dar es Salaam Hong Kong Karachi
Kuala Lumpur Madrid Melbourne Mexico City Nairobi
New Delhi Shanghai Taipei Toronto

With offices in

Argentina Austria Brazil Chile Czech Republic France Greece
Guatemala Hungary Italy Japan Poland Portugal Singapore
South Korea Switzerland Thailand Turkey Ukraine Vietnam

OXFORD and OXFORD ENGLISH are registered trade marks of
Oxford University Press in the UK and in certain other countries

© Oxford University Press 2011

The moral rights of the author have been asserted

Database right Oxford University Press (maker)

First published 2011
2015 2014 2013 2012 2011
10 9 8 7 6 5 4 3 2 1

No unauthorized photocopying

All rights reserved. No part of this publication may be reproduced,
stored in a retrieval system, or transmitted, in any form or by any means,
without the prior permission in writing of Oxford University Press, or as
expressly permitted by law, or under terms agreed with the appropriate
reprographics rights organization. Enquiries concerning reproduction
outside the scope of the above should be sent to the ELT Rights Department,
Oxford University Press, at the address above

You must not circulate this book in any other binding or cover
and you must impose this same condition on any acquirer

Any websites referred to in this publication are in the public domain and
their addresses are provided by Oxford University Press for information only.
Oxford University Press disclaims any responsibility for the content

ISBN: 978 0 19 442295 6   Book
ISBN: 978 0 19 442296 3   CD-Rom
ISBN: 978 0 19 442297 0   Pack

Printed in China

This book is printed on paper from certified and well-managed sources.

ACKNOWLEDGEMENTS

*The authors and publisher are grateful to those who have given permission to reproduce
the following extracts of copyright material:* p.155 'Towards a model of test evaluation:
using the Test Fairness and the Test Context Frameworks' by Antony John
Kunnan in *Multilingualism and Assessment* by Lynda Taylor and Cyril J Weir (eds),
2008. Cambridge University Press. Reproduced by permission; p.211 Screenshot
of a Microsoft Excel 2007 Workbook containing three Worksheets and p.212
Screenshot of a Microsoft Excel 2003 Workbook containing one Worksheet.
Used with permission of Microsoft; p.130 Example of an analytic rating scale.
Used by permission of the ESL Service Courses, University of California, Los
Angeles; pp.138–142 ACTFL Proficiency Guidelines: Speaking (American Council
on the Teaching of Foreign Languages 1999. Used by permission of the American
Council on the Teaching of Foreign Languages.

Figures by Oxford Designers and Illustrators: p.115 Figure 6.1; p.188 Figures 10.1–
10.4; p.211 Figure 11.1; p.212 Figure 11.2; p.226 Figures 12.1–12.3; p.227 Figures
12.4–12.7; p.229 Figure 12.8; p.230 Figure 12.9; p.231 Figure 12.10; p.232 Figures
12.11–12.12; p.239 Figure 12.13; p.245 Figure 13.1–13.4; p.245 Figures 13.5–13.6;
p.246 Figures 13.7–13.12; p.260 Figures 14.1–14.2; p.263 Figures14.3–14.4

*Although every effort has been made to trace and contact copyright holders before
publication, this has not been possible in some cases. We apologise for any apparent
infringement of copyright and, if notified, the publisher will be pleased to rectify any
errors or omissions at the earliest possible opportunity.*

CONTENTS

PREFACE

This book would never have been started, much less finished, without the help and encouragement of a number of people. In particular, I am grateful to Julia Sallabank, who originally encouraged the project and oversaw its initiation at OUP; Julia Bell, the editor who very supportively oversaw the process of turning a manuscript into a finished product; two anonymous reviewers, who provided a number of helpful suggestions; Lynda Taylor, my content editor, who challenged me on points large and small, and really helped make this book much stronger and clearer; James Greenan, the copy editor, who helped polish the text, providing many valuable suggestions on points throughout, in a way that only an informed nonspecialist could; and Publishing Manager Catherine Kneafsey and Editor Natasha Forrest, who were also of assistance during the writing process. Of course, the blame for any remaining errors, omissions, and infelicities rests with me.

I owe a great debt of thanks to many others, for encouragement, advice, error spotting, and many other things. In particular, these included (in alphabetical order): Ben Bangs, Kyle Crocco, Chad Davison, Jan Eyring, Juan Carlos Gallego, Peter Groves, Jinkyung Stephanie Kim, Antony Kunnan, Nancy Lay, Ashley Kyu-Youn Lee, Lorena Llosa, Michelle Luster, Mary Ann Lyman-Hager, Teruo Masuda, Gary Ockey, Rene Palafox, Amparo Pedroza, Vanessa Russell, M. Trevor Shanklin, Simeon Slovacek, Hyun-Jung Suk, Debbie Thiercof, Xiaoming Xi, and Cheryl Zimmerman. Thanks also to the other students in my language testing course at California State University, Fullerton, and the participants in two summer workshops at the San Diego State University Language Acquisition Resource Center, who provided the impetus for developing the materials that developed into this book, and gave extensive feedback in class as things evolved.

I also wish to extend my appreciation to the American Council on the Teaching of Foreign Languages, the UCLA ESL Service Courses Program, and the University of Cambridge Press for their gracious permission to reproduce material here.

Thanks are also due to Lyle Bachman, not only for teaching me about language assessment, but training me in how to think about and approach it as well; and to Dilin Liu, for advising me to specialize in testing, rather than some other area of applied linguistics.

Finally, I wish to thank my family for their encouragement and support throughout this process. In particular, my wife Eva has waited while her husband practically disappeared to sit at the computer writing. She has endured far too many days, nights, and weekends without my company, as our dog Odo would wander back and forth to check on each of us, and as the writing and editing process dragged on. And on. And then on some more. This book would not have been possible without her love, support, patience, and understanding.

LIST OF ACRONYMS AND ABBREVIATIONS

α	Cronbach's alpha
λ	cut score
Φ	index of dependability
ϕ	item phi; phi correlation coefficient
ρ	Spearman rho
$\Phi(\lambda)$	Phi(lambda)
AYL	assessing young learners
B, B-index	Brennan's B-index
B*	B-index for polytomous data
CAS	computer-automated scoring
CAT	computer-adaptive testing
CBT	computer-based testing
CI_{CRT}	criterion-referenced confidence interval
CRT CI	criterion-referenced confidence interval
CRT	criterion-referenced testing; criterion-referenced test
DI	difference index
DI*	difference index for polytomous data
G theory	generalizability theory
ID_{UL}	item discrimination
ID^*_{UL}	item discrimination index for polytomous data
IF	item facility
IF*	item facility for polytomous data
IRT	item response theory
M	mean
Mdn	median
Mo	mode
NRT	norm-referenced testing; norm-referenced test
p	item facility
P&P testing	paper-and-pencil testing

pb(r)	point-biserial item discrimination index or correlation coefficient
Q	semi-interquartile range
r	Pearson product-moment correlation coefficient (usually refered to as "Pearson *r*")
$r_{\text{item-total}}$	correlation between a polytomous item and total score (a Pearson *r*)
$r_{\text{item-mastery}}$	correlation between a polytomous item and test mastery/non-mastery
r(pb)	point-biserial item discrimination index or correlation coefficient
$r_{\text{p-bis}}$	point-biserial item discrimination index or correlation coefficient
r_{pbis}	point-biserial item discrimination index or correlation coefficient
s	standard deviation
s^2	variance
SD	standard deviation
SEM	standard error of measurement
VPA	verbal protocol analysis
WBT	web-based testing

INTRODUCTION

Language teachers often have to develop or choose tests or other assessments, whether for their whole school or their own classes, but often they do so with little or no training in what to do. Certainly, this was true for me the first time I was put in charge of testing for a language program, and I remember having little or no idea where to start. This book is intended to give teachers some idea of where to start, and to help them make better-informed decisions. The tests that they use should then be ones they can feel happier about using—there are few things as disheartening as working hard on a project, and doing the best job one can, but at the same time being sure there were important things done wrong or left undone, and having no idea what they were.

Who This Book Is For

The book is intended for two groups: students in introductory language testing courses (and naturally their instructors), and language teachers who need to create tests for themselves or their school or program, or who have test results that need analyzing. I have tried to make it something that will be useful for both groups, a textbook for students like the ones I teach in my own testing course, and a handbook or guide for teachers who may have no training in language assessment but who nonetheless have to make tests or make sense of testing data.

The Aims of This Book

The goal of the book is to help current and future teachers learn to develop and analyze their own tests. It should also be useful for helping teachers to choose from among commercially available tests, to decide to develop their own if nothing on the market is suitable, or to adapt existing tests to better meet their needs. It is *not* intended as a guide to important language tests in use around the world, although it should help readers to make better sense of the information test publishers provide, or help them realize when there is something off-base, incomplete, or suspicious-sounding about what is being claimed. By the end of the book, readers will be better placed to make informed decisions about assessment programs and the use of testing at their institution. Expertise in test writing and test analysis is generally achieved through years of practice and experience, but this book will provide pre-service and in-service teachers with a valuable introduction to the tools necessary for these tasks, as well as useful advice for those interested in learning more on various topics.

The Organization of This Book

This book is organized into two parts, conveniently labeled "Part I" and "Part II." Part I addresses fundamental concepts of language assessment, explains how to plan, write, and administer tests, provides a conceptual overview of how to score and analyze test results, and gives an overview of test validation procedures, as well as a basic orientation to several more advanced topics in language testing.

Part II explains in detail the quantitative procedures that should be used to describe test results, identify problematic test questions, estimate measurement error, and so forth. Each of these chapters begins with an explanation of the concepts, and is followed by one or two practice worksheets. Each worksheet is accompanied by detailed directions on how to complete it using Microsoft Excel. The DVD inside the back cover of this book contains the Excel files used in the worksheets, a completed version of each file showing the correct formulas, and video tutorials demonstrating how to do the worksheets. The tutorials use Flash, and should be viewable in any Flash-enabled web browser, although they have only been tested in Mozilla Firefox, Google Chrome, and Microsoft Internet Explorer. Each tutorial consists of a recording of my computer screen as I work through a worksheet, and includes my step-by-step narration of the process.

For a detailed listing of the topics covered, please see the Table of Contents.

How to Use This Book

My practice when using this book with my own class, as part of a 15-week, 45-hour introductory course on language testing, is to cover two chapters a week, one from Part I and another from Part II. I spend two weeks apiece on Chapters 15 and 18, however, since each has two worksheets. Doing this gives the students time to move through the statistical portion of the book at a pace of one lesson per week, rather than two per week concentrated at the end of the course. Given that many language teachers have a certain amount of math anxiety, spreading the quantitative portions out, rather than compressing them, strikes me as less stressful for both students and instructors. This approach of interleaving the two parts also allows midterm exams, if they are used in a class, to assess both conceptual and quantitative aspects of the text, and it gives those students who are having initial difficulty with the math more time to catch up.

Why Excel?

Some readers may wonder why this book uses Excel for the quantitative chapters. In some cases, the question is asked in the sense of "Why do we need to do math when we are testing language?" To that, I would answer that if we want to say how well students did on a test, we will not be able to speak in more than vague generalities—unless we can use descriptive statistics (Chapter 12), or graph their performance (Chapter 13). Furthermore, we will not know which test questions are doing a good job ("good job" being defined later in the book; see Chapters 5, 15, and 16), which incorrect answers to multiple-choice questions are working and which are not (Chapter 17), or how consistent scores are on a test (Chapters 6, 18, and 19). We will not be able to say how closely related scores were on two different parts of a test, or on two different tests (Chapter 14). And of course, if we want to average our students' grades at the end of a course (Chapter 11), the process is far neater, faster, and less painful with Excel than with paper, pencil, and a calculator or abacus. I would also point out that Excel is not a program for people who enjoy doing math, but rather a program for people who need to do some math but would rather tell a computer to do it for them.

Other readers will answer "Yes, yes, but why not something more powerful, such as" (insert the name of your favorite statistics package here). For more advanced statistical procedures, I certainly would not recommend Excel, since it is not really a statistics program. For the analyses covered in this book, however, it is quite adequate, and even preferable in some regards. First and foremost, nearly everyone around the world with access to a computer has access to it, and it is far cheaper than most statistics programs. Furthermore, most statistics packages cannot do certain types of item analyses (particularly calculating the upper-lower item discrimination, B-index, or distractor point-biserials) without programming or other complex procedures. As a program for entering data, Excel is at least as flexible as anything else. Language teachers will probably find Excel more approachable than most statistics packages, and I would further argue that entering the formulas for themselves will help readers better understand what they are doing. And finally, figures generated in Excel can be reformatted rather easily, and are easily pasted into other applications such as Microsoft Word or Powerpoint.

Using the Glossary

When any of us first begin studying language testing, there is a great deal of new terminology to be learned. Even when the concepts are simple, the number of new terms being bandied about can be confusing at times. I have therefore included a glossary in this book, to make it faster and easier to look up terms that have been forgotten from earlier chapters, and to make studying easier for those readers who are using this as the textbook in a class on language assessment. At over 275 entries, including abbreviations, acronyms, and Greek letters, it is rather comprehensive, and covers all the terms introduced in bold throughout the book.

Notes on Terminology

Finally, for the sake of clarification, I should point out that I will often treat the terms *test* and *assessment* as almost interchangeable in this book. "Assessment" is a more superordinate term that includes tests, as well as any other tool (e.g., portfolios) used to make decisions about students' levels of language ability. Tests, on the other hand, are assessments that tend to be somewhat formal, and are often used for making high-stakes decisions—in terms of the grades assigned at the end of courses, if nothing else. Many people have additional assumptions about what tests are and what they look like, but as this book will show, many of those assumptions are based on what people have encountered in the past, and should not necessarily be taken as guidelines for good testing practice. Similarly, I will use the terms *examinee* and *test taker* interchangeably. I will sometimes also use *student*, particularly when the context is clearly related to assessment in the context of a class, language program, or school.

PART I

INTRODUCTION

Part I of this book deals with fundamental testing concepts, including consideration of the reasons for testing, how we look at tests and test scores, and some of the more common types of test tasks, before moving on to a discussion of the process of planning and creating tests. It presents conceptual overviews of the quantitative topics of analyzing items (test questions) and the consistency of scoring, but postpones the relevant calculations until Part II of the book. It then discusses the procedures for creating scoring rubrics or rating scales for speaking and listening tests, procedures for test validation and administration, and concludes with brief overviews of several additional topics that, while important in language testing research and practice, require greater coverage than is possible in an introductory textbook.

Each chapter in Part I includes recommendations for further reading on the topics covered, as well as discussion questions asking readers to relate the content of the chapter to teaching and testing situations with which they are familiar—whether as teachers or learners of a language.

1 WHAT ARE WE TESTING AND WHY?

Introduction

A key assumption made in this book is that tests are tools. We will begin by examining how this affects the ways in which we view tests, which leads to consideration of some common test purposes and types, followed by several contrasting paradigms, or ways of looking at tests. The question of what we want tests to tell us comes next, along with a discussion of how well a test needs to perform its appointed task and how we can judge this. The chapter concludes with an explanation of why graphs and descriptive statistics provide a crucial means of looking at test results.

Tests as Tools

One of the most important things to keep in mind when making or using language tests is that tests and other assessments are tools. We want to use a test or assessment for a particular reason, to do a certain job, not "just because." We should have in mind what that reason is, and who is likely to be taking the test, before we start planning the test—let alone before we start writing it. Almost without fail, the reason for giving the test will have something to do with making decisions about students, or other people (for example, prospective students, prospective employees, or people wanting to have their language ability certified for some purpose). These decisions, naturally, should inform the way that we design our tests (Mislevy 2007).Keeping in mind that a test is a tool can do a lot to clarify our thinking about how to use it. A particular tool is better for some tasks than for others, as anyone who has ever used pliers to remove a screw can understand. Similarly, a certain test might work quite well for one purpose, but not so well for something else. Some tools are poorly made, and are not useful for much of anything; so are some tests, particularly those that are random collections of questions thrown together without any planning. Likewise, some tools are well made, but are highly specialized; in the same way, a given test might be intended for a particular purpose, such as assessing the English-speaking ability of air traffic controllers, and it might do a wonderful job performing that task, but it might not be a good indicator of a doctor's ability to converse with nurses and patients.

Often, there may be several options available for a tool, some high-priced and some cheap, but one of the cheaper alternatives may do the job quite well enough, and while the more expensive options might work even better, they may not be better *enough* to justify the extra expense. Finally, to draw the tool analogy to a close, we should always keep in mind that nobody asks whether someone has a good tool that they can borrow. If someone needs a hammer, they ask for one, not for a screwdriver or wrench! In spite of this, though, it is an all-too-common occurrence for a teacher to ask colleagues if they know any good tests that can be used.

Keeping this firmly in mind, we will next consider some of the purposes we use tests for, and some of the ways we look at test results.

Test Purposes and Types

As Brown (1995) points out, language tests are normally used to help make decisions, and there are a number of types of decisions that they can be used for. We generally refer to tests, in fact, by the type of decision they are used to make. I think it is useful to divide these test and decision types into two broad categories: those that are closely related to a teaching or learning curriculum, and those that are not. I use this distinction because curriculum-related tests all have a specific domain—the curriculum—to which we can refer when planning and writing these tests. In contrast, when a test is not based on a particular curriculum, we have the burden or freedom (depending on one's point of view) of deciding what specifically it *should* be based on.

These types of tests are summarized in Table 1.1. Brief consideration, of course, will show that many tests are used for more than one purpose; I will refer to several common types of overlap in the following discussion. This is not necessarily problematic.

Furthermore, as will become evident shortly, the dividing line between one type of test and another is not always as clear and sharp as we might pretend. Nevertheless, there are several clearly identifiable types of decisions that are informed by testing, for which some sort of classification system is useful. Because the actual use of a test may change from what was originally planned, it is important to think in terms of types of *decisions* more so than types of tests *per se*; however, it is common in actual usage to *refer* to types of tests as a convenient shorthand.

Curriculum-related decisions	Other decision types
Admission (sometimes including screening)	Proficiency
Placement	Screening
Diagnostic	
Progress	
Achievement	

Table 1.1 Test Purposes and Types

Curriculum-Related Tests

The first type of curriculum-related test that a new student might encounter is an **admission test**, which is used to decide whether a student should be admitted to the program at all; this could of course be viewed as a screening test for a language program (see below), illustrating that, as noted earlier, the lines between categories can often be rather fuzzy. A related type of test is a **placement test**, which is used to decide at which level in the language program a student should study. The student then gets "placed" into that level—hence the name. In many cases, a single test might be used for both purposes: to decide whether a student's language ability is adequate for even the lowest level in the program (admission decisions), and if they pass that threshold, to decide which level is most appropriate for them (placement decisions).

Diagnostic tests are used to identify learners' areas of strength and weakness. Sometimes diagnostic information is obtained from placement (or admissions) tests, but sometimes diagnostic tests are administered separately once students have already been placed into the appropriate levels. Some language programs also use diagnostic tests to confirm that students were placed accurately. This can be a good idea, especially if a program is not highly confident in its placement procedures, but it is debatable whether this is actually a diagnostic purpose *per se*. Diagnostic information can be used to help teachers plan what points to cover in class, to help them identify what areas a student may need extra help with, or to help students know which areas they need to focus on in their learning.

Once students are placed appropriately, teachers may wish to find out whether or how well their students are learning what is being taught. **Progress tests** assess how well students are doing in terms of mastering course content and meeting course objectives. This is done from the point of view that the learning is still ongoing—that is, that students are not expected to have mastered the material yet. Many progress decisions in the classroom do not involve testing, however, but are made informally, in the midst of teaching (see, for example, Leung 2004). This is often referred to as monitoring, or "just paying attention," and is assumed to be a fundamental part of teaching, but this does not make it any less a form of assessment. More formally, we often refer to smaller progress assessments as quizzes. However, to the extent that we are using these assessments—quizzes, tests, or whatever—to grade students, we are assessing something other than progress. **Achievement tests** are those that are used to identify how well students have met course objectives or mastered course content. To a large extent, the question of whether a particular test or quiz is an achievement or progress test depends upon how it is being used. To the extent that the test is used to make decisions about what or how fast to teach, it is a progress test, and to the extent that it is used to make decisions about how individual students have learned what they were supposed to, it is an achievement test.

For example, imagine that a test is given in the middle of a course. It is used to assign grades for how well students have learned the material in the first half of the course, but it is also used by the teacher to decide whether any of those points need to be reviewed in class. In such a case, the test is both a progress and an achievement test. As a second example, consider a test given at the very end of a course. This test is used to assign grades to students—to make decisions about how much learning they have achieved in the course—so it is purely an achievement test. In considering whether a test is actually serving as an assessment of progress, achievement, or both—regardless of what it is being *called* by a teacher or program—the key is to think in terms of the type(s) of decisions being made. This is especially important when the actual use of a test has changed from what was intended when it was originally designed.

Moving beyond the level of an individual course, achievement tests can also be used at the level of the school or language program for decisions about whether to promote students to the next level or tier of levels, or for program exit or graduation decisions. Often, of course, practicality dictates that achievement testing for such purposes be combined with end-of-course achievement testing.

Finally, there are two additional types of test-based decisions that closely relate to language curricula and programs, but which do not involve their "own" types of tests. The first involves program evaluation—one source of evidence to use when evaluating a program's effectiveness is tests. While we may want to consider the results of placement tests—and how good a job of placing students they seem to be doing—we may also want to examine achievement test results. In particular, if achievement tests are used at the end of a course, or for graduation, and if these tests are clearly tied to the goals and objectives (Brown 1995) of the course or program, then student performance on those tests should tell us something about how well the program is working.

A second type of curriculum-related decision that tests can help with involves the curriculum planning process. When trying to identify the needs of learners, or—in the case of a new program—prospective learners, we may wish to give a test to the students or potential students to see what they already know and what they still need to learn. Any of the types of tests just discussed might be used for this, although diagnostic, placement, and achievement tests are probably the most likely. One other type of test that might be used, however, is proficiency testing, which—unlike the types just described—is *not* generally tied to a particular language program.

Other Types of Tests

There are two closely related test types that are not usually associated with any of the aspects of a language curriculum, but with which teachers should be familiar nonetheless. The first and most important of these is **proficiency tests**, which assess an examinee's level of language ability, but do so without respect to a particular curriculum. Typically, this involves assessing more than one narrow aspect of language ability; for example, one well-known proficiency test, the Test of English for International Communication (TOEIC; Educational Testing Service 2009b) has long included an assessment of both listening and reading ability, and now includes an optional test of speaking and writing. Similarly, the five Cambridge Main Suite exams all include assessments of reading, writing, speaking, and listening, as well as "use of English" at the more advanced levels (University of Cambridge ESOL Examinations 2008).

When proficiency tests are used to make selection decisions—most commonly about whether someone is sufficiently proficient in the target language to be qualified for a particular job—they are called **screening tests**. Technically, the admission tests discussed above are a type of screening test, but in an academic context. We will limit the use of the term, however, to those tests that involve non-academic selection decisions.

Ways of Looking at Tests

Besides classifying tests by the types of decisions they are used to inform, we can also view them in several other ways. These involve considering tests in terms of frameworks for interpreting results, the things that examinees have to do during the test, and the ways that the tests are scored.

Norm-Referenced and Criterion-Referenced Testing

One major way in which test results can be interpreted from different perspectives involves the distinction between norm- and criterion-referenced testing, two different frames of reference that we can use to interpret test scores. As Thorndike and Hagen (1969) point out, a test score, especially just the number of questions answered correctly, "taken by itself, has no meaning. It gets meaning only by comparison with some reference" (Thorndike and Hagen: 241). That comparison may be with other students, or it might be with some pre-established standard or criterion, and the difference between norm- and criterion-referenced tests derives from which of these types of criterion is being used.

Norm-referenced tests (NRTs) are tests on which an examinee's results are interpreted by comparing them to how well others did on the test. NRT scores are often reported in terms of test takers' **percentile scores**, that is, the percentage of other examinees who scored below them. (Naturally, percentiles are most commonly used in large-scale testing; otherwise, it does not make much sense to divide test takers into 100 groups!). Those others may be all the other examinees who took the test, or, in the context of large-scale testing, they may be the **norming sample**—a representative group that took the test before it entered operational use, and whose scores were used for purposes such as estimating item (i.e. test question) difficulty and establishing the correspondence between test scores and percentiles. The norming sample needs to be large enough to ensure that the results are not due to chance—for example, if we administer a test to only 10 people, that is too few for us to make any kind of trustworthy generalizations about test difficulty. In practical terms, this means that most norm-referenced tests have norming samples of several hundred or even several thousand; the number depends in part on how many people are likely to take the test after it becomes operational.

The major drawback of norm-referenced tests is that they tell test users how a particular examinee performed with respect to other examinees, *not* how well that person did in absolute terms. In other words, we do not know how much ability or knowledge they demonstrated, except that it was more or less than a certain percentage of other test takers. That limitation is why criterion-referenced tests are so important, because we usually want to know more about students than that. "About average," "a little below average," and "better than most of the others" by themselves do not tell teachers much about a learner's ability *per se*. On the other hand, **criterion-referenced tests (CRTs)** assess language ability in terms of how much learners know in "absolute" terms, that is, in relation to one or more standards, objectives, or other criteria, and not with respect to how much other learners know. When students take a CRT, we are interested in how much ability or knowledge they are demonstrating with reference to an external standard of performance, rather than with reference to how anyone else performed. CRT scores are generally reported in terms of the percentage correct, *not* percentile. Thus, it is possible for all of the examinees taking a test to pass it on a CRT; in fact, this is generally desirable in criterion-referenced achievement tests, since most teachers hope that all their students have mastered the course content.

Note also that besides being reported in terms of percentage correct, scores may also be reported in terms of a **scoring rubric** or a **rating scale**, particularly in the case of speaking or writing tests. When this is done with a CRT, however, the score bands are not defined in terms of below or above "average" or "most students," but rather in terms of how well the student performed—that is, how much ability he or she demonstrated. A rubric that defined score bands in terms of the "average," "usual," or "most students," for example, would be norm-referenced.

One important feature of CRTs is that they normally include the use of a **cut score**; that is, a particular score is established as a standard for meeting the criterion, for passing or failing, or for being considered to have demonstrated mastery or non-mastery of the material. Frequently, there will be more than one cut score on a given CRT. This is the case, for example, in placement testing: A cut score divides each pair of adjacent levels (for example, a five-level curriculum will require four cut scores). In classroom grading, there are also multiple cut scores; in the American system, for example, the traditional cut scores are 90%, 80%, 70%, and 60%, for assigning the grades of A, B, C, D, and F. In cases where there is plus/minus grading, there are 12 cut scores: A+/A, A/A-, and so on.

Generally speaking, CRTs are most commonly tied to language curricula, and report how much of the curriculum students have mastered, what portions they still need to master, or what level of the curriculum would be most appropriate for them. On the other hand, one common use for NRTs is for proficiency testing, and thus such tests will report test takers' ability in relation to that of others who have taken the test. It is important to keep in mind, however, that while proficiency tests do not *need* to be norm-referenced, it can be easier to develop this type of test, which merely ranks or orders test takers, than a CRT proficiency test, which requires that results be reported in terms of a framework of language ability.

One noteworthy example of a CRT proficiency test is the American Council on the Teaching of Foreign Languages Oral Proficiency Interview (Swender, Breiner-Sanders, Laughlin, Lowe, and Miles 1999), which rates examinees in terms of the ACTFL Speaking Proficiency Guidelines (American Council on the Teaching of Foreign Languages 1999). Rather than numerical scores, the OPI classifies test takers as being at various levels: Novice-Low, Novice-Mid, Novice-High, Intermediate-Low, Intermediate-Mid, and so on. Another example of a CRT proficiency test is the IELTS (International English Language Testing System; University of Cambridge ESOL Examinations 2009), which assigns scores from 1("non user") to 9 ("expert user"), along with brief descriptions of the language ability of test takers at each level.

Similarly, most tests which integrate multiple skills (for example, reading and writing; see below for a discussion of integrated tests) tend to be CRTs, but that is not an automatic thing. In fact, it is impossible to tell merely by looking at a test whether it is a CRT or NRT. The key is not the purpose, or the types of test tasks, but the way in which scores are interpreted—in terms of other people's performance, in terms of the overall amount of knowledge or ability demonstrated, or perhaps even in some combination of the two, since it may be that a test combines features of both a norm-referenced and criterion-referenced approach. When students' performance is interpreted in terms of the class or group average, or in comparison to "the average student," those are norm-referenced interpretations. In particular, when teachers decide that an average score is a C, and that a certain number of points above average is a B, and so on, that test is being interpreted as an NRT, even if the teacher uses the *term* criterion (for example, "I have set the criterion for earning an A at two **standard deviations** above the mean, so only the top two percent of students will receive this grade"). When we make a criterion-referenced interpretation, we are concerned with how well a student did without reference to anyone else's score. This does *not* mean that averages and other **descriptive statistics** are not useful in CRTs, but it means we do not use them in the same way that we would in NRTs. (See Chapter 12 for further discussion of descriptive statistics, why they are used, and how they are interpreted.)

Summative vs. Formative Assessment

Another way of looking at and using tests and other assessments also involves two **interpretive frameworks**, but these frameworks have more to do with when tests are administered, and the purposes the results are used for. **Summative assessments** are typically given at the end of a unit, course, program, etc., and they provide information about how much students learned. They are therefore closely related to achievement tests, and in fact, most achievement testing is largely summative, and summative testing usually aims to assess learner achievement. On the other hand, **formative assessments** take place while students are still in the process of learning something and are used to monitor how well that learning is progressing (see, for example, Leung 2004). They are therefore closely related to progress assessment, and to the extent that the results of an assessment are used to guide the subsequent teaching and learning process, such assessment is formative. One way to keep the distinction between these two perspectives clear is to remember that summative assessments are used to sum up how well someone did, and formative assessments are used to shape or form what is being taught.

These two assessment types are usually viewed as being a dichotomy, but they are probably better thought of as being the endpoints of a continuum. For example, if a teacher informally assesses how well his students are mastering something being taught that day, without assigning any grades, this is clearly formative, and not summative at all. Similarly, if a student is required to take a test in order to graduate from a program, that is clearly a summative assessment. On the other hand, however, if a teacher gives a quiz over material that has been covered recently, and uses the results to both assign grades and decide whether to review the material further or move on to something else, the quiz is clearly performing both summative and formative functions, respectively. As an additional, learner-centered example, if a course includes a quiz at the end of every lesson, it could be put to multiple uses. If learners use the quiz to decide whether they are satisfied with how much they have learned on the topic, that would be a summative function, while if they use it to decide whether they need to review the material further before moving on, that would be a formative use of the quiz.

As a final note on this topic, a similar distinction is often made in the area of educational evaluation, where programs, courses, and so forth can be evaluated from a summative or formative perspective.

Objective vs. Subjective Testing

Several other ways of looking at tests are fairly common, but nevertheless offer mistaken or inaccurate perspectives. One of these is the false distinction between objective and subjective testing. A so-called **objective test** is one that can be scored objectively, and therefore uses selected-response questions (particularly multiple-choice questions, but sometimes true-false or matching questions as well). A **subjective test**, on the other hand, is one that involves human judgment to score, as in most tests of writing or speaking. As testing researcher Lyle Bachman (Bachman 1990) has pointed out, however, there are several problems with these terms. First of all, we should consider where the questions on an "objective" test come from. Even the most principled expert planning decisions about what to assess and how to do it are somewhat subjective, as are any decisions made in the course of writing the actual test.

For example, imagine the case of teachers creating a final exam for a course on academic reading. Before they start writing the test, they make decisions as to what topics to use for reading passages, how long passages should be, how many passages and questions to include on the test, what types of questions they need (for example, main idea, reading for details, scanning, and inference questions), and how many of each type they want. Then, when they start writing the test, they make decisions about which reading passages to copy, or make decisions throughout the course of writing their own passages. Every question that they write is the product of multiple decisions about its content, intended purpose, and what choices they want to include. No matter how appropriate these decisions are, every one of them is clearly subjective to one degree or another.

On the other hand, "subjective" tests are not necessarily as subjective as their label might suggest. With the use of clearly written scoring rubrics (also referred to as rating scales), and rater training and **norming** using example responses, much of the subjectivity in scoring can be reduced. If appropriate record keeping and statistics are used, it can be monitored and reduced even further. As an example, if a language program uses a placement test that includes a writing section, just having teachers read the writing samples and assign a score based on their individual judgment would be highly subjective. In contrast, if the program had a clear scoring rubric, trained teachers in how to apply it, and kept track of how consistent scoring was for individual teachers and for all the teachers as a group, much of the subjectivity would be taken out of the process. It could still be *argued* that the scoring rubric was subjectively derived, but that argument could probably be countered fairly successfully. Thus, the terms objective and subjective should at most be used to refer to the scoring method used, not the overall test itself, and even then, the scoring is not quite as sharp or fuzzy as those two labels might imply.

The important question is therefore not whether a test is "objective" or "subjective," but where subjectivity and measurement error will come into play, and how that subjectivity and error can best be reduced. Generally speaking, this requires that any decisions about the test—including decisions about its planning, creation, administration, and scoring—be made consciously, that is, in a carefully considered manner. Reflective decisions are more likely to have some principled basis and thus be more defensible than those that are made implicitly or reflexively, without consideration or forethought. Obviously, making all decisions *conscious* decisions requires planning, which will be discussed in greater detail in Chapters 3 and 4. The need to make defensible decisions, and to show that assessments are appropriate for their intended uses, will be discussed later in this chapter, and in greater detail in Chapter 8. Once a test has been constructed, there are ways to estimate the level of measurement error, and to identify test questions that are likely causing a disproportionate share of that error; these topics are the focus of the quantitative chapters of this book and Chapters 5 and 6. Methods of scoring "subjective" (i.e. writing and speaking) tests more consistently are the subject of Chapter 7.

Direct vs. Indirect Testing

A second problem revolves around the distinction between **direct** and **indirect tests**, which is less a false distinction than a misnomer. So-called "direct" tests are those that require examinees to use the ability that is supposed to be being assessed; for example, a writing test that requires test takers to write something, or a speaking test that requires examinees to speak. In contrast, indirect tests are those that attempt to assess one of the so-called (see Savignon 2001) "productive skills" through related tasks that do not require any speaking or writing. Instead, they rely upon tasks that will be easier and/or faster to grade; for example, an indirect test of writing might include a multiple-choice test of grammatical knowledge, error detection, knowledge of the rules of rhetorical organization, and so on. Similarly, an indirect test of speaking might include a test of listening comprehension and/or the ability to select the response that best completes a short dialog. In other words, rather than attempting to assess the ability itself, these tests assess related abilities, in the hope that this will provide an accurate enough estimate of an examinee's ability. Naturally, there is the potential in doing this that the resulting test will be convenient to administer and score, but will provide little or no useful information about someone's writing or speaking ability.

What is problematic about this distinction is that the so-called "direct" tests are themselves indirect (Bachman 1990). Note that it is not the "direct" tests themselves that are at issue, but rather the label they are being given. The problem relates to the distinction between competence and performance; that is, if an assessment requires students to do something, and the resulting performance is then scored, or otherwise evaluated, we can only observe that performance. Fortunately for those of us in the testing business, that performance can generally be taken as an *indication* of the underlying competence, but the performance is not the competence itself. We generally assume that good performance on a speaking or writing test results from high ability levels, but if someone does poorly, the reason(s) may be less clear: Perhaps it is a question of weak language ability, but it may also be a matter of unfamiliarity with the task, or even nervousness, among other things. Other factors could also lead a high-ability test taker to receive a poor score on a performance test. Some examples include unfamiliarity with the subject matter being talked or written about, emotional distress, misunderstanding what sort of response was expected, and a negative personal reaction to or by the person scoring the test. Thus, it is probably more accurate to refer to such tests as being more authentic or more communicative, and as perhaps tending to have greater **construct validity**. Despite the point I am raising here, though, the terms *direct* and *indirect* are still widely used.

Finally, it should be noted that the term **semi-direct tests** is generally used for speaking tests that require the test takers to record their speech rather than talk directly to a human interlocutor. These tests are generally tape-mediated or computer-mediated, as in the case of the TOEFL iBT speaking test (Educational Testing Service 2009a), Computerized Oral Proficiency Instrument (COPI; Malabonga, Kenyon, and Carpenter 2005), and Computer Assisted Screening Tool (CAST; Language Acquisition Resource Center at San Diego State University 2009; Malone 2007). This type of test is clearly quite similar to direct testing, in that it obviously assesses speaking ability by having examinees speak, rather than listen or read. It is the lack of a live interlocutor with whom the test taker can interact reciprocally, though, that distinguishes *semi-direct* from *direct tests*.

Discrete-Point vs. Integrated Tests

Another important distinction between types of tests is the one between discrete-point and integrated assessments. Both approaches have strengths and weaknesses, which means that test designers must give careful thought to the trade-offs involved in choosing one, the other, or both. A **discrete-point** test is one that uses a series of separate, unrelated tasks (usually test questions) to assess one "bit" of language ability at a time. This is typically done with multiple-choice questions, and was long the format used for standardized language tests of reading, listening, grammar, and vocabulary. Although this hardly makes for lifelike language use, this approach to test design does in fact have several redeeming features. For one thing, having each question or task unrelated to the others, aside from the fact that they all assess the same ability, satisfies an important statistical assumption underlying **item response theory** (**IRT**; see, for example, Hambleton, Swaminathan, and Rogers 1991; Embretson and Reise 2000). IRT is a powerful statistical methodology commonly employed in large-scale standardized testing, and is very useful for—among other things—controlling item and test difficulty and estimating examinees' ability levels.

Another main attraction to discrete-point testing is that if a student gets an item wrong, it is presumably because of a lack of ability in a specific area, and not interference from some other thing that is being simultaneously tested—for example, getting a reading question wrong on a discrete-point test cannot stem from a lack of writing ability. Furthermore, because each question is so brief, discrete-point tests also allow the coverage of a large number of points, whether these are topics, situations, vocabulary items, or grammatical structures. They can also be used to assess a wide variety of communicative functions or language use tasks, although how *well* they might assess the ability to perform a particular function or task is open to debate.

Finally, discrete-point tests are useful for testing very specific areas of language, such as the grammar points that have been covered in a course. To continue that example, students taking a discrete-point grammar test will not be penalized for a lack of knowledge of other points that were not taught. Similarly, they cannot use their knowledge of other points to compensate for their lack of mastery of what has been taught; that is, they cannot "write around" or "talk around" their gaps.

Unfortunately, although discrete-point tests offer these benefits, this comes at the price of authentic language use. Very seldom in real life does anyone use language one discrete point at a time—outside language tests and highly structured classroom practice, language use tasks tend to involve the integration of multiple skills, and language users can often use strength in one area of language ability to compensate for weakness in another. Thus, discrete-point tests provide an incomplete picture of what learners can actually *do* with the language. This is the reason for the development of **integrated tests**, which require examinees to use multiple aspects of language ability, typically to perform more life-like tasks. Examples might include taking notes over a listening passage and then writing a summary, or writing something about one or more texts read during the test. Such tests more closely resemble real-life language use tasks, and thus require more communicative language use.

Since authenticity and communicative language use are things that are fundamental to the communicative approach to language teaching, one might wonder why all the language tests used in programs claiming to follow that approach are not integrated. The reason, as it turns out, is that integrated tests create their own set of problems. The first, and perhaps most easily addressed reason, is that integrated tests are more difficult to score than discrete-point multiple-choice questions. This challenge can be dealt with by establishing clear scoring rubrics, and training raters in how to use them. (The development of scoring rubrics will be dealt with in greater detail in Chapter 6.)

A second problem raised by the use of integrated tests is that it is often more difficult to interpret scores that result from them. For example, if test takers score highly on an integrated reading and writing task, we can probably assume that they both read and write well. If they do poorly on the test, though, is it because they are poor readers, poor writers, or both? Without some additional measure of reading and/or writing, we cannot be sure.

Another issue has to do with how broad an integrated test can be in terms of what it is covering. When we give a test, we want it to tell us something about how students will perform *outside* the test environment. In a single test, we cannot possibly cover every topic, situation, vocabulary item, rhetorical mode, literary genre, notion, communicative function, language use task, grammatical structure, and so on, that we might find important; as a result, we must be selective and use a representative *sample* from all the areas about which we wish to make claims. Because integrated tasks typically take up as much time as a larger number of discrete-point tasks, they reduce the number of points that can be sampled in a given test.

For example, a teacher might have covered four grammatical structures and vocabulary associated with four topics, and now wishes to assess their students' ability to comprehend them in reading and use them accurately in writing. This teacher plans to use integrated tasks, but only has time to include three tasks on the test. Each task will target one structure and one topic covered in the class. This plan is probably reasonable. On the other hand, if the teacher had covered 10 topics and 10 structures, and only wanted to include one task on the test, that would be rather problematic. Unfortunately, there is no hard-and-fast rule for determining what constitutes an adequate sample on a test, so teachers must have a clear rationale to support any decisions they make, a point that will be discussed later in this chapter, and then in greater detail in Chapter 8.

In deciding between discrete-point and integrated tests, besides the factors already discussed, there is also the matter of what effect the test might have on the teaching and learning process. If teachers are encouraged to use communicative language practice activities both inside and outside the classroom, but then use decontextualized tasks to assess their reading, listening, grammar, and vocabulary separately, this sends a mixed message about the importance of achieving communicative competence in the target language. Furthermore, if discrete-point tests are imposed from above, they tend to send an *un*mixed message that communicative practice does not matter. This decreases the desire and motivation of students to achieve communicative competence, since they will be assessed on the basis of something else. It also puts pressure on teachers to focus on developing discrete skills in isolation so as to better prepare students for their tests. On the other hand, the best way to prepare students for integrated tests would probably be to include extensive communicative language practice, both in class activities and as part of homework and other assignments.

As a final point on this topic, it is worth mentioning the idea of using **independent speaking and writing tasks**, which is probably the most common approach to assessing speaking and writing. In these tasks, test takers react to a prompt or interlocutor, but do not have to process significant amounts of written or spoken text—that is, they do not have to comprehend a reading or listening passage in order to respond. This should not be considered a discrete-point approach to testing speaking or writing, however, particularly since multiple aspects of speaking or writing could be assessed in these tasks (for example, vocabulary use, grammatical accuracy, fluency, or pronunciation in a speaking test). It is probably also worth pointing out that there is not always a clear line between integrated and independent speaking and writing tasks—that is, it is probably better to view the two types as the two ends of a continuum, rather than as discrete categories.

Performance Assessments: Focus on Task Completion vs. Focus on Language Use

McNamara (1996: 6) perhaps best explains **performance assessments**, describing them as assessments that require "actual performances of relevant tasks … rather than more abstract demonstration of knowledge, often by means of paper-and-pencil tests." He further distinguishes two ways of viewing second language performance assessments: the *strong sense* and the *weak sense*. The difference between the two perspectives lies in the criteria used to evaluate the performance. The **strong sense of language performance assessment** is concerned with how well a task is performed, using real-world criteria; the level of linguistic accuracy displayed only matters to the extent that it interferes with or enables task performance, making "adequate second language proficiency … a necessary but not a sufficient condition for success on the performance task" (McNamara 1996: 43).

In contrast, the **weak sense of language performance assessment** is concerned with the level of the language used in performing the task. The purpose of the task is to elicit a sample of language to be evaluated; performance of the task, as such, is secondary, and if task completion or fulfillment is considered in the scoring, it is typically done with reference to language. In language teaching and assessment, we are generally more concerned with the weak sense of performance assessment; the strong sense is more likely to come up in vocational testing contexts.

What we Want Tests to Tell us

Now that we have examined decisions that tests can help us make, and several ways of looking at tests and test results, it seems appropriate to discuss what it is that we hope to learn when we administer a test. First and foremost, we assume that a test or other assessment is providing information about one or more **constructs**. A construct is the ability that we want to assess, but which we cannot directly observe—for example, we cannot judge a student's level of reading ability just by looking at them, or by opening up their head and looking inside. We therefore have examinees *do* things, such as answering questions on tests, which provides us with an indirect indication of how much of a particular construct they possess. That is, based on their performance, we make inferences about how much of the construct they possess. In testing in a school or language program, the construct is probably based on the curriculum or syllabus being used, which in turn is (presumably) based on some theoretical model of language ability and its acquisition (see, for example, Bachman and Palmer 1996; Canale and Swain 1980; Purpura 2004). On the other hand, when tests—most notably proficiency tests—are not based on a particular syllabus or curriculum, the construct will be based directly on a theoretical model.

We also expect that what people do when they take a test is going to tell us something about how well they will use language *outside* the test. Our concern may be with how they would perform "out there" in the real world, or it may be with how they would use language in a course or program—although presumably what goes on in the classroom is tied somehow to real-world language use. Bachman and Palmer (1996) have coined the term **target language use (TLU) domain** to refer to the contexts outside the test, whether in the real world or in the classroom, where test takers will use the language. When students take tests, we make generalizations about how they will perform in these contexts—in the TLU domain—based on their performance and scores. Put another way, students take tests and receive scores based on how they did. We then make certain inferences or predictions about their ability to use language outside the test, in the TLU domain. Based on those scores, we make decisions: what level a new student should study in, whether the student has learned enough of the material we have taught, and so on. The process for how this takes place is summarized in Figure 1.1.

Students perform tasks on a test. The tasks will, presumably, provide information about students' ability (i.e. the construct(s) of interest)

Students get scores for how well they perform those tasks

Based on those scores, we make inferences about each student's ability to use the target language (inferences about constructs, as contextualized in the TLU domain)

Based on these beliefs about their ability levels, we make decisions

Figure 1.1 How Tests Are Used to Make Decisions

As noted earlier, we can view test performance as indicating something about test takers' language ability—that is, how much of the construct they possess. We must also keep in mind, though, that a performance is a *contextualized* use of language, and therefore also depends on the features of that context (Chapelle 1998). Thus, how well language learners do on a particular test task (for example, answering a reading comprehension question, writing an essay, or taking part in a role-play) is a result of two things: their language ability and other attributes (for example, background knowledge, personal assertiveness, level of concern over detail, and tolerance for ambiguity), and the characteristics of the task (Bachman 2002b). It therefore follows that if we view the test as sampling tasks from the language use context(s) of interest—that is, the ones to which we wish to generalize on the basis of test scores—we must take care to sample broadly enough. Otherwise, any claims that performance on the test can be generalized to performance "out there" in the real world or in the classroom will not hold up to examination. The same thing is true about claims that performance on an achievement test is an indication of how much students have learned in a course. Without adequate sampling of the topics, situations, genres, rhetorical modes, functions, notions, structures, and tasks that were covered in class, it is not possible to claim, in fairness, that the test provides a clear picture of what students have or have not achieved.

As mentioned earlier, there is no simple rule for what level of sampling is "adequate." Obviously, it will not be possible to include examples of every relevant TLU task on a single test (see Figure 1.1). How much is "good enough" depends on the extent to which a test designer can make a convincing case that the coverage is broad enough and representative enough of the TLU domain(s) of interest (i.e. of the non-test language use contexts), and provide any necessary support for that argument. One way to ensure this is by systematically analyzing and modeling the TLU domain, and using the results of this process as the basis for planning and writing the test (Bachman and Palmer 1996; Mislevy and Haertel 2007).

How Good Is Good Enough?

Obviously, no test is going to be perfect. What matters most is that it should be useful for its intended purpose (Bachman and Palmer 1996), and that it should do its job with fairness (Kunnan 2004). Evaluating the usefulness of a test is best done on a systematic basis. Bachman and Palmer propose doing this through the consideration of several **qualities of usefulness**, which are summarized in Table 1.2. The various qualities are all important to making sure a test is useful for its intended purpose. One or more will often be prioritized in a given situation, but not to the extent that the others are ignored. Test developers need to decide how important each quality is, and set minimally acceptable levels for it. In other words, besides prioritizing, it is important to decide what the lowest level or worst outcome is for each one that one could accept before deciding that the test could not do its job adequately. Chapter 3 will discuss the qualities in greater detail, as well as how to set minimally acceptable levels for each of them. Later on, Chapter

8 will address the question of how to make the argument that the test really does perform its job to a satisfactory degree.

Quality	Definition
Reliability	consistency of scoring, estimated statistically
Authenticity	the degree to which test tasks resemble TLU tasks
Construct Validity	the degree to which it is appropriate to interpret a test score as an indicator of the construct (i.e. ability) of interest
Impact	effects of the test on people and institutions, including (but not limited to) **washback**—the effect of a test on teaching and learning
Practicality	the degree to which there are enough resources to develop and use the test

Table 1.2 Bachman and Palmer's Qualities of Usefulness

Before concluding this discussion of test usefulness, however, it seems appropriate to raise an issue related to the quality of **reliability**, the notion of measurement error. While reliability and measurement error will be the focus of Chapters 6, 18, and 19, it is worth noting here that no test score is a perfect indicator of language ability, as tempting as it may be to pretend otherwise. Rather, it is only an *estimate* of examinee ability, and like any estimate, is subject to a certain margin of error. Reliability, or the consistency of scoring, involves determining how much effect error has on test scores. Error can be caused by a variety of factors involving the test itself, the people taking the test and conditions in which they take it, and the way in which it is scored. While some error is inevitable, the goal of much of this book is to teach readers how to plan, write, and administer tests in such a way as to help minimize this error.

Why Graphs and Descriptive Statistics Matter

We conclude this chapter with a discussion of a particular way of looking at test results, and why teachers should concern themselves with it: the use of descriptive statistics and graphs. The best place to start might be with the question that many readers are subconsciously (or even consciously!) asking: *Why* do we need to bother with all that? Many teachers, especially in their capacity as novice test developers, may wonder. Experts, professionals, and people involved in large-scale testing need to, of course, but why do classroom teachers need to bother? After all, a fondness for math was probably not the reason most of them chose language teaching as a career!

Carr (2008b) notes a number of reasons why it is worth teachers' while to use graphs (see Chapter 13) and **descriptive statistics** (see Chapter 12). The first reason is probably the least convincing to the statistically skeptical: descriptive statistics are important for helping us decide whether certain statistical tests are appropriate. There are a number of such tests, and although they fall beyond the scope of this book, they are still very important. One common example (known as the *t*-test) is used when we have two sets of test scores (for example, two tests taken by the same class) and we want to know whether the difference between them is small enough to be the result of chance.

Another reason is that these tests can help us choose the correct **correlation coefficient**. Correlation coefficients are used when we want to learn exactly how closely related two sets of numbers are (see Chapter 14). Which correlation coefficient is appropriate will depend on the nature of our data, but we do not *know* the nature of the data without first calculating descriptive statistics.

Descriptive statistics are also important because the same formulas are used in calculating other useful things. In particular, they are useful as part of calculating the reliability of a test (see Chapters 18 and 19), or in determining which test questions have done a good job (see Chapters 15 and 16).

At a more fundamental level, descriptive statistics and visual representations of data are important because they give us basic information about how examinees did when they took a test. They tell us how well most students performed, but also provide information about the rest of the group as well. In particular, they tell us whether test scores were distributed the way we expected, wanted, or even needed. For example, at the end of a unit or course, we expect most of the students to have mastered the material covered. We do not know whether this is the case, though, until we administer some sort of assessment and look at the overall results. The "looking at" process is done with descriptives and graphs, unless one's class is so small (i.e. only a handful of students) that one can "eyeball" the scores to see that they are more-or-less what was expected.

Finally, this also involves a matter of testing ethics, as the International Language Testing Association Code of Ethics (2000) states that information about tests must be communicated both accurately and "in as meaningful a way as possible." Since it is impossible to discuss patterns of test performance in any meaningful way without using numbers, or graphs illustrating numbers, we are rather stuck. For example, graphs can help us see at a glance how many students were assigned to each level on a program's placement test, or how many students received an A, B, C, D, or F on a final exam. Similarly, descriptive statistics can help us make exact comparisons between two groups, as when we want to compare the scores of two classes that took the same test.

The point of all this is not to persuade you that you should necessarily *enjoy* the process of creating graphs and calculating statistics, but that it really does matter. As for whether the average language teacher can really ever learn to do these things properly, the answer is *yes*, something that I hope the second part of this book will prove to you.

Summary

This chapter began by pointing out that tests are tools, to be used for specific purposes, and then described the most common of those: placement, admission, diagnosis, progress, achievement, proficiency, and screening. It then explored perspectives from which we can view tests, including norm- vs. criterion-referencing; summative vs. formative purposes; so-called objective vs. subjective testing; the arguably misnamed direct, indirect, and semi-direct tests; and discrete-point vs. integrated tests. The chapter subsequently introduced the notion of constructs, and how they are contextualized within a target language use (TLU) domain, before taking up the qualities of test usefulness and the related issue of measurement error. It then addressed the importance of graphs and descriptive statistics as an additional, crucial way of viewing test results.

Further Reading

American Council on the Teaching of Foreign Languages. 1999. 'ACTFL proficiency guidelines—speaking' (revised 1999). Retrieved March 29 2008, from http://www.actfl.org/files/public/Guidelinesspeak.pdf.

Bachman, L. F. 1990. Chapter 3 'Uses of language tests'. *Fundamental Considerations in Language Testing.* Oxford: Oxford University Press.

Bachman, L. F. and **A. S. Palmer.** 1996. Chapter 1 'Objectives and expectations', Chapter 2 'Test usefulness: Qualities of language tests'. *Language Testing in Practice.* Oxford: Oxford University Press.

Brown, J. D. 1995. Chapter 4 'Testing'. *The Elements of Language Curriculum: A Systematic Approach to Program Development.* Boston: Heinle and Heinle Publishers.

Canale, M. and **M. Swain.** 1980. 'Theoretical bases of communicative approaches to second language teaching and testing'. *Applied Linguistics* 1: 1–47.

Carr, N. T. 2008b. 'Using Microsoft Excel to calculate descriptive statistics and create graphs'. *Language Assessment Quarterly* 5 (1): 43–62.

International Language Testing Association. 2000. *Code of ethics for ILTA.* Retrieved July 10 2009, from http://www.iltaonline.com/index.php?option=com_content&view=article&id=57 &Itemid=47.

Kunnan, A. J. 2004. 'Test fairness' in M. Milanovic. and C. J. Weir (eds.). *European Language Testing in a Global Context: Proceedings of the ALTE Barcelona Conference, July 2001: 27–48.* Cambridge: UCLES/Cambridge University Press.

Leung, C. 2004. 'Developing formative teacher assessment: Knowledge, practice, and change'. *Language Assessment Quarterly* 1 (1): 19–41.

McNamara, T. 1996. Chapter 1 'Second language performance assessment'. *Measuring Second Language Performance.* London: Addison Wesley Longman.

Purpura, J. E. 2004. Chapter 3 'The role of grammar in models of communicative language ability', Chapter 4 'Towards a definition of grammatical ability'. *Assessing Grammar.* Cambridge: Cambridge University Press.

University of Cambridge ESOL Examinations. 2009. *Information for Candidates.* Retrieved June 6 2010, from http://www.ielts.org/PDF/Information_for_Candidates_2009.pdf.

Discussion Questions

1   Has most of the language testing you have been part of (either taking or giving tests) been discrete-point or integrated? How has each type affected your language teaching or learning?

2   Besides the test uses listed here, can you think of any other uses that language tests are put to?

3   Think of a language test with which you are familiar.
    a   What was its purpose?
    b   Was it norm- or criterion-referenced?
    c   Was it summative or formative?
    d   Was it discrete-point or integrated?

4   Consider a language program in which you have studied or taught, and think of a purpose for which a performance assessment would be appropriate in that context. Which would you feel more appropriate for that test: the strong or weak sense of language performance assessment?

5   Imagine that you are planning a language proficiency test. What construct(s) would you include on your test? What target language use domain(s) would you want to generalize to—i.e. make claims about—on the basis of this test?

6   Consider the qualities of usefulness listed in Table 1.2. How important would you view each of them as being in the following contexts, and why?
    a   A progress assessment in a language class
    b   An end-of-course achievement test in a university language course
    c   A language proficiency test used by employers to make hiring decisions
    d   The placement test for a university-level language program

2 TASKS—THE BUILDING BLOCKS OF TESTS

Introduction

This chapter should probably be viewed more as a list of some things to keep in mind when creating tests than as a list of options from which to randomly choose. It is intended to serve as a handy reference and source of ideas for different test tasks that teachers can use when developing tests, but this is not the final chapter in the book. Consequently, if you stop reading at the end of this chapter, your tests will look as though they had been written by someone who only read the first two chapters of a testing book. Chapters 3 and 4 will address how to plan the test itself; in particular, Chapter 3 details how to select appropriate tasks on the basis of what we are trying to assess and our reasons for giving the test. After all, you will not really know what task types you need until you have considered what your needs *are*, which is a crucial early part of the planning process. Nearly all of the test tasks you use on your own tests *will* look like the ones described here, but that does not mean that something is necessarily a bad idea merely because it is *not* included here. Similarly, just because something *is* described here does not mean it would necessarily be a good choice in your particular case.

Why Focus on Task Types at This Point?

The question naturally follows, then: Why include this section describing various task types now, rather than later, following the discussion of planning and choosing task types? In fact, I almost didn't! In the end, though, just as it is handy to know what sorts of building materials are available before creating the blueprints for a house, it seems useful to have teachers keep in mind the possibilities described here while planning their tests. This, therefore, is meant as a partial listing of the options that are available: the building blocks from which you can choose when you plan your tests. It is intended to help make new testers aware of what some of the possibilities are, and to indirectly suggest that "good" and "professional" do not always mean "multiple-choice."

Unfortunately, this last point actually needs to be emphasized. Many people, both teachers and students, are convinced that "real" tests of the serious, professionally developed sort must always be multiple-choice. Years ago, when I was teaching in an intensive English program, I had to grade final exams and turn in course grades in under 16 hours—preferably within *three* hours! I therefore created 100-question multiple-choice final exams for two of my courses. As little as I knew about testing at the time, I knew enough to be dismayed when someone who had never *seen* the tests described them as "wonderful." After all, they were multiple-choice, and we had optically scanned answer sheets … What more could anyone ask for? There are good reasons why standardized tests are almost always multiple-choice—although this may change in the near future (see Chapter 10)—but it does not always follow that all multiple-choice tests are good, nor that all good tests are multiple-choice.

On the other hand, automatically choosing a particular format simply because it is *not* multiple-choice would also be ill-advised. Similarly, looking through the tasks listed here and choosing one or two before doing any other planning would also be very unwise. To continue the house-building metaphor, it would be as bad an idea as buying some building materials and then starting to build a house, without having made any blueprints first.

Task Format

Before proceeding any further, it is important to establish the terminology that will be used here. By **task format**, I mean what a test task "looks like," in terms of what sort of input test takers must process, and how we expect them to respond (for example, choosing an option, writing one word, or performing a role-play). Other writers have sometimes referred to this as "task type" (Bachman and Palmer 1996), "item format" (Brown and Hudson 2002), "test method" (Bachman 1990), "method" (Allen and Yen 1979), "response format" (Famularo 2008; Shin 2008), or "technique" (Alderson 2000). I have chosen "task format" for three reasons. First, it implicitly suggests that tests are not necessarily composed entirely of items, or questions. Second, it makes clear that we are considering the "shape" of a task, as opposed to what ability it is intended to assess. Finally, it emphasizes the point that the format includes *what* students are responding to, not just the *way* that they are supposed to respond.

When discussing task formats, there are three important types of classifications that we can make; these give a fairly good idea of what a given task's format will be. The first of these involves the type, or format, of response that a particular task calls for. **Selected response** tasks require the examinee to choose the correct answer from among several options, where "several" can mean as few as two, or as many options as can be squeezed onto one page. (Note that I am not recommending this "maximum squeeze" approach! I am only pointing out that this would be an example—a bad one—of selected response.) **Constructed response** tasks, on the other hand, call for the examinee to write or say something in response. Constructed response tasks can be further subdivided into **limited production** and **extended production** tasks (Bachman and Palmer 1996). Limited production tasks call for examinees to provide a short answer, which may be as short as one word, or as long as a sentence (if written) or an utterance (if spoken). Extended production tasks require responses that are longer than one sentence or utterance. They may only be two sentences or utterances long, or they might be much more extensive.

The second way of categorizing task formats is the distinction between *items* and *prompts*. An **item** is a question that requires a short answer, or the selection of an appropriate response; thus, items are always selected response or limited production tasks. When we talk about "test questions," items are what we usually have in mind. A **prompt**, on the other hand, usually asks the test taker to provide an extended response. This is the sort of task format most commonly used with speaking and writing assessments.

The third classification has to do with whether a test task is *passage-based* or *independent*. **Passage-based tasks** require examinees to read or listen to material in order to perform the task, as with reading comprehension questions. An important point with these tasks is that the questions cannot be answered, or tasks cannot be performed, without comprehending the passage. If test takers can do the tasks without reading or listening to the passage, after all, how can they be passage-based? This topic of ensuring **passage dependence**—that is, the need to comprehend a reading or listening passage in order to answer questions about it—is addressed further in Chapter 5, but suffice it to say for now that this fundamental point is neglected all too often by teachers writing tests of reading and listening comprehension. **Independent tasks**, on the other hand, do not require the processing of any additional material; test takers can respond to the task based solely on the item or prompt itself. Examples of independent tasks would be a grammar item that does not have any relationship to a reading or listening passage, or a speaking or writing prompt that is not based on a reading or listening passage.

Where Test Tasks Come From

Norris and his colleagues (Norris et al. 1998: 25) discuss two approaches to developing tests: *construct-based* and *task-centered*. (They actually state that these are two approaches to developing performance assessments, but the two approaches apply equally well to test development in general.) These approaches are somewhat reminiscent of McNamara's strong and weak senses of performance assessment, but the two sets of distinctions are not the same, and are not necessarily even parallel. **Construct-based test development** starts out by considering the construct that is being assessed, and selecting or creating test tasks that will tap into it; that is, tasks that will elicit evidence showing how much of the construct each examinee has. **Task-centered test development**, on the other hand, starts with deciding which tasks from the TLU domain—typically real-world language use tasks— are of greatest interest, sampling from among those tasks, and adapting those selected tasks for use on the test. Sampling is necessary because not everything can be included in the test. Similarly, adaptation is needed because we are usually simulating real-life tasks in a classroom, not following students around in the real world and scoring how they do "out there."

In either case, as Bachman (2002b) points out, we need to keep in mind both constructs and the tasks which are used to assess them. Constructs, after all, are the whole point of the test. Test users make a decision—placement, achievement, etc.—based on what they believe about how much of the construct each student has. These inferences about constructs are based on test scores, which depend on how well students perform the tasks on the test— for example, how many questions they get right. At the same time, however, we should make our tasks authentic—that is, they should resemble TLU domain tasks as much as possible, at least to the extent permitted by available resources. Ignoring authenticity is highly problematic, because if test tasks do not resemble TLU domain tasks, this limits the degree to which we can generalize to that domain (Bachman and Palmer 1996). Thus, if we want to make statements about what examinees can do with language in the real world, the tasks they perform on the test cannot be entirely divorced from real-world tasks.

Focusing only on the task aspect leads to problems with how well we can extrapolate from test performance and make claims about performance on other tasks not actually included in the assessment. Ignoring the resemblance between test tasks and real-world tasks, and focusing on constructs alone, however, does not work either. This is why Bachman (2002b) argues that we must adopt both task- and construct-based approaches in our test design; that is, while we may start planning our tests from one or the other perspective, we must address both sets of issues.

Regardless of their origins, however, test tasks tend to fall into several predictable formats. Ways of classifying these formats were described above; what follows next is a discussion of what several of the more common formats are, what they are typically used to assess, and a few points to keep in mind when assessing particular constructs. Chapters 3 and 4 will then discuss in further detail the planning of which task formats to include in a given test, which depends on the specific ways in which we define the construct(s) we wish to assess on a given test, as well as on the TLU domain to which we wish to generalize.

Commonly Used Task Formats

Before going on to describe a number of task formats and their more common uses, it is important to point out that a particular task format should not be chosen merely because it looks interesting, nor merely because it seems easy to implement. This is not meant as an argument that teachers should plan tests that are boring and impractical, but rather that someone developing a test should attempt to make principled decisions. Novelty, convenience, and expediency are important, but they should not be our only concerns. As noted earlier, guidelines for selecting particular task formats are covered in Chapter 3. Chapter 4 then explains, once a particular task format has been chosen, how to write the specifications for it—that is, how many options there should be in a multiple-choice question, how long responses to a writing prompt should be, and so on. Advice on actually writing the items and prompts, and creating or selecting reading and listening passages, is provided in Chapter 5. Finally, a task format should not be chosen simply because it is listed below; while I would certainly not argue that any of these task formats are inherently inappropriate options, that is not quite the same thing as arguing that a particular one is a good idea in a particular situation. Choose the tool that will best serve the purpose you have in mind.

Selected Response Tasks

Selected response tasks include some of the best-known task formats used in assessment. They are all item-based tasks, and can be used in association with reading or listening passages, or by themselves. Perhaps the best recognized of these task formats is **multiple-choice**. In multiple-choice tasks, as with any item-based task, examinees are presented with the **item stem**, the portion of the item that poses the question being asked. Below this are several **options**, *answer choices*, or *alternatives*, the possible answers from which the test taker must choose. The correct option is called the **key**, and the incorrect answers are the **distractors**. Multiple-choice items are popular for a number of reasons, including ease of scoring. Unfortunately, while they are easy to write, it often proves difficult to write *good* questions without training and experience. On the other hand, it is entirely too easy to write *poor* ones. (How to write better questions, how to identify stronger and weaker ones, and tips for improving poor items will be discussed in Chapter 5.) There are also concerns over how well this task format can assess language ability, although research also exists supporting its use. For example, in the area of reading comprehension, some research (for example, Rupp, Ferne, and Choi 2006) indicates that test takers read differently when taking multiple-choice tests than they would otherwise. On the other hand, Freedle and Kostin (1994) report three related studies which indicate that tests using this format can be construct-valid.

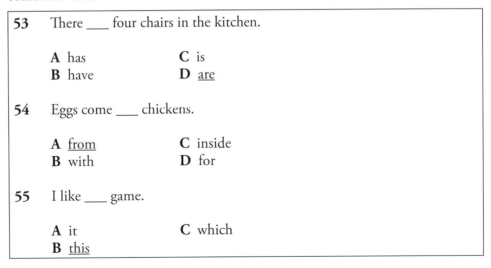

53	There ____ four chairs in the kitchen.	
	A has	**C** is
	B have	**D** <u>are</u>
54	Eggs come ____ chickens.	
	A <u>from</u>	**C** inside
	B with	**D** for
55	I like ____ game.	
	A it	**C** which
	B <u>this</u>	

Figure 2.1 Examples of Multiple-Choice Questions From a Test For Beginning-Level Students

8	Where is the conversation taking place?
	A <u>at a bookstore</u> **C** in a museum
	B in a library **D** at a university
24	The operator works for a _____ company.
	A telephone **C** <u>computer</u>
	B game **D** music

Figure 2.2 Examples of Multiple-Choice Questions From an Intermediate-Level Listening Comprehension Test

True-false questions are essentially multiple-choice items with only two answers; aside from being easier than ordinary multiple-choice items to guess correctly, however, they are also considerably harder to write well, and often wind up becoming trick questions—that is, they tend not to have one unambiguously correct answer. One way that teachers sometimes try to counter this is by having students correct false statements to make them true, or underline the part of the stem that makes the item false; this, however, requires the items to be scored as limited production questions, which is a different task format. It also requires that the scoring key take into account how to treat questions that were true, but which are altered by students to make *other* true statements.

Another commonly used selected response task format is **matching**, a selected response format in which the correct option is accompanied by a relatively large number of distractors, many of which are the correct answers to other items. Matching can be a useful task format, but it is easy to go wrong with these tasks and make them more a matter of logic and the process of elimination, rather than tools for assessing the construct of interest. One way around this is to include more alternatives than there are questions or blanks. It should be pointed out that matching tasks are not limited to cases where students write the letter of the correct choice or draw a line connecting a list of words to a list of stems or pictures. They also include tasks where students write in a word from a list or word bank, which would therefore include information transfer tasks where the information to be written down is in a list. Matching tasks can be easy to write, but as with the other selected response formats, there are several ways in which it can be rather easy to go wrong. These will be discussed later in Chapter 5.

The final selected response format that I will discuss is **ordering tasks**, which ask examinees to arrange words, sentences, or paragraphs into the appropriate order. Such tasks may be useful for assessing sensitivity to rhetorical organization, for example, but they suffer from the same problem as many matching tasks—that is, unless there are more options than questions, it becomes easier to guess the correct answers as more and more questions are answered.

Selected response tasks probably owe most of their popularity to the ease with which they are scored. That is separate, of course, from the important question of how *selecting* an answer compares with *providing* an answer. Research (for example, Brown 1980; Chapelle and Abraham 1990; Shohamy 1984; Wolf 1993) confirms what most of us might expect: selected response tasks tend to be easier than their limited production equivalents. The extent to which selected response might assess something qualitatively different from limited production, however, is less clear. Selected response tasks will also tend to be less authentic than their limited production equivalents.

Limited Production Tasks

Like selected response tasks, limited production tasks are typically item-based, and can be either passage-based (for example, reading or listening comprehension items) or independent (for example, various types of short-answer grammar questions). Most commonly, these are **short-answer questions**, although other task formats are possible, such as information transfer tasks *without* a list of the words or phrases that students are supposed to write. Other examples of task formats besides short-answer questions include **fill-in-the-blank** (also known as *gap-fill*) items, usually one sentence long; **sentence writing or combining tasks**, such as when students are given a set of words with which to form a sentence; completing a blank or **incomplete graphic organizer**; and completing an incomplete outline. These two tasks may be used to assess sensitivity to the rhetorical structure of a passage (for example, Vongpumivitch 2004), or the ability to recognize main ideas, major ideas, and supporting details (for example, Shin 2008). Limited production tasks require a written response, ranging in length from one word to a phrase, or perhaps as much as a sentence. It is also possible to have spoken or written questions that require a short spoken response, but this is much less common. Good limited production items are generally somewhat easier to write than good selected response items, but they pose two difficulties of their own, both involving scoring.

Short-answer item:

1   What did Alice follow down the hole?

     a rabbit

Fill-in-the-blank item (revised version of short-answer item above):

1   Alice followed a(n) __rabbit__ down the hole.

Sentence combining item:

17   *Lions / not / eat / vegetables*

     Lions do not eat vegetables.

Figure 2.3 Examples of Some Limited Production Tasks From a Reading Comprehension Test

	Classifying Polygons		**Classifying Polygons**

I Triangles have three sides

    A _____

    B Isosceles triangles have two equal sides

    C _____

II _____

    A Irregular quadrilaterals have no parallel sides

    B Trapezoids have two parallel sides

    C _____

        1 _____

        2 Rhombus: a parallelogram with four equal sides

        3 Rectangle: a rhomboid with four right angles

        4 Square: a rhombus with four right angles

III Pentagons have five sides

IV _____

V _____

VI Octagons have eight sides

I Triangles have three sides

    A <u>Right-angle triangles have one 90° angle</u>

    B Isosceles triangles have two equal sides

    C <u>Equilateral triangles have three equal sides</u>

II <u>Quadrilaterals have four sides</u>

    A Irregular quadrilaterals have no parallel sides

    B Trapezoids have two parallel sides

    C <u>Parallelograms have two pairs of parallel sides</u>

        1 <u>Rhomboid: a parallelogram with unequal adjacent sides and no right angles</u>

        2 Rhombus: a parallelogram with four equal sides

        3 Rectangle: a rhomboid with four right angles

        4 Square: a rhombus with four right angles

III Pentagons have five sides

IV <u>Hexagons have six sides</u>

V <u>Heptagons have seven sides</u>

VI Octagons have eight sides

Figure 2.4 Example of an Incomplete Outline Task From a Reading Comprehension Test

The first issue, and probably the most widely recognized one, is that short-answer questions take longer to grade or score than selected response items, making them less practical for testing beyond the level of the individual classroom, as well as in cases where a teacher has a large number of students, little time in which to grade tests, or both. This is especially true when the desired answers are longer than a single word or phrase, although this is becoming less of a problem with the advent of **web-based testing (WBT)** and increasingly practical methods for **computer automated scoring (CAS)**, as will be discussed in Chapter 10.

The second problem has to do with the scoring key. As a rule, most questions will have more than one possible correct answer, particularly when learners are above the most basic level. Therefore, the scoring key needs to include all synonyms or other alternative answers that are considered acceptable. If only one teacher is doing all the scoring, this becomes less necessary; on the other hand, the larger the number of tests being scored, the more important it is to write these decisions down, for the sake of consistency. This is even more true when partial credit (i.e. less than full credit, or fewer points than the maximum possible) is being awarded for certain answers that are deemed partially correct, but not adequate for receiving full credit. It might seem that experienced teachers should be able to apply common sense regarding which responses are close enough and which ones are not. Unfortunately, this does not work as well as one might expect: Teachers often disagree, sometimes strongly! Since it should not matter to a student which teacher happens to be grading their paper, luck should be removed from the equation through a carefully specified scoring key.

Deletion-Based Tasks

Deletion-based tasks involve taking a written passage and deleting words or portions of words, which are then replaced with blank spaces. Test takers must then fill in these blanks, either by writing in the empty space or by selecting from a range of options. They are most commonly a subset of limited production items, but they can also be written using selected response formats. For this reason, I will treat them as a separate category of task format.

Cloze Tests

Probably the best-known, most prototypical type of deletion-based task is the **cloze test**. In a cloze test, single words throughout a passage are replaced with blanks, and students must write the missing words in the blanks, or select the correct word in the case of multiple-choice cloze. Normally, the first two sentences or two will be left intact, so readers can gain a sense of the passage. In **fixed-deletion cloze**, the words are deleted randomly—that is, every *n*th word is deleted, where *n* is some number chosen in advance. For this reason, this task format is also known as *nth-word deletion cloze* or *random deletion cloze*, since the deletions are at evenly-spaced intervals, which makes it effectively random which words (and which *types* of words) will be deleted. Obviously, the fewer words between deletions, the harder it will be to answer correctly; therefore, n is usually at least 5 (Alderson 1983), but often 10 or more.

Fixed-deletion cloze in second language testing was originally proposed as a means of assessing overall language proficiency (Oller 1979). Subsequent studies have found that it can assess grammatical competence in some cases, and textual competence—that is, understanding of cohesive ties—in others (Chapelle and Abraham 1990). It may be that these inconsistent results are because of the random nature of the deletions; if so, Bachman (1985) points out that switching to rational deletion (see below) would allow teachers to assess the specific areas in which they are interested.

Original Passage (Carroll 1865)

Alice opened the door and found that it led into a small passage, not much larger than a rat-hole: she knelt down and looked along the passage into the loveliest garden you ever saw. How she longed to get out of that dark hall, and wander about among those beds of bright flowers and those cool fountains, but she could not even get her head through the doorway, "and even if my head *would* go through," thought poor Alice, "it would be of very little use without my shoulders. Oh, how I wish I could shut up like a telescope! I think I could, if I only know how to begin." For, you see, so many out-of-the-way things had happened lately, that Alice had begun to think that very few things indeed were really impossible.

Random Deletion Cloze (n = 7)

Alice opened the door and found that it led into a small passage, not much larger than a rat-hole: she knelt down and looked along the passage into the loveliest garden you ever saw. How she longed _____ get out of that dark hall, _____ wander about among those beds of _____ flowers and those cool fountains, but _____ could not even get her head _____ the doorway, "and even if my _____ *would* go through," thought poor Alice, "_____ would be of very little use _____ my shoulders. Oh, how I wish _____ could shut up like a telescope! _____ think I could, if I only _____ how to begin." For, you see, _____ many out-of-the-way things had happened lately, _____ Alice had begun to think that _____ few things indeed were really impossible.

Rational Deletion Cloze (prepositions, conjunctions, relative pronouns, and other connectors)

Figure 2.5 Examples of Some Deletion-Based Tasks (note that these examples are briefer than would be a good idea in real life)

Alice opened the door and found that it led into a small passage, not much larger than a rat-hole: she knelt down and looked along the passage into the loveliest garden you ever saw. _____ she longed to get out _____ that dark hall, and wander about _____ those beds of bright flowers _____ those cool fountains, _____ she could not even get her head _____ the doorway, "and even _____ my head *would* go through," thought poor Alice, "it would be _____ very little use _____ my shoulders. Oh, how I wish I could shut up _____ a telescope! I think I could, _____ I only know _____ to begin." For, you see, so many out-of-the-way things had happened lately, _____ Alice had begun to think _____ very few things indeed were really impossible.

C-Test (n = 7; "odd" letters deleted; blanks shifted one to the left for one-letter words)

Alice opened the door and found that it led into a small passage, not much larger than a rat-hole: she knelt down and looked along the passage into the loveliest garden you ever saw. How she longed t_____ get out of that dark hall, a_____ wander about among those beds of bri_____ flowers and those cool fountains, but s_____ could not even get her head thr_____ the doorway, "and even if my he_____ *would* go through," thought poor Alice, "i_____ would be of very little use wit_____ my shoulders. Oh, how I wi_____ I could shut up like a tele_____! I think I could, if I only kn_____ how to begin." For, you see, s_____ many out-of-the-way things had happened lately, th_____ Alice had begun to think that ve_____ few things indeed were really impossible.

Figure 2.5 Examples of Some Deletion-Based Tasks (note that these examples are briefer than would be a good idea in real life) (continued)

Aside from questions about what, exactly, it measures, another issue with fixed-deletion cloze involves the starting point for deletions. Specifically, changing the exact position at which the deletions start may lead to large changes in the scores on two cloze tests based on the same passage, even with as many as 50 blanks. Porter (1978) created two tests based on the same passages, with the only difference between them being that deletions in one test occurred one word earlier than in the other. Scores on the two tests had surprisingly low correlations, indicating that to a large extent, the two were measuring substantially different things. Subsequent research by Sciarone and Schoorl (1989) found that if this problem is to be avoided, about 75 blanks is the minimum number of blanks if acceptable-word scoring is used, and 100 blanks for exact-word scoring (see below for an explanation of these two types of scoring). This presumably has to do with adequacy of sample size: Since words are being randomly selected for deletion, a certain number have to be chosen for a given "sample" to be representative of the text as a whole. Two *unrepresentative* samples of words, after all, can hardly be expected to be comparable. Thus, for fixed-deletion cloze, if we want the minimum of 75 blanks needed to ensure representative sampling of various language features (assuming *n* is from five to ten words) a passage of at least 375–1,000 words would be required.

A second approach to cloze testing is **rational-deletion cloze**, also referred to sometimes as *gap-fill* tasks, in which words of a specific type (for example, connectors, nouns, or prepositions) are deleted. Of course, deletions should not be clustered together too closely, as sufficient context needs to be provided for test takers to be able to infer what belongs in each blank. One way to avoid this is to set a target for the number of deletions in a passage, and then spread them more-or-less evenly throughout, leaving the first sentence or two of the passage intact. Much like fixed-deletion cloze, it is helpful to start from the end of the passage and work backwards, but trying to delete the target words at *roughly* similar intervals; obviously, *identical* intervals, as used in *n*th-word deletion cloze, will not be possible here.

Rational-deletion cloze can be used to assess a number of different constructs, including vocabulary (for example, deleting nouns), cohesion (for example, deleting various cohesion markers, including content words in some cases), or various aspects of grammar (for example, deleting prepositions). Indeed, many common grammar exercises are arguably modified versions of rational-deletion cloze, such as passages in which blanks are inserted before every noun, with ø to be inserted when no article is required. Another example is passages with infinitives in parentheses next to each deleted verb; students must then conjugate the verbs based on the context provided by the passage. Obviously, these tasks can be used for assessment as well.

By definition, the blanks in rational-deletion cloze are not a random sample of the words in the passage. Thus, two rational-deletion cloze tests based on the same passage and targeting the same construct(s) will probably have similar patterns of deletions. Scores on the two tests will also probably be very similar, since they are assessing the same things. This presents an advantage over fixed-deletion cloze, in that it is not necessary to have such a large number of deletions.

A variant of rational-deletion cloze, which I will label **summary cloze**, is intended to assess reading comprehension. It involves writing a summary of a reading passage, and choosing the deletions that would be required to demonstrate comprehension of the original passage; that is, each word deleted provides information that could serve as the focus of a multiple-choice or open-ended comprehension question.

As noted above, cloze tasks can also employ selected response, either multiple-choice or matching. Deletions for selected response cloze tests can be fixed or rational, depending on the intended purpose of the assessment. Of course, this raises the question of whether limited production or selected response is more appropriate in a particular situation, a question that teachers should consider carefully before making a decision.

Aside from how the deletions were made, cloze tests are also distinguished by the method used to score them. **Exact word scoring** requires that test takers supply the word that was in the original passage; any other word, regardless of how well it might fit in the blank, is counted wrong. This arbitrary method poses serious issues of fairness, of course, since in many cases answering correctly might be a question of luck, not of language ability. Language testing expert J. D. Brown perhaps phrases it best: "There is something inherently repugnant about counting an answer wrong, which is actually correct, simply because the author of the original passage did not choose to use that word" (Brown 1980: 316). In contrast, **acceptable response scoring** is an approach that counts any reasonable response as correct. It is also possible to expand this to include partial credit for incorrect answers that are close to correct; how close is "close enough" must be decided in advance by the test writer or test development committee.

Research by Brown (1980) comparing exact-word, acceptable-word, and multiple-choice scoring indicates that multiple-choice cloze tends to be the easiest of the three, but discriminates the most poorly between high- and low-ability test takers. Exact-word scoring is the most difficult of the three, and discriminates only slightly better than multiple-choice cloze. Acceptable-word scoring, however, does the best job of differentiating between high- and low-ability examinees, with an average difficulty level between those of the other two methods.

C-Tests

A **C-test** is similar to a cloze test, but with the second half of every *n*th word deleted. As with cloze tests, the very beginning of the passage should be left intact to give examinees a sense of the passage. C-tests are most commonly used as measures of general language proficiency—at least, in terms of written language— and in particular, seem to assess both vocabulary knowledge and grammar (Eckes and Grotjahn 2006). Some studies have further indicated that they assess knowledge of derivational and inflectional morphology (Chapelle 1994) and the strategic use of vocabulary knowledge and semantic associations (Babaii and Ansary 2001). In a cloze method comparison study, Chapelle and Abraham (1990) found that scores on a C-test were higher than on fixed- or rational-deletion cloze tests based on the same passage. C-test scores were also the most highly correlated with scores on a multiple-choice vocabulary test, as well as with a test of **field independence** (a cognitive style associated with more analytic processing, as opposed to **field dependence**, which is more holistic). (For a general discussion of field independence/dependence and its relationship to second language acquisition, see Chapelle and Green 1992; and Johnson, Prior, and Artuso 2000.)

Extended Production Tasks

Extended production tasks, as explained earlier, are intended to elicit responses that will be longer than a single sentence or utterance. They are almost always *prompt*-based, whereas limited production and selected response tasks are overwhelmingly *item*-based. Extended production tasks can be either *independent* or *passage-based*. An essay prompt, whether it is a short single-sentence question or an entire paragraph, is one very common example of an independent extended production task. Passage-based extended production tasks are, of course, integrated tasks by definition; some examples are provided in Table 2.1. Regardless of the specific task, it is important to specify the scoring criteria and procedures before the test is administered. This will be discussed later in Chapter 7. I will divide extended production tasks into three categories here: those with *written* responses, those with *spoken* responses, and **portfolios**.

Nature of the integration	Example of a possible response
Listening and speaking	giving a short spoken reaction
Listening and writing	writing a summary of the listening passage
Reading and speaking	giving a spoken summary of the passage
Reading and writing	writing an essay reacting to the passage

Table 2.1 Examples of Passage-Based (i.e. Integrated) Extended Production Tasks

Extended Production Tasks With Written Responses

Written responses to extended production tasks can range in length from several sentences or a single paragraph up to an entire essay; in non-test assessments, where students have time to work at home, they can even include full-length research papers. These tasks include more than traditional writing prompts, however. One example of another task format is **recall tasks**, in which students write as detailed a summary as they can remember after listening to or reading a passage. In the case of reading, they are often allowed to read the passage as many times as they wish before putting it away and beginning their responses. In the case of a listening recall task, they might be permitted to listen more than once, or they might be allowed to take notes during the listening and then review them prior to writing. Recall tasks are more commonly used as research tools than for academic purposes, since they involve not only language ability, but memory as well. (In fact, many native speakers—including this author, in his native language—might even find such a task difficult!)

Written summaries of reading or listening passages are another extended production format, and are just what the name would indicate. Their primary difference from recall tasks is that test takers are allowed to refer to the passage (or their notes, in listening) when writing. Because they do not depend on a learner's memory, they are more suitable for curriculum-related assessment purposes. Not surprisingly, research by Riley and Lee (1996) indicates that students writing summaries provide more main ideas than students performing recall tasks. Interestingly, recall tasks seem to yield responses where a higher proportion of the ideas are details, as opposed to main ideas. For summary tasks, however, the pattern is reversed, with students' responses containing more main ideas than details. Given these patterns, then, any time we deem comprehension of main ideas to be more important than the ability to remember specific details—whether important ones or not—summary tasks are probably more appropriate.

Dictation is another familiar and transparent term, and integrates listening ability with writing ability; thus, if the ability to write down what a student hears is of interest, it may be a useful task format. Aside from its use as a pedagogical task (see, for example, Natalicio 1979; Reinders 2009), dictation has also been used to assess knowledge of lexical "bundles" (Nekrasova 2009) and responsiveness to instruction on a particular syntactic feature (for example, Sheen 2009), and has been viewed by many (for example, Fouly and Cziko 1985; Oller 1972; Stansfield 1977, 1985; Young 1987) as an indicator of overall language proficiency. *Note-taking* is a related task format that may be appropriate in academically oriented language programs. Its main difference from dictation is that the goal of note-taking is not, of course, to write down every word that was heard. Two common questions faced when creating a dictation or note-taking task are how many times the passage should be repeated, and how quickly or slowly it should be read. The answers depend to a large extent on the generalizations about language ability that teachers wish to make. Thus, if examinees could listen to the passage multiple times outside the test, then it would be more authentic for them to hear it multiple times during the test as well. Likewise, if they would only hear it once in the real world, or in the classroom outside testing situations, then it would be more authentic to only let them listen once during the test. Authenticity must be balanced, though, with the practical matter of how many times most students will *need* to listen in order to be able to write what they heard. It is also important to consider the extent to which students will need extra time to write—even native speakers may have difficulty keeping up with fast speech.

Suggestions for developing scoring rubrics for recall, summary, dictation, and note-taking tasks will be discussed in Chapter 7.

Extended Production Tasks With Spoken Responses

Spoken responses to extended production tasks can vary greatly in length, depending on the amount of preparation time provided, the amount of input about which learners are to speak, and the format of the task. They may be as short as a few utterances (essentially, "spoken sentences"), a short monolog of 30 seconds, or a very short conversation. They can also include a lengthy conversation, or a speech or presentation of the same length as a "real" one in the TLU domain. Of course, the appropriate length will vary depending on the TLU domain task on which the assessment is based. When appropriate "real world" tasks are too long to be practical for use in classroom or other assessment settings, it may be appropriate to simulate a specific *portion* of the longer task.

The most prototypical extended production speaking task is perhaps the *interview*. Interviews can be highly scripted, with specific prompts which must be asked, or from which interviewers must choose. Follow-up questions may not be allowed, or may be required; in the latter case, the prompts serve more as jumping-off points for the interview. Other interviews are much more free-formed, however (for example, the ACTFL Oral Proficiency Interview; see Swender et al. 1999), with no set list of prompts from which to start. In more open-ended interviews, however, it is necessary to specify what sorts of things (topics, functions, structures, etc.) should be discussed or elicited. More open-ended formats also, naturally, require more training and experience to perform properly.

It has long been recognized (see, for example, van Lier 1989) that in many ways, interviews are not necessarily reflective of normal conversation. Most spoken interaction in the real world does not consist of Person A asking Person B a series of questions, with Person A selecting all the topics to be discussed, and making all the decisions about when to move on to the next topic. This does not necessarily mean that the interview is fatally flawed as a means of speaking assessment, but this issue of discourse authenticity has led to interest in alternative approaches to speaking assessment.

One such approach is the **group oral interview** (Folland and Robertson 1976), in which pairs or small groups of students discuss one or more specific topics; these may be a list of questions or topics, or a reading or listening passage. How small is "small enough" to be manageable is a question that will depend on a number of factors, such as the proficiency levels of the students, differences between their levels, their talkativeness, their shyness, how long the interview will last, how many raters are available to score the interactions, and how many interviewees a rater can evaluate simultaneously. Whether the interviewer(s) should be involved in the discussion—and if so to what extent—is another consideration to be borne in mind. Finally, although the group oral obviously offers the benefit of greater efficiency, and may permit the observation of discourse features not likely to emerge in traditional interviews, there are also concerns about the validity of score interpretations resulting from its use.

In summarizing research on the group oral, testing researcher Gary Ockey concludes (Ockey 2009b) that studies have presented mixed results. I interpret this as indicating that like most task formats, the group oral format *can* be used to produce useful results, but—like *any* format—does not possess any magical "inherent validity" that guarantees good results in every case. Ockey recommends that to make the group oral more useful, it must be implemented in a way that will be appropriate for the testing context, and students taking it need to be familiar with the testing format. He also notes that the complex nature of this test format means that a number of variables can influence examinee performance in ways that are still poorly understood, with sometimes unexpected results. (For example, Ockey's study finds that assertive test takers tend to score more highly when grouped with less-assertive test takers than when they are grouped with other assertive examinees. On the other hand, non-assertive test takers' scores are *not* affected by the assertiveness of other group members.) Thus, given the complexity and incomplete understanding of the variables involved in this task format, it should probably be used with caution in high-stakes settings, although that is not to say that it should never be used in such settings. In classroom settings, however, group testing may be the only way to make speaking assessment possible.

Another speaking task format closely related to the group oral is *role-play tasks*; in fact, it could be argued that it is merely an extension of the group oral interview. Role-plays provide the benefit of assessing learners' ability to engage in various types of speech acts, or to perform a wider variety of language functions, than would be the case in a discussion. Role-plays also make it possible to assess the ability to speak in a wider range of situations, and about a wider range of topics. They are particularly appropriate if students are used to engaging in role-plays in class, as there are fewer concerns then with task format familiarity. Role-plays are usually easier to plan for two speakers than for larger numbers, although careful planning and a bit of creativity can help teachers increase the number of students to be included in a given interaction. Roles and background information must be clearly specified, of course, so that examinees will know how they are expected to perform. This is often done by providing the information on note cards, which the other students are not allowed to see. The language used on these role cards, of course, should be at a level equivalent to or below the language the examinees are expected to be producing, so that reading ability does not interfere with someone's ability to display their speaking ability.

When writing these role cards, of course, it is crucial that the directions be clear, specific, and understandable to the students. Nothing ruins a good role-play quite as much as having one of the students doing the opposite of what was intended. When a restaurant is supposed to be out of the special of the day, and the "waiter" was instructed to suggest another dish instead, it can ruin the entire task if the waiter instead simply takes the order as given. The "customer" then has no chance to ask questions about the rest of the menu, complain, demand to see the manager, or engage in any other speech acts beyond saying "Thank you."

Another somewhat simpler speaking task format is the *monolog*, which is often employed in speaking assessments in which responses are recorded (for example, the Internet-Based TOEFL, or iBT; Educational Testing Service 2009). Students may prepare a monolog in advance in some cases (for example, when they are required to memorize a poem beforehand), but memorized speeches or poems may be of limited value in terms of generalizing to communicative language ability. Thus, students are more frequently asked to respond to a prompt or prompts without having seen them in advance. These prompts may take the form of a number of different tasks and functions, including giving opinions, one-person role-plays (for example, "*Imagine that I am your friend, and you want to ask me to come to your house to help you move some furniture. Call me on the telephone and ask me to help you.*"), narrating the story told by a series of pictures, describing a picture, or interpreting graphs. (Note that these tasks can be used in interview-based tests as well.) One important consideration for those planning monolog-based speaking tests is whether to allow time (ranging perhaps from a few seconds to one minute) for planning an unrehearsed response. The rationale for such time is that even in one's first language, it may take time to process pictures or graphs, consider opinions on an issue, and so forth.

Outside of certain Language for Specific Purposes (LSP) contexts, graph and picture comprehension is not something language teachers want to test, *per se*; rather, graphs and pictures are tools for eliciting samples of language. Xi (2005) recommends against including graphs with too many visual "chunks," particularly when test takers are not all used to reading graphs. She further recommends allowing planning time to help compensate for some examinees' lack of graph familiarity. Naturally, this advice would apply equally to interview-based tests that included graphs, picture narration tasks, and so forth.

A final type of speaking task format that includes extended production responses is *reading aloud*, also referred to as oral reading. This task format is perhaps best suited to the assessment of pronunciation ability (see, for example, Celce-Murcia, Brinton, and Goodwin 1996)—including both segmentals (vowels and consonants) and suprasegmentals (stress, rhythm, intonation, connected speech, etc.)—and reading fluency (especially in first language reading; see, for example, Crosson and Lesaux 2009; Deeney 2010; Wanzek et al.). My personal experience in the classroom has also indicated that it can provide an indication that second language learners have difficulty with derivational and inflectional suffixes. On the other hand, it seems unlikely to provide much useful information about an examinee's command of grammar (aside from inflection), vocabulary, or any other components of communicative language ability.

Portfolios

Portfolios are collections of student work from a course, and are useful for showing a student's development and improvement. Portfolios are most commonly associated with writing, but they can be used in the assessment of speaking as well, as will be discussed below. Portfolios of student writing are probably already familiar to many teachers, and provide a more comprehensive picture of a student's writing ability than can be gotten from performance on a single timed occasion. Writing portfolios can show the development of a student's writing ability. They also provide a means of assessing students without having to worry about how test anxiety might impede performance. When pre-writing and drafts are included in the portfolio, they can provide a way to prevent—or at least detect—plagiarism. For example, a poor outline and three mediocre, barely-improving drafts of a paper, followed by a perfect final draft, may be cause for suspicion. A perfect final paper on an entirely different topic is even more suspicious.

On the other hand, writing portfolios are not without their drawbacks. For example, they do not reveal anything about how well a student can perform with limited time; this can be addressed, of course, by also using timed writing assignments to assess students. Perhaps the most serious issue, however, is that sometimes it can be difficult to tell how much of the portfolio is indicative of students' independent writing ability, as opposed to what they can do with assistance. This depends, of course, on the amount and nature of the assistance provided to students, and even when that assistance is considerable, portfolios can still be quite useful. For example, teachers can learn about student achievement by examining whether pieces from later in the course "evolved" into finished products more quickly than those written earlier. Similarly, comparing the quality of final drafts from early and late in the course can provide information on achievement (admittedly, scaffolded achievement), even if drafts are not included in the portfolio.

Although they seem to be more commonly associated with writing, portfolios can also be useful for assessing student progress and achievement in speaking ability.

The process is somewhat more involved than with writing portfolios, of course, since recordings of student speech must be made and organized. If students can record their speech digitally, this is much more feasible. In many cases, it may be necessary to train teachers and students in how to record, convert, copy, etc.

Whatever the recording format being used, it is important to specify to students what should be included, in terms of content and length. Options include recording of regular spoken journal "entries" (with or without assigned topics or prompts), interactions with native speakers or other students outside class, and even speaking activities in class. When recordings are being made of monologs, or student-to-student dialogs, it is important to keep in mind that these will generally be recordings of the students' *best* work. Students should therefore be encouraged to re-record themselves if they catch errors, but not to repeat the process so many times that they begin to sound unnatural, as if they were delivering a recited performance.

Regardless of whether they are spoken or written, it is essential to keep in mind *why* a portfolio is being used for assessment—that is, what information is it expected to provide about a student's language ability? As with any of the task formats described in this chapter, that question should be answered before the tasks are chosen.

Translation as a Task Format

Translation may fall under limited or extended production, depending on the length of the material to be translated. Probably the most important thing to keep in mind, though, is that translation is a good way to assess the ability to translate. As a means of assessing reading, writing, speaking, listening, grammar, vocabulary, discourse competence, or sociolinguistic competence, however, it is probably somewhat questionable. It can potentially *involve* any or all of these areas, but by virtue of that very fact, it is difficult to make defensible claims about any particular one of them.

Summary

In this chapter, we have looked at several ways to classify task formats. One of these is the distinction between selected and constructed response tasks, with constructed response further broken down into limited and extended production. We also considered the differences between items and prompts, and passage-based versus independent tasks. We compared task- and construct-based approaches to test design, noting that both TLU domain tasks and **construct definitions** must be kept in mind, regardless of which we approach we say we are following. Now that we have reviewed some of the options available when making a test, the next chapter will take up the question of how to choose from among them. This will be done as part of the test planning process, once decisions have been made about test purpose, constructs, TLU domains, and requirements for test usefulness. Chapter 4 will then address what specific details need to be specified about each test task—essentially, a plan for exactly how to write the test—and Chapter 5 will provide advice for what to do while writing various types of items and prompts or selecting or creating listening and reading passages, as well as how to identify which questions in item-based tests need improving.

Further Reading

Bachman, L. F. 1990. *Fundamental Considerations in Language Testing.* Oxford: Oxford University Press.
For a discussion of input, response, and the relationship between them, see Chapter 5.

Bachman, L. F. 2002b. 'Some reflections on task-based language performance assessment'. *Language Testing* 19: 453–476.

Bachman, L. F. and **A. S. Palmer.** 1996. *Language Testing in Practice.* Oxford: Oxford University Press.

For more on classifying input and responses, see their test task characteristics framework on Chapter 3, particularly the sections dealing with characteristics of the input and expected response.

Brown, J. D. and **T. Hudson.** 2002. *Criterion-Referenced Language Testing.* Cambridge, UK: Cambridge University Press.

See Chapter 3 for a discussion of task formats, which the authors refer to as item types.

Celce-Murcia, M., D. M. Brinton, and **J. Goodwin.** 1996. *Teaching Pronunciation: A Reference for Teachers of English to Speakers of Other Languages.* Cambridge, UK: Cambridge University Press.

Chapter 12 deals with testing and evaluation in the English pronunciation classroom, and Appendix 13 includes a one-page diagnostic passage for learners to read aloud.

Norris, J. M., J. D. Brown, T. Hudson, and **J. Yoshioka.** 1998. *Designing Second Language Performance Assessments* (Technical Report 18). Honolulu: University of Hawai'i, Second Language Teaching and Curriculum Center.

Discussion Questions

1   What are some examples of testing situations where (a) passage-based items and (b) independent items might be more appropriate?

2   What would you say are some of the benefits and drawbacks of using multiple-choice and short-answer items to assess the following areas of ability?
    a Reading comprehension
    b Listening comprehension
    c Writing ability
    d Speaking ability
    e Grammatical competence
    f Vocabulary knowledge

3 For a language class which you have taught, or have taken yourself, think of an achievement test (for example, a chapter or unit test, midterm exam, or final exam), and how part of it could be converted to a rational-deletion cloze test:
  a What were some of the constructs (for example, grammatical structures, lexical categories, reading strategies) the test was supposed to assess?
  b What category of words might you delete from a cloze passage in order to assess this construct?

4 In general, what do you think are some of the advantages and disadvantages of using each of the following response formats to assess grammar and vocabulary?
  a Selected response
  b Limited production
  c Extended production

3 PLANNING AND DESIGNING THE TEST

Introduction

In this chapter and in the next one as well, we will begin applying the concepts from Chapters 1 and 2 by focusing on **test specifications**, i.e. the plans for a test, which are used as an outline when the test is written, and as directions for the people writing the test. After a discussion of why we need to bother with planning tests in the first place, rather than just writing them, we will move to discussing what to include in specifications. The approach used here will divide the specifications into three parts or stages. The first of these will be the specifications of the **test context and purpose**, which include fundamental decisions about the test that need to be made before we can actually plan the content of the test. The chapter will then pose the question of whether any existing tests can be used, and suggest answering that question based on the requirements decided upon in the context and purpose specifications. For those cases where it is preferable to create a new test, the chapter will conclude by explaining what needs to be included in specifications of the test's overall structure. Chapter 4 will then continue the discussion of specifications, explaining what needs to be included in the specifications of the individual test tasks.

Why Do we Need to Plan Tests?

Just as we need to plan before we write a paper or report, we need to plan before we write a test. The longer or more important the test is, or the more versions (forms) we will need, the more planning we need. Similarly, the more people involved in writing the test, the clearer and more detailed our plans need to be. This is for fairly simple, logical reasons. Often one person or a committee will plan a test, but the actual writing of the test questions or prompts will be done by a larger group—perhaps all of the teachers in the school or program, or perhaps all of the full-time teachers. This might be the case, for example, when a program or school is creating a new placement test for incoming students. When people will be writing the test who were not involved in the planning stage, any assumptions, expectations, etc. must be spelled out. Otherwise, it becomes much more difficult for a coherent test to be produced.

Another example of a situation that requires detailed test planning is when a teacher or program will need to give a number of similar tests, quizzes, or other assessments at regular intervals. Examples of these would be chapter or unit tests, final exams, or weekly quizzes. A similar situation exists when teachers are expected to write their own tests, but the tests are supposed to follow a similar format. In all of these cases, for the assessments to be truly similar, there must be generic specifications. The specific content from the chapter or unit, course, or week in question can then be plugged into those specifications.

For example, imagine a course that includes grammar and writing, and that covers a different grammar point every week. The teacher wants to use weekly writing assignments to assess how well students have mastered the latest grammar structure. Since the teacher wants the assignments to be consistent from week to week, differing only in the grammar points they focus on, he or she decides to write a set of generic specifications. The specifications for creating writing prompts will specify that each week's prompt must elicit the structure(s) just covered. Similarly, the **scoring rubric** for the assignments needs to include assessment of how accurately learners used the target structure. It may also include other grammar points covered previously, or grammar in general, but must give some priority to the current target structure(s). The generic specifications for both the prompts and the rubric will refer to "the target structure(s)." which are different for each week—perhaps the past progressive one week, and *if* clauses another week.

As another example, a language program might want to use generic specifications for all the intermediate level courses. The specifications then might require that a certain number of new words introduced in the course be included in any reading or listening passages. Naturally, what those new words might be would differ from course to course.

Writing Specifications

In this book, the specifications for a test are divided into three categories: specifications of the **test context and purpose**, specifications of the overall **test structure**, and specifications for individual **test tasks**. For reasons of length, specifications for individual **test tasks** will be discussed in Chapter 4. As explained in Chapter 1, a test should be used to give information about how well someone can use the target language in a particular language use context—usually in the real world. Therefore, the three categories of specifications should all be based on the language use context(s) of interest, because we want to generalize from test results to those domains. In other words, we want test performance to tell us something about how students would do *outside* the test, so we need to base the test on those non-test language use situations.

Test Context and Purpose Specifications

Specifications of the test *context and purpose* are somewhat different from the other two categories. Specifications for the test *structure* and the various *tasks* included on the test both provide guidelines for what the test should look like, and what test writers should do when writing questions or prompts, writing or selecting passages, etc. Test context and purpose specifications, on the other hand, state how the test will be used, how results will be interpreted, and why the test is being given in the first place.

Why Context and Purpose Specifications Matter

As stated earlier, tests and other assessments are tools, and the correct tool has to be used for a given job. Before we decide what tool is most appropriate, though, we have to know what that job *is*.

Unfortunately, this is usually people's favorite test development step to skip. These things are often left implicit by teachers, or even programs, when tests and other assessments are being planned. This is unfortunate, as not having fundamental assumptions clear from the start often leads to confusion later. Plans for the general shape of the test (the test structure specifications) may not focus on the things that are actually important, and decisions about individual tasks (specifications for the individual test tasks) may not make sense in terms of what the test is supposed to be doing. The result can be tests that omit important sections, or place too much or too little emphasis on particular sections or constructs. It can also lead to poor decisions and inconsistency in terms of reading and listening passages, question writing, prompt writing, and scoring rubrics.

If someone is designing a test as part of a project in a testing course, skipping this stage can be particularly disastrous. This kind of "project test" is almost always artificial, in that it is not an organic part of the program for which it is being written. The test will usually not be used ever again after the student finishes the testing course. In fact, such tests are often written for classes that the testing students are not teaching themselves, making the test writers even further removed from the context where the test would theoretically be used. Because the test writers are *really* writing the test to satisfy a course requirement, they often fail to see the importance of this step, and skip it. Unlike a teacher developing a test for a specific real-world purpose, such students do not have an intuitive sense of what the test should *do* and how it will be used. This usually leads to questionable decisions about what to include in the test, resulting in a test that would not serve its (theoretically) intended purpose very well. It also means that the project does not do a very good job of fulfilling its intended purpose: giving the students practice with test development and creation. Then, when the testing students are trying to write about their test, they have difficulty explaining why they did what they did, and find it a challenge to write a coherent report. If they actually administer the test and analyze the results, confusion about test purpose and interpretive framework can lead to a mishmash of misinterpreted data and questionable conclusions.

Thus, if someone is creating a test and cannot explain why they are doing something, they probably do not have a good reason for doing it, and should reconsider the purpose of the test and then revise their plans accordingly. It is not that the particular choice in question is *necessarily* going to be a bad choice, but that they are trying to use a particular tool without having first decided what they are trying to do with it.

In contrast, if someone is developing a test for a real-world purpose in their language course or program, they already may be taking for granted many of the points that follow. It is safer, though, to make these decisions explicit, rather than leaving them as unstated assumptions. Putting them down in writing makes it easier to spot inconsistencies, and easier to discuss them with colleagues or others working in the development process. Sometimes such unstated assumptions turn out not to have been shared by everyone involved in the process! This can serve also as insurance against assumptions accidentally "drifting" as the test is being planned and written, and can help prevent inconsistencies between the various portions of the test.

What to Include in Context and Purpose Specifications

What the context and purpose specifications should include is summarized in Table 3.1. The first thing to decide, of course, is the purpose(s) of the test: That is, why are you doing all this in the first place? What decision(s) will be made based on test results?

Component	Explanation
Purpose(s) of the test	What decision(s) will you make based on test results?
Construct(s) to be assessed and their definitions	What are the constructs, and what do you view them as including?
Interpretive framework	Criterion-referenced or norm-referenced?
Target language use (TLU) domain and common/important task types	What language use context(s) outside the test should test results generalize to? What should the test tell you about what students can do in those contexts?
Characteristics of test takers	Who are the people who will take your test, what are they like, and what do they probably know?
Minimum acceptable levels for each of the qualities of usefulness	What is the lowest level you would be willing to accept for each one, and how do you prioritize them?
Resource plan	What resources do you need to create and use this test, and what resources are available?

Table 3.1 Summary of What to Include in Specifications of the Test Context and Purpose

The next point to consider is what constructs the test is intended to assess, and how they are defined. The **construct definitions** include what the constructs are regarded as including (see Table 3.2 for some examples of common components of construct definitions for reading, writing, speaking, listening, and grammar). For example, if a test is intended to assess reading, should "reading" include skimming or scanning, both, or neither? Skimming and scanning might be important things to include in certain situations, but not in others. Likewise, if a writing assessment is being planned, is the ability to produce logical, meaningful, and appropriately organized content important, or is control over linguistic accuracy the only concern?

Construct	Elements often included in construct definitions
Listening	Listening for the main idea, listening for major points, listening for specific details, listening for the gist, inferencing, predicting, determining the meaning of unfamiliar vocabulary from context, distinguishing fact from opinion, determining speaker's intent, note-taking
Reading	Reading for the main idea, reading for major points, reading for specific details, reading for the gist, inferencing, predicting, skimming, scanning, determining the meaning of unfamiliar vocabulary from context, distinguishing fact from opinion, sensitivity to rhetorical organization of the text, sensitivity to cohesion of the text, identifying author purpose or tone, paraphrasing texts
Speaking	Grammar, vocabulary, segmental pronunciation (vowels and consonants), suprasegmental pronunciation (for example, stress, rhythm, intonation, prominence, connected speech phenomena), content, organization, cohesion, task performance, appropriate use or performance of language functions, sociolinguistic appropriacy
Writing	Grammar, vocabulary, content, rhetorical organization, cohesion, task performance, use of appropriate rhetorical mode, register
Grammar	Ability to use structures accurately, ability to comprehend structures, control at the sentence level, control at the discourse or suprasentential level, accuracy of forms, accuracy of meaning (Purpura 2004); may relate to grammar in general, or to specific forms covered in the course or program
Vocabulary	Ability to recognize and understand words and phrases, define or explain them, use them appropriately in context (at the sentential and/or discourse/suprasentential levels); ability to recognize and understand collocations, define or explain them, and use them appropriately in context; may relate to vocabulary in general, or to specific words and phrases taught in the course or program

Table 3.2 Examples of Common Components of Construct Definitions

In the case of testing at the program level (as in placement testing, or exit testing), the answer should largely depend on what is covered in the program's curriculum. That is, things should be included in the construct definition to the extent that they are included in the curriculum. In the case of classroom testing, however, the question can be a little more complex. When developing generic specifications for quizzes and tests, or for a single major test, the focus usually needs to be on what was covered in the portion of the class to which the assessment pertains. Besides that focus, however, a teacher must decide the extent to which *previous* material, or material from other courses, should be included.

For example, in a class that focuses on speaking and does not include explicit instruction in grammar, to what extent should the teacher include grammatical accuracy when evaluating their speaking ability? In this case, the construct definition would probably only include grammatical accuracy in terms of whether it interfered with effective communication, required listener effort, or was distracting to listeners. In a class that *did* include some teaching of grammar, however, the teacher would probably want the construct definition for speaking to include grammatical accuracy, with a focus on the structures that had been taught in the portion of the course being assessed. The construct definition might also include mention of communicative effectiveness, listener effort, and how distracting the learner's errors are. In addition, the teacher *might* choose to place some emphasis on structures that had been taught previously in that course (i.e. before the preceding test), although presumably less than on the structures currently being taught.

As test development and validation expert Stephen Sireci has pointed out, when we are talking about educational testing (whether at the course or program level), "… there is often a thin distinction between a construct and a content domain" (Sireci 2007: 478). Fortunately, if the course or program has a clearly defined curriculum, we can base the construct definitions on its *goals and objectives* (Brown 1995; Eyring 1996; also referred to as *learning outcomes* or *competencies*). If there are no such clearly stated targets for student learning, the test design process may help point out the need for better development of the curriculum.

With respect to construct definitions for grammar, I have not included metalinguistic knowledge, that is, the ability to *explain* rules rather than to *use* them. When speaking of communicative competence, we are not concerned with "*stating* a rule but [with] *using* a rule in the interpretation, expression, or negotiation of meaning" (Savignon 2001: 17). With respect to construct definitions for vocabulary knowledge, it should also be pointed out that collocations can include things such as prepositions, the knowledge of which is often treated as part of grammatical competence. There can be considerable overlap at times between syntax and lexis, of course, which are sometimes referred to together as "lexicogrammar," as both facets of language are involved in determining the correct grammatical form, what that form means, and when or why it is used (Celce-Murcia and Larsen-Freeman 1999).

Finally, three additional points about constructs and construct definitions bear mentioning. First, it is important that these be thought through logically. For example, if a teacher is assessing writing, and wants the construct definition to include spelling, but not grammar, that may be hard to justify. Second, constructs are not limited to reading, writing, speaking, listening, grammar, and vocabulary. There is no reason that they cannot be based on any of the other components of communicative competence, such as functions or pragmatics (see, for example, Canale and Swain 1980; Bachman and Palmer 1996). Finally, it may be advisable for teachers to undertake a brief review of the language acquisition and/or language assessment literature for advice on construct definitions. This might include looking at models of language ability (for example, Canale and Swain 1980; Bachman 1990; Bachman and Palmer 1996), or descriptions of the components that might be included in the definition for a particular construct (see, for example, Alderson 2000 for a discussion of how to define reading ability; Douglas 2000 for construct definitions in tests of language for specific purposes; and Purpura 2004 for grammatical ability).

Once the constructs have been defined, the next point to specify is whether to interpret the test results in comparison with one or more criteria or cut-off points (for example, for placing into different levels, earning certain letter grades, or satisfying a requirement for being considered "proficient") or to interpret results in terms of how well others did (for example, how far above or below average each student's score was). This decision as to the interpretive framework to adopt will most likely follow from the purpose of the test (review Chapter 1 for explanations of test purposes and the norm- and criterion-referenced frameworks). In the context of tests for language programs or courses, any tests that teachers develop will usually be criterion referenced.

It is also important to decide in advance what the target language use domain will be. As explained in Chapter 1, test results should give information about how students would perform in contexts outside the test. Many people are tempted to say "The results should tell us about their ability to communicate in the real world," but it simply is not feasible to create a test that will relate to every imaginable real-world context that students might encounter. It is therefore necessary to select one or more specific contexts (topics, situations, tasks, etc.) about which we wish to make claims. We also must make decisions about what we want to be able to say students can *do* in those contexts, in terms of tasks and functions.

Following this, it is necessary to describe the people who are likely to take the test. A given test might be appropriate for one group of examinees, but not for another. Some of the most important things to specify are the examinees' language proficiency levels, first language backgrounds, countries and/or cultures of origin, educational backgrounds, reasons for studying the language, overall educational goals, ages, levels of life experience and world knowledge, and their degree of familiarity with the target language culture. When tests are being developed for vocational or language for specific purposes programs, levels of topical or content knowledge must also be specified. Although most of these things may seem like nothing more than common sense, it is important to write them down explicitly. One reason for this is that including them in the test specifications helps make it less likely that we will forget or ignore what *should* be obvious. Another reason is that not everyone involved in the planning and writing of the test may share the same assumptions about the prospective students' background.

Chapter 1 introduced Bachman and Palmer's (1996) list of qualities that make a test useful: reliability, authenticity, construct validity, impact, and practicality. For each of them, we must decide in advance what the minimally adequate level is that we can accept in our test. We must also decide how to prioritize them, and strike an appropriate balance among them. After all, nobody has infinite resources for test development, so it will be impossible to make *everything* a maximum priority.

For instance, since reliability—the consistency of scoring—must be estimated statistically, a specific numerical target must be set. For **high-stakes tests** (tests with serious or important consequences for test takers or other stakeholders), this is usually set at .80 or higher. Reliability will be the subject of Chapter 6, but for now, imagine a television with a poor signal. Much of the screen will be showing random interference; a reliability of .80 is analogous to saying that 20% of the picture will be "snow," and 80% will actually be the program you are trying to watch. Are you satisfied with 20% measurement error, do you require 10% or less, or is 30% good enough in your situation?

Construct validity and authenticity differ from reliability in that they are qualitative notions, and are not expressed statistically. The minimum acceptable level for construct validity must also be selected before proceeding any further. That is, test scores will be used to make inferences, or judgments, about the language ability of test takers. How appropriate do those judgments need to be? Put another way, how good a job must the test do of reflecting the constructs you are planning to assess? Similarly, how closely must the test tasks resemble TLU domain tasks for the test to have a satisfactory level of authenticity? Points on which to compare tasks include the input to which students must respond (listening or reading passages, conversational or writing prompts, etc.), and how they are expected to respond. Comparisons should also include topics, language functions, and the linguistic characteristics of input and students' expected responses.

The impact of a test is best examined in terms of both its size and how positive or negative it is. Therefore, when setting minimum acceptable levels for impact we need to decide how *large* the impact needs be, and how *positive* the impact needs to be. Often, people developing a test may say, for example, that the test should have at least a moderately positive impact. This is a nice start, but what does it mean in practical terms? To achieve meaningful, positive impact, or to avoid noticeable negative impact, we need to elaborate on what such statements mean, putting them into more concrete terms. One way to do this is to list all the potential effects the test might conceivably have, including effects that seem unlikely but are still *reasonably* possible. In the case of a single school or language program, the list of important effects will commonly include four areas: how students will study or learn, what and how teachers will teach, impact on students and teachers personally, and effects on the program or school in general. (Note that the first two types of effects, and arguably the third type, fall under the heading of **washback**, the effect of a test on teaching and learning. Naturally, this also includes the curriculum which is being taught or studied.)

Once all of the reasonably foreseeable consequences have been listed, they should be classified as *desirable* or *undesirable*. As Samuel Messick, a pivotal figure in the development of validity theory, has pointed out, these consequences must be consistent with social values, and must be sufficiently positive to justify the use of the test (Messick 1989a). In the final step, the setting of the minimum acceptable levels, decisions must be made as to which potential consequences absolutely must be avoided, and which desirable ones absolutely must be achieved. *Test fairness* might also be considered here as well; see Chapter 8 for a brief discussion of Kunnan's (2004, 2008) Test Fairness and Test Context Frameworks.

Perhaps the most commonly discussed aspect of impact is *washback*, the effect of a test on teaching and learning. This includes effects on all aspects of the curriculum, including materials and teaching approaches, as well as on what the students do to learn and to prepare for tests. Indeed, this aspect of impact is so important that washback is sometimes confused with impact, rather than being seen more properly as a crucial *part* of impact. Trying to plan tests that seem likely to cause positive washback is important, because teachers *will* wind up teaching to the test, at least to some extent. In fact, as Hargis (2003) points out, tests can essentially *become* the curriculum. Thus, in a program focusing on developing communicative competence, and rooted in the communicative approach, tests need to support the teaching approach, not sabotage it. If language is assessed communicatively, then the only way to prepare for such tests will be by practicing actual communication in the target language. Tests can then be used to support the curriculum, rather than undermine it.

On the other hand, if the test is outside your control, then you may be reading this book in order to gather ammunition to use against it. In the meantime, until you can bring about some sort of change, there may be little or nothing that you can do about curriculum–assessment mismatches, but at the least, being able to articulate exactly why there is a real problem may be comforting, and can help highlight where efforts need to be focused in trying to bring about change.

The last of Bachman and Palmer's qualities of usefulness, practicality, is intimately tied to the final component of the test context and purpose specifications: the resource plan. A test is practical if there are enough resources available to create, administer, and score it.

The most important types of resources are probably time, space, materials and equipment, and personnel. They can also include the money to pay for these things, or to pay for *more* of them—more classrooms, more paper, more computers or audio equipment, or more hours of extra work from teachers or secretaries. Table 3.3 provides a number of examples of what resources are commonly required, especially for "large" tests, such as those administered at the program or school level. Most of these needs exist in miniature for classroom testing as well, though. In large- or even medium-scale testing, there is also the matter of resources to *report the scores*. For example, if several hundred people will expect to receive their scores at noon next Tuesday, and results need to be explained and discussed for several minutes per student, you need to plan accordingly.

Type of resource	Examples
Time	Time for planning the test, writing the test, reviewing the test, pilot testing, reviewing pilot testing results, revising the test, administering the test, scoring the test, organizing and reporting results
Space	Rooms for teachers to meet about writing the test, rooms for administering the test, space for students to line up to register or check in for a test, rooms for interviews or other speaking tasks, places for students to wait before taking speaking tests, rooms for teachers to meet to score tests, storage space for old test results, storage space for old tests
Materials and equipment	Paper, pencils, optical scanning sheets, copy machines, audio-visual equipment (especially for listening tests), optical scanning machines, computers for writing the test and keeping records, computers for administering computer-based tests, number stamps (for numbering each test), rubber bands, location/directions signs, signs asking for quiet, tape for signs, tables and chairs for registration or check-in, boxes for tests, sound systems, recordings, extension cords, chalk or dry-erase markers
Personnel	People to plan the test, people to write the test, people to make recordings, students to take the test during pilot testing, people to review the pilot testing results and revise the test, people to produce the test, people to administer the test, people to score the test, people to report the results to students

Table 3.3 Examples of Resources Often Required For Testing

Regarding one aspect of space requirements—storage space for old tests and test results—it is worth pointing out that in some cases, laws or policies may require that old tests be kept for a certain length of time. This may be as short as one academic term after the test, perhaps, but sometimes might even be as long as five years or more. It is important to find out what the legal and/or institutional requirements are in a given place, and to follow them. Personal information should be kept confidential, so storage needs to be secure as well, with access restricted; in some places there may be strong legal requirements for this, but even when there are not, professional ethics require it (International Language Testing Association 2000). At the same time, test takers may have rights to review their tests (not just the test results); what these rights are will, again, vary across jurisdictions, but they need to be respected scrupulously. Even when examinees' *legal* rights are limited, and confidentiality of test materials is an overriding concern, people should be entitled to at least some explanation for and justification of their test results when they are unhappy with the outcome.

Setting the minimum acceptable level for practicality and formulating a resources plan essentially means deciding what resources are necessary, identifying what is available, making plans for what will be needed when, and deciding whether there is enough "cushion" in the plan (in terms of time, money, etc.) to handle unexpected problems. It also includes taking into account any externally imposed limitations—for example, if an achievement test can only be administered during regular class hours, or if school policy requires that all placement testing take less than three hours on a given morning, with results available later that same day.

Another example of an externally imposed limitation during the development of a test might be if teachers were not given the time necessary to develop the test. Writing test specifications in a thoughtful manner, writing a well-constructed test following those specifications, and reviewing their work prior to actually giving the test, these things all take time. Furthermore, operational testing should be preceded by a pilot or trial administration and subsequent revisions. To the extent that any of these receive short shrift due to time (or staffing) constraints, the quality—and usefulness—of the test will suffer. It also should be kept in mind that professional test developers and those creating their first test will not work at the same pace, or need the same level of effort and revision to produce high-quality tests. As with any skill, experience matters; therefore, the testing expertise and experience of the person or team planning and writing a test needs to be taken into consideration too, and considered as part of the resource plan.

Evaluating Existing Tests

Once it has been decided what the test needs to do, one option to consider is whether existing tests will meet your needs. At the program or school level, this could mean looking at existing tests. It could also include looking at any tests currently being used by the program and deciding whether they already suit the purpose at hand. At the classroom level, existing tests may be produced by the publisher of a textbook. The quality of these tests can vary, even if teachers are following the book without any deviation. The more that a teacher goes beyond the textbook, of course, the greater the chance that the textbook test will not be adequate without at least some supplementation. Similarly, if a teacher is considering a test written by another teacher for the same course, it must be examined carefully.

Evaluating an existing test, wherever it came from, is mostly a matter of considering each of the components of the test context and purpose specifications. Questions about test purpose are not always easily answered—just because a test was designed for one purpose does not mean it cannot be used for others, but the question should still be asked. Similarly, a norm-referenced test might be useable as a criterion-referenced test, and vice versa, although not always—this will particularly depend on what difficulty level was being targeted when the items were being written. More clearly, it is important to make sure that the constructs assessed by the existing test are comparable to those that need to be assessed in your situation. The existing test should generalize to the TLU domain(s) with which you are concerned, and the students for whom the test was written should be similar to yours. Finally, it is important to ask whether the minimum level for each of the qualities of usefulness will be met if the existing test is used.

If those questions can all be answered satisfactorily, then there is no point in "reinventing the wheel." On the other hand, the rest of this chapter addresses what planning will be required if existing tests will *not* meet a teacher's or program's needs.

Specifications of the Overall Test Structure

Once we have specified the context and purpose of the test, the next step is to plan what the test will look like. In a nutshell, this means deciding what **task format(s)** to use, and how many of them. In other words, what will students *do* when they take the test (for example, write a paragraph, perform a role-play, or read something and answer multiple-choice questions about it), and how many questions or prompts will there be in each section of the test?

For many people, this is the starting place when they create a test, but skipping ahead and starting here is usually a serious mistake. If the reasons for giving the test and how the results will be interpreted are not clear, the resulting test is less likely to serve its intended purpose well. It may not be appropriate for the students taking it if who they are and what they are like are not kept in mind. If decisions about how important various qualities are (for example, authenticity or impact) are not made in advance, and the test "just gets written" anyway, it will not reflect the priorities that the teacher(s) planning the test would have wanted to set, had they taken time to reflect. Finally, if the test is planned or written without considering the available resources, it may prove impractical to use. Alternatively, in a drive for practicality without actually considering what resources are available, teachers may wind up with a test that is quite practical to use, but is not useful enough in other ways.

So, what goes into planning the test's structure? The first step is to consider the construct definitions that were written as part of the context specifications. If something is included in the construct definition, it will need to be assessed. Typically, each construct will be the subject of a separate section. Every construct must have at least one section that is assessing it; otherwise, it will be left out of the test. Similarly, each section of the test will be intended to engage a specific construct, or portion of a construct. For example, if you wish to assess reading, listening, and writing, you will normally have three sections, rather than trying to assess the three constructs in one combined section.

This is not true for integrated tasks, however, since integrated tasks always assess more than one construct. It is important to keep in mind that integrated tasks do complicate the interpretation of test results, unless the construct definition reflects the integrated nature of the task, rather than two separate constructs. For example, as discussed in Chapter 1, using an integrated reading and writing task will make it difficult to disentangle the effects of reading ability and writing ability. If the construct is defined as the ability to read information and write about it, however, test scores become more interpretable in terms of the construct being assessed. Of course, using such a blended construct means that we cannot make statements about reading and writing as separate abilities. In any case, we cannot report scores for something, or say that it is included in what we are assessing, unless we actually assess it—whether independently, or as part of an integrated task. Of course, this also applies to language "subskills" as well.

Additionally, it must be decided how important each section (and/or construct) is in relation to the others. Are they all equally important, or are some constructs twice as important, or half again more important, than others? Do students need to demonstrate a certain level of ability in each area, or can a greater level of ability in one construct compensate for lower ability in another? For example, if a test assesses reading and listening, are the two abilities equally important, or is one more important than the other (and if so, how much more important)? Can a student's strong reading ability compensate for weak listening ability, or must students do well in both areas?

Once the number of sections has been decided on, the next step is to decide which *task format(s)* (see Chapter 2) to use in each section. Each task within a section will also have a task format—that is, a particular task will be a multiple-choice question, essay prompt, short-answer question, matching question, etc. This decision should be made at this stage of the process, *not earlier*. (If it was made previously, though, why was that format chosen? Does the choice still make sense?) It should not be a random or arbitrary choice (for example, automatically assuming that any test of reading, listening, or grammar must be multiple-choice, or that vocabulary tests must use either multiple-choice or matching); rather, it needs to be one that can be defended if necessary. Choosing which format(s) to use involves striking a balance among the qualities of usefulness, and choosing the one(s) that will best assess the construct covered in each section of the test. This frequently involves making tradeoffs between construct validity and authenticity on the one hand, and practicality on the other. Obviously, this step needs to wait until the various qualities have been prioritized, and the construct(s) identified. Making these decisions prematurely is like buying shoes without checking the size or trying them on, which is why they should be based on the decisions made earlier, in the test context and purpose specifications. (Of course, poor choices can be made to work, after a fashion, just as it is possible to make shoes fit by cutting off their toes or stuffing them with newspaper!)

These decisions in turn may lead to a reconsideration of the minimum levels set previously, and/or a rebalancing of the priorities set for them. By this, I do not mean that serious, considered decisions need to be abandoned as soon as they threaten to become slightly inconvenient. It is true, however, that unrealistic decisions can sometimes seem perfectly reasonable until it becomes time to put them into operation.

When deciding which task format(s) to use, Bachman and Palmer (1996) recommend that TLU tasks should be adapted whenever possible. This adaptation means making them usable in the context of the test, or taking salient parts of TLU tasks and using or adapting them so as to make them practicable. Essentially, it this is no different from what teachers do when they adapt real-life tasks to classroom activities, whether by simplifying them, providing some form of scaffolding, or narrowing their focus or length. As Bachman (2002b) points out, however, not tying test tasks to construct definitions makes it hard to generalize about how well students would do on other tasks besides the ones specifically included on the test. Thus, while we should try to choose representative tasks from the TLU domain, we must make sure that they will give us information about our construct(s), as defined in the test specifications. Unfortunately, the need for construct representation and practicality means that we may sometimes be forced to use task formats that are not adapted from TLU domain tasks (Bachman 2002b; Bachman and Palmer 1996). Obviously, this sort of decision involves a trade-off between authenticity on the one hand, and practicality on the other.

Steps in the process		Comments
1	Review construct definitions.	Each construct will usually be the focus of one or more sections of the test.
2	Choose task format(s) for assessing each construct, or for each aspect of each construct.	Choose the task format(s) that will best permit you to assess your construct, while remaining sufficiently practical that you can actually write and use the test.
3	Decide how many of each task (questions, passages, prompts, etc.) to use in each section.	If you want to report a separate score for a certain construct, or a particular aspect of a construct, you need to have enough tasks or ratings to give you a *consistent* score.

Table 3.4 Summary of How to Write Test Structure Specifications

When task formats have been selected for assessing each construct, we must decide how many of each task to use. For example, for a reading test, how many passages and questions do we need? There must be enough questions (or other tasks) to provide a reasonably reliable score. What constitutes "reasonably reliable" is something that you decided previously, in the test context specifications. How to estimate the reliability of these results will be discussed in Chapter 6, but it is a basic truth that the fewer scores (questions, tasks, ratings, etc.) there are, the lower the reliability will be. As a rule of thumb, I find that it is easier to achieve an adequate reliability level on item-based tests when there are at least 20–30 well-written items.

A further complication here is that if we want the results to include specific information about various aspects of each construct, there must be enough tasks for each of them to provide reliable results. For example, if a teacher is writing a diagnostic listening comprehension test and wants to include (i.e. report, or use in some fashion) a score for making inferences when listening, they must use enough inference questions to get a reasonably reliable score. Even reporting scores for just a few "subskills" will require increasing the length of the test significantly. *Not* using enough questions to get a reasonable level of scoring consistency means that while they may report separate scores, those scores will probably not be worth very much, given the high level of measurement error that will go into them.

Summary

This chapter began by reviewing the importance of planning tests before writing them, whether on a test-by-test basis, or as generic specifications when a number of similar tests (or quizzes) need to be created over different sets of content. It then discussed the context and purpose specifications, which detail the test purpose(s), the construct(s) to be assessed and their definitions, the interpretive framework for the test (NRT or CRT), the TLU domain, characteristics of the intended test takers, minimal acceptable levels for the qualities of usefulness, and a resource plan. We then moved on to consider the possibility of using existing tests, and advocated using the context and purpose specifications as the basis for performing this evaluation. This was followed by an explanation of what to include in specifications of the overall test structure, when no suitable existing tests are available. These specifications, based on the context and purpose specifications, are simply a listing of (1) the task format(s) to be used to assess each construct, or each aspect of each construct, and (2) how many of each task (items, passages, prompts, etc.) to use in each section. Chapter 4 will take up the question of what to include in the specifications for each of the individual test tasks that are listed in the test structure specifications.

Further Reading

Note: More reading suggestions for test specifications can be found in the Further Reading section of Chapter 4. Below are references for models of language ability and potential ideas for what to include in construct definitions.

Alderson, J. C. 2000. Chapter 1 'The nature of reading', Chapter 4 'The reader: defining the construct of reading ability'. *Assessing Reading*. Cambridge: Cambridge University Press.

Bachman, L. F. 1990. *Fundamental Considerations in Language Testing*. Oxford: Oxford University Press.
See Chapter 4, "Communicative language ability."

Bachman, L. F. and **A. S. Palmer.** 1996. Chapter 4 'Describing language ability: Language use in language tests'. *Language Testing in Practice*. Oxford: Oxford University Press.

Buck, G. 2001. Chapter 2 'What is unique to listening', Chapter 4 'Defining the construct'. *Assessing Listening*. Cambridge: Cambridge University Press.

Canale, M. and **M. Swain.** 1980. Theoretical bases of communicative approaches to second language teaching and testing. *Applied Linguistics* 1: 1–47.

Douglas, D. 2000. Chapter 2 'Specific purpose language ability'. *Assessing Language for Specific Purposes.* Cambridge: Cambridge University Press.

Fulcher, G. 2003. Chapter 2 'Defining the construct'. *Testing Second Language Speaking.* Harlow, UK: Pearson Longman.

Luoma, S. 2004. Chapter 4 'Speaking scales', Chapter 5 'Theoretical models'. *Assessing Speaking.* Cambridge: Cambridge University Press.

Purpura, J. E. 2004. Chapter 4 'Towards a definition of grammatical ability'. *Assessing Grammar.* Cambridge: Cambridge University Press.

Read, J. 2000. Chapter 6 'The design of discrete vocabulary tests', Chapter 7 'Comprehensive measures of vocabulary'. *Assessing Vocabulary.* Cambridge: Cambridge University Press.

Weigle, S. C. 2002. Chapter 1 'Introduction', Chapter 2 'The nature of writing ability', Chapter 4 'Research in large-scale writing assessment'. *Assessing Writing.* Cambridge: Cambridge University Press.

Discussion Questions

1 Consider a language program in which you have studied or taught. Think of one or more purposes that could be served by a single test, and briefly specify:
   a the purpose(s) of the test
   b what construct(s) the test should assess
   c how the construct(s) should be defined—that is, what should be included in each one
   d the interpretive framework (NRT or CRT) that would be most appropriate
   e the TLU domain(s) to which the test should relate
   f characteristics of the test takers
   g minimum acceptable levels for each of the qualities of usefulness
   h the resources that would probably be available in this program for developing this test.

2 For the same test, for each construct—or each aspect of each construct, if you are subdividing the construct(s)—how many task formats would you use, and which ones?

3 For each of the task formats you listed in Question 2, how many of that task would you include?

4 For the same language program, *or* for a different one with which you are familiar, what is an example of tests or quizzes that might be improved by using generic specifications to plan them?

4 WRITING THE SPECIFICATIONS FOR INDIVIDUAL TEST TASKS

Introduction

Chapter 3 introduced the importance of planning tests before they are written. It described what needs to be included when writing the specifications of the *context and purpose of a test*, and the specifications of the *overall test structure*. Those first two stages of specifications report the decisions that have been made about what job the test is meant to do, and what the overall test will look like in terms of the number of sections, the task format(s) in each section, and how many tasks (i.e. the number of questions, prompts, passages, etc.) there will be. There is still one stage left in the planning process, however: writing specifications for the various *task formats* being used in each section. Once this is finished, and ideally a few sample tasks have perhaps been written, it will be time to start writing the test itself. The test writing process is addressed in Chapter 5. It largely consists of following directions; these directions are the specifications for the overall test and for the individual tasks. This chapter will begin with a list of general considerations, followed by a discussion of specific points to keep in mind when planning certain common item types. It will conclude with a word about the iterative nature of creating test specifications, and a brief discussion of how to reverse engineer the specifications of existing tests.

Specifications For Individual Tasks: General Considerations

Test task specifications need to be written separately for each section, and for each type of question or prompt. These are descriptions of how each task is to be written, and go beyond merely identifying the task format to be used, which is done in the test structure specifications. For example, reading and listening questions need separate specifications, and "reading for the main idea" questions need separate specifications from inference questions. Similarly, multiple-choice and short-answer questions based on the same listening passage also need separate specifications. There may be overlap in the specifications for two different tasks, even extensive overlap, but each task needs its own description.

These specifications need to include a number of points, which are summarized in Table 4.1. The purpose and the construct definition(s) for each task will be drawn from the test context and purpose specifications. Essentially, every portion of the construct definition will be covered by at least one set of task specifications; otherwise, that portion of the construct has been neglected, and needs to be added. Likewise, any task must be relevant to one of the constructs being assessed, or it has no business being included on the test. There is sometimes a temptation to use a *non*-integrated task to engage or assess two constructs simultaneously, as with a single multiple-choice question that is intended to assess both grammar and vocabulary, or two separate grammar points. This often results in the task doing a mediocre job of assessing each one. The same concern applies if the specifications include specific portions of a construct (for example, a list of specific grammar points, semantic categories, or reading subskills). Therefore, if a selected response—or perhaps even limited production—task format is used, a given question should only target one construct or portion of a construct. The various parts of the multi-part construct do *not* necessarily need separate test sections, however.

To a certain extent, each task will have already been described in the overall test structure specifications, by specifying its task format. Merely saying that students will write a short paragraph, or that they will listen to things and answer both short-answer and multiple-choice questions about them, is only a start. Neither of these examples gives enough information for someone who will be writing the test, though. More details about what to include in task descriptions will be provided below.

When specifying the scoring method, there are several points to cover. For question-based task formats (for example, short-answer and multiple-choice questions), will the scoring be **dichotomous**, with questions scored as correct or incorrect, with nothing in between? Or will it be **polytomous**, that is, with more than one scoring category, as is the case when partial-credit scoring is used? Polytomous scoring is usually discussed in measurement literature as relating to questions worth more than one point; for example, a question potentially worth three points might be scored as 0, 1, 2, or 3. Conceptually, however, it also applies to single-point questions that can receive partial credit.

For limited production tasks, model answers should be described in terms of what they must include or "look like." The actual model answers themselves will be written later, when the questions are being written. Some guidance needs to be provided at this point, though, for the teacher(s) writing them. In particular, if scoring will be polytomous, this section should address two interrelated points. First, what makes some questions worth more than others? For example, items requiring two-part answers might be considered worth more points than those with one-part answers, or it might be decided that certain item types will be worth more than others because they are believed to require a higher level of ability than others, or are more difficult. Second, what sorts of answers will tend to be worth less (or more) than others? Obviously, these points must be discussed in rather general terms at this stage—they are intended as directions for teachers writing the test, not the questions and scoring key themselves. If more than one person will be writing questions, though, it is useful to have all this worked out in advance, so that questions written by different teachers are as similar as possible.

Specifications component	Comments
Purpose, and construct definition(s) for the task	Taken from the overall test specifications, which were based on the context and purpose specifications
Description of the task	Descriptions of questions, prompts, or reading or listening passages (depending on the task format being used), and time allowed to complete the section.
Scoring method	Including: • For questions: right/wrong, or partial credit? • For limited production tasks: model answer descriptions, and essential response components • For extended production tasks: considerations the scoring rubric must address, and type of scoring rubric
Sample task	Example of each type of prompt, question, and reading or listening passage

Table 4.1 What to Include in the Specifications For Individual Tasks

For extended production tasks, the **scoring rubric** does not need to be written, adapted, or selected yet, but the things it will address do need to be specified. Scoring rubrics are the topic of Chapter 7, where they will be discussed in detail. At this stage, what is most important are the various considerations that it must address. For a writing test, will the scoring rubric need to include vocabulary use? Grammatical accuracy? Should it rate how well students performed the task? Does it need to include penmanship, spelling, or punctuation? These are the sorts of things that should be listed here. It is a good idea not to delay this step until later, since it will help focus the writing of prompts, making them more likely to elicit the types of writing (or speaking) that need to be assessed. It may also be helpful to decide now the type of scoring rubric to use: *analytic*, or *holistic*. In **analytic scoring**, each category of concern is rated separately (for example, grammatical accuracy, content, organization, etc.), with the scores then combined. In **holistic scoring**, the performance is given just one overall rating, which is based on the various categories of concern taken together as a whole.

Finally, there should be some sample or example questions, prompts, and passages to help make the specifications more concrete. This is particularly important if more than one person is creating the test, since it will help the test writers have a better idea of what they should be producing. It can also be useful for tests produced by a single person, if the specifications will be used repeatedly to create new tests—whether as generic specifications for tests used throughout the course, or as specifications for alternative forms (i.e. versions) of the same test, for use in different years. The task specifications might be clearly written, but other teachers (or the same teacher, months later) may need an example to help them understand more quickly and accurately. In addition, it may be a good idea to include bad examples, to provide an idea of what to avoid. In some cases the sample items, prompts, and passages could also be contained in a separate document from the specifications; particularly in large-scale testing organizations (i.e. those with at least several thousand test takers per year), the specifications and examples might be spread out into guidelines for item writers, guidelines for interviewers, and so on, with each document designed with a different audience in mind. Typically, though, the fewer the people involved in planning and writing the test, the more sense it probably makes to keep things simple in terms of the number of documents used.

Much of the following discussion relates to describing tasks, not only the things that should be included in the specifications for various tasks, but is also intended to point out decisions that need to be made. Teachers often handle most of these points implicitly, as basic assumptions, but it is best to make everything the result of explicit decisions. Tests should not be written a certain way just because no other alternatives were ever considered.

Specifications For Item-Based Task Formats

Most language tests make heavy use of *items*—that is, selected response and limited production questions. As with task specifications in general, the things that need to be included are primarily a matter of clarifying details. Table 4.2 presents a listing of the components needed in the specifications for multiple-choice questions, true-false questions, short-answer questions, and deletion-based tasks (specifically, cloze tests). One important term to review here is *item stem*, which is the part of an item that actually poses the question. In a multiple-choice question, the stem is the portion before the *options* (which are also referred to as the *answer choices*). In short-answer and true-false questions, of course, there is nothing *but* the stem. Another useful term to reintroduce here is *distractors*, the incorrect choices in a multiple-choice or matching question.

While some of the points outlined in Table 4.2 are fairly self-explanatory, several others may require a bit of clarification or amplification. The first three points in Table 4.2 (language of presentation, number of distractors, length of stems and options) are the same for all three selected response task formats, and they will be addressed in the following section, since they pertain almost exclusively to reading and listening comprehension questions. They are included in the table, though, for ease of reference while writing specifications. Similarly, ways of describing vocabulary and grammatical difficulty are discussed in the section on how to write specifications for reading and listening passages.

For multiple-choice questions	For short-answer questions
• Whether items are presented in the L1 or L2 • How long the item stem and options are • Which vocabulary and grammatical structures are to be used (or avoided), if any • How many options there are	• Whether items are presented in the L1 or L2 • Whether responses are accepted in the L1, L2, or both • Whether linguistic accuracy is included in scoring criteria (for answers in the L2) • Which vocabulary and grammatical structures are to be used (or avoided), if any • How long item stems are • How long responses should be • What is the maximum number of pieces of information to ask for • Whether polytomous or dichotomous scoring is to be used; if polytomous, how many points per item, or per piece of information
For true-false questions • Whether items are presented in the L1 or L2 • Whether "false" items need to be corrected • How long the item stems and options are • Which vocabulary and grammatical structures are to be used (or avoided), if any	

For matching questions
• Whether items are presented in the L1 or L2
• How many distractors there are
• How long the item stems and options should be
• Which vocabulary and grammatical structures are to be used (or avoided), if any
• Which part(s) of speech are to be used (for one-word answers)
	For deletion-based tasks
	• What type of deletions is to be used: fixed vs. rational
	  – For fixed (random, *n*th-word) deletions: how many words between deletions
	  – For rational deletions: what the criteria are for selecting deletions, and what the minimum number of words is between deletions
	• How many deletions there should be
	• How long the intact text at the beginning of the passage should be
	• Whether multiple passages, or only one passage, can be used to reach the number of deletions
	• Passages: same as for reading comprehension passages

Table 4.2 Considerations and Task Specification Components Required For Item- and Deletion-Based Task Formats

Two points about the specifications for matching tasks also bear further comment. First, regarding the number of options, it is important that matching tasks have more options than questions, so that the last few cannot be answered—or their answering facilitated—through the simple process of elimination. Second, if one-word options are being used in a matching section, particularly on vocabulary tests, using more than one part of speech (for example, mixing nouns, verbs, and adjectives) in the list of options can help students answer correctly through the process of elimination, rather than by actually knowing the answers.

Finally, the last two points regarding short-answer questions are interrelated, and may also require some clarification. Obviously, every short-answer question will require at least one piece of information to be answered correctly. In some cases, however, there may be two or more things that must be provided in order to receive full credit. For example, a reading question might require test takers to find two pieces of information in a story. Similarly, a grammar question requiring students to use the correct verb tense might require both the correct tense *and* agreement with the subject. In such cases, the maximum number of "bits" of information should be decided in advance, as well as the question of whether to use partial credit scoring—that is, whether items will be scored *dichotomously* (completely right or wrong, for one point or zero), or *polytomously* (with partial credit available, either by making the item worth more than one point, or by using fractional scoring (for example, a score of ½ or 0.5).

Specifications For Reading and Listening Comprehension Questions

One of the first points to consider when specifying comprehension tasks is to decide which language to use when presenting the questions. There is often an assumption that the questions should all be presented in the target language, but this is not necessarily a requirement, particularly when students share the same L1. In particular, when listening or reading comprehension is being assessed, this point needs to be considered carefully. Not surprisingly, presenting questions in the L1 seems to reduce test difficulty, especially for students with lower levels of language proficiency, or with short-answer questions (Rahimi 2007; Wolf 1993). Using L1 questions to assess L2 comprehension is also one way to avoid using items that are written with language that is more difficult than the language of the passages themselves. As Kirschner, Wexler, and Specter-Cohen (1992: 545) point out, the construct of interest is normally the ability to comprehend what is in the *passage*, in spite of some teachers' claims that "understanding the test questions is part of the test."

Furthermore, in the case of short-answer comprehension questions, the language of the response should also be specified. Especially at lower levels, responding in the target language may interfere with students' ability to demonstrate how much they really comprehended (see, for example, Brantmeier 2006; Wolf 1993). On the other hand, however, there will also be cases where it is precisely the L2 response that is of interest (for example, in short-answer grammar or vocabulary items).

None of this means that comprehension questions should necessarily be written in students' L1, or that students should respond to short-answer questions in their L1. Even when this is possible, it may not prove to be a good idea—teachers should consider whether the idea would be appropriate in their testing contexts. The decision, of course, should be made based on the construct definition(s) around which the test is being designed. To reiterate a point made above, the language in the comprehension questions (and the language in any responses students are expected to write) should not be more difficult than the language of the passage(s) to be read or heard. Using the L1 in these tasks is merely one possible way to address that issue, particularly at lower levels of language ability.

Finally, in cases where answers will be written in the L2, a decision also needs to be made as to whether linguistic accuracy should be considered when scoring, aside from when it renders answers unclear or factually wrong. A frequent response to this question is, "Of course it should!" The decision should, though, be based on the construct definition, rather than on instinct. If the construct is defined as "the ability to comprehend written text and answer questions using accurate language," then including accuracy of language use in the scoring guidelines is appropriate. The task format itself might be less appropriate, however. This sort of construct definition sounds rather close to what we might expect in an integrated test; therefore, in this scenario, it might be a good idea to reconsider both the construct definition and the task format. For example, would it be more appropriate to assess the ability to comprehend written text by asking students to write something about a written text (i.e. not just answer questions about the text)? Or are there reasons (for example, practicality, or common TLU domain tasks) for staying with the original form of the construct definition? If the construct is revised, will providing short answers to questions be the most useful way to assess it? There is no single correct answer to this question, of course—what matters most is being able to justify the choice that is eventually made.

Besides the language of the items and the students' responses, another point bears emphasizing: Inferences about specific reading and listening "subskills" can only be justified when the test actually requires students to use those subskills in order to answer questions. This seems to be particularly difficult when vocabulary-in-context items are being planned, as opposed to items testing vocabulary *knowledge*. **Vocabulary-in-context items** require examinees to identify the sense of a word that is being used in a passage, or to identify the meaning of an *unfamiliar* word using context clues. The focus is not on whether students already know the meaning of the word(s) in question—in fact, they should not—but rather whether they can infer the meanings of new, unfamiliar words from context.

Finally, for listening comprehension tests, there is the additional question of whether to let students preview the questions before listening to the passage. (See Sherman 1997 for research into the effects of previewing questions.) In real life, people usually know why they are listening to something (Mendelsohn 1994), so allowing students to preview questions helps to make the test task more authentic in that regard. Similarly, questions of how many times to let students listen to a passage should be answered in terms of authenticity (for example, certain recordings can be played multiple times in real life, whereas other real-world listening tasks may only be heard once). An additional consideration, of course, is how the students' level compares to that of the passage: Passages that are more difficult than those which students can normally handle may require additional chances to listen, whereas relatively easier passages might be presented to the test takers only once.

Specifications For Reading and Listening Comprehension Passages

In addition to writing the specifications for listening and reading comprehension items, the passages themselves must be planned as well. This may be somewhat easier when tests relate to a specific course.

General Considerations

One of the most important things, of course, is that any passage must be able to support questions of the sort called for in the specifications. For example, if the test structure specifications call for a mix of comprehension questions that will assess reading for specific details, drawing inferences, identifying the main or important ideas, and scanning, the passages need to be selected, adapted, or written so that they can be used for those purposes. If the test uses a series of short reading passages that leave nothing significant *un*stated, then inference questions will not be possible. Similarly, if scanning is included, then passages that would be suitable for scanning (for example, schedules, catalogues, or hotel listings) must be used.

Table 4.3 lists some of the most important things to include when writing specifications for a reading or listening passage. Many of these features apply equally to both reading and listening. For example, obviously, longer passages will tend to be more difficult, regardless of whether they are spoken or written. Likewise, how familiar the topic of the passage is also plays an important role in how difficult students will find the materials to process (see, for example, Alderson and Urquhart 1985, 1988; Lee 1986; Leeser 2007). Furthermore, certain topics may produce a negative emotional response—for example, a reading passage about national disasters might be distressing for students who have recently survived one themselves. Therefore, passage specifications need to include rules or guidance on what will be considered appropriate topics. Almost as important, perhaps, is the degree of topical specificity of the passage. That is, how accessible will the material be to a nonspecialist who is listening to or reading it? For example, a listening passage about predicting earthquakes might be full of technical terminology, and difficult for non-geologists to understand; or it could be at a more general level, and comprehensible to anyone with sufficient general language ability. All this, of course, requires familiarity with the students and what they are likely to already know.

Vocabulary is another important area to consider when planning listening or reading passages. Of course, in classroom testing, it may also be helpful to consider what words have been taught as part of the syllabus or curriculum—this is an obvious and useful starting point. In addition to this, though, other indicators of vocabulary should be considered as well. The level of vocabulary used in a passage can be described in several ways, including *lexical variation, lexical sophistication,* and *lexical density* (Read 2000). Variation is most commonly measured by the **type-to-token ratio** of the passage, that is, the total number of words in the passage divided by the number of different word forms; for example, if a particular word occurs five times in a passage, it counts as five *tokens* but only one *type*.

Sophistication of vocabulary has to do with how many low-frequency words are used in the passage. Word frequency is best determined by using **corpus**-based research. Cobb (2007) provides a practical discussion of how to do this in English. Also, it should be pointed out that in some cases, relatively infrequent words may have been learned as part of the class, and would thus be acceptable—or even necessary—in the passage.

Lexical density has to do with the proportion of words that are lexical, or content words, as opposed to grammatical, or function words. Information about all three ways of describing the vocabulary of a passage can be obtained using free software (Nation, n. d.) available at http://www.victoria.ac.nz/lals/staff/paul-nation/nation. aspx, or by using free Web-based applications (Cobb, n. d.) available at http:// www.lextutor.ca/.

Syntax is also an area that should be included in the specifications for a reading or listening passage. A variety of approaches can be and have been employed to analyze syntactic complexity, including counting **T-units** (essentially, an independent clause and any dependent clauses that are attached to it, Hunt 1965) and estimating their density (for example, number of T-units per 100 words), or counting the frequency of grammatical structures such as infinitive clauses, use of the passive voice, etc. (Carr 2006). At the classroom or program level, however, where the test is based upon a set curriculum, it may be simplest to consider what structures have been taught, and try to limit the passages to those.

Table 4.3 also includes two additional groups of points: several that apply specifically to reading, and others that apply specifically to listening. These will be addressed separately below.

Reading Comprehension Passages

With respect to reading, perhaps the most notable item is one that is *not* included in the list: *readability*. Readability formulas are easily used, and can often be applied using the same word processing software that teachers are using to write the test in the first place. Their use can be very tempting—they are easy to obtain, and concrete—and they may be appropriate for L1 reading, but research has indicated that they are poor indicators (at best) of text difficulty (Carrell 1987). In fact, because they tend to be based on the number of syllables (Alderson 2000; Carrell 1987), they are in effect an indicator of vocabulary complexity, which is probably better evaluated using the methods discussed above.

The *genre* of a reading passage is also something to include in the specifications. Here, I am using this term to refer to the type of passage—that is, what sort of text the passage is an example *of*. A few examples include magazine advertisements, billboard advertisements, business letters, personal letters, short stories, newspaper articles, magazine articles, academic journal articles, movie schedules, and train or bus schedules. It bears pointing out that in applied linguistics the term *genre* is typically used somewhat more broadly, and describes types of communicative events, which are categorized in terms of their communicative purposes, as well as their components and organization (Basturkmen and Elder 2004). This broader definition would subsume *rhetorical mode* (the type and purpose of a piece of writing, which also influence how it is structured), as well as what I am referring to as "type of speech act" under listening passages, and potentially register as well. I am separating all of these, however, because I believe that doing so makes the process of writing specifications clearer, and makes it less likely that important considerations will get ignored.

Finally, the specifications for reading passages should also include the *rhetorical mode(s)* to be used in passages—for example, whether the passage should be narrative, expository, cause-and-effect, persuasive, problem-solution, etc., in its organization and purpose.

Listening Comprehension Passages

In planning the type(s) of listening passages to include on a test, the first consideration is the type(s) of speech act to include. Among other things, this includes deciding whether a specific passage type should be a monolog or dialog, whether it should be transactional or interactional communication, and the genre of the speech act as well. Some examples of listening passage genres include commercials, announcements, news or weather broadcasts, academic lectures, telephone messages, conversations between friends, interactions between customers and service personnel, and conversations between supervisors and employees. Whatever selection is made, it is crucial that the type(s) of speech act be authentic. It is almost always a bad idea to simply read aloud a written passage, such as a narrative, when assessing listening comprehension. For reasons of authenticity, there are very few cases in which it might be appropriate to assess students on their ability to understand stories that have been read aloud.

The register, or level of formality, used in a passage is also something important, and should match the speech act and its participants. What communicative functions (for example, apologizing, asking permission, offering advice, etc.) are desirable in listening passages should also be specified. A single test *may* not be able to include enough material for all of the functions on the list to be included on a given form (i.e. version) of the test, so if any are considered more or less important than the others, this should be included in the specifications as well.

In addition, there are several points that relate to pronunciation and delivery that must be specified, starting with the speed of speech. Some aspects of the use of *suprasegmentals* may also need to be specified—for example, for very low-level students learning languages such as English, which normally include linking and other means of connecting words within an utterance, it may be necessary to speak each word in isolation, that is, without connecting it as in normal speech. Because this sort of modified listening input is highly inauthentic, however, it should be used only when test takers would be unlikely to comprehend normal speech. On the other hand, if certain suprasegmental features are considered important (for example, English tag questions eliciting agreement vs. confirmation, or yes-no questions vs. open-choice alternative questions; see Celce-Murcia, Brinton, and Goodwin 1996), the specifications should mention them. Likewise, if certain features such as the intonation patterns used in sarcasm are to be avoided, this should be specified as well.

Another concern that should be included in the specifications is what accent patterns or dialects should be included or avoided (see, for example, Taylor 2008). For example, speakers with strong regional accents in the target language might be unintelligible to examinees at lower levels of proficiency. On the other hand, more advanced learners should be able to comprehend common or important accents, and it might be important for the specifications to include this. Of course, deciding how heavy someone's accent is a subjective question, but this should also be taken into consideration as well. For example, in a test aimed at intermediate-level learners of English as a foreign language, it would probably be reasonable to include examples of British and North American English, and perhaps Australian or New Zealand accents as well. At the same time, a very strong accent from the Southeastern United States, Scotland, or New York City might make a speaker a poor choice for recording listening passages on that test.

Another point that should be included in the specifications for listening comprehension passages is any aspects of authentic discourse that should be included or avoided. Among other things, these might include hesitations or fillers, interruptions, repair, or clarification questions.

A final point about listening specifications that may not be entirely clear to some is the distinction between *scripted, unscripted,* and *semi-scripted* passages (Geddes and White 1978). **Scripted passages** are just that—they are written out and then read or performed verbatim. All too frequently, however, these passages *sound* scripted, and may resemble written language use more than the patterns used in actual spoken language (Burns and Joyce 1997). On the other hand, **unscripted passages** are recordings of naturally occurring speech. Their authenticity is obviously quite high, but it can be very difficult (or even impossible) to find such a recording that will be appropriate in terms of all the categories discussed here. **Semi-scripted passages**, therefore, can serve as a useful compromise, offering control over the necessary features, while still sounding authentic. They are, essentially, a plan or outline for a listening passage, which is then improvised according to that plan. Semiscripts can vary, from perhaps as general as the cue cards for a role-play, to as specific as a turn-by-turn outline of what should be said, without providing the actual words.

How "tightly" (i.e. specifically) to write the specifications for a semiscript is partly related to the question of how important standardization of the passages is. The less detailed the specifications for a semiscript, the more likely it is that versions performed by different people *using the same specifications* will be very different from each other. If that is undesirable, then a greater degree of specificity should be added. In any case, regardless of how detailed the semiscripts are (i.e. role-play-like with very little other specification, vs. outline-like, with turn-by-turn descriptions of what to say), the specifications must still take into account all of the considerations listed in Table 4.3, as would be true for any other passage.

Often, it may be necessary to use existing reading or listening passages, particularly for **low-stakes tests** (tests where the consequences for test takers and other stakeholders are not so serious or important), when the extra work of developing new ones is impractical. It may be very difficult to find passages that exactly match the specifications, however, so it may become necessary to modify them somehow. In reading passages, this is usually done by making changes to the grammatical structures and vocabulary that are used. The same sorts of changes may also be made when adapting listening passages, but it will also be necessary to re-record the passages. Even if the grammar and vocabulary are left unchanged, it may be necessary to re-record for better sound quality (for example, because there was too much background noise in the original), or for any of the other features included in Table 4.3. Whether passages are used as-is or adapted, however, it may be necessary to gain permission from the copyright owner before using them in tests. While intellectual property laws vary across jurisdictions, authors still deserve fair and responsible treatment. Even if something is available for free on the Internet, that does not automatically mean it is fair game!

Both listening and reading	
• Length • Topic • Topical specificity • Vocabulary (variety, frequency/familiarity, density) • Syntax	
Reading	**Listening**
• Genre • Rhetorical mode	• Type of speech act • Register • Communicative functions to be included • Speed of speech • Use of suprasegmentals • Accent of the speaker(s) • Aspects of authentic discourse to be included or avoided • Scripted, unscripted, or semi-scripted

Table 4.3 Considerations to Include in Listening and Reading Passage Specifications

One final point about writing specifications for reading and listening passages is that, as with test items and prompts, ideally, a sample passage should be included with the specifications, to serve as a model for the people writing or selecting passages. Even if original passages are going to be used for the actual test, it is appropriate here to use a preexisting one to illustrate what the final product should look or sound like.

Specifications For Vocabulary and Grammar Tests

For both vocabulary and grammar tests, there are three main considerations to bear in mind, above and beyond those that apply to specifications for any other type of test. First, it is important to keep in mind the distinction between the ability to *recognize* a word, or *comprehend* a structure, and to *use* that word or structure accurately. Second, at times there may be a need to consider the *range* of vocabulary or grammatical structures that have been acquired, in addition to the *degree of mastery* that has been achieved over the words or structures that are actually produced (Laufer and Goldestein 2004). Note that this concern with both range and degree of mastery will apply equally when vocabulary or grammar is included in a scoring rubric for speaking or writing tasks.

Finally, it may be appropriate in some cases to use polytomous scoring, in order to simultaneously assess control over form and meaning (Purpura 2004). This approach can be applied to multiple-choice questions as well as limited production tasks, with one point being given for accuracy of form and another for accuracy of meaning. (Note that it is not strictly necessary to make each item worth two points; if each item were worth one point, then the two aspects of the response would be worth half a point apiece.) An example of this might be a question about using modals for suggestions. On the test paper, there is a three-line excerpt from a dialog. Speaker A says, "Should we go to the beach today, or go hiking in the mountains?" A blank space is provided for Speaker B's response, and then Speaker A replies, "OK, let me get my boots on." The test taker is supposed to write Speaker B's response in the blank space. In this example, one point would be awarded for making a suggestion about hiking in the mountains, and one point would be awarded for using an appropriate modal, such as *should*, perhaps also taking into consideration the form of the main verb.

Specifications For Speaking and Writing Prompts

Any prompt is intended to elicit a particular sort of response. The task specifications for prompts are instructions for how to write those prompts, and need to make clear what sort of response is desired. When writing these specifications, it is probably helpful to write the directions that will be given to students when they take the test, as this may make the task of writing the prompts clearer. This, along with the description of the task format in the specifications for the overall test, is an important starting point. When a teacher is writing a prompt, they need to make sure that, taken together, the directions and the prompt itself will give students a fair chance to do well on whatever the task is. This is much more likely to happen if it is obvious to that teacher what they are supposed to be asking the students to do. To ensure that, therefore, there should be a description of the responses that the prompts are intended to elicit.

For example, if it is a writing prompt, is the goal for students to produce a few sentences, an entire paragraph, or a properly organized essay? Whatever the case, the prompt should be likely to elicit that kind of response from students who have an appropriate level of language ability. The specifications should therefore state this clearly, as well as the nature of the communication that the prompt should attempt to elicit. This includes the purpose of the communication; thus, for writing, the genre and rhetorical mode should be specified. For speaking, it includes the type of speech act, register, communicative functions, and any other aspects of discourse that should be elicited. For both speaking and writing, the specifications should detail the desired length of the expected responses; the topics of the prompts, and how topic-specific the prompts can be; and even broad statements about vocabulary or grammatical patterns that students are supposed to produce. This list probably sounds familiar, as these are most of the things that need to be included when writing the specifications for reading and listening passages.

Of course, the most important thing is that the specifications should also describe the prompts themselves. As Weigle (2002) points out, this portion of the specifications includes a description of the language that should be used in prompts (especially any grammatical structures or vocabulary that should be used, or avoided), as well as a description of any input being provided to examinees (reading or listening passages, pictures, graphs, etc.).

More on Specifications For Interview-Based Speaking Tests

When a speaking test is being created, the decision may be made to rely entirely on prompts and ask a fixed set of questions to all of the students. (It is possible, of course, to produce multiple forms of such a test, but any students taking the same form would be asked the same set of questions.) This is particularly the case when a "semi-direct" test is being planned, or when role-plays or other directed tasks are being used. It is common as well as for longer speaking tasks (for example, giving a speech, talk, or other monolog), and for short, one-sentence questions (for example, *What is your name?*, or *What color is the book?*) such as might be appropriate in a course for students with very low levels of speaking ability.

In tests administered one-on-one by a teacher or other rater, however, speaking tests often take the form of interviews. In effect, the teachers performing the interview must spontaneously create unwritten prompts as the interview progresses. These can be relatively free-form and wide-ranging, but generally, the less structure is imposed upon the interviewer, the more training is needed in how to perform these interviews efficiently. When interviewers are given more structure and fewer options, on the other hand, less training will generally be required.

These two approaches to interviewing—unguided interviews and rigidly fixed sets of questions—can be treated as the two ends of a continuum. In the real world, however, almost all interview tests avoid both extremes. For example, even when all examinees are to be asked the same set of questions, follow-up questions may be asked, which will naturally introduce some variation from one interview to the next. After all, as Cangelosi (1990) points out, one of the strengths of interview tests is that they allow for clarification. Similarly, most teachers will find it less stressful to have a list of questions or topics from which to choose, so they are not forced to make them up as they go along.

A step in the direction of greater flexibility is when interviewers are given a list of potential questions to ask, and are allowed to select from that list. Here, questions may be grouped into categories by topics, functions, or grammatical structures they are intended to elicit (for example, questions that would be likely to require students to speak in the past tense). Such a list is particularly helpful if the interview is part of a placement or proficiency test, where students with a wide variety of ability levels might take the same test. In these cases, the list may be grouped by level of difficulty or sophistication; or, if the questions are grouped by topic, they may be grouped *within* each topic according to difficulty. Having such a list in those cases means the teachers doing the interviewing do not have to think up questions on the spot. In addition, it can be helpful in keeping the questions asked of different examinees broadly comparable, and ensures that questions get asked about the topics, functions, grammatical structures, etc. that need to be sampled on the test. Sometimes, the number of questions may not be specified; instead, the specifications may call for the conversation to last a certain minimum length of time, include questions involving a certain number of topics or grammatical structures, etc. In other cases, the policy for ending the interview might be to continue until the teacher has a good enough sense of the speaker's performance to assign a score.

In some cases, the interview may have a certain amount of structure, but still be rather free-form in terms of the specific questions asked. This would be the case, for example, if the teacher is given a list of topics, functions, or structures to attempt to elicit, but is not given any specific questions. (For example: "Ask a question about three of the following five topics: family, eating in restaurants, clothing, hobbies, and travel.") In these situations, interviewers will often be told to use their judgment as to which items on the list to address, and in what order.

On a cautionary note, it should be pointed out that researcher Ann Lazaraton has reported inconsistencies in the support or accommodation provided by raters during interviews, identifying eight different types that were used to greater and lesser degrees by interviewers in her study (Lazaraton 1996). Furthermore, Lazaraton also identified differences in the difficulty of questions asked by different raters (Lazaraton 2002). Of course, these findings raise the possibility of differences in interlocutor support and question difficulty affecting test takers' scores. Therefore, the amount of this support that is permissible should be addressed in the directions given to interviewers, as well as any guidelines for how raters should take into consideration the amount of assistance when assigning scores. Similarly, if lists of specific questions are not provided to interviewers, they should at least be given instructions regarding what to ask, in terms of topic, vocabulary, and grammatical structures, at a minimum.

Like traditional one-on-one interviews, group interviews or group discussion tasks can also vary in terms of how structured they are. Students may be directed to ask each other specific questions, perhaps with follow-up (especially for higher-level students, and with the amount of follow-up perhaps included in the scoring). At advanced levels, they may be given one or more topics to discuss, rather than specific questions. Whichever approach is followed, it is clearly more effective to provide students with questions or topics to discuss, rather than to tell them to just start talking. These lists will keep the task more focused, and make it less likely that they will sit there just looking at each other, wondering what to do, instead of talking.

Whatever approach is decided upon, it must be described in the task specifications. If lists of questions will be used, then the categories, difficulty levels, etc. of the various questions should be specified, so that those writing the questions will have clear guidance on what to produce. This is, of course, no different from specifying any other type of speaking prompt. If only lists of topics are to be used, either the topics should be listed, or the basis for deciding on them should be specified here. For example, for an achievement test, this might mean merely specifying use of the topics from the second half of the course, the grammar focus of the current unit, or something similar. For a diagnostic speaking test administered at the beginning of the course, it might mean saying that the topics will be those that are covered during that term. In particular, saying only that the topics will be "those covered in the course" might be appropriate when the specifications are generic ones that are to apply to multiple courses, or to more than one test within the same course. Likewise, even if questions are to be written, rather than simple lists of interview topics, a set of generic specifications might specify writing the questions based on topics, functions, etc. covered in the course. The *generic* versions of these specifications for writing questions would look very similar to those for an interview test in which interviewers would only be supplied a list of topics.

Specifications Development as an Iterative Process

Many teachers who are writing test specifications for the first time are under the impression that once they have made a decision, they are bound by that decision for the rest of the project. In fact, though, previous decisions can be revisited, and in fact, very frequently *need* to be. It may become clear that changes will be needed while the specifications are still being written, or problems may arise when it comes time to write the actual test. In either case, after the earlier sections are changed, anything that has been written (i.e. other portions of the specifications, or actual questions, prompts, and passages) needs to be reviewed, to make sure it conforms to the newly revised specifications, not to the original ones. Very often, of course, the changes in earlier material are needed because a problem was identified later on, but the parts between these two sections need review and reconsideration. Similar revisions may also become necessary after pilot testing, and again during operational testing, as new issues or problems emerge. For example, specifications describing listening passages may have seemed perfectly clear when they were written, but when someone actually has to *use* those descriptions to write or select texts, critical omissions may suddenly become apparent.

An example of this took place once in an academic English testing project with which I was involved. The test development team videotaped a university lecture, identified a segment that was self-contained and of the proper length, and wrote all the comprehension questions for the passage. It was only after a three-hour item-writing meeting that everyone agreed that despite coming from a general education course, the passage was too technically-oriented, and would be highly problematic for students not studying engineering or the physical sciences. (The person leading that day's meeting had been under the mistaken impression that *everyone* already understood the basics of stellar formation—the process by which stars are formed from large clouds of dust and gas in space. As it turns out, however, that was not the case, and I apparently watch too much *Star Trek*.) This had not been part of the specifications previously, and they were altered to exclude most science passages in the future. In addition, by making such additions to the specifications, they are made a permanent part of the "institutional memory," and not dependent on someone remembering to mention them later on when new people are brought onto the testing team. Making the changes "official" by adding them to the specifications can thus save people later on from having to rediscover the hard way why the changes were a good idea.

Reverse Engineering Specifications From an Existing Test

Sometimes, there is already a test, or part of a test, and a teacher is asked by a supervisor to "make the new one look like this." Perhaps there were once specifications, and they were lost, or perhaps there never were any, just a rough idea of how the test was supposed to look. In either case, before writing the new version of the old test, specifications need to be drawn up. Fortunately, this process is not very different from that for writing specifications from scratch. In fact, it is arguably somewhat easier. In order to "reverse engineer" the specifications that are implicit in the test, we follow the steps for writing the three levels of specifications: *test context and purpose, overall test structure,* and *individual tasks.* Rather than making decisions, though, here we are basically figuring out what the intentions of the creators of the original test were and what decisions they made. .

In the process of doing this, it may become apparent that there were inconsistencies in what was being done previously, or that some point in the specifications was clearly ignored. In such cases, teachers need to decide whether to adjust the specifications accordingly on their own, or seek approval or directions from a supervisor or the other teachers involved in the project. Which path will be more appropriate will depend, of course, on the situation. These points are almost certain to come up, though, since in most cases the test probably really was written without using any specifications. The resulting product should be much improved, however, since it will essentially be a better-planned, more internally consistent version of a test that the institution already liked.

Summary

Chapter 3 began the discussion of test specifications, starting with explanations of the context and purpose specifications and specifications for the overall structure of the test. This chapter then took up the topic specifications for individual test tasks. After pointing out general considerations, it dealt with what to include in the specifications for item-based tasks, and raised issues specific to assessing reading and listening comprehension, including the details of planning for reading and listening comprehension passages. The chapter then addressed some considerations relevant to testing vocabulary and grammar before moving on to cover the writing of specifications for speaking and listening prompts and interview-based speaking tests. A brief discussion then followed pointing out that the development of specifications is an iterative process, with changes sometimes occurring in response to problems identified during the test writing process. The chapter concluded by offering a few pointers on reverse engineering specifications from an existing test.

Now that we have considered the purposes of tests and several ways to classify them, the choices available to us in terms of task formats, and how to plan a test, Chapter 5 will address the actual writing of the test, and will provide guidelines for how to implement the plan contained in the specifications.

Further Reading

Note: This list includes suggestions for further reading on all three stages of the specifications design process: context and purpose, overall test structure, and individual test tasks.

Alderson, J. C. 2000. Chapter 5 'A framework for test design', Chapter 6 'Tests in the real world: test purpose'. *Assessing Reading.* Cambridge: Cambridge University Press.

Alderson, J. C., C. Clapham, and **D. Wall.** 1995. Chapter 2 'Test specifications'. *Language Test Construction and Evaluation.* Cambridge: Cambridge University Press.

Bachman, L. F. and **A. S. Palmer.** 1996. Chapter 3 'Describing tasks: Language use in language tests', Chapter 5 'Overview of test development'. *Language Testing in Practice.* Oxford: Oxford University Press.

Buck, G. 2001. Chapter 5 'Creating tasks', Chapter 6 'Providing suitable texts', Chapter 7 'Designing and constructing complete assessments'. *Assessing Listening.* Cambridge: Cambridge University Press.

Davidson, F. and **B. K. Lynch.** 2002. *Testcraft: A Teacher's Guide to Writing and Using Language Test Specifications.* New Haven, CT: Yale University Press.

Douglas, D. 2000. Chapter 5 'From target language use to test tasks'. *Assessing Language for Specific Purposes.* Cambridge: Cambridge University Press.

Fulcher, G. 2003. Chapter 3 'Tasks for second language speaking tests', Chapter 5 'Test specifications'. *Testing Second Language Speaking.* Harlow, UK: Pearson Longman.

Luoma, S. 2004. Chapter 3 'Speaking tasks', Chapter 6 'Developing test specifications', Chapter 7 'Developing speaking tasks'. *Assessing Speaking.* Cambridge: Cambridge University Press.

Purpura, J. E. 2004. Chapter 5 'Designing test tasks to measure L2 grammatical ability', Chapter 6 'Developing tests to measure L2 grammatical ability'. *Assessing Grammar.* Cambridge: Cambridge University Press.

Read, J. 2000. Chapter 6 'The design of discrete vocabulary tests', Chapter 7 'Comprehensive measures of vocabulary'. *Assessing Vocabulary.* Cambridge: Cambridge University Press.

Weigle, S. C. 2002. Chapter 5 'Designing writing assessment tasks'. *Assessing Writing.* Cambridge: Cambridge University Press.

Discussion Questions

You may find it helpful to base your answers here on the same test you used in the discussion questions for Chapter 3.

1 Consider a language test that you have taken, administered, or are otherwise familiar with that included reading and/or listening comprehension. For the reading or listening portion of the test only:

   a What task format(s) were used?
   b Was the scoring dichotomous (right/wrong) or polytomous (partial credit)?

   Imagine you are in charge of revising the test, and make decisions about the following points. Provide your rationale for each decision.

   c What task format(s) will you include?
   d Will you use dichotomous or polytomous scoring?
   e For each task format, what decisions will you make regarding the points in Table 4.2?
   f How many passages will you include?
   g For each passage, what decisions will you make regarding the points in Table 4.3?

2 Consider a language test that you have taken, administered, or are otherwise familiar with that included speaking and/or writing ability. For the speaking or writing portion of the test only:

   a What task format(s) were used?
   b Was the scoring rubric analytic or holistic?

   Imagine you are in charge of revising the test, and make decisions about the following points. Provide your rationale for each decision.

    c What task format(s) will you include?

    d How many prompts will you include? If this is a speaking test, will you use prompts, an unguided interview format, or something in between?

    e What purpose of communication, genre, rhetorical mode, etc. will test takers be expected to provide?

3 Consider a language test that you have taken, administered, or are otherwise familiar with that included a separate section on grammar and/or vocabulary. For the grammar or vocabulary portion of the test only:

    a What task format(s) were used?

    b Was the scoring dichotomous (right/wrong) or polytomous (partial credit)?

Imagine you are in charge of revising the test, and make decisions about the following points. Provide your rationale for each decision.

    c What task format(s) will you include?

    d Depending on whether it is a grammar or vocabulary test, will this/these format(s) require examinees to recognize words/comprehend structures, or use words/structures accurately?

    e Will you use dichotomous or polytomous scoring?

    f For each task format, what decisions will you make regarding the points in Table 4.2?

5 WRITING THE TEST

Introduction

The test specifications detail how the test is supposed to be constructed. Specifically, they include the decisions as to which task formats are most appropriate for each section of the test. Once the specifications have been completed, the next step is to begin writing the test itself. This chapter will discuss a number of things to do during the test writing process that will result in a better, more useful test.

Following the Plan

Writing the test should begin with a review of the specifications, since these are the instructions for how to write the test. The next step should be to write the directions for the students taking the test, if these were not written as part of the specifications. As a rule, they will need to be written for each section or group of tasks. Keeping in mind what students are supposed to be doing can help test writers keep the questions, prompts, passages, and so forth consistent with the plan in the specifications.

Perhaps the most important thing to keep in mind is something we have been hearing most of our lives: *Follow the directions*. After all, there is no sense in making a plan and then ignoring it. It makes no difference whether the person writing the test is the same one who wrote the specifications, is part of the group that wrote them, or is helping make a test designed by others. The plan may be adjusted as the project develops, but this needs to be the result of a conscious, considered decision, not a case of plans accidentally "drifting." In particular, the test should be written using the same tasks that the specifications describe, with the same balance. Someone with no experience in using formal test specifications may find this confusing, so I will use two examples to clarify the point I am trying to make here. In the first case, imagine a reading test with specifications that call for a mix of three types of questions: reading for the main idea, drawing inferences, and reading for specific details. In that case, the teachers writing the test need to write all three types of questions, and *not* simply write main idea items. Similarly, imagine a writing test's specifications stating that the two prompts should elicit a variety of rhetorical modes (persuasion, narration, description, etc.). In this case, if all the prompts are for persuasive essays, the specifications are not being followed.

When more than one person is writing the test, an extra level of planning is required to make sure that the group as a whole follows the specifications, even if the individual members are all doing so. That is, each person needs to be given specific duties, so that each section of the test is addressed. Merely telling all the teachers involved in the project, or even all the teachers in the language program or school to write five questions and turn them in, with no further instructions, is inadequate at best. Doing that will result in a collection of random elements, and the test would be a waste of time for teachers and students alike. Saying that everyone should write ten questions following the specifications and meet again in a week is better, but probably *not* specific enough; rather, the types of questions need to be specified.

Writing Passage-Based Test Tasks

Tests of listening and reading comprehension present an added dimension of complexity for test writers, above and beyond what is found with simple assessments of speaking, listening, grammar, or vocabulary that do not include input that must be processed and comprehended. This need to process and respond to input not only involves the passages themselves, but also has important implications for the questions. Most of the points about reading and listening comprehension questions will focus on selected response and limited production tasks, but some issues will apply to extended production tasks as well.

General Considerations For Reading and Listening Passages

It is important to start by creating or selecting appropriate reading and listening passages. The simplest way to do this is to follow the specifications in terms of length, vocabulary, syntax, topical content, etc. In cases where the specifications were vague, teachers creating or selecting the passages should make notes about what they do, and share these with the rest of the test development team, so that tighter specifications will result. It is quite likely, especially the first time that they are used to guide item writing, that the passage specifications will need to be revised in this fashion, particularly those for listening passages. What seemed clear during the process of writing the task specifications (see Chapter 4) may be revealed to be too broad and unspecific when actually put to use. For this reason, it is crucial to develop a clear construct definition for reading or listening comprehension (as part of the test context and purpose specifications; see Chapter 3) before writing the task specifications; this construct definition will benefit from careful thought about what elements it should include, and should be guided by the relevant literature.

One of the most important requirements for a good reading or listening passage is that it needs to be able to serve as the basis for the tasks that will be based upon it; otherwise, it is useless. For example, if a listening test is supposed to include several questions that require inferencing, at least several of the passages need to include something that is implied, so that the questions can be written. If the passages are all very short and simple, with all information stated explicitly, it may not be possible to write inference questions. If the passage is too short, it may be possible to ask about its topic, but there may not be a main idea of the sort found in longer types of passages, such as lectures. (The same issue applies, of course, with reading passages—not just listening passages.) Similarly, a reading test that includes scanning needs to use a text that is of the sort for which scanning would normally be considered appropriate (for example, schedules, timetables, or listings for hotels or restaurants). Furthermore, it is probably also a good idea to control (or limit) the time allowed on scanning tasks, so that students do not have time to read the entire text carefully, even if they want to.

If teachers find, during the test-writing process, that the specifications call for passages that are too short for the tasks they need to write, the specifications need to be amended to include longer passages. I saw this become necessary once in a project to develop a high-level academic reading test. In order for the passages to "stand on their own" (i.e. make sense, and seem complete, covering a single main proposition), it was necessary to allow passages that were half as long again as had originally been intended. Of course, if individual passages become longer, this may also require reducing the number of passages used on the test.

Creating or Selecting Listening Passages

There are several points unique to listening passages that do not really apply to selecting or creating reading passages. Many principles are equally relevant to creating good reading or listening passages (particularly attention to grammar, vocabulary, length, and topical content). Similarly, there are parallel issues—using the appropriate rhetorical mode(s) in reading, and using appropriate speech activities (for example, transactional or interactional communication) or functions (for example, persuading, apologizing) in listening passages. These similarities do *not* mean, however, that listening passages should resemble reading passages that have been read aloud. Indeed, poor authenticity because of too much resemblance to written language is a common problem with scripted listening passages, as was previously explained in Chapter 4.

One obvious issue with producing listening comprehension passages is that the sound quality must be good enough for students to hear what is being said without undue effort. The audio needs to be clear enough to be satisfactory when the test is administered, *not* merely clear when sitting next to the speakers or listening with headphones. As a general rule, the larger the room, the clearer the recording needs to be. Of course, if a listening test is going to include video for greater authenticity, the quality of the visuals needs to be good enough to be useful. My own experience with trying to obtain genuine videos of TLU speech for listening comprehension tests has taught me that there are three areas that can determine whether a clip is acceptable or not: appropriacy of the topic, clarity of the audio, and visual quality. It is fairly easy to get video of genuine speech (unscripted, actually taken from the

TLU domain) where two of these requirements are met, but getting all three at an acceptable level requires careful preparation or very good luck.

A further point that relates to audio quality is the use of background noise, whether in a genuine recording, or inserted to scripted or semi-scripted recordings to "set the stage" and enhance authenticity. This is seldom used in testing materials, however, presumably for the same reasons that can make it problematic in teaching materials: It is very easy to overdo this, and if the noise continues during the actual speech of the recording, it can have a major effect on the clarity of the passage, at least for non-native speakers. Native-speaking teachers should be particularly cautious here, as the background noise may not interfere at all with their own listening. Passages with background noise during the talking should therefore be used with caution, if at all. If recordings of genuine, unscripted language use are being considered for use on the test, background noise levels should be explicitly considered as part of the process of reviewing the passages.

In their seminal article introducing the use of semi-scripted passages, Geddes and White (1978) recommend getting at least two "takes" of each passage, and either using one or the other, or editing them together (which is a much simpler, cheaper, and faster task today than it was in 1978) to get a complete usable recording. This is a good idea even when scripted passages—which can be rehearsed, unlike semi-scripted recordings—are being used, as even these can be difficult to read perfectly the first time through. Furthermore, problems that went unnoticed during the recording session may seem painfully obvious later on, when the recordings are reviewed. Therefore, a minimum of two takes is probably very sound advice. (As a point for comparison, note that professional test developers spend significant amounts of money using actors in professional recording studios in order to ensure they capture exactly the right quality of audio or video; thus, in comparison, recording multiple takes is not such a heavy demand!)

Additionally, it is important that the speakers who are used in recordings have clear voices, and speak loudly and clearly enough for the recordings to be of useable quality. Voices should also be distinct from each other in dialogs—having two people who sound similar to each other will be particularly confusing for students who are trying to comprehend what is being said. This is one reason that many listening passages used for tests and classroom materials often use one male and one female voice. Using two males or two females is fine, of course, as long as their voices are not too similar to each other.

A final point to keep in mind is the need to avoid nonstandard dialects or accents, unless comprehending them is specifically part of the construct being assessed. For some languages, accent patterns, and dialects, this can be a greater cause for concern than in others. The degree to which this will be a problem depends on how different the dialect is that the speaker is using, or how heavy their accent pattern is. Naturally, the degree of concern will probably also depend on how advanced the learners are who are taking the test. For more advanced students, understanding a variety of dialects or accent patterns may be a very reasonable expectation.

General Suggestions on Item Writing

There are three overarching considerations to keep in mind when writing test questions, be they selected response or limited production. These relate to questions themselves being clear to the students and construct-relevant; asking questions that cannot simply be answered through logic or background knowledge, without actually knowing the answer *per se*; and maintaining item independence.

Keeping Questions Clear and Construct-Relevant

When writing test questions, one of the first things to keep in mind is that the questions themselves should be as easy to read as possible, and ought not to serve as an additional source of difficulty on the test (Kirschner, Wexler, and Specter-Cohen 1992; Thorndike and Hagen 1969). This, of course, is the reason for *considering* asking questions in the students' L1, as discussed in Chapter 4.

The test specifications are supposed to describe various parts of the construct, and which tasks and task formats will be used to assess each of them. If the specifications are followed when writing the test, every part of the construct(s) will be assessed, and everything on the test will assess part of the construct(s) of interest. This is a point that teachers sometimes miss when creating tests, and they sometimes wind up writing items that do not actually relate to the construct that they need to be assessing. Thorndike and Hagen also caution against writing trick questions; this is of particular importance in a language test, since we are concerned with students' language ability, not their ability to solve puzzles. They further warn against basing items on trivial details or distinctions, unless those details are part of the construct that is being targeted for assessment. For example, if we are trying to assess knowledge of verb tenses, we should not make knowledge of articles necessary in order to get an item correct.

Not Giving Away the Answers

The test questions are intended to tell how much of the construct a student has. It is only logical, therefore, that answering the question correctly should depend on having and applying that particular ability. For example, items that give away the answers to other items should obviously not be used. This issue seems to be a more frequent problem with multiple-choice than with short-answer questions, perhaps because the options on multiple-choice give more chances to give clues to test takers; nevertheless, limited production questions can create the same problem as well. In particular, Cangelosi (1990) cautions that **completion** (also called **fill-in-the-blank**, or **gap-fill**) items can help students to answer correctly without knowing the answers on their own. Similarly, all the options for a selected response item should be plausible; otherwise, it becomes easier to guess the correct answer using the process of elimination. Likewise, questions should not be asked that can be answered using common sense or general knowledge alone.

The message is about a change in schedule for a(n) _____.

A <u>business meeting</u>
B doctor's appointment
C airline flight

The meeting time has been changed from _____.

A 8 am to 9 am
B <u>9 am to 10 am</u>
C 10 am to 11 am

Figure 5.1 Example of One Item Giving Away the Answer to a Previous Item (through the reference to "meeting"). Both items are based on the same listening comprehension passage, a recorded phone message.

In passage-based tasks, one of the ways to avoid this issue is to make sure that the items all have **passage dependence**, that is, that answering a question correctly requires comprehending the listening or reading passage on which it is based. This seems like nothing more than ordinary common sense, and of course, it is nothing more than that. Nevertheless, it has long been recognized as an important issue (see, for example, Connor and Read 1978; Hanna and Oaster 1978–1979; Perkins and Jones 1985; Powers and Wilson 1993 ; Tuinman 1973–1974), even in some commercially produced tests (Keenan, Betjemann, and Olson 2008).

According to the passage, there are now over _____ dance schools in Italy.

A two hundred
B <u>two thousand</u>
C two hundred thousand
D two million

The research center uses the panda blood samples for:

A creating super-pandas
B <u>research and storage</u>
C comparison with bears and cats
D display purposes

Figure 5.2 Examples of Multiple-Choice Items with Poor Passage Dependence Because They Have One or More Implausible Options (the supposedly correct answer is underlined for each of the above items; these questions are taken from different tests)

Probably the best way to evaluate the passage dependence of a set of test questions is simply to try answering them without reading or listening to the passage. Any that can be answered without the passage have poor passage dependence, and need to be revised or replaced. Since the person writing the questions is probably too familiar with the passage to do this, it is best to ask a colleague who has not read or heard the passage to try to answer the questions. Before doing this, however, it is probably a good idea for the person writing the test to try taking it themselves. This can help them find problematic questions beforehand, not just in terms of passage dependence, but also in terms of other errors as well (for example, multiple-choice questions with no correct answer, or two correct answers; or short-answer questions that do not have *any* good answers).

Maintaining Item Independence

Item independence is, despite its name, *not* the opposite of *passage dependence*. Rather, it means that getting one item right should not depend on answering others correctly—individual items should be independent of each other in that sense. (The assumption of independence is especially important in **item response theory**, an advanced statistical methodology that will be discussed briefly, on a conceptual level, in Chapter 10.) By definition, this principle is violated at least to some extent by any passage-based test, but this violation is generally small enough to be ignored. Note that item independence overlaps with passage dependence in that if one question gives away the answer to another one, this interferes with both passage dependence and the independence of the items. The most important thing here for teachers to keep in mind is probably to avoid overlapping items. In other words, two items should not pose the same question, even with slightly different wording.

The reading passage is about the _____ airplane in the world.

A biggest
B first
C oldest
D <u>fastest</u>

The engineers in the passage are trying to make a _____ airplane.

A huge
B <u>fast</u>
C small
D fuel-efficient

Figure 5.3 Two Contiguous Items That lack Item Dependence (both are asking about essentially the same piece of information; any examinee who can answer one can answer the other)

Item Writing For Selected Response Task Formats

On top of the practices that need to be followed in creating any type of item-based test task, *selected response tasks*—multiple-choice, true-false, and matching questions—introduce a few additional factors to which teachers need to pay attention. Thorndike and Hagen (1969) point out one that applies to all three formats: it is important to make sure that there is no pattern to the responses, even if this would make grading faster. Some way must be found to randomize the order, whether it is through truly randomizing the options, alphabetizing them, or something else. For multiple-choice questions, it is particularly important to randomize the order in which the correct option appears.

Multiple-Choice Questions

Many people believe that multiple-choice questions are easy to write. In fact, they are easy to write *poorly*, and many are, as most teachers have never been trained in how to write them. It is not terribly hard to learn, though, as good item writing mostly involves attention to detail and an awareness of several rules, rules which generally seem obvious *after* they have been explained. Before discussing how to use this task format more effectively, however, it might be useful to review a few terms presented in Chapter 2. The *stem* is the portion of the item that poses the question being asked, or the "question" part of a multiple-choice item. The *options, answer choices,* or *alternatives* are the potential answers from which students choose. The correct option is called the *key*, and the incorrect answers are the *distractors*.

One important principle to keep in mind when writing multiple-choice questions is that the items should be written so they are as easy to read as possible, while remaining clear and unambiguous (see, for example, Cangelosi 1990; Haladyna, Downing, and Rodriguez 2002; Thorndike and Hagen 1969). To implement this principle, Thorndike and Hagen suggest avoiding redundancy in the options by putting as much information as possible into the stem, but at the same time restricting the stem to only the information needed to pose the question. At the same time, however it is important to be clear and unambiguous, so that students understand what they are being asked.

Along these same lines, most experts (see, for example, Haladyna, Downing, and Rodriguez 2002; Thorndike and Hagen 1969) also recommend avoiding negatives, particularly *not*, whenever possible, as these can make the questions more difficult to read. This advice is often given to people writing multiple-choice questions in content areas, for tests that will be delivered in students' native languages. In language tests, therefore, it seems likely that this would be an even greater area of concern. Occasionally, however, it is impossible to avoid this; in such cases, words such as *not, except,* etc. should be highlighted very obviously, preferably in **bold face** and either ***italicized***, <u>underlined</u>, or printed in **CAPITAL LETTERS**. It is probably a good idea to attempt to limit the use of these words to the stem, and avoid them altogether in the options if possible. Similarly, *none of the above* and *all of the above*-type options should probably be avoided, for similar reasons. There also seems to be a consensus that "multiple multiple-choice" items, such as those offering choices between "1 and 2," "1 and 3," are a bad idea, even in content area assessment (Cangelosi 1990; Haladyna et al. 2002); in language assessment, they are likely to be an even worse idea. (Note that this contrasts with the evaluation by the same authors of what I will call *multiple true-false*, which is described in the true-false section below.) This is supported by the findings of Sireci, Wiley, and Keller (1998), who found problems with this multiple-choice format even when used mostly with educated native speakers (specifically, on a certified public accountant examination).

As for avoiding ambiguity, one of the ways to do this is by ensuring that there is one answer that is clearly the best. There should be one option that is clearly correct, not two or more that are partially correct. As obvious as this sounds, it is worth taking time to review all the items for just this point before the test is administered, that is, to make sure that there is one and only one correct answer to each question. When there is extensive, repeated editing and revision, embarrassing accidents can sometimes find their way into the test. As Cangelosi (1990) points out, the options should not overlap, either, but should instead be distinct from each other. Otherwise, as he notes, students will be better able to answer questions correctly using deduction, not the ability being assessed.

Vocabulary item with no correct answer:

An <u>over-the-counter</u> drug is medicine that is:

A only sold with a doctor's permission.
B administered to people at the hospital.
C used only for serious illnesses.

Reading item with multiple correct answers, but no overlapping options:

One of the issues faced by travelers is:

A packing their luggage
B getting around town
C <u>selecting souvenirs</u>
D finding a good hotel

Listening item with severely overlapping options:

Orange County:

A has the largest concentration of Vietnamese people in California.
B is one of the locations with the most Vietnamese residents in California.
C <u>has the largest concentration of Vietnamese people in the U.S.</u>
D is one of the locations with the most Vietnamese residents in the U.S.

If A is true, B is true as well; if C is true, A, B, and D are also true; and if D is true, B must also be true. Additionally, the item was intended for use at a university in Orange County, and anyone living there would know that both A and B are correct, and probably C and D as well. This item was deemed unsalvageable.

Figure 5.4 *Examples of Ambiguous Multiple-Choice Questions*

On a related note, options should not give away the answers to other questions, nor should they give hints to the correct answer for that question, or even facilitate guessing. One common type of error in writing multiple-choice items relates to this, as well as to the avoidance of ambiguity: writing overlapping options. This occurs when one option is a logical subset of another (for example, *dog* and *animal*), or two options are similar (or even identical) in meaning (for example, *hot* and *warm*, or *hat* and *cap*).

What is the main idea of the passage?

A Kevin and Kate went to Italy to buy a house.
B Kevin and Kate bought a house in Italy and made new friends.
C <u>Kevin and Kate bought a house in Italy and remodeled it.</u>
D Kevin and Kate enjoy spending time at their new home in Italy.

The remodeling took a long time to finish, but it:

A <u>was worth the effort.</u>
B was hard work.
C gives them an excuse to travel to Italy more often.
D is the perfect place to entertain friends and neighbors.

Figure 5.5 Example of One Reading Comprehension Item Giving Away the Correct Answer to Another One (the stem of the second question gives away the answer to the first one; note also the inconsistency between the lengths of options A and B vs. C and D in the second question)

Another important point is that options should all "pull their weight" on the test. That is, each one should be chosen by some of the students who answer incorrectly; any options that do not get chosen are doing no more good than if they were not there in the first place. One important consideration here is to make sure that all distractors are plausible, without being so close to correct that there are two correct answers. A careful balance must be struck here, as Rupp, Ferne, and Choi (2006) have—unsurprisingly—found that greater plausibility of distractors is associated with greater item difficulty, and it would be a mistake to make all of the questions highly difficult. Again, however, *implausible* distractors are a waste of space on the test.

One issue that can render options implausible is if they are not syntactically parallel. An exception to this would be when the item is assessing grammar, as long as there is an even distribution of different structures—either all of the options use equally different structures, or groupings of structures are evenly divided (for example, in a verb tense question, having two options use verbs set in the past and two use verbs set in the present). For any other type of questions, however, the same grammatical structures (clause or phrase types, parts of speech, etc.) need to be used in all the options for a given question.

In a manner similar to multiple-choice grammar items, the semantic field of multiple-choice options needs to be considered carefully as well. The options should all come from the same semantic field, should come from different semantic fields, or the fields should be balanced equally (for example, on a four-option question, have a pair of options from each of two semantic fields, as illustrated in Figure 5.6). Note, of course, that this guideline applies mainly to short, even one-word options, as longer options are less likely to have a single identifiable semantic field. Rupp et al. (2006) report that semantic similarity among options is associated with increased item difficulty. Thus, as with plausibility, a careful balance must be struck.

Vocabulary item with grammatically inconsistent options:
The doctor gave the patient some _____.

A <u>medicine</u>
B stethoscope
C surgical

Vocabulary items with grammatically consistent options:
The doctor used a _____ to listen to the patient's heart.

A scalpel
B <u>stethoscope</u>
C syringe

The doctor said the patient needed a(n) _____.

A <u>operation</u>
B pulse
C thermometer

Grammar item with options that are all different parts of speech, but still acceptable:
The doctor said the patient needed to have an _____.

A operable
B operate
C <u>operation</u>

Reading comprehension item with options from inconsistent semantic fields:
In the story, the man bought two _____ tickets.

A airplane
B bus
C <u>movie</u>
D train

Acceptable alternation between options from different semantic fields:
The patient had a small cut. The doctor used _____ to treat it.

A anesthesia
B <u>a bandage</u>
C a prescription
D X-rays

In the story, the man bought two _____ tickets.

A airplane
B concert
C <u>movie</u>
D train

Figure 5.6 Examples of Consistency and Inconsistency in the Grammar and Semantic Field of Multiple-Choice Options

Likewise, options should be similar in length. All of these points, as well as others (for example, pragmatic function), can be summarized in one general principle: Do not write an option that will be the "odd man out" for a given item.

A final point involves the number of options that should be written. There are partisans for both the three- and four-option multiple-choice question, and even some who support the occasional use of binary response questions—that is, two-option multiple-choice. Some might even believe that since five-option questions are harder to write, that must "obviously" prove that they are superior, since they seem to reduce the potential for guessing even further! After reviewing the results of a number of studies, Haladyna et al. (2002) argue that because the number of effective distractors (i.e. distractors chosen by more than a tiny number of test takers) is often low on four-option multiple-choice, three-option questions can be equally effective in most cases, and two-option may work just as well in many cases.

True-False Questions

Simple true-false can be problematic, especially for inexperienced test writers. It is relatively easy to write trick questions, even unintentionally, and there is greater potential for guessing because there are only two options. Furthermore, many statements simply end up being neither entirely, unambiguously true nor false, only *mostly* true or false, or *usually* true or false. Cangelosi (1990) notes that this is particularly true of statements involving judgment, rather than description. He further cautions against true-false stems that are literally true, but are meant to be false. As an example of such a stem, a reading passage might tell of a store employee who was not allowed to leave work early one day when he felt sick. For the question *The cashier could not leave work early*, the teacher probably intends the answer to be "true," but the cashier physically *could* have left, albeit at the risk of becoming unemployed. Thus both answers are arguably correct. Thorndike and Hagen (1969) offer several suggestions for ways to deal with these issues, including avoiding negatives, avoiding ambiguous or indefinite terms of degree or amount (*frequently, usually, mostly,* etc.), confining each stem to a single idea or concept, and keeping true and false statements roughly equal in length.

One adaptation of the true-false format that seems to eliminate some of the drawbacks mentioned above is **multiple true-false**, which appears to work acceptably well (Cangelosi 1990; Haladyna et al. 2002). These are items with stems along the lines of "Choose all that apply," followed by a list of binary-choice (i.e. *true/false, yes/no,* etc.) options. Since there can be a fairly large number of items, and as they seem to lend themselves to being less tricky or absolute than most traditional true-false questions, Haladyna et al. report that reliability can achieve reasonable levels. (Reliability was introduced in Chapters 1 and 3, but will be covered in detail in Chapters 6, 18, and 19.) Among other things, high reliability would suggest that examinees were attempting to answer the questions to the best of their ability, rather than randomly guessing.

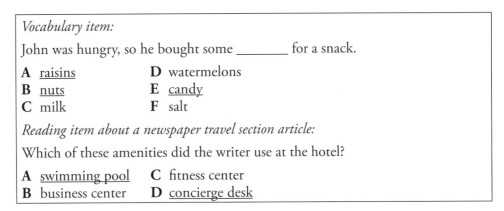

Vocabulary item:

John was hungry, so he bought some _____ for a snack.

A <u>raisins</u>   **D** watermelons
B <u>nuts</u>   **E** <u>candy</u>
C milk   **F** salt

Reading item about a newspaper travel section article:

Which of these amenities did the writer use at the hotel?

A <u>swimming pool</u>   **C** fitness center
B business center   **D** <u>concierge desk</u>

Figure 5.7 *Examples of Multiple True-False Items*

Matching Items

In language courses, matching seems particularly common as a means of assessing vocabulary. While there appears to have been far less research devoted to this task format than to multiple-choice, matching seems especially popular in classroom testing. On the other hand, Haladyna and his colleagues note that while it seems to be used frequently in textbooks, it is very uncommon in standardized testing in the United States (Haladyna et al. 2002). This is not the case elsewhere, however; for example, the IELTS and all five Cambridge Main Suite exams include matching tasks (see University of Cambridge ESOL Examinations 2006a, 2006b, 2007a, 2007b, 2008a, 2008b). Their rarity in high-stakes U.S. testing is surprising, given the format's popularity at the classroom level, most likely due to the ease with which it is constructed. It would seem that as long as there are more options than blanks, guessing would not be an important factor. In fact, one of the few studies on the subject (Zimmerman, Williams, and Symons 1984) demonstrated that reliability can be even higher for matching than for multiple-choice questions.

Existing research (for example, Haynie 2003; Shaha 1982, 1984) appears to have mostly involved using matching in *content area* assessment, not in the assessment of *language*. The format therefore seems to have been studied primarily as a tool for testing declarative knowledge. The closest parallels to assessing declarative knowledge in language courses, of course, are assessing vocabulary (see Budescu 1988), or possibly posing simple factual statements about a reading or listening passage. It might therefore be best to be cautious in using this task beyond those contexts in high-stakes testing. This is consistent with Haladyna et al.'s (2002) conclusion that matching is quite acceptable in classroom testing, but that high-stakes use should await additional research.

Item Writing For Limited Production Tasks

In this section I will address both short-answer questions and deletion-based tasks. (Note that multiple-choice cloze tasks will also share many of the same concerns as other multiple-choice questions.) Both formats have the attraction that students are actually *providing* responses, rather than *selecting* them. This is generally more authentic than selected response, but these tasks require more time to score.

Short-Answer questions

One attractive benefit provided by short-answer questions is that in tests of grammar or vocabulary, they can force students to *produce* the correct forms, not merely *recognize* them. In tests of reading or listening comprehension, they can increase the passage dependence of items, as students must actually provide the correct response. This is true regardless of whether they are permitted to respond in the target language or in the L1. When responses are given in the target language, the tasks are presumably more authentic than equivalent selected response ones would be. At the same time, comprehension questions with L2 responses do assess writing to a certain extent, which can alter the construct being assessed. For this reason, we must be careful about including grammar or vocabulary use as part of the scoring criteria when assessing reading or listening ability. By the same token, if the focus of a short-answer question is vocabulary, grammar is unlikely to be part of the construct, so any decision to include it as part of the scoring criteria (beyond the point at which it ceases to interfere with communication) needs to be justifiable in terms of the construct definition—that is, if grammar is not included in the construct definition for vocabulary, it should not be part of the assessment criteria.

In cases where we *do* want to include grammar or vocabulary use in the scoring of listening and reading comprehension questions, this needs to be included in the construct definition; if it is not included, but we decide that it is nevertheless an important consideration in scoring, the construct definition needs to be revised accordingly (for example, from "the ability to comprehend reading passages" to something along the lines of "the ability to comprehend reading passages and answer questions about them with appropriate control over grammatical structures").

Similar principles apply for including elements such as spelling, penmanship, or punctuation in the scoring of short-answer questions. These are probably most appropriately included in construct definitions for tests assessing learners at relatively high proficiency levels, who are be planning to work or study in environments where these types of errors might be less tolerated. Still, they must be included in the construct definition if they are to be part of the basis for scoring, and the construct definition changed if they were not originally included.

As just stated, it is essential that an item assesses the construct of interest—for example, if a supposedly listening-only item assesses sentence writing skills as much as it does listening comprehension, it is a poor listening item. Therefore, in writing these tasks, we must take into consideration the expected level of writing ability of the students who will be taking the test. Continuing the example, asking advanced students to provide a phrase or a short sentence in answering a comprehension question is reasonable; expecting beginning level students to write a complete sentence or two in order to answer a question may be asking too much. The scoring procedure may help mitigate the issue, however, if it is decided not to penalize for grammatical or vocabulary errors that do not interfere with the expression of meaning.

When writing short-answer questions, it is important that they be clear and unambiguous. Cangelosi (1990) cautions that overly simplistic short-answer items can be ambiguous, and Thorndike and Hagen (1969) caution that the directions and questions should be clear and specific enough that test takers have no doubt what they are supposed to do, making the only problem one of whether they know the answer or not. It is therefore important that questions be phrased clearly, so that if students do not know how to answer, it is because of a lack of language ability, not a failure to guess which of several potential meanings was intended. This seems like common sense, of course, but it is sometimes easier said than done. Most teachers can attest that all too often, a question that seemed clear and reasonable while the test was being written proves to be problematic when actually posed to the students.

The *most* effective way to deal with this, I have found, is to write the scoring key as part of writing the questions themselves. If a teacher cannot write a model answer to the question, it is unlikely the students will be able to either, so the question needs to be revised or dropped—preferably revised. The key should include a list of all acceptable answers, and if polytomous (partial credit, in this context) scoring is to be used, the value to be assigned each anticipated answer should be included. Naturally, not every acceptable or partially acceptable response can be anticipated, but the more specific the scoring key is, the better thought out the items themselves will be.

Deletion-Based Tasks

Deletion tasks such as cloze, gap-fill, and C-tests seem fairly simple to construct, on the face of things. There are several things that can be done, however, to produce better results. Some things to keep in mind are the need to come up with an appropriate value for *n* (even in rational-deletion cloze, the deletions should be at *roughly* even intervals, although perfection here is not a goal, nor even possible), and to determine whether one passage or several will be needed to generate enough blanks; what constitutes "enough" should have been decided as part of the process of writing the specifications. For random (i.e. fixed-deletion) cloze, the findings by Sciarone and Schoorl (1989) should be kept in mind here: specifically, for the deletions to be sufficiently random that it does not really matter *exactly* which word was the starting place for deletions, there need to be at least 75 blanks for acceptable word scoring, and 100 for exact word scoring. Fewer deletions may still provide a suitable level of reliability, but scores will be difficult to interpret, as the set of deletions being used will probably not be representative of the words in the passage as a whole. Note, however, that this restriction applies to fixed-deletion cloze, *not* to rational-deletion cloze tasks. When there is some principled basis for making deletions (for example, words in a particular grammatical category, or that are on a list of vocabulary words that are to be assessed), these heavy requirements are not applicable. It is therefore probably a good idea for teachers to avoid *fixed*-deletion cloze in favor of *rational*-deletion cloze. Doing so allows us to target whatever construct or portion of a construct that we were interested in assessing in the first place. It also helps us avoid the issues of longer testing time and examinee fatigue, and makes it unnecessary to find suitable passages that are long enough to support that many deletions.

When selecting or writing the passages on which the task will be based, the same considerations apply as for selecting or writing any normal reading passage. In rational-deletion cloze, however, there is the added requirement that the text include enough of the type of word being targeted for deletion. When the deletions are to be made, the best procedure for creating fixed-deletion cloze passages is perhaps to begin counting backwards from the end of the passage, deleting every *n*th word.

As with short-answer questions, a scoring key should be developed at the same time as the task itself. In this case, however, it is less to ensure that the deletions are plausible than to make sure that it is done in good time, and that the list of possible answers is available for review along with the rest of the test.

Writing Prompts For Extended Production Tasks

General Considerations

It is essential that directions and prompts be clear and specific about what students are supposed to do when they respond. When administering writing tests, and tape- or computer-mediated speaking tests, it will not always be possible for students to ask for clarification as to what they are supposed to do. Therefore, the expected response should be described clearly in terms of the criteria that will be used to judge it. For example, if a letter-writing task will be scored without consideration of grammatical accuracy, as long as the response is comprehensible, examinees should be told as much. On the other hand, if an essay will be scored on the basis of grammatical accuracy, vocabulary use, content, and organization, those categories should be disclosed to the test takers in the directions. If the response to a speaking prompt is supposed to include specific things, such as a particular piece of information, that should be part of the question posed by the prompt as well. In particular, when a teacher is attempting to elicit a particular grammatical structure, such as a specific verb tense, the prompt needs to be worded in such a way that students cannot appropriately avoid that structure. If this step is not taken, it will be unfair to penalize such responses, even if they are not what the teacher had in mind.

On a related note, if a test is to include an interview section, besides writing the interview questions—which are really just prompts, of course—some guidance for follow-up questions should be written as well. This should include instructions or reminders for the interviewers about what the point of the question is so that if students do not answer it in the intended fashion the first time, the interviewer can try to redirect them, giving them a chance to show whether their initial response was a result of not having sufficient language ability, or simply not getting the point of the question. One example of this might be a question asking test takers to describe an experience, or narrate the story shown in some pictures. In English conversation, this can be done using either of two time frames: the past or the present. If the point is to get the test takers to describe events in the past, the teacher might stop a student and ask them to tell the story using the past tense. Admittedly, prompting someone to use a specific verb tense might raise a question about their ability to perform without prompting, but in my experience, few students who require prompting because of a lack of control over verb tenses will be able to sustain the appropriate time frame consistently, even after being reminded.

Where to Get Ideas For Prompts

One of the best ways to come up with writing or speaking prompts is to base them on language use tasks in the TLU domain. In language assessment—particularly at the level of a classroom, program, or school—we are usually concerned with what McNamara (1996) calls the "weak sense" of performance assessment. That is, the test task is a way to obtain a language sample from the test takers. We may consider task completion or effectiveness as *part* of the scoring, but our main concern is with the language that students use to complete the task, rather than with the completion of the task itself. In addition, the test tasks that are used as the basis for prompts should be viewed as *samples* of the overall "universe" (in the statistical sense) of all possible tasks in the TLU domain. Therefore, the most important, most common, and most prototypical TLU tasks will generally be the most appropriate candidates for adaptation as test tasks.

When TLU domain tasks—that is, real-life language use tasks—are being adapted for use on a test, a good place to start is by describing the TLU tasks themselves. Decisions will already have been made as to the construct definition, TLU domain, and what some of the most common or important tasks are. At a minimum, the description of a given TLU task should include the setting of the activity (the setting in a role-play, for example, would include the purpose of the interaction, the identities of and relationships between the speakers, as well as the time and place of the interaction), the language input that the speaker would receive in real life, how the speaker would be expected to respond in real life (by giving an explanation, asking a favor, apologizing, etc.), and the length of the expected response. (See Bachman and Palmer's 1996 task characteristics framework for a more rigorous description of the features of TLU domain and test tasks.) It should be pointed out that this procedure is just as applicable to writing tasks as it is to speaking. The only real difference is that slightly different information needs to be provided; for example, the rhetorical mode of a piece of writing, rather than the language function, and the intended audience for a letter, rather than the identities of the speakers.

The task description may need some adaptation in order to work in a testing situation, of course, just as authentic learning activities must be adapted from the real-life tasks they reflect. Note that not all of the information may be included in the prompt itself, but—depending on the task—some of it might be incorporated into the directions, the scoring rubric, or the instructions for interviewers. In the case of a role-play, some of the information provided to each student might be incomplete, with the missing information given to a student's partner.

Obviously, when the prompts are in the form of interview questions, this approach to adapting TLU tasks will not be appropriate. When more authentic language use tasks are desired, however, it should result in prompts that are clearly enough defined that students will know what is being asked of them. This will give them a fair chance to perform to the best of their abilities.

Reviewing Passages, Items, Keys, and Prompts Before Pilot Testing

If a teacher is working on a test for use in their own class, the planning and writing of the test will likely be a solitary affair. When a test is for use at the school or program level, however (for example, a placement test, or a promotion test), there may be multiple teachers working together on it. Various members of this test development team will, as a rule, be assigned specific portions of the project, with the rest of the committee reviewing each person's work. Perhaps the most emotionally sensitive portion of this process is the reviewing of test items. Newcomers to this process must quickly learn to grow thick skins, and not take personally the inevitable criticism of their passages, questions, and prompts. Indeed, for many people, the first time they are told—by colleagues, even friends—that several of their items were unclear, or not congruent with the specifications, their reaction is similar to that of a new mother who has been told her baby is ugly. Unfortunately, sometimes the "baby" really is ugly, and the task needs revision or replacement. This should not be taken as a sign of personal criticism, and should be accepted in good grace as part of an important and ongoing learning process. It is worth keeping in mind that the more tasks a particular teacher creates, the more their work will draw criticism.

The process of reviewing items, passages, keys, and prompts needs to be approached collegially. One person should be in charge of recording all changes that are agreed upon, and whenever possible, decisions should be made by consensus. If one person is officially in charge of the group, it is important that he or she not enforce decisions upon the others, unless there are tremendous differences in test-writing expertise. Likewise, being the loudest or most stubborn group member does not make one's ideas more correct than everyone else's. Interestingly enough, there appears to be very little empirical research on the process of testing committee dynamics (but see Kim et al. 2010, for a rare example). Davidson and Lynch (2002) also discuss the group dynamics of test development teams at some length, including one study they performed on the revision process.

As mentioned previously in Chapter 3, it may prove necessary to revise the test specifications during the item writing process. Things that seemed perfectly clear beforehand may suddenly seem insufficiently precise once teachers start writing test questions or looking for passages to include in (or create for) a test. This can be especially true when the people—usually teachers—writing tests or parts of tests were not involved in creating the specifications. This lack of clarity can manifest itself as people having no idea where to start, since they do not have sufficiently clear guidance as to what they are supposed to be producing. Insufficient clarity or detail can also be the culprit when teachers' items or passages are too disparate. Sometimes, of course, that can be the result of a failure to follow directions; the best way to prevent *that* is to provide examples as part of the specifications; review the specifications and sample items during a training meeting or workshop; and choose test writers who are willing to try to follow directions, rather than doing things their own way.

The development and use of specifications is an iterative process (Bachman and Palmer 1996; Davidson and Lynch 2002). Whether they are working alone or as part of a team, teachers must be prepared to review and revise the specifications if necessary. Such alterations may become necessary for the reasons discussed above; in other cases, it may become necessary to revise some time later, when something has changed. When such changes are made, however, it is crucial that test developers go back and make sure that the test tasks already written under the old specifications will fit under the revised ones.

Compiling the Test

Once the test has been written, reviewed, and revised, it must be "packaged," that is, the tasks put together and the test copied so that it can be administered. Tasks that assess the same construct should be put together, and within each of those sections, tasks with the same format should be placed together. For example, if a test has a grammar section, all of the grammar items should be placed together. If it uses a mix of multiple-choice and short-answer items, all of the short-answer questions should be together, and all the multiple-choice questions should be together. Within each of these groupings of items, it is usually better to try to arrange them from easier to harder, to the extent that this can be judged in advance (for example, by complexity of grammatical structures, infrequency of vocabulary, etc.). Once a test has been piloted, of course, item difficulty estimates can be used for ordering. The exception to these rules is reading and listening tests; for these, it is best to group items by passage. For items based on a passage, it is best to put them in the same order as the parts of the passage with which they deal. Items relating to the passage as a whole usually go first or last.

For reading comprehension tests, it is better to put the items on the same page as the passage when possible. Failing that, the test should be arranged so that it will be easy for students to look back and forth between the questions and the passage.

Item Analysis: A Conceptual Overview

Once the test has been written and reviewed, it needs to be pilot tested; that is, given to a sample of the students who will take it "officially," to make sure that the test is functioning as well as hoped. One of the most important things to be learned from this pilot testing involves finding out how well the questions did their jobs, and which ones might need improvement. This is done by looking at three sets of numbers: estimates of how difficult an item is, estimates of how well each question separated those who did well on the overall test from those who did poorly, and distractor analysis for selected response tasks. These three concepts, along with how to *calculate* the various estimates, are explained in Chapters 15–17, and the related concept of correlation is explained in Chapter 14. The rules of thumb discussed below are summarized in Table 5.1.

In classical test analysis, item difficulty is expressed as the **IF (item facility)** or *p*-value, or IF* or *p** for polytomous items (see Chapter 15). The difficulty level is used as a basis for evaluating items in *norm*-referenced tests (NRTs). For *criterion*-referenced tests, though, there is no equivalent rule; that is, items should not generally be flagged for revision or replacement merely because their difficulty levels are too high or too low.

Item discrimination can be estimated using either the *correlational* or *subtractive* method (correlation, the relationship between two sets of scores, is explained in Chapter 14). The formulas are virtually the same for NRTs and CRTs, but they are applied to different sets of numbers, which is what differentiates the NRT and CRT formulas (see Chapters 15 and 16, respectively).

	NRT	**CRT**
Difficulty	$.30 \leq IF \leq .70$	N/A*

Discrimination
  Correlational
  Subtractive
	$r_{\text{p-bis}} \geq .30$
	$ID_{UL} \geq .40$
		$\phi \geq .30$
		$B \geq .40$

*Only reported to assist in interpretation of other results.

Table 5.1 Rules of Thumb For Interpreting Item Analyses

The **discrimination indices** for CRT are dependent on **cut scores**—that is, they tell us how good a job the question does of separating masters from non-masters, passing students from failing students, etc. Therefore, if there are multiple cut scores (as discussed in Chapter 1), the discrimination for an item must be calculated separately for each cut score (for example, if there are four cut scores, each item will have four discrimination values–these may be either **B-index** or **item ϕ** estimates, depending on the approach being used). In cases where the cut scores have not been set yet, or if they are not very well trusted, or are under review, it makes sense to include the **point-biserial** in CRT item analyses as well, as a source of additional information. This suggestion may be somewhat unorthodox, but since the point-biserial shows the relationship between item score and total test score, it seems that this would be useful information when there is some sort of problem with the cut scores on which the B-index or φ is based.

Generally speaking, in NRT analyses, discrimination should probably be prioritized somewhat over difficulty. This does *not* mean that difficulty should be ignored, but if an item has very high discrimination, and the difficulty is a little outside the target range, the item should probably be a lower priority for revision. Any changes, in fact, run the risk of reducing the high discrimination value. By the same token, though, it is important in an NRT to have items as close to the IF = .50 line as possible—that is, half of the test takers answering it correctly and half incorrectly. (See Chapter 15 for an explanation of why this is important.)

As a final note regarding interpreting these indices, it bears pointing out that the rules of thumb in Table 5.1 are appropriate for high-stakes testing. They are important for seeing to it that each question on the test is pulling its own weight in terms of contributing useful information, and helping the overall test achieve a satisfactory level of reliability (typically .80 or higher; see Chapter 6). On teacher-made tests, however, especially for classroom use, lower levels may be acceptable; the trade-off here is that the lower the discrimination of each item, the more items will be needed to achieve a satisfactory level of reliability. (See Nelson 2001, for a review of what various experts have suggested as appropriate thresholds for difficulty and discrimination.)

In rare cases, it may be necessary to discard an item completely, but usually it is simpler and more efficient to revise it instead. Once items have been flagged as needing revision, it is useful to look at how well the distractors on these items performed. That is, if certain options were never or almost never chosen by any test takers, they need to be reworded or replaced. As a general guideline, the poorer the discrimination, the more likely that several options will have been chosen by few or no students, *or* that one of the distractors was attractive to too many high-ability students. How to calculate the percentage of students that chose each option will be discussed in Chapter 17; interpreting the percentages is a fairly straightforward exercise, and although there is a rule of thumb that 10% of examinees should choose each option, the interpretation is somewhat subjective. We can also examine the point-biserial correlations for each option, the procedure for which is explained in Chapter 17 as well. When a distractor is attractive to many high-ability examinees, that usually indicates that the item as written is tricky, unclear, or otherwise problematic. That distractor, the key, or the stem may need to be revised to fix the situation.

When performing item and distractor analysis, it is very useful if teachers can identify patterns in terms of what is wrong with problematic items. This will be useful when additional items are written later, and once a pattern is discerned, it may help point the way to a consistent technique for fixing the current crop of questions. All revisions should be made keeping in mind the constructs that are being assessed.

Finally, once revisions have been made to problematic items, it is desirable to re-pilot the test if time and other resources permit this. Re-administering the test will allow us to see whether the changes had the effect we anticipated, and whether additional modifications still need to be made. In terms of deciding how important this is in a given situation, it is necessary to consider the stakes of the test, the resources needed to re-administer it, the previous level of reliability, and how extensive the revisions have been to the original version. If a test already had a satisfactory or near-satisfactory reliability level, most of the revisions were probably minor anyway (for example, mostly revising distractors), and a second round of pilot testing may not be necessary. On the other hand, if extensive revisions were necessary, with many items being rewritten or even replaced, re-piloting the test is probably going to be rather important.

Summary

This chapter began by presenting important considerations to keep in mind when writing passage-based tests, before moving on to discuss general suggestions about item writing. It then discussed the process of writing selected response, limited production, and extended production tasks, along with strategies and advice for doing so. After recommending that all portions of the test be reviewed before pilot testing, it provided suggestions for compiling the test. It then concluded by explaining the conceptual basis for item analysis, one of the goals of which is increased reliability for the test as a whole. In the next chapter, we will look at the issue of reliability, or scoring consistency, in greater depth.

Further Reading

Item-Writing and Related Research

Davidson, F. and **B. K. Lynch.** 2002. *Testcraft: A Teacher's Guide to Writing and Using Language Test Specifications.* New Haven, CT: Yale University Press.

Haladyna, T. M., S. M. Downing, and **M. C. Rodriguez.** 2002. 'A review of multiple-choice item-writing guidelines for classroom assessment'. *Applied Measurement in Education* 15 (3): 309–334.

Kim, J., Y. Chi, A. Huensch, H. Jun, H. Li, and **V. Roullion.** 2010. 'A case study on an item writing process: Use of test specifications, nature of group dynamics, and individual item writers' characteristics'. *Language Assessment Quarterly* 7 (2): 160–174.

Rupp, A. A., T. Ferne, and **H. Choi.** 2006. 'How assessing reading comprehension with multiple-choice questions shapes the construct: A cognitive processing perspective'. *Language Testing* 23 (4): 441–474.

Examples of a Variety of Task Formats

University of Cambridge ESOL Examinations. 2006a. *Key English Test: Information for candidates.* Retrieved June 18 2010, from http://www.candidates.cambridgeesol.org/cs/digitalAssets/105327_3812_6Y05_KET_IforC_w.pdf

University of Cambridge ESOL Examinations. 2006b. *Preliminary English Test: Information For Candidates.* Retrieved June 18 2010, from http://www.candidates.cambridgeesol.org/cs/digitalAssets/105331_3813_6Y05_PET_IforC_w_Eng.pdf

University of Cambridge ESOL Examinations. 2007a. *Certificate of Proficiency in English: Information For Candidates.* Retrieved June 18 2010, from http://www.candidates.cambridgeesol.org/cs/digitalAssets/113322_cpe_infoforcand.pdf

University of Cambridge ESOL Examinations. 2007b. *IELTS Handbook 2007.* Retrieved June 18 2010, from http://www.cambridgeesol.org/assets/pdf/resources/IELTS_Handbook.pdf

University of Cambridge ESOL Examinations. 2008a. *Certificate in Advanced English: Information For Candidates For Examinations From December 2008.* Retrieved June 18 2010, from http://www.candidates.cambridgeesol.org/cs/digitalAssets/121084_cae_infoforcand_dec08_E.pdf

University of Cambridge ESOL Examinations. 2008b. *First Certificate in English: Information For Candidates For Examinations From December 2008.* Retrieved June 18 2010, from http://www.candidates.cambridgeesol.org/cs/digitalAssets/121063_fce_infoforcand_dec08_E.pdf

Discussion Questions

1 This chapter presents a number of rules for writing multiple-choice test questions.
   a How many of these rules had you heard of before?
   b Which of these rules have you seen violated on a test before?
   c Are there any other guidelines for multiple-choice questions that you have heard of, but that are not mentioned here?

2 In Figure 5.4, the second item is a reading comprehension item asking about issues faced by travelers. What could be done to the stem to make it acceptable, without changing the options?

3 Look at the two items in Figure 5.5.
   a How could the first item be rewritten so as to limit redundancy?
   b The second item has two options that are noticeably longer than the other two. How serious a problem do you think this is? Why?
   c How could the second item be rewritten to make the options more comparable in length?

4 What might be problematic with changing Option C, "surgical," to "surgery" in the first example of Figure 5.6?

6 CONSISTENCY OF MEASUREMENT

Introduction

Previous chapters discussed what can be done to plan and write a test properly, on the assumption that a well-planned and well-written test has the best chance of being useful for its intended purpose. Chapter 5 also raised the topic of looking at how students performed on specific items, and using this information to identify which items need revision. This process will in turn boost the overall *reliability* of the test, that is, its consistency of scoring or measurement. As we will see, reliability is, strictly speaking, used to refer to the scoring consistency of norm-referenced tests, and **dependability** refers to the consistency of criterion-referenced tests. In order to gain a better understanding of both concepts, in this chapter we will discuss the concept of reliability, examine different approaches to calculating reliability, and learn how to use reliability to estimate the accuracy of individual scores. Following this, we will explore how to improve a test's reliability by lengthening it, address the dependability of test scores and classification decisions, and consider how to estimate reliability and dependability in performance tests (i.e. tests that include speaking and writing). The chapter will then conclude with a discussion of how to interpret reliability and dependability estimates. It should be pointed out now that this chapter contains several formulas used in calculating reliability and dependability. None of these formulas are actually *used* in this chapter—they are included here, however, for two reasons: on the assumption that each one should accompany the conceptual discussion of its use, and so that readers who are comfortable with algebra can use them to get a better feel for concepts (for example, the impact of the number of items on reliability).

Understanding Reliability

As was explained earlier, *reliability* refers to the consistency of scoring, and is estimated statistically. Technically, it should be noted that reliability is usually used to refer to scoring consistency in norm-referenced tests (NRTs), and the term *dependability* is used for scoring consistency in criterion-referenced tests (CRTs). We will begin by considering just what is meant by scoring consistency.

A fundamental concept in measurement theory is that any measure or assessment will be imperfect, and contain at least a small amount of error. For example, if we were to do something as simple as measuring 100 people's heights, there would be a certain amount of error. Some people might not stand up straight, and some might stand on their toes. We could misread someone's height, or the markings on the measuring stick or tape could even be somewhat faulty. Now, in fact, most real-life measurements of height are quite accurate, but imagine if we decided to measure height with extreme precision—in millimeters, or sixteenths of an inch. We would then encounter a great deal more error, because of the scale on which we were working. At that level of *intended* precision, even something uncontrollable, such as a person's spine settling during the day, would lead to errors. In fact, the same person measured on three separate occasions might be told three different heights. Just as measuring the same person several times and averaging the numbers together should yield a more accurate result, we generally use more than one indicator of ability in language tests—this is why, for example, there are very few reading tests with only one question.

If measurement of such apparently simple, visible characteristics such as physical height can include error, then certainly attempts at measuring constructs— invisible abilities inside students' heads—such as language ability will be subject to error as well. The entire purpose of estimating reliability and dependability is to identify how much measurement error there is, which helps inform us as to the usefulness of our tests and lets us know if we need to make improvements that will reduce the margin of error to an acceptable level.

Classical reliability theory (commonly referred to as **classical test theory** or **classical true-score theory**) is rooted in this concept of measurement error, as well as the related notions of **observed score**, or the score that a person actually receives on a test, and **true score**, the score that a person would receive with perfect measurement, that is, if there were no measurement error—assuming such a thing were possible. An observed score is considered, then, to be the combination of measurement error and the student's true score; likewise, measurement error is the difference between his true score and observed score. Formally speaking, reliability is defined as the ratio of *true score variance* to *observed score variance*. That is, it tells us how much variance in people's scores comes from variance in their true scores. If the concept of score variance is a little confusing, it may help to consider that (1) not all scores on a test are the same, so there is variation from one test taker to the next, and (2) for a single person, there will be variation in how well they do on the different items or other tasks—that is, they will do better on some things than on others, get some questions right and others wrong, etc. Mentally substituting the word "variation" for "variance" in this context can help as well.

Another way of looking at the concept of true score is to imagine that someone takes the same test 100 times, but without remembering what was on the test the previous times. Presumably, the person's scores will not be identical every time, but they will probably be fairly close to each other, with some slight variation from test to test. If we average all 100 scores together, that average will probably be their true score. This example can also help illustrate the relationship between true scores and reliability. If there were a lot of variation in that person's 100 test scores—that is, if they were rather far apart much of the time—the test would have low reliability. By the same token, if the scores were all clustered very close to each other, the test would have very high reliability.

Reliability values range from .00 (no measurement, all error) to 1.00 (perfect measurement, without any error), although neither extreme ever occurs in practice. It is very important to understand that reliability is *not* the proportion of test takers whose scores were accurate. Rather, the error and precision of a test apply to the scores of all the people who take it. A reliability of .80 (a common minimally acceptable level in high-stakes testing) means that 80% of each person's score comes from his true score, and 20% is based on measurement error; repeating an analogy from an earlier chapter, this may be easier to understand in terms of a television picture with 80% picture and 20% static or "snow." While we cannot tell which part of the score came from error and which did not, we can take steps to identify what *caused* the error. This is the purpose of item analysis (see Chapters 5 and 15–17), as well as several more advanced statistical methods such as **generalizability theory** and the **many-facet Rasch model** (see Chapter 10 for explanations and conceptual overviews of these two approaches).

Approaches to Estimating Reliability

There are several ways in which we can estimate the reliability of a test. These will be classified here in terms of whether they require that a test be administered once (**internal consistency reliability** estimates) or twice (**parallel forms** and **test-retest reliability** estimates).

Parallel Forms and Test-Retest Reliability

Since we cannot directly obtain someone's true score we must find other ways to estimate reliability. Both make use of *correlation*, a mathematical estimate of the degree of relationship between two sets of numbers (explained further in Chapter 14). One of these other approaches is *test-retest reliability*, in which students take the same test twice, and the reliability estimate is the correlation between their two scores. Aside from the logistical issue of having to administer the test twice, there is also the problem that if the two administrations are close enough together, students are likely to do better the second time because of familiarity with the test. On the other hand, if the two administrations are spread out enough for students to forget about what was on the test the first time, there is the possibility that they might learn something during the time between the test administrations, which would improve their scores on the retest. In this case, their true scores would not be the same on the two occasions, making the test look less reliable than it really is. Conversely, if the test takers are not currently studying or being otherwise exposed to the target language, and the two test administrations are not close together, the test takers may lose a certain degree of language ability, resulting in lower scores the second time because the *true* scores were lower. This, too, would make the test look less reliable than it actually is.

The other approach that requires two test administrations is *parallel forms reliability* (often called *alternate forms reliability*). A *form* is a version of a test that is written to the same specifications as others. It uses the same task formats, assesses the same constructs, and so forth, but contains different tasks (prompts, questions, passages, etc.). In slightly simplified terms, *parallel forms* (or *alternate forms*) are forms of the same test that yield the same scores; if a student takes two truly parallel forms of a test, his or her score will be the same on both forms. This, of course, is an ideal case; in actual practice, parallel forms are never *perfectly* parallel ("strictly parallel"), so scores on different forms of a test will not be *exactly* identical, although they may be close enough for the difference not to matter ("essentially parallel"). The parallel forms reliability of a test, then, is the correlation between two forms of the test. This requires having two forms, however, and getting the same group (the larger the better) to take both of them.

It is seldom practical to administer a test twice, or to administer two forms to the same group, of course. While it is important to establish that different forms of a test are parallel, creating two merely for the sake of checking reliability is probably not a good idea. The issue of practicality is one compelling reason why many people use another type of approach, one that only requires administering a test once. Nevertheless, even if test-retest and parallel forms reliability are not generally practical approaches to implement, it is useful to understand both of them. Test-retest reliability is helpful in explaining the concept of true scores, and parallel forms reliability is important to establish when there are two or more forms of a test, so we can be sure they are equivalent.

Internal Consistency Reliability

To get around these problems, *internal consistency reliability* approaches have been developed. These only require administering a test once, and as the name suggests, look at the extent to which different parts of the test are measuring the same thing; or, to look at it differently, the degree to which they are measuring it in the same way. The simplest of these—known as **split-half reliability**—divides the test questions into two halves and correlates the scores on the halves. The safest way to do this is to divide the questions on an odd-even basis, i.e. odd-numbered questions in one half and even-numbered questions in the other half, as correlating the original first and second halves will often mean comparing sections of the test that are not similar at all. The resulting correlation must then be adjusted upwards, using the **Spearman-Brown prophecy formula**, which will be discussed in greater detail below. This formula is used here to adjust for the fact that essentially, the two halves are being treated as two tests, imitating the procedure for test-retest or parallel forms reliability. In fact, of course, the real test is twice as long as either half. All things being equal, a test with more items will produce more reliable scores, so an adjustment must be made to keep the actual reliability from being underestimated.

One problem with split-half reliability is that an odd-even split might not produce precisely comparable halves. As Wainer and Thissen (2001) point out, some ways of performing the split might work better, and others might give worse results. There are many possible ways of splitting the test, and they report that there are 92,378 potential ways to split a 20-item test in half; for a 30-item test, there are 77,558,760. Fortunately, we do not have to worry about trying all the possible combinations, nor do we have to settle for hoping that an odd-even split will prove adequate. Instead, we can use **Cronbach's alpha**, which is probably the most widely-used estimate of internal consistency reliability. The formula for alpha is:

$$\alpha = \frac{k}{k-1}(1 - \frac{\sum s_i^2}{s_x^2})$$

where k = the number of items on the test,

　　　　 s_i^2 = the **population variance** (see Chapter 13 for an explanation of how to calculate this) for an individual item on the test,

　　　　 $\sum s_i^2$ = the sum, or total, of all these **item variances**, and

　　　　 s_x^2 = the *population* variance of the total test score—that is, after the total score is calculated for each student, the variance of those scores is calculated.

(Note that another version of this formula is sometimes presented; both versions yield identical results, but this one is somewhat simpler algebraically.) Rather than dealing with two presumably parallel halves of the test, Cronbach's alpha treats all of the items as parallel measures of the construct (i.e. each item has the same difficulty and the same variance as all the others; Bachman 2004), and "is equivalent to computing the average for all possible splits" (Wainer and Thissen 2001: 33), with the Spearman-Brown correction for length already included. Practice calculating alpha is included in Chapter 18; the formula is presented here, though, as a reference.

This sounds so much simpler than administering a test twice and correlating the scores, or splitting it in half, correlating, and adjusting, that one might wonder why anyone would ever bother with another approach. Indeed, its relative convenience makes alpha quite popular, as do the conceptual advantages it provides over estimating split-half reliability, and the issues involved in test-retest and parallel forms reliability. There are a few caveats to keep in mind, though, when using alpha. In particular, there are two assumptions that must be met: the assumptions of *homogeneity* and *item independence*. Failing to satisfy these assumptions can lead to inaccurate results.

To the extent that the various items are not *parallel* measures (i.e. do not have the same difficulty levels and variances), alpha will underestimate the actual reliability of the test (Allen and Yen 1979; Bachman 2004; Wainer and Thissen 2001). The less parallel the items are (i.e. the greater the differences among items in terms of difficulty levels and variances), the worse this underestimate will be. How do we make sure that a test or section of a test has relatively parallel items? Perhaps the most important thing is that it should have *homogeneous* content—that is, that it assesses *one* construct. To the degree that the same group of items is assessing more than one construct, it will not be internally consistent, and the internal consistency reliability will be reduced. For example, a grammar test with 60 items based on three separate grammatical structures might be fairly homogeneous, if written properly. On the other hand, a test of 20 reading comprehension questions 20 listening comprehension questions, and 20 grammar questions might have a low reliability if those 60 items were analyzed together. Then again, if all 60 items were of comparable difficulty, the reliability might be acceptable after all.

What complicates things even further is that, if we try to achieve high reliability by pursuing strict homogeneity of content, that may result in a narrowing of the assessment, and of the construct. In an extreme case, this could give us a test that has high internal consistency reliability, but is not particularly useful. We therefore should try not to lump together constructs that are highly disparate, while at the same time making sure we cover the construct with adequate breadth—that is, not omitting important aspects of it simply out of concern for reliability.

In addition to the assumption of homogeneity, Cronbach's alpha assumes that items are *independent* of one another. In other words, performance on one item is not related to performance on another, aside from the fact that both are assessing the same ability (Hambleton, Swaminathan, and Rogers 1991). You may recall that we discussed item independence in Chapter 5 in the context of avoiding overlapping items. Bachman (2004) notes that violating this assumption will lead to an overestimation of alpha. A violation of this assumption could occur, for example, in tests of reading or listening comprehension, if the items based on a single passage are more closely related to each other than to the rest of the items. Another example, and probably a more serious violation of this assumption, would be if students needed to answer one question correctly in order to answer another one.

Fortunately, although there are probably small violations of this assumption in every passage-based test, they are rarely severe enough to be a cause for concern. As long as the items are *essentially* independent, that is good enough. In cases where we *do* need to evaluate the degree of independence or dependence on a test (for example, because we are concerned because the reading passages on a test are very different from each other), however, we can look at the correlations among items, and see if those correlations are all roughly similar, or if some groupings of items are more closely interrelated than others.

The assumptions of homogeneity and independence have important implications for how Cronbach's alpha is calculated. When a test consists of several sections, each targeting a different construct or set of constructs (for example, one separate section each for reading, listening, and grammar), it will almost certainly be inappropriate to base alpha on the entire test. This is because the overall test would automatically be heterogeneous in content (i.e. the different sections would not be assessing the same construct, and the items would thus not be parallel measures), and performance on items within a given section would probably be related, introducing item dependence. Thus, separate estimates should be computed for each of the sections, rather than reporting one value for the entire test. If a composite reliability is needed for the overall test (for example, a test of reading, writing, speaking, listening, and grammar), **multivariate generalizability theory** (see Brennan 2001) should be used. (An extensive treatment of generalizability theory is beyond the scope of this book, although the topic is introduced very briefly in Chapter 10.)

Another assumption of Cronbach's alpha, implicit in the formula, is that there is some variation in the ability levels of the people taking the test. As total test score variance increases, alpha increases as well. Therefore, if the examinee sample is truncated somehow—that is, includes only test takers in a narrow ability range for example, for example, only high-ability or only low-ability test takers—alpha will be underestimated as well.

As a final note, two additional formulas are often mentioned in connection with Cronbach's alpha. These are **K–R20** and **K–R21**, also sometimes abbreviated KR–20 and KR–21, or KR20 and KR21. They take their names from the article in which they were introduced, which was written by Kuder and Richardson (1937). As with the point-biserial and phi coefficients (see Chapter 5), they are simplifications of a more complicated formula that only work with dichotomously scored test items. In the era before computers as we know them today even existed, when calculations were made using paper, pencil, a slide rule, and a mechanical adding machine, these were invaluable time savers. Today, however, if calculations are being done on a computer, the savings in time is negligible. In fact, if reliability is being calculated in Excel (as in Chapter 18), the full Cronbach's alpha formula turns out to be slightly less work. The main reason they are included here is that there are rare occasions when teachers might not have ready access to a computer, or might only have descriptive statistics for a test (explained in Chapter 12), but not information on individual items (in which case K–R21 could still be used). Otherwise, they are primarily of historical interest now. The formulas are:

$$\text{K–R20:}\ \ r_{xx'} = \frac{k}{k-1}\left(1 - \frac{\sum pq}{s_x^2}\right) \quad \text{and} \quad \text{K–R21:}\ \ r_{xx'} = \frac{k}{k-1}\left(1 - \frac{M(k-M)}{ks_x^2}\right)$$

where
- $r_{xx'}$ = reliability,
- k = the number of items on the test,
- p = IF, item facility, the proportion of students answering the item correctly,
- q = $1 - p$, the proportion of students answering the item incorrectly,
- $\sum pq$ = the sum, or total, of pq for all of the items, added together,
- s_x^2 = the *population* variance of the total test score, and
- M = the mean, or average, of the test scores.

Again, these formulas only work with dichotomous (i.e. scored 0 or 1) data; for polytomous data, it is necessary to use the full Cronbach's alpha formula. For dichotomous data, K-R20 will yield results equal to alpha. (Note, however, that for polytomous data, KR–20 and KR–21 will yield meaningless results!) Furthermore, K–R21 will equal K–R20 if all item difficulties are equal; to the extent that they are not (and in real life, they will *never* be exactly equal), K-R21 will underestimate the true reliability of the test. Because it only requires basic descriptive statistics, however, K-R21 can be used to get a rough estimate of the lower bound of reliability (i.e. the actual value for alpha will be no lower than K-R21).

Estimating the Accuracy of Individual Scores

If a test is to be useful, its reliability must be sufficiently high that the results can be trusted to mean something. The greater the amount of measurement error, the less meaningful or useful the scores become. It is important that we know the reliability for a test—essential, in high-stakes situations—but that does not tell us much about how accurate an individual's test score is. That is, we know there is *some* measurement error involved in any test, so when a student receives their score on a test, we do not expect that observed score to be their true score. If the test is fairly reliable, we might suspect that their true score is not very far away from the observed score, but we do not know how close it might be.

Fortunately, there is a formula that lets us estimate how close the two scores—true and observed—are. The **standard error of measurement (SEM)** provides a confidence interval about a test taker's observed score, telling us how likely it is that their true score is within a certain range around (i.e. a certain distance from) his observed score. The level of confidence is related to the normal distribution, which has the famous bell-shaped curve seen in Figure 6.1. As it shows, it is 68.26% likely that an examinee's true score will be within one SEM of their observed score. Put another way, this is the probability that the distance from observed score to true score is not more than one SEM. It is even more likely (95.44%) that the true score is within two SEMs of the observed score, and it is almost a certainty that it the true score and observed score will be no more than three SEMs apart. The formula for calculating the SEM is $s_x \sqrt{1 - \alpha}$, where s_x is the standard deviation for total test scores, and α is reliability. (Note that while alpha is used here, the formula works with any other NRT estimate of scoring consistency.) Chapter 18 includes practice in calculating the SEM.

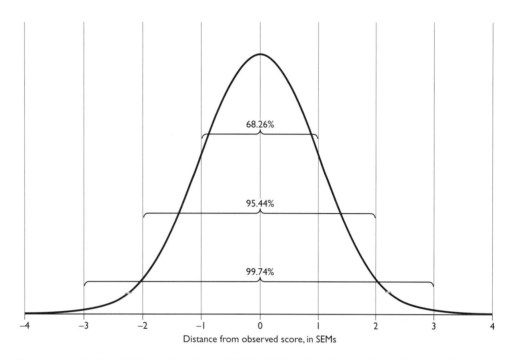

68.26%

95.44%

99.74%

-4   -3   -2   -1   0   1   2   3   4

Distance from observed score, in SEMs

Figure 6.1 Likelihood That a True Score Will Be Within One, Two, or Three Standard Errors of Measurement of the Observed Score

The formula indicates that as reliability goes up, the SEM goes down, but as the dispersion of the test scores (i.e. how spread out test scores are; see Chapter 12) goes up, the SEM rises with it. A test with a reasonably high reliability might nevertheless have a large SEM, which is one strong reason that the SEM should be reported along with the reliability of a test. It should be pointed out here that this discussion has assumed that the SEM is constant at all levels; this is not in fact the case, however. While it is possible to calculate the SEM at different specific score levels (the **conditional SEM**, or CSEM; see, for example, Lord 1984), that discussion lies beyond the scope of this book, and use of the SEM will be quite adequate for classroom testing, and probably for most tests used at the school or program level.

Improving the Reliability of a Norm-Referenced Test

Once the reliability of a test has been estimated, we may be satisfied with the results, and go on to some other project. All too often, though, pilot testing will reveal that the reliability is too low. In Chapter 5, we discussed the use of *item analysis* to help identify poor items for review, so that they could be improved. As the formula for alpha on page 111 suggests, however, a larger number of test questions can also improve reliability; that is, as k grows larger, $\frac{k}{k-1}$ gets closer to 1; as *k* grows smaller, the rest of the formula is multiplied by a smaller number, thereby shrinking alpha. The Spearman-Brown prophecy formula was mentioned previously in the discussion of correcting for shorter test length when calculating split-half reliability. The formula is more commonly used for two other purposes, however: estimating the effect on reliability of changing the length of the test, and estimating how many items would need to be added to achieve a particular target level of reliability. The formula is:

$$r_{new} = \frac{mr_{old}}{1+(m-1)r_{old}}$$

where r_{new} = the reliability after changing the length of the test,

r_{old} = reliability before changing the length of the test, and

m = the factor by which the length of the test will be changed.

Note that the formula is usually presented using *k* instead of *m*, but many language teachers find that notation somewhat confusing, probably because *k* is also used elsewhere to indicate the total number of items on a test. I have therefore adopted Wainer and Thissen's (2001) use of *m*, and changed the subscripts of the correlation terms to something that I hope will seem more intuitive. It is important to remember that *m* is *not* the number of items on the test, and it is *not* the number of items the test needs to add. Thus, if we want to increase the length of the test by 50%, *m* will equal 1.5, or 150% of the original length of the test. If we double the number of items, *m* will equal 2, and if we cut the number of items by 50% for some reason, *m* will equal 0.5.

If the goal is to estimate the impact of changing the length of the test by a specific amount, we need to decide how much to change it—for example, we may decide to increase the number of items by 50%. Alternatively, if the reliability is quite high but the test is too long, we might want to see what the effect would be of shortening it by 25%. In either case, this gives us *m*, and we use that and r_{old} to solve for r_{new}.

On the other hand, if we want to lengthen the test enough for it to reach a particular target level of reliability, we use the current reliability (r_{old}) and the target reliability level (r_{new}), and solve for *m*. Examples of using the formula both ways—to predict the effects of a particular change in length, or to estimate how much change is needed to reach a particular target reliability—are provided in Chapter 18.

Score Dependability

Dependability, as explained earlier, is scoring consistency for a criterion-referenced test. It is always slightly lower than the reliability for the same test because of differences between the NRT and CRT paradigms. As mentioned in Chapter 1, norm-referenced testing is used to make relative decisions—that is, to rank people by ability. A CRT is used to estimate students' ability levels without respect to those of other learners; these are called absolute decisions. To return to the analogy of measuring people's heights, merely ranking people by height, from short to tall, is simpler than providing accurate measurements for each person's height. Ranking is also likely to be more accurate.

To estimate the CRT dependability index Φ, or phi, normally requires the use of **generalizability (G) theory**. (Note that this is the capital Greek letter phi, pronounced *fee*. The lower-case version (ϕ) is usually used to denote **item ϕ**, a CRT discrimination index.) It is not feasible to explain G theory in any detail in this book (see Chapter 10 for a brief description and list of suggested readings), but nevertheless, teachers often need to be able to estimate dependability in some way. Fortunately, Brown (1990) provides a shortcut formula to estimate Φ using Cronbach's alpha and a few descriptive statistics. The drawback to the formula is, unfortunately, that it only works with dichotomous data. The formula is:

$$\Phi = \frac{\frac{ns^2}{n-1}(KR20)}{\frac{ns^2}{n-1}(KR20) + \frac{M(1-M)-s^2}{k-1}}$$

where n = the number of people who took the test,

   s^2 = the variance (using the *population* formula) of test scores, in proportion-correct metric (the decimal equivalent of the percentage of questions that were answered correctly; for example, a proportion-correct score of .80 means that the student answered 80% of the questions correctly),

   KR20 = the reliability of the test, using Cronbach's alpha or the K-R20 formula

   M = the mean of the proportion scores, and

   k = the number of items on the test.

It is crucial that proportion-correct scores be used for s^2 and M, not raw total scores. Thus, if there are 25 questions on a test, and the average score is 19.75 out of 25, the proportion score of .79 should be used in the formula (19.75 ÷ 25 = .79). Similarly, the variance should be computed for the proportion scores; if it has been calculated already for raw scores, however, Brown points out that the proportion score variance is equal to the raw score variance divided by k^2.

Note further that I have used K-R20 here, rather than alpha or $r_{xx'}$, in order to emphasize that this shortcut only works with dichotomous data. It does not really matter, of course, which dichotomous formula is used, as the result will be the same. The hyphen is omitted from K-R20 in the formula for clarity, because equation formatting makes it look like K – R20, which could be mistaken for "K minus R20."

There is also a CRT equivalent for the SEM, called the **CRT confidence interval (CI$_{CRT}$, or CRT CI)**, which is interpreted much like the SEM. Brown and Hudson (2002) extend Brown's (1990) work to provide a similar shortcut for estimating this when dichotomous scoring is used:

$$CI_{CRT} = \sqrt{\frac{M(1 - M) - s^2}{k - 1}}$$

As with the shortcut for Φ, the mean and variance must be computed using proportion scores.

As a final note on score dependability, lengthening a criterion-referenced test—all things being equal—will raise dependability, just as doing so raises reliability on a norm-referenced test. Unfortunately, however, we cannot use the Spearman-Brown prophecy formula as we can with NRT. There are ways of getting equivalent information using generalizability theory, but these approaches are beyond the scope of this book.

Classification Dependability

In criterion-referenced testing, dependability of scores is naturally an important issue. As was discussed in Chapter 1, however, CRT is also frequently concerned with classifying students as being above or below some cut score. Students are then categorized as masters or non-masters, although more commonly teachers and programs will refer to passing and failing, placing into one level or another, or receiving a particular grade rather than a higher or lower one. For each of these decisions there is a cut score; in the case of placement testing or assigning letter grades, there will be multiple cut scores for the same test. Just as Φ gives us an indication of the dependability of *scores*, we are interested in the dependability of these *classifications* as well. There are two basic types of classification dependability estimates—both called *agreement indices*—that can be used: **threshold loss** and **squared error loss agreement indices**. They are called agreement indices because they estimate how much agreement—consistency—there would be in the results if students were tested and classified repeatedly.

One approach, *threshold loss agreement indices*, treats all classification errors as being equally severe. From this perspective, if a person is classified at the mastery level, but in truth they should have been below the cut score, it does not matter whether their true score was only slightly below the cut score, or was far below it. The same is true if they should have received a score above the cut score, but did not because of measurement error, and were instead misclassified as a non-master. This perspective is probably most appropriate when very high-stakes decisions are being made; in the context of testing at the class, school, or program level, however, it is probably less useful. Interested readers can find a full discussion of the two main threshold loss agreement indices, the agreement (p_o) and kappa (κ) coefficients, in Bachman (2004) and Brown and Hudson (2002).

An approach that is probably more useful in curriculum-based testing is the use of *squared error loss agreement indices*. From this perspective, classification errors are less serious if the student's true score is close to the cut score, and more serious if their true score is farther away from the cut score. In other words, small errors are not deemed as serious as large ones in this way of thinking, unlike the threshold loss agreement indices, which treat all errors as being equally bad. Probably the

most straightforward and most popular squared error loss agreement index is
$\Phi(\lambda)$, which is pronounced "fee lambda." It is probably also the most appropriate
such agreement; see Brown (1990) for a summary of the research indicating the
problems with its primary competitor, Livingston's (1972) criterion-referenced
reliability coefficient $k(X, Tx)$. Like Φ and the CI_{CRT}, $\Phi(\lambda)$ is derived from
generalizability theory, but also has a shortcut formula for use with dichotomous
data (Brennan 1992; adapted to the notation used in this book):

$$\Phi(\lambda) = 1 - \frac{1}{k-1}\left[\frac{M(1-M) - s^2}{(M-\lambda)^2 + s^2}\right]$$

where k = the number of items on the test,

M = the mean of the proportion scores,

s^2 = the population variance of the proportion scores, and

λ = the cut score.

It should be noted that $\Phi(\lambda)$ is lowest when the cut score is equal to the mean of
the proportion scores on the test. At that point, $\Phi(\lambda)$ is equal to Φ (Brennan 1980).

Because $\Phi(\lambda)$ is *cut-score dependent* (i.e. it changes when the cut score changes),
when there is more than one cut score, it must be calculated separately for each
one. To spell out the implications of $\Phi(\lambda)$ being lowest at the mean, the closer a
cut score is to the mean of the test scores, the lower the classification dependability
will be at that cut score. The farther away from the mean a cut score is, the greater
the classification dependability will be for that cut score.

In contrast, Φ and the CI_{CRT} are only calculated once for a given set of scores,
as they estimate *score* consistency, not classification consistency, and thus do not
depend on the cut score. While Φ is important in that it tells us how consistent
our scores are, $\Phi(\lambda)$ is also very important, because we want to know how
accurately our test separates students into various groups: letter grades, course
levels, passing/failing, etc.

Besides $\Phi(\lambda)$, the CI_{CRT} is also quite important with respect to classification
accuracy—that is, if there is a reasonable chance (as indicated by the size of the
confidence interval) that a student's true score could be on the other side of a cut
score, we must consider the possibility that the student is being misclassified. We
may, therefore, decide in some situations to err on the side of liberality, adjusting
the cut score downwards by one or two confidence intervals. In other situations,
however, we may find it prudent to err on the side of caution, adjusting the cut
score upwards, so that test takers are not likely to pass accidentally. Alternatively,
we may leave the cut scores alone, and instead try to get additional information
(solicit comments from teachers, conduct an interview, reexamine a writing
sample, etc.) to help determine whether the test taker's observed score might be
on the wrong side of the cut score—that is, to help us decide whether, due to
measurement error, a student passed or failed inappropriately, was placed into the
wrong level, or received the wrong grade.

Estimating the Reliability and Dependability of Performance Tests

This chapter has focused on assessing the consistency of scoring in item-based tests, such as are commonly used to assess reading, writing, vocabulary, and grammar. Consistency is also important in *rated* tasks, however, such as are commonly used in the assessment of speaking or writing.

Reliability of ratings is often addressed by reporting the **inter-rater reliability**, that is, the degree of consistency across scores by different raters. The related concept of **intra-rater reliability**, the consistency of the ratings by a single rater, is not used as commonly, since it would require that raters score the same performance twice. When there are only two raters, this is handled by reporting the correlation between the scores from the two raters, generally the **Spearman** ρ (rho; see Chapter 14), as the vast majority of rated scores will be ordinal data. The *Spearman-Brown prophecy formula* (discussed later in this chapter, and in Chapter 18) is then applied, in order to adjust for the fact that each rating constituted half of the test (i.e. $m = 2$ when there are two raters, following the notation used in this book). When there are several ratings, the **Fisher's Z-transformation** is applied to each one, the scores are averaged together, and the average is converted back into a correlation coefficient.

The vast majority of testing situations only use one or two raters per speaking or writing performance; when ratings are unreliable, it is usually simpler and cheaper to hire better raters, train raters better, and adjust the scoring rubric (see Chapter 7). Most people will therefore need to use Fisher's Z-transformation very rarely, if ever. As a reference for those rare situations when it might be needed, however, the formula (simplified from Neter, Kutner, Nachtsheim, and Wasserman 1996)

is $Z = \dfrac{1}{2} \ln \left(\dfrac{1 + r}{1 - r} \right)$. The reverse of the formula, for converting an averaged Z back to a correlation, is $r = \dfrac{e^{2Z} - 1}{e^{2Z} + 1}$.

As Bachman (2004) points out, however, inter-rater reliability gives us useful information about overall rater agreement, but does not tell us anything regarding the overall consistency of the scores that are being reported. This is empirically confirmed in research by Fleenor, Fleenor, and Grossnickle (1996), which indicates that reliability and inter-rater agreement estimates provide distinctly different information. Thus, while it is a good idea to report the correlations between different raters' scores, an overall reliability estimate is also needed. One approach to doing this is to use Cronbach's alpha, with each score treated as one "item." (Note that if certain subscales are being weighted differentially, the formula for alpha should be applied to the *weighted* scores.) Ideally, generalizability theory (Brennan 2001; Shavelson and Webb 1991), and possibly **many-facet Rasch theory** (Linacre 1989), would be used instead of alpha, particularly for important tests. Used in conjunction, they can provide quite powerful information about rated performances (see, for example, Bachman, Lynch, and Mason 1995); unfortunately, though, they require more statistical background than many language teachers are interested in acquiring. For those who are interested, however, brief overviews of these two topics are provided in Chapter 10, along with some recommendations for further reading.

Interpreting Estimates of Reliability and Dependability

As was mentioned earlier in this chapter, a common rule-of-thumb value for reliability and dependability in high-stakes testing is that it should be .80 or greater. This is not an absolute standard *per se*, but it seems to be a very common target. In lower-stakes situations such as testing at the classroom, program, or school level, a lower value may be acceptable. The question is, of course, how much measurement error is too much. Thorndike and Hagen (1969) point out that a test with low scoring consistency is better than nothing, but that having a value above .80 does not automatically mean the test is ideal. Although reliability/ dependability is only one of the qualities of usefulness that we need to consider, it has a great deal to do with whether test scores mean anything, or are a collection of near-random numbers. Personally, I am quite uncomfortable with a level below .70 even in classroom situations. I am displeased and concerned below .80, in fact. I am completely unwilling to accept anything at .67 or less, on the grounds that a third of the score variance was due to measurement error.

There is no clear standard for what constitutes an excessively large standard error of measurement, or CRT confidence interval. One good idea, however, is to convert the SEM or CI_{CRT} to a percentage metric, and use personal judgment to decide whether it is uncomfortably large. For most teachers, deciding whether the margin for error is too large or not is much more intuitive than answering the same question about the reliability or dependability index. Choosing an acceptable SEM or CI_{CRT} value and using that to determine what level of reliability should be targeted, while not a common approach, would constitute an empirical approach to deciding on the acceptability of a particular value for reliability or dependability: If the SEM or CI_{CRT} is too large, improvements in alpha or Φ (respectively) will help reduce it to a more acceptable level.

As for how to improve the reliability and dependability, in this chapter we have focused on making the test longer. Another approach, sometimes even more useful, is to use item analysis (see Chapters 5 and 15–17) to flag certain items as problematic and needing review. Once the poorly discriminating items have been revised, scoring consistency will improve. (Chapters 18 and 19 will offer practice in actually *using* the formulas discussed in this chapter.)

Note, however, that all of the steps and procedures discussed in this chapter are things we can do after the test has been planned, written, and administered. Other things can be done beforehand, during the planning and writing of the test, to increase *in advance* the likelihood of achieving good scoring consistency.

For example, using clear test specifications and writing high-quality items are two things that can do a lot here, and should reduce the number of items that will be flagged for revision—that is, items that will reduce the reliability or dependability of the test. Other procedures that can help with the consistency of scores are to use appropriate scoring rubrics and properly trained raters (discussed in Chapter 7), and to ensure that tests are administered properly, minimizing any extraneous impact of testing procedures on scores (see Chapter 9). And of course, consistent scoring is not the only quality of usefulness with which we need to be concerned, as noted in Chapters 1 and 3. It is an important precondition for one of the other qualities of usefulness, however—construct validity—and establishing the reliability or dependability of a test is an important part of the test's validation argument, which will be discussed further in Chapter 8.

Summary

In Chapter 6, we began by exploring the concept of reliability and dependability—scoring consistency for norm- and criterion-referenced tests, respectively. We considered ways of estimating reliability, including those that require testing twice (test-retest and parallel forms reliability), as well as internal consistency approaches (split-half reliability and Cronbach's alpha), which only require administering one test a single time. This chapter then raised the issue of estimating the accuracy of individual scores by providing an estimate of the margin of error, the standard error of measurement (SEM). We then discussed using the Spearman-Brown prophecy formula to estimate the effect on reliability of lengthening a norm-referenced test, or to see how much longer it would need to be in order to reach a particular reliability target. We next took up the topic of dependability, the criterion-referenced equivalent of reliability, with a focus on Φ, the index of dependability for scores; the CRT confidence interval (CI_{CRT}), which estimates the CRT margin of error, as the SEM does for NRT; and $\Phi(\lambda)$, which estimates how consistently examinees are classified as belonging in a particular group (for example, passing vs. failing, which level of a program they would place into, or what letter grade—A, B, C, D, F—they would receive). This was followed by a discussion of how to interpret reliability and dependability estimates, and we noted that, in addition to adding to test length, other steps and practices can help to increase the consistency of test scores. The chapter concluded with a reminder that while extremely important, reliability is not the only quality of usefulness of concern, although it plays a vital role in demonstrating construct validity.

Further Reading

Allen, M. J. and **W. M. Yen.** 1979. Chapter 3 'Classical true-score theory', Chapter 4 'Reliability'. *Introduction to Measurement Theory.* Monterey, CA: Brooks/ Cole Publishing Company.

Bachman, L. F. 2004. Chapter 5 'Investigating reliability for norm-referenced tests', Chapter 6 'Investigating reliability for criterion-referenced tests'. *Statistical Analyses for Language Assessment.* Cambridge: Cambridge University Press.

Kunnan, A. J. and **N. T. Carr** (in press). 'Statistical analysis of test results' in C. Chapelle (ed.). *The Encyclopedia of Applied Linguistics.* Addison-Wiley.

Nelson, L. R. 2001. *Item Analysis for Tests and Surveys Using Lertap 5.* Retrieved June 28 2009, from http://assess.com/xcart/product.php?productid=235&download=1&next=1&file=Lertap5Man.zip

Wainer, H. and **D. Thissen.** 2001. 'True score theory: The traditional method' in D. Thissen and H. Wainer (eds.). *Test Scoring.* Mahwah, NJ: Lawrence Erlbaum Associates.

Discussion Questions

1 In the section on Cronbach's alpha, an example is used of a test with 60 items: 20 reading comprehension, 20 listening comprehension, and 20 grammar.
   a Suppose that this test had an acceptable reliability level, in spite of mixing constructs together. Besides items having comparable difficulty levels, what about this test might have helped increase the reliability?
   b Now, suppose that alpha for the combined 60 items is low. A colleague suggests reporting alpha separately for each of the three sections. Why might this yield better results?

2 For norm- and criterion-referenced tests, many of the same concerns apply when it comes to consistency of measurement, but there are differences, including different terms used for parallel concepts. For both NRT and CRT, how would you summarize what needs to be estimated in the following three areas? Do they all apply equally to both NRT and CRT?
   a Consistency of *scoring*
   b Consistency of *classification*
   c Margin of error

3 Consider a language test that you have taken, administered, or are otherwise familiar with that included items—whether selected response or limited production.
   a Would it be more appropriate to consider this test norm- or criterion-referenced?
   b How many sections did the test include (for example, reading, listening, grammar, vocabulary, etc.)?
   c What estimates of reliability or dependability should be estimated for it, and for what? (For example: Should Cronbach's alpha or Φ be used, and should it be calculated separately for each section, for the test as a whole?)

4 Consider a language test that you have taken, administered, or are otherwise familiar with that included speaking and/or writing ability. For the speaking or writing portion of the test only:

   a Would it be more appropriate to consider this test norm- or criterion-referenced?

   b What task format(s) were used, and how many tasks were there?

   c What estimates of reliability or dependability should be estimated for it?

7 RATING SCALES FOR EXTENDED PRODUCTION TASKS

Introduction

As was noted in Chapter 1, it is a misnomer to refer to performance assessments, such as tests of speaking and writing, as "subjective." The tasks themselves are not necessarily any more subjective than other task formats. In fact, they are *arguably* less subjective, given that they are generally more authentic than other, less performative task formats. The nature of the scoring in performance assessments, of course, is the source of the word "subjective," since these tasks are generally rated using human judgment. Much of the purpose of this chapter is to point out ways to reduce the degree of that subjectivity, however, so that test scores are as consistent as possible. This chapter discusses how to do this by explaining various types of rating scales, followed by a section on how to develop or adapt rating scales for use in a particular testing situation. It then takes up procedures for training and norming raters, and for performing the actual ratings themselves. By the end of the chapter, readers will see that by using appropriate rating scales, rater training, and rating procedures, it *is* possible to achieve consistent scoring of speaking and writing tasks. The degree of this consistency can then be estimated and reported using the procedures described in Chapter 6.

Rating Scales and Scoring Rubrics

I will generally use the term *rating scale* here, but will occasionally use the term *scoring rubric* as well. These terms all refer to a set of generic descriptions of student performance which can be used to assign scores to an individual student's performance in a systematic fashion. A rating scale has several levels or **score bands**, each of which has its own description of what performance looks like at that level. The **descriptors**, or descriptions of performance within a particular score band, should be based on the construct definition that was written as part of the context and purpose specifications (see Chapter 3).

Analytic vs. Holistic Rating Scales

When discussing rating scales, we very frequently classify them as either *holistic* (sometimes referred to as "global," or "unitary") or *analytic* (sometimes called "componential"). In **holistic scoring**, a student's performance on a task (or set of tasks) is judged in terms of its overall quality, or the overall level of ability displayed, and a single rating is given to their performance of the task(s), usually in the form of a grade or number. All of the descriptors for a given level or score band are grouped together. Note that various performance features which are to be evaluated will probably be listed in the same order within each band. This is done for the purposes of clarity, to make reading them easier for the raters. The feature descriptions within a band will not be considered separately, however, and in particular, they will not be given separate scores. An example of a holistic rating scale is provided in Figure 7.1. (Note that unlike many holistic scales, this one focuses entirely on language use.) This scale is used in the ESL Placement Examination at the University of California, Los Angeles, a test of academic writing ability. Most of the students who take this test have a high level of English proficiency, but the rating scale must also include descriptors that will cover the small number of test takers who have lower levels of language ability.

 ESLPE COMPOSITION RATING SCALE
REVISED FALL 2000

6   Exempt from ESL Service Courses

- Grammar is near native-like with little or no evidence of ESL errors. There may be basic writer developmental errors (for example, spelling, sentence fragments and run-ons, interference from oral language).

- The writing exhibits a near native-like grasp of appropriate academic vocabulary and register and there are few problems with word choice OR the writing is fluent and native-like but lacks appropriate academic register or sophisticated vocabulary.

- Cohesion between paragraphs, sentences, and ideas is successfully achieved through a variety of methods (transitional words and phrases, a controlling theme, repetition of key words, etc.).

5   **ESL 35**

- The number and type of grammatical errors are limited and usually follow a discernible pattern; these include errors in article usage, noun number, subject/verb agreement, verb form (tense/aspect) and word form.

- Meaning is never obscured by grammar or lexical choices that are not native-like.

- The writing exhibits fluency, which is achieved through a variety of simple and complex sentence structures. These are usually constructed appropriately, although there may be some problems with more complex grammatical structures (for example, subordination or embedding relative clauses).

Figure 7.1 Example of a Holistic Rating Scale (used by permission of the ESL Service Courses, University of California, Los Angeles)

- Register and vocabulary are generally appropriate to academic writing.
- Cohesion is adequate and achieved through the use of transitional words and phrases.

4   ESL 33C

- Grammar errors may occur in article usage and noun number, subject/verb agreement, verb form (tense/aspect), word form/choice, relative clause formation, passive voice, and coordination and subordination.
- Errors are noticeable, but rarely obscure meaning.
- The writing is less fluent than the 5 paper. It may sound choppy because there are too many simple sentences. Or there may be too many complex sentences that are too long to process. Or there may be some non-native-like sentence fragments and run-ons.
- Vocabulary may be repetitive or inaccurate, and the register may exhibit a lack of academic sophistication.
- There may be a limited lack of cohesion and difficulty with paragraphing.

3   ESL 33B

- Patterns of errors occur in article usage and noun number, subject/verb agreement, verb form (tense/aspect), and/or word form.
- Errors are noticeable and occasionally obscure meaning.
- Although there is a good basic knowledge of sentence structure, the writing lacks fluency because of errors in or avoidance of relative clauses, passive voice, and/or coordination and subordination. There may be some non-native-like sentence fragments and run-ons.
- Vocabulary is inaccurate in places and may rely on repeating words and expressions from the prompt.
- The writing exhibits a basic knowledge of cohesive devices but these may be misapplied, or the devices used may not create cohesion.

2   ESL 33A

- Frequent patterns of errors occur in article usage and noun number, subject/verb agreement, verb form (tense/aspect), and/or word form.
- Errors are noticeable and obscure meaning.
- Although there is a basic knowledge of sentence structure, this is not consistently applied. The writing exhibits errors in and avoidance/absence of relative clauses, passive voice, and/or coordination and subordination. There are non-native-like sentence fragments and run-ons.

Figure 7.1 Example of a Holistic Rating Scale (used by permission of the ESL Service Courses, University of California, Los Angeles) (continued)

- Vocabulary is generally basic and word choice is inaccurate. The writer may rely on repeating words or expressions from the prompt. The register can often resemble either a conversational narrative or a stilted, confusing attempt at academic discourse.

- Although there is some use of cohesive devices, it is neither consistent nor always effective, and may be simple and repetitive in many cases.

1   Pre-University

- Pervasive patterns of errors occur in article usage and noun number, subject/verb agreement, verb form (tense/aspect), and word form.

- Except in very simple sentences, meaning is frequently obscured.

- A basic knowledge of sentence structure is lacking, and there are frequent errors in and/or avoidance of relative clauses, passive voice, and/or coordination and subordination. When sentences are complete, they are often simple or are expressions learned as "chunks".

- Vocabulary is quite basic, and more sophisticated attempts at word choice are often inaccurate or inappropriate. The register is often too conversational for academic purposes or, if an academic tone is attempted, it is incomprehensible.

- There may be attempts to use cohesive devices but they are either quite mechanical or so inaccurate that they mislead the reader.

0   No Response

Figure 7.1 Example of a Holistic Rating Scale (used by permission of the ESL Service Courses, University of California, Los Angeles) (continued)

In **analytic scoring**, the descriptors are grouped into several **subscales**, which are essentially smaller (i.e. more narrowly focused) scoring rubrics that are each concerned with a specific performance feature or portion of the overall construct, as illustrated in the example rating scale in Figure 7.2. (This scale was used for the UCLA ESL Placement Examination until it was replaced by the holistic scale in Figure 7.1; see Carr 2000). Each subscale is considered separately, and receives its own rating. The difference between analytic and holistic scoring is not what qualities are described in the rating scale, but whether various portions of the construct definition are each considered separately, or taken together as a whole. Of course, after the separate scores have been assigned on an analytic rating scale, we can always add or average them together to create a composite score for the overall performance.

UCLA ENGLISH AS A SECOND LANGUAGE PLACEMENT EXAM COMPOSITION RATING SCALE
REVISED SEPTEMBER 1993
CONTENT

9–10 The essay fulfills the writing task well and treats the topic with sophistication. The main idea is clear and well-developed. Support is relevant, thorough and credible.

7–8 The essay addresses the writing task appropriately* and is developed competently. The main idea is clear and competently developed, but with less sophistication and depth than the 9–10 paper. Arguments/ideas are competently supported.

5–6 The essay addresses the writing task adequately, but may not be well-developed.
OR The essay only addresses part of the topic, but develops that part sufficiently. The main idea is clear but may not be fully developed. Ideas/arguments may be unsupported or unrelated to main idea.

3–4 The essay only partially fulfills the writing task OR the main idea is somewhat clear, but requires the reader to work to find it. The essay contains unsupported or irrelevant statements.

1–2 The essay fails to fulfill the writing task, and lacks a clear main idea and development. Most ideas/arguments are unsupported, and ideas are not developed. OR Not enough material to evaluate.

Note: *Appropriate* is defined as addressing all aspects of a writing topic, for example, all characteristics in questions involving choices. Furthermore, all parts of the writing task should be touched on in the writer's response.

RHETORICAL CONTROL

9–10 Introduction and conclusion effectively fulfill their separate purposes: the introduction effectively orients the reader to the topic and the conclusion not only reinforces the thesis but effectively closes off the essay. Paragraphs are separate, yet cohesive, logical units which are well-connected to each other and to the essay's main idea. Sentences form a well-connected series of ideas.

7–8 The introduction presents the controlling idea, gives the reader the necessary background information, and orients the reader, although there may be some lack of originality in the presentation. The conclusion restates the controlling idea and provides a valid interpretation but not as effectively as the 9–10 paper. Paragraphs are usually cohesive and logically connected to the essay's main idea. Sentences are usually well-connected.

Figure 7.2 Example of an Analytic Rating Scale (used by permission of the ESL Service Courses, University of California, Los Angeles)

5–6   Introduction presents the controlling ideas but may do so mechanically or may not orient the reader to the topic effectively. The conclusion does not give the reader new insights or may contain some extraneous information.

      Paragraphs may exhibit a lack of cohesion or connection to the essay's main idea. Sentences may not be well-connected.

3–4   Introduction and conclusion do not restate the controlling idea. Introduction fails to orient the reader adequately, and the conclusion may be minimal or may not be tied to the rest of the essay. Paragraphs often lack cohesion and are not appropriately connected to each other or to the essay's main idea. Sentences are not well-connected.

1–2   Introduction and conclusion are missing or unrelated to rest of the essay. There is no attempt to divide the essay into conceptual paragraphs, or the paragraphs are unrelated and the progression of ideas is very difficult to follow.
      OR Not enough material to evaluate

LANGUAGE (Grammar, Vocabulary, Register, Mechanics)

9–10   Except for rare minor errors (esp. articles), the grammar is native-like. There is an effective balance of simple and complex sentence patterns with coordination and subordination. Excellent, near-native academic vocabulary and register. Few problems with word choices.

7–8   Minor errors in articles, verb agreement, word form, verb form (tense, aspect) and no incomplete sentences. Meaning is never obscured and there is a clear grasp of English sentence structure. There is usually a good balance of simple and complex sentences both appropriately constructed. Generally, there is appropriate use of academic vocabulary and register with some errors in word choice OR writing is fluent and native-like but lacks appropriate academic register and sophisticated vocabulary.

5–6   Errors in article use and verb agreement and several errors in verb form and/or word form. May be some incomplete sentences. Errors almost never obscure meaning. Either too many simple sentences or complex ones that are too long to process. May be frequent problems with word choice; vocabulary is inaccurate or imprecise. Register lacks proper levels of sophistication.

3–4   Several errors in all areas of grammar which often interfere with communication, although there is knowledge of basic sentence structure. No variation in sentence structure. Many unsuccessful subordinated or coordinated structures. Frequent errors in word choice (i.e. wrong word, not simply vague or informal). Register is inappropriate for academic writing.

Figure 7.2 Example of an Analytic Rating Scale (used by permission of the ESL Service Courses, University of California, Los Angeles) (continued)

> 1–2   There are problems not only with verb formation, articles, and incomplete sentences, but sentence construction is so poor that sentences are often incomprehensible. Sentences that are comprehensible are extremely simple constructions. Vocabulary too simple to express meaning and/or severe errors in word choice. OR Not enough material to evaluate.

Figure 7.2 Example of an Analytic Rating Scale (used by permission of the ESL Service Courses, University of California, Los Angeles) (continued)

If all this discussion of "portions of the construct definition" is unclear, keep in mind that the construct definition for a speaking or writing test—or section of a test—will almost always include more than one component (see Table 3.2 for examples of some common components of construct definitions). For example, the construct definition for a hypothetical intermediate-level speaking test might include grammatical accuracy, pronunciation, and accurate use of vocabulary. If this construct definition only contains these three features or categories, by implication we have now decided to exclude a number of other things from our consideration. These excluded things could be included in another scoring rubric, just not this one. For example, we have effectively decided that we will not grade the content of responses, nor their organization, cohesion, or coherence. We are following a very weak approach to performance assessment in this case, in that we are not concerned with the success of task performance *per se*, but will only grade the language used. On the other hand, if we are unhappy with excluding one of these categories, and want to include it in the scoring rubric, we must revise our test context and purpose specifications accordingly. Finally, once we have made a final decision about our construct definition, we must decide how to structure the rating scale. If we decide to consider grammar, pronunciation, and vocabulary together, and give a single score to each student on a given task, then we are using a holistic rating scale. If we give separate scores for grammar, pronunciation, and vocabulary, we are using an analytic rating scale.

It should be noted that whether to use an analytic or holistic rating scale is a separate decision from the number of tasks to score. Each student may be assessed on several tasks, with a score (holistic) or scores (analytic) being given on each one of the tasks; or each student may be assessed on a single task, again using either a holistic or analytic approach. Outside interview testing, however, it is probably a bad idea to give a single score (or set of scores, with analytic scales) to multiple tasks. If nothing else, scoring each task separately will lead to greater reliability or dependability. On the other hand, only giving one score or set of scores to several performances (speaking tasks, writing tasks, etc.) means that variation across tasks will be ignored. This is especially important if the tasks differ in terms of language functions, topical content, etc. Some tasks will lend themselves to evaluating certain criteria more readily, while the nature of other tasks allows for a focus on some other feature(s); if we do not score these tasks separately, we lose the different pieces of information that each one can provide us. Furthermore, teachers will probably be swayed most by their first impressions and what they hear at the end, with anything in between likely to count for less. At the same time, however, the number of tasks (and subscales, in an analytic rating scale) needs to be chosen carefully, as the more separate judgments a rater has to make within a limited timeframe, the more stressful and cognitively difficult this may be. Furthermore, the more rushed the judgments are, the greater the likelihood that the reliability of ratings will suffer.

Holistic scales have the advantage of requiring fewer decisions, and can therefore be faster. If a school or program is administering a test to a large number of students, and has to pay teachers extra to rate the speaking or writing section(s), this means holistic scoring may be somewhat cheaper than analytic. Aside from this advantage, however, holistic scoring often comes up short against analytic scoring. For example, holistic scoring cannot provide information on separate aspects of language ability. Therefore, it is rather common for two students to receive the same scores for different reasons—one may have good pronunciation and poor grammar, and the other may have good grammar but an accent that makes comprehension difficult. Analytic scoring is therefore far more useful for providing diagnostic information, in terms of what areas of a student's writing or speaking are stronger or weaker.

A related issue is that when something besides linguistic accuracy is considered, holistic scoring may combine abilities that are not necessarily closely related. For example, in native speaker writing, linguistic accuracy often goes hand in hand with the ability to generate good content that is appropriately organized. Few native speakers will produce weak content using excellent grammar and word choice, and few will write an essay with strong, well-organized content and poor language use. This is probably why holistic scoring seems so widely used in assessing L1 composition. In L2 writing, however, someone may have excellent content and organization, but issues with language, or vice versa. Above a certain minimal level of language ability, L2 students' linguistic accuracy is often quite distinct from their ability to generate content and organize it coherently. The same principle holds for speaking as well. Therefore, analytic ratings are often better able to describe the performance of second language writers and speakers. The main exceptions to this are at very low levels of proficiency, where students cannot generate much meaningful content anyway; at very advanced levels, where linguistic accuracy is not much of a factor; and in cases where *only* linguistic accuracy is being assessed, and where students have fairly evenly developed profiles in terms of grammatical accuracy, vocabulary development, etc. Even then, though, as Weigle (2002) points out, non-native speakers often have uneven developmental profiles.

Another advantage of analytic rating scales is that they also give greater control over rater behavior. Returning to the example of an intermediate level speaking test mentioned above, imagine that we create two versions of the rating scale. Both versions use the same descriptors, but one rubric is analytic, and the other holistic. The only difference is that in the holistic scale the descriptors for grammar, pronunciation, and vocabulary are all grouped together within a given scoring band, while in the analytic scale, they are separated into three subscales. In the holistic scoring scenario, one rater may give greater emphasis to grammatical accuracy, a second rater may be more concerned with pronunciation, and a third with vocabulary use. Thus, a student's score will depend on which rater(s) score their performance; such a dependence is fundamentally unfair. In the analytic scenario, however, each rater has to consider the three categories separately, and give each one its own score. Then, if we have decided as a school or program that all three areas are equally important, we can simply average (or add; mathematically, it comes out the same) the scores together. On the other hand, if we decide, say, that grammar and vocabulary are both twice as important as pronunciation, we can use a weighted average or total. In this case, the composite score would equal (Grammar x 2 + Vocabulary x 2 + Pronunciation) ÷ 5, or Grammar x 0.4 + Vocabulary x 0.4 + Pronunciation x 0.2. Whatever is decided, this gives the test developers greater control over how the various aspects of the construct definition are prioritized.

Weigle (2002) cites research indicating that analytic scales are easier to use for new or inexperienced raters. She further points out that analytic scoring is obviously superior in terms of the feedback it provides, by virtue of yielding separate scores for different aspects of the performance.

Finally, holistic scoring can be consistent, especially if a clear rating scale is used by well trained, normed raters. Nevertheless, all things being equal, a comparable analytic rating scale will be even more reliable or dependable. As was explained in Chapter 6, having more items on a test means higher reliability. Put differently, more *scores*, or pieces of information about a test taker's ability, will translate to greater consistency, whether the additional scores are the result of more items, more prompts or tasks, more subscale scores, or more raters.

"Trait" Scales

In addition to the analytic-holistic distinction, another way of classifying rating scales involves the degree to which they are tailored to a specific test task. **Primary trait scoring** refers to using a *holistic* rating scale that includes features of the specific test task. A related concept is **multiple-trait scoring**, which refers to using an *analytic* rating scale that includes features of the specific test task. For example, on a writing test, one task might require students to write an informal post card message to a very close friend about a vacation they are taking. They are given several pictures of things they have done or seen on their trip, and are required to mention at least three of them in their postcard message. A primary- or multiple-trait scale for this task would probably include in its descriptors mention of what to do if students referred to one or two pictures, or none. The descriptors might also include instructions to raters on how to penalize for excessively formal messages. As another example, if an integrated reading and writing task involved writing a summary of a reading passage, a trait-based scale would probably include mention of specific details, and how important it would be to include certain ones, or certain numbers of details. (For a clear introduction to ways to score recall or summary tasks, see Alderson (2000).) In contrast, *non-trait* scales in these examples could be used with any postcard writing task, or any summary writing task.

"Objective" Scoring Approaches For Speaking and Writing

So-called **objective scoring for extended response tasks** does not seem to be used very widely, probably for good reason. The term includes several different attempts at speeding up the rating process, and making it less subjective and more mechanical. One example includes the use of several yes-no questions, such as "Does the student use appropriate grammar in the essay?" The number of "yes" answers is counted, and then this number is used to provide a score. One problem with this "yes-no question" approach, however, is that frequently the answer is "somewhat," "frequently, but not always," or "with certain structures, yes, but not with others." This may then lead teachers to give half points, or other fractions, to each question, but without firm definitions as to what the difference is between 0.0 and 0.5, or between 0.5 and 1.0. Furthermore, when the test is used with students with a wide variety of levels (as in a placement test, for example), the definition of "adequate" or "appropriate" may be unclear. After all, what is considered appropriate grammar use at the beginning levels is unlikely to be the same as what is seen as "appropriate" coming from more advanced learners. (Unfortunately, I believe the program in which I encountered this method *did* use it for placement testing!)

Another attempt at objective scoring involves counting the numbers of errors in a response, or part of a response. The errors may be weighted based on how severe they are deemed to be. The total is then divided by the number of words in the response, and this number is used as the score. As Bailey (1998) points out, however, decisions about error gravity involve a certain degree of subjectivity, something these approaches are intended to avoid! She also notes that error counting only addresses what students have done wrong, and gives them no credit for the positive aspects of their performance—that is, what they did *right*.

An approach related to error counting is to count the number of **T-units** (essentially, an independent clause and all the subordinate clauses associated with it) and error-free T-units, and compute various ratios with them (for example, number of words per T-unit, or ratio of words in error-free T-units to total words), as was done by Robb, Ross, and Shortreed (1986). Although this may be the most promising of the so-called objective methods, it still suffers from several shortcomings. In particular, all errors count equally, unless error gravity judgments are incorporated, which then renders the procedure less than objective. In addition, the greater complexity of this approach probably makes it at least as time-consuming as the ordinary rating process.

Developing or Adapting Rating Scales

When it comes to writing a new scoring rubric, or adapting or adopting an existing one, the first place to start is with the construct definition contained in the test context and purpose specifications. If an existing rating scale can be found that covers all of its components, and no extraneous ones, the next step is to consider whether it will work with the tasks that will be included on the test. For example, a rating scale designed for use with essays is probably not appropriate for use in scoring paragraphs, letters, or summaries of reading passages. A further point to examine is whether the descriptors for the various levels seem to describe the writing or speaking of the students who will be taking the test, or whether they are more appropriate for a different group of students. In particular, does the number of levels in the rating scale seem appropriate? Are there so many levels that it is hard to differentiate them, or are there so few levels that a given level seems too broad?

Most likely, no preexisting rating scale will be a perfect fit to the specifications for a different test, unless it was designed for use in a similar program, for similar purposes, with similar students. If one can be found, of course, that is wonderful. More commonly, however, it is necessary to make modifications to an existing rating scale, or to create a new one entirely. Thus, asking "Does anyone have a good scoring rubric that I can borrow?" is a misguided question, unless it is qualified by specifying a great deal more information about what the rubric is supposed to do. Adapting an existing rubric can involve just minor wording changes, or extensive modifications resembling the creation of a completely new rating scale. There seems little need to comment here on slight adjustments to the wording of descriptors, such as adding or changing a word here and there, and in any case, the results of such minor revisions will need to conform to the same principles as new rating scales; thus, the following discussion will focus on how to develop new rating scales.

Developing Rating Scales: First Steps

Developing a scoring rubric should begin with the construct definition contained in the test specifications. The components of the construct definition will dictate what points need to be addressed in the descriptors. Various portions of the construct definition may be combined together, or treated separately—for example, if the construct definition for a speaking test refers to both segmental and suprasegmental pronunciation, a decision must be made as to whether to describe these two things separately, or together, in the scoring rubric. A related decision that must also be made early on is whether to use an analytic or holistic rating scale. If an analytic scale is going to be created, the decision about what portions of the construct definition to combine or address separately will have obvious ramifications for the number of subscales to be included; typically, though, there will be one subscale per component of the construct definition (Bachman and Palmer 1996). At the same time, what counts as a "component" may be a subjective question, as in the example of segmental and suprasegmental pronunciation. Furthermore, it can be tempting at times to include as many subscales as possible, for the sake of thoroughness. This will make the scale difficult or impossible to use, though. As a general rule, three to five subscales seems most common; more than five becomes difficult for raters, and risks making their task too complex.

In assessments that are intended to replicate real-world tasks from the TLU domain, sometimes it may also be appropriate to include a subscale—or potentially more than one, if the task is suitably complex, or involves a need for technical knowledge as well—relating to how well the task was performed. This sort of addition is particularly appropriate in language for specific purposes (LSP) testing (see Douglas 2000), which will be discussed further in Chapter 10.

Once the number of components or subscales has been decided on, it is time to decide on the number of levels and write the descriptors for each one. Fulcher (2003) classifies approaches to creating rubrics as either *intuitive* or *empirical*. **Intuitive rating scale development** is when one or more teachers or other experts base the scale on their expert judgment, knowledge of the teaching and testing context, and so on. This is essentially the same as Bachman and Palmer's (1996) recommendation to base descriptors on either a theory of language development, or a syllabus or curriculum. It therefore might just as fairly be called a *theory-based, syllabus-based,* or *curriculum-based* approach. In the case of language for specific purposes assessments, consideration may also be given to real-life criteria used for assessing non-test communication (see Douglas 2001; Jacoby and McNamara 1999).

At the school or program level, **empirical approaches** generally involve looking at a sample of actual learner performances, dividing them into groups based on the level of performance, and then describing the characteristics of the written or spoken responses at each level. It should be noted that this is something of an oversimplification of Fulcher's description. I am deliberately limiting the discussion of empirical approaches here to what is likely to be of use to teachers, schools, and language programs, as opposed to large-scale testing organizations and assessment researchers, who may choose to implement more complex procedures (see, for example, Fulcher 1996, and North 1997; see Fulcher 2003, and Luoma 2004 for discussions of additional methods and references to examples of studies using them).

When the performances are being divided into different levels or bands, there are two ways to go about separating them, one *norm-referenced* and one *criterion-referenced*. If the divisions are based on features within the performances themselves, as opposed to some outside standard, this would be an inherently *norm-referenced* approach; in other words, the levels in the rating scale do not necessarily reflect anything to do with the language program or curriculum. The resulting rating scale would accurately describe students' current performances, but the description might not be terribly relevant to any particular language curriculum. Dividing the speaking or writing performances in this way, then, might be more appropriate in a proficiency testing situation, rather than in curriculum-related testing. In contrast, if the writing or speaking performances were divided on the basis of preexisting levels in the program—that is, the compositions or interviews of students in Level 1 would be grouped together, then those of the Level 2 students, etc.—the approach would be *criterion-referenced*, and the scale would be directly tied to the program's curriculum. Using this second approach, however, would depend to some extent on the students having already been placed in the appropriate levels.

Writing the Descriptors

When it comes time to actually write the descriptors, there are a number of things to keep in mind. One of the first is that the rubric should provide a verbal description of performance at various levels, not just say "A," "B," "C," and so on in each category. Similarly, it is a bad idea for the rubric to contain references to levels in the program (for example, "Fluency and accuracy resemble what would be expected of students in Level 3," or "Shows greater fluency than Level 2 student, but without the accuracy expected in Level 4"), especially with analytic scoring. Even if the levels of the rubric *are* meant to correspond to levels in a language program (say, on a placement test), the raters should be evaluating each performance in terms of how it resembles the descriptors, not how it resembles their own internal understanding of performance at a given level of the curriculum. Even experienced teachers who "know what Level 3 students in our program are like" need actual written descriptors, as they may not *really* "know" the same thing, or have the same impressions, and worse yet, may not even realize that they are not in agreement with each other. Thus, continuing the example, rather than *mentioning* Level 3 directly, a band descriptor should confine itself to describing the fluency and accuracy of students at that level.

Furthermore, focusing on the level, not the descriptors, makes it more likely that raters will generalize from overall performance to all of the subscales, during analytic scoring. It is fine to write descriptors that describe each level, with one score band corresponding to one level in the program, but the process of developing these descriptors may not be as cut-and-dried as might be anticipated beforehand. Teachers should therefore discuss the descriptors *before* they are used. Finally, another advantage of having descriptors that actually describe performance at each level—as opposed to merely labeling each score band by its level—is that scores can then be used to provide diagnostic feedback.

Bachman and Palmer (1996) provide important guidelines for establishing the top and bottom of rating scales. The lowest band should be zero, indicating a failure to respond, or examinee responses that were off topic or demonstrated no evidence of the construct. This does not mean zero language ability, merely that the task was not addressed, or that no evidence of the construct was provided. The highest level on the scale should reflect *mastery* of a given component of the construct definition. This is *not* necessarily the same thing as perfection, or being "native-like"; mastery must be viewed in the context of the test at hand. For example, a rating scale for role-plays performed in class in an intermediate-level conversation course would not define mastery in the same way that a rating scale would for role-plays in an advanced course in the same program.

It is also important to decide in which of two ways the rating scale will be interpreted. The most common approach is to assign scores based on which band a student's speech or writing most resembles, i.e. the "best fit" approach. If the response is inconsistent, raters must decide which one best describes what was said or written. Some tests may instruct raters that when a case cannot be decided, they should assign the lower score; others may say to give the higher one. The other way to use rating scales, however, is to assign a score to a student based on the lowest level that they consistently demonstrate, or "sustain." This is the philosophy in the ACTFL Oral Proficiency Interview (OPI; see Swender et al. 1999), the rating scale for which is provided in Figure 7.3. Thus, a student at the intermediate high level usually functions at the advanced level, but not always—that is, they *occasionally* perform at the intermediate level (suffer a communicative "breakdown," in ACTFL parlance), so they are not continuously sustaining performance at the advanced level. It is this combination of never slipping *below* the intermediate level, but being unable to perform consistently at the advanced level without any breakdowns ("sustain the advanced level"), that characterizes the intermediate high level.

SUPERIOR

Speakers at the Superior level are able to communicate in the language with accuracy and fluency in order to participate fully and effectively in conversations on a variety of topics in formal and informal settings from both concrete and abstract perspectives. They discuss their interests and special fields of competence, explain complex matters in detail, and provide lengthy and coherent narrations, all with ease, fluency, and accuracy. They explain their opinions on a number of topics of importance to them, such as social and political issues, and provide structured argument to support their opinions. They are able to construct and develop hypotheses to explore alternative possibilities. When appropriate, they use extended discourse without unnaturally lengthy hesitation to make their point, even when engaged in abstract elaborations. Such discourse, while coherent, may still be influenced by the Superior speakers' own language patterns, rather than those of the target language.

Superior speakers command a variety of interactive and discourse strategies, such as turn-taking and separating main ideas from supporting information through the use of syntactic and lexical devices, as well as intonational features such as pitch, stress and tone. They demonstrate virtually no pattern of error in the use of basic structures. However, they may make sporadic errors, particularly in low-frequency structures and in some complex high-frequency structures more common to formal speech and writing. Such errors, if they do occur, do not distract the native interlocutor or interfere with communication.

ADVANCED HIGH

Speakers at the Advanced-High level perform all Advanced-level tasks with linguistic ease, confidence and competence. They are able to consistently explain in detail and narrate fully and accurately in all time frames. In addition, Advanced-High speakers handle the tasks pertaining to the Superior level but cannot sustain performance at that level across a variety of topics. They can provide a structured argument to support their opinions, and they may construct

---

Figure 7.3 ACTFL Proficiency Guidelines: Speaking (American Council on the Teaching of Foreign Languages 1999; used by permission of the American Council on the Teaching of Foreign Languages) (continued)

hypotheses, but patterns of error appear. They can discuss some topics abstractly, especially those relating to their particular interests and special fields of expertise, but in general, they are more comfortable discussing a variety of topics concretely.

Advanced-High speakers may demonstrate a well-developed ability to compensate for an imperfect grasp of some forms or for limitations in vocabulary by the confident use of communicative strategies, such as paraphrasing, circumlocution, and illustration. They use precise vocabulary and intonation to express meaning and often show great fluency and ease of speech. However, when called on to perform the complex tasks associated with the Superior level over a variety of topics, their language will at times break down or prove inadequate, or they may avoid the task altogether, for example, by resorting to simplification through the use of description or narration in place of argument or hypothesis.

ADVANCED MID

Speakers at the Advanced-Mid level are able to handle with ease and confidence a large number of communicative tasks. They participate actively in most informal and some formal exchanges on a variety of concrete topics relating to work, school, home, and leisure activities, as well as to events of current, public, and personal interest or individual relevance.

Advanced-Mid speakers demonstrate the ability to narrate and describe in all major time frames (past, present, and future) by providing a full account, with good control of aspect, as they adapt flexibly to the demands of the conversation. Narration and description tend to be combined and interwoven to relate relevant and supporting facts in connected, paragraph-length discourse.

Advanced-Mid speakers can handle successfully and with relative ease the linguistic challenges presented by a complication or unexpected turn of events that occurs within the context of a routine situation or communicative task with which they are otherwise familiar. Communicative strategies such as circumlocution or rephrasing are often employed for this purpose. The speech of Advanced-Mid speakers performing Advanced-level tasks is marked by substantial flow. Their vocabulary is fairly extensive although primarily generic in nature, except in the case of a particular area of specialization or interest. Dominant language discourse structures tend to recede, although discourse may still reflect the oral paragraph structure of their own language rather than that of the target language.

Advanced-Mid speakers contribute to conversations on a variety of familiar topics, dealt with concretely, with much accuracy, clarity and precision, and they convey their intended message without misrepresentation or confusion. They are readily understood by native speakers unaccustomed to dealing with non-natives.

Figure 7.3 ACTFL Proficiency Guidelines: Speaking (American Council on the Teaching of Foreign Languages 1999; used by permission of the American Council on the Teaching of Foreign Languages) (continued)

When called on to perform functions or handle topics associated with the Superior level, the quality and/or quantity of their speech will generally decline. Advanced-Mid speakers are often able to state an opinion or cite conditions; however, they lack the ability to consistently provide a structured argument in extended discourse. Advanced-Mid speakers may use a number of delaying strategies, resort to narration, description, explanation or anecdote, or simply attempt to avoid the linguistic demands of Superior-level tasks.

ADVANCED LOW

Speakers at the Advanced-Low level are able to handle a variety of communicative tasks, although somewhat haltingly at times. They participate actively in most informal and a limited number of formal conversations on activities related to school, home, and leisure activities and, to a lesser degree, those related to events of work, current, public, and personal interest or individual relevance.

Advanced-Low speakers demonstrate the ability to narrate and describe in all major time frames (past, present and future) in paragraph length discourse, but control of aspect may be lacking at times. They can handle appropriately the linguistic challenges presented by a complication or unexpected turn of events that occurs within the context of a routine situation or communicative task with which they are otherwise familiar, though at times their discourse may be minimal for the level and strained. Communicative strategies such as rephrasing and circumlocution may be employed in such instances. In their narrations and descriptions, they combine and link sentences into connected discourse of paragraph length. When pressed for a fuller account, they tend to grope and rely on minimal discourse. Their utterances are typically not longer than a single paragraph. Structure of the dominant language is still evident in the use of false cognates, literal translations, or the oral paragraph structure of the speaker's own language rather than that of the target language.

While the language of Advanced-Low speakers may be marked by substantial, albeit irregular flow, it is typically somewhat strained and tentative, with noticeable self-correction and a certain "grammatical roughness." The vocabulary of Advanced-Low speakers is primarily generic in nature.

Advanced-Low speakers contribute to the conversation with sufficient accuracy, clarity, and precision to convey their intended message without misrepresentation or confusion, and it can be understood by native speakers unaccustomed to dealing with non-natives, even though this may be achieved through repetition and restatement. When attempting to perform functions or handle topics associated with the Superior level, the linguistic quality and quantity of their speech will deteriorate significantly.

Figure 7.3 ACTFL Proficiency Guidelines: Speaking (American Council on the Teaching of Foreign Languages 1999; used by permission of the American Council on the Teaching of Foreign Languages) (continued)

INTERMEDIATE HIGH

Intermediate-High speakers are able to converse with ease and confidence when dealing with most routine tasks and social situations of the Intermediate level. They are able to handle successfully many uncomplicated tasks and social situations requiring an exchange of basic information related to work, school, recreation, particular interests and areas of competence, though hesitation and errors may be evident.

Intermediate-High speakers handle the tasks pertaining to the Advanced level, but they are unable to sustain performance at that level over a variety of topics. With some consistency, speakers at the Intermediate High level narrate and describe in major time frames using connected discourse of paragraph length. However, their performance of these Advanced-level tasks will exhibit one or more features of breakdown, such as the failure to maintain the narration or description semantically or syntactically in the appropriate major time frame, the disintegration of connected discourse, the misuse of cohesive devises, a reduction in breadth and appropriateness of vocabulary, the failure to successfully circumlocute, or a significant amount of hesitation.

Intermediate-High speakers can generally be understood by native speakers unaccustomed to dealing with non-natives, although the dominant language is still evident (for example use of code-switching, false cognates, literal translations, etc.), and gaps in communication may occur.

INTERMEDIATE MID

Speakers at the Intermediate-Mid level are able to handle successfully a variety of uncomplicated communicative tasks in straightforward social situations. Conversation is generally limited to those predictable and concrete exchanges necessary for survival in the target culture; these include personal information covering self, family, home, daily activities, interests and personal preferences, as well as physical and social needs, such as food, shopping, travel and lodging.

Intermediate-Mid speakers tend to function reactively, for example, by responding to direct questions or requests for information. However, they are capable of asking a variety of questions when necessary to obtain simple information to satisfy basic needs, such as directions, prices and services. When called on to perform functions or handle topics at the Advanced level, they provide some information but have difficulty linking ideas, manipulating time and aspect, and using communicative strategies, such as circumlocution.

Intermediate-Mid speakers are able to express personal meaning by creating with the language, in part by combining and recombining known elements and conversational input to make utterances of sentence length and some strings of sentences. Their speech may contain pauses, reformulations and self-corrections-

Figure 7.3 ACTFL Proficiency Guidelines: Speaking (American Council on the Teaching of Foreign Languages 1999; used by permission of the American Council on the Teaching of Foreign Languages) (continued)

as they search for adequate vocabulary and appropriate language forms to express themselves. Because of inaccuracies in their vocabulary and/or pronunciation and/or grammar and/or syntax, misunderstandings can occur, but Intermediate Mid speakers are generally understood by sympathetic interlocutors accustomed to dealing with non-natives.

INTERMEDIATE LOW

Speakers at the Intermediate-Low level are able to handle successfully a limited number of uncomplicated communicative tasks by creating with the language in straightforward social situations. Conversation is restricted to some of the concrete exchanges and predictable topics necessary for survival in the target language culture. These topics relate to basic personal information covering, for example, self and family, some daily activities and personal preferences, as well as to some immediate needs, such as ordering food and making simple purchases. At the Intermediate-Low level, speakers are primarily reactive and struggle to answer direct questions or requests for information, but they are also able to ask a few appropriate questions.

Intermediate-Low speakers express personal meaning by combining and recombining into short statements what they know and what they hear from their interlocutors. Their utterances are often filled with hesitancy and inaccuracies as they search for appropriate linguistic forms and vocabulary while attempting to give form to the message. Their speech is characterized by frequent pauses, ineffective reformulations and self-corrections. Their pronunciation, vocabulary and syntax are strongly influenced by their first language but, in spite of frequent misunderstandings that require repetition or rephrasing, Intermediate-Low speakers can generally be understood by sympathetic interlocutors, particularly by those accustomed to dealing with non-natives.

NOVICE HIGH

Speakers at the Novice-High level are able to handle a variety of tasks pertaining to the Intermediate level, but are unable to sustain performance at that level. They are able to manage successfully a number of uncomplicated communicative tasks in straightforward social situations. Conversation is restricted to a few of the predictable topics necessary for survival in the target language culture, such as basic personal information, basic objects and a limited number of activities, preferences and immediate needs. Novice-High speakers respond to simple, direct questions or requests for information; they are able to ask only a very few formulaic questions when asked to do so.

Novice-High speakers are able to express personal meaning by relying heavily on learned phrases or recombinations of these and what they hear from their interlocutor. Their utterances, which consist mostly of short and sometimes

Figure 7.3 ACTFL Proficiency Guidelines: Speaking (American Council on the Teaching of Foreign Languages 1999; used by permission of the American Council on the Teaching of Foreign Languages) (continued)

incomplete sentences in the present, may be hesitant or inaccurate. On the other hand, since these utterances are frequently only expansions of learned material and stock phrases, they may sometimes appear surprisingly fluent and accurate. These speakers' first language may strongly influence their pronunciation, as well as their vocabulary and syntax when they attempt to personalize their utterances. Frequent misunderstandings may arise but, with repetition or rephrasing, Novice-High speakers can generally be understood by sympathetic interlocutors used to non-natives. When called on to handle simply a variety of topics and perform functions pertaining to the Intermediate level, a Novice-High speaker can sometimes respond in intelligible sentences, but will not be able to sustain sentence level discourse.

NOVICE MID

Speakers at the Novice-Mid level communicate minimally and with difficulty by using a number of isolated words and memorized phrases limited by the particular context in which the language has been learned. When responding to direct questions, they may utter only two or three words at a time or an occasional stock answer. They pause frequently as they search for simple vocabulary or attempt to recycle their own and their interlocutor's words. Because of hesitations, lack of vocabulary, inaccuracy, or failure to respond appropriately, Novice-Mid speakers may be understood with great difficulty even by sympathetic interlocutors accustomed to dealing with non-natives. When called on to handle topics by performing functions associated with the Intermediate level, they frequently resort to repetition, words from their native language, or silence.

NOVICE LOW

Speakers at the Novice-Low level have no real functional ability and, because of their pronunciation, they may be unintelligible. Given adequate time and familiar cues, they may be able to exchange greetings, give their identity, and name a number of familiar objects from their immediate environment. They are unable to perform functions or handle topics pertaining to the Intermediate level, and cannot therefore participate in a true conversational exchange.

Figure 7.3 ACTFL Proficiency Guidelines: Speaking (American Council on the Teaching of Foreign Languages 1999; used by permission of the American Council on the Teaching of Foreign Languages)

In part, the choice between these two interpretations—the "best fit" and "lowest sustained level"—is philosophical; however, the first ("most resembles") approach is probably easier to implement in most cases. The second ("sustains the level") approach is probably primarily useful if, for some reason, it is important to identify the lowest level at which a student ever performs. Since we are more commonly concerned with students' typical performance, or even the best of which they are capable, the second approach will seldom be appropriate.

Descriptors should be kept as brief as possible, while still including enough detail to be clear. Obviously, this is something of a tradeoff. It is best to write descriptors positively, in terms of how much ability, knowledge, accuracy, control, etc. the student demonstrates. These can often be written in terms of how limited or extensive particular qualities are (for example, no or almost no ability, limited ability, basic ability, extensive ability). They can also be written by describing both the *level of accuracy or control* over something (particularly grammar or vocabulary) and the *range* demonstrated. As much as possible, descriptors should focus on what test takers show they can do, not on what they cannot do—in other words, negative phrasing should be avoided when possible. This is more difficult to do at lower proficiency levels, which tend to contain more references to what students can't do yet.

Furthermore, descriptors should be parallel across levels. In other words, if a certain aspect of the response is addressed in the descriptors for one score band, it should be addressed in the descriptors at other levels as well. For example, if the rating scale for a writing test mentions essay structure in the descriptors for several score bands, other levels should also address essay structure, or something comparable (for example, paragraph structure at lower levels). At the same time, however, they should be written without reference to the other levels—that is, descriptors should not say "better than Level X" or "not as accurately as students at Level Y." This requirement for descriptors that are parallel at each level, but not co-dependent upon the descriptors for other levels, means that writing descriptors can be a challenging task. This is particularly true when there is little difference between two or more bands on a given subscale. Frequently, this difficulty results in heavy use of adverbs and quantifiers (for example, "mostly," "somewhat," "occasionally"); scale developers must be careful to use these words carefully, and to avoid ambiguity. Ambiguous descriptors will lead raters to impose their own criteria, and while a given rater *might* apply their own idiosyncratic criteria consistently, other raters would be using their own personal interpretations of the scale, meaning that inter-rater reliability would suffer.

Other things that can be important to include are the extent to which a listener or reader would find something clear or unclear, would be distracted by errors, or would have difficulty understanding due to errors. The degree of listener or reader effort necessary to comprehend the response is also something that can be included, as is the degree to which errors interfere with communication. In speaking, the degree of interlocutor sympathy needed can also be a useful consideration to include in descriptors, as can mention of the likely impact of being familiar with non-native speech or writing, or of being familiar with the student's L1.

Something to avoid, however, is using the "educated native speaker" as a standard for accuracy, or as an ideal interlocutor in the rating scale. I have no desire to rekindle the "native speaker wars" here, being something of a moderate on the subject myself. Certainly, many people find "*the* native speaker," as Lantolf and Frawley (1985) put it, a useful notion, even if it is an ideal that is never really observed. That, of course, is the problem: Not all native speakers speak (or write) the same, meaning that—as Lantolf and Frawley point out—the "typical native speaker" is more or less an average of how native speakers are believed to communicate. For example, native speakers of North American English cannot agree on whether ə and ʌ are one sound or two. The same is also true for ɔ and ɑ, although at least the latter question is better recognized as being a regional variation. Problems arise, however, when different people disagree about what the Platonic ideal of the native speaker *is*, exactly. Therefore, rather than describing performance in terms of a native speaker whom nobody has ever met, descriptors should be defined "in terms of the relative presence or absence of the abilities that constitute the domain," that is, "in terms of relative degrees of ability" (Bachman and Clark 1987: 30). This is the approach that has been outlined in this chapter. We may assume that educated native speakers would demonstrate complete mastery over all grammatical structures, but our descriptors do not need to include that point, and raters will probably rate more fairly if they are not focusing on comparing students to native speakers, but instead are comparing the students' performance to the various descriptions of it in the rating scale.

Two final considerations that might be included in a rating scale involve the role of the interlocutor. The first is ratings of interlocutor competence or cooperativeness in group oral or role-play tasks. McNamara and Lumley (1997) report that when raters perceive an examinee's interlocutors as less interactionally competent, they tend to compensate by giving higher scores to the examinee. Ratings of the other speaker(s) in a test taker's group should not be included in the scores *per se*, but the act of considering this point would help raters to examine it consciously, and thus take it into consideration when scoring the other aspects of the interview. Finally, Lazaraton (1996) further suggests including a rating for the degree of interlocutor support (for example, scaffolding provided by an interviewer) that proves necessary during an interview.

Rater Training and Norming

Once the rating scale has been written, and raters have been selected, there still remains a problem. Even with the clearest rating scale, different raters may not understand or apply it the same way. The purpose of rater training, therefore, is to help lead them to apply it in the same manner, interpreting the descriptors in the same way. Research (Bonk and Ockey 2003; Weigle 1994, 1998) has shown that untrained raters are less consistent, and that training is particularly important with inexperienced raters, and can help them to become more consistent in their ratings. It is less effective, however, in helping raters become less severe or lenient—although they *do* tend to become more consistent. Naturally, this topic is not very relevant to most classroom grading situations, but if students in a program or school are all given the same test (for example, a placement test, or a common final exam for a given level), the ratings should be comparable. In other words, it should not matter to a student which teacher happens to be rating their speaking or writing test.

The rater training process begins by having the raters review the rating scale. Explanations should be provided for each of the subscales, as necessary. Raters should then be shown examples of compositions or recorded speaking tasks that have been judged to be clear, unambiguous examples of that particular score band, and there should be discussion or explanation of why that particular response received the score that it did. After examples of each level have been reviewed, the raters should be shown several examples to rate on their own, with this followed by more discussion, including what led raters to give the scores that they did. In more formal settings, this procedure may be followed by a test for the raters, to see how well they can apply the rating scale following the training. Not being sufficiently accurate can be cause for repeating the training, or not being used as a rater.

As Ockey (2009b) points out, the training should also advise the raters not to compare test takers to each other; instead, they should compare an examinee's performance on each task to the descriptors in the rating scale. This becomes particularly important in the context of pair or group speaking tasks, of course, but the issue is not confined to that context alone. Another point, specific to interview testing, involves types of interlocutor support that will be allowed. Lazaraton (1996: 166) calls for "training on the role of the interlocutor in the assessment." In other words, interviewers should be told whether they should provide scaffolding (for example, repeating questions slowly with overarticulation, supplying vocabulary, or correcting mistakes), and encouraged to attend to what they do during the test. In particular, they should take note of how much interaction in the interviewing was their own scaffolding, and how much was the student communicating.

It is a good idea if experienced, fully-trained raters still review the rating scale before using it again, and perhaps do some practice scoring, especially if it has been a long time since the last time they rated. This procedure is sometimes referred to as **rater norming** (or *rater standardization*), although that term also refers to a group of raters meeting to review a sample of responses, and then determine how strictly or leniently they should score on that particular occasion.

Note that the first time that raters are being trained to use the rating scale, prior to any pilot testing, it will be difficult—if not impossible—to provide any examples of student writing or speaking. If there is access to writing samples or recordings of speech from similar tests, or even classroom tasks similar to the intended test tasks, however, these benchmark samples can be used during the initial training session.

As a final note, in some cases, it is impossible for raters to meet for training in person. If appropriate self-training materials are provided, however, it is still possible to achieve a high degree of consistency (Kenyon 1997). Such materials are probably more difficult to create than those used in on-site rater training, of course, given the additional detail required. Self-training is therefore probably only a good idea in those unusual situations when circumstances make it absolutely necessary. Nonetheless, web-based delivery of rater training is becoming increasingly common and can be highly effective.

Rating Procedures

There are only a few general rules that bear pointing out regarding the procedures used in rating speaking or writing tasks. One is that the higher the stakes, the more important it is to have multiple ratings of each performance, whether it be written or spoken. Having two raters instead of one will improve reliability, and is an important step in helping to minimize the subjectivity of ratings. If two teachers have been trained in applying the rating scale and give similar scores, we can be much more confident about reporting and using those scores. With writing tests, or recorded speaking tests, it is obviously simpler, as raters do not have to read or listen simultaneously. In most situations beyond the individual teacher's class, two raters per performance is the norm.

In the case of speaking assessments, either the raters should be in the same room, or one should view a recording. If both are present during the test, either both can speak, or one can speak and the other merely observe and score (although this teacher usually winds up saying a little as well). Teachers normally take turns filling these roles. Even if two raters are present during a speaking test, it is preferable to record the performance anyway, although this may not be possible in all situations. When it can be done, however, recording allows tests to be reviewed, and in the case of rating disagreements, makes it possible to bring in a third rater to settle the matter (see below). In classroom testing, the performances can be used as pedagogical tools (for example, for self- or peer correction activities), and also used for rater training later on. On a practical note, the first thing in each recording should be to ask each student's name, and to say the date of the test. This may seem unnecessary, but it can prove extremely difficult to match "the student in the red sweater" to a name on a roster.

Even if a speaking test is being recorded, the ratings should be assigned *during* the test; thus, if a rater does not feel she has heard enough to assign scores, she can extend the test a bit. Raters should not assign fractional scores—that is, if a rater has trouble deciding between, say, a 2 and a 3 on a five-point scale, there should be directions accompanying the rating scale on how to resolve this problem. As stated previously, the most common approach will be to specify that all borderline cases should be given the lower score, or that they should receive the higher score; which one depends on the purpose and context of the test. For example, in a test of speaking ability for brain surgeons, I would recommend the more stringent approach. The reason that half-point scores are problematic is that this effectively creates additional score bands throughout the rating scale, and these half point "bands" have no descriptors. Thus, two raters might put the threshold for giving an extra half point at different levels, which will lead to inconsistent scoring. As tempting as it may be sometimes, using half scores is a bad idea. If there appears to be too much distance between the bands of a rating scale, then additional levels should be added to it before the next administration.

Raters' scores should be independent of each other, and a pair of raters should only share their scores with each other *after* they have been given. When raters disagree by more than one band overall, the best way to handle the disagreement is *not* by negotiation or compromise, but by bringing in a third rater. The two closest scores are then used, and the more disparate one removed, except that when the third rating is exactly in the middle of the other two, all three scores are averaged together. Negotiation and compromise are only appropriate when there is simply no trained third rater available, for whatever reason. Negotiating the disagreement is a bad idea, because the more accommodating person may actually be better applying the rating scale. Similarly, being more persuasive, more persistent, or more senior is not the same as being more accurate. Not having independent ratings defeats the entire purpose of having a second rater, and therefore risks producing inflated reliability results.

Summary

In this chapter, we began by discussing several ways to classify rating scales for speaking and listening tests—analytic vs. holistic; "trait" scales, which are tailored to a specific task; and so-called "objective" scoring approaches. This was followed by considerations involved in the decision of whether to adapt an existing rating scale, or develop a new one. When creating a new scoring rubric, it was emphasized that the correct starting point is the construct definition decided upon in the test specifications (discussed in Chapter 3). Different options for deciding the number of levels to include in the scale were explained, as well as guidelines for writing descriptors. We then looked at the importance of proper rater training and norming, and suggestions for how this can be carried out. The chapter concluded with a discussion of appropriate procedures for carrying out the actual rating process. At this point, we are ready to analyze the test results, considering descriptive statistics and distributions of scores (see Chapters 12 and 13), as well as reliability or dependability (see Chapters 6, 18, and 19), depending on whether the test is norm- or criterion-referenced. These results will also play a role in the forming of our validity argument, which is the topic of Chapter 8.

Further Reading

Readings on developing rating scales

Alderson, J. C. 2000. 'The free-recall test' (pp. 230–232), 'The summary test' (pp. 232–236). *Assessing Reading.* Cambridge: Cambridge University Press.

Bachman, L. F. and **A. S. Palmer.** 1996. 'Scoring as levels of language ability' (pp. 208–219), 'Using rating scales' (pp. 219–222), 'Deriving test scores' (pp. 223–225). *Language Testing in Practice.* Oxford: Oxford University Press.

Douglas, D. 2000. Chapter 2 'Specific purpose language ability'. *Assessing Language for Specific Purposes.* Cambridge: Cambridge University Press.

Fulcher, G. 2003. Chapter 4 'Rating scales'. *Testing Second Language Speaking.* Harlow, UK: Pearson Longman.

Luoma, S. 2004. Chapter 4 'Speaking scales'. *Assessing Speaking*. Cambridge: Cambridge University Press.

Weigle, S. C. 2002. Chapter 6 'Scoring procedures for writing assessment'. *Assessing Writing*. Cambridge: Cambridge University Press.

Additional Examples of Rating Scales Available Online

ACTFL Proficiency Guidelines – Writing:
http://www.actfl.org/files/public/writingguidelines.pdf

Cambridge ESOL Common Scale for Writing: 29
(not used for scoring tests, but to help interpret performance across the Cambridge tests in terms of the Common European Framework of Reference levels; see p. 29):
https://www.teachers.cambridgeesol.org/ts/digitalAssets/109701_fce_hb_dec08.pdf

General Impression Mark Scheme for Writing: 28
(one of two scales used to score writing on the First Certificate in English exam; see p. 28).
https://www.teachers.cambridgeesol.org/ts/digitalAssets/109701_fce_hb_dec08.pdf

iBT Speaking: http://www.ets.org/Media/Tests/TOEFL/pdf/Speaking_Rubrics.pdf

iBT Writing: http://www.ets.org/Media/Tests/TOEFL/pdf/Writing_Rubrics.pdf

IELTS Speaking Scale (Public Version):
(user-oriented version of the scale, which is very close to the version actually used to score the test):
https://www.teachers.cambridgeesol.org/ts/digitalAssets/114292_IELTS_Speaking_Band_Descriptors.pdf

IELTS Writing Scale (Public Version): 28
(user-oriented version of the scale, which is very close to the version actually used to score the test):
https://www.teachers.cambridgeesol.org/ts/digitalAssets/113300_public_writing_band_descriptors.pdf

Discussion Questions

1 It was pointed out earlier in this chapter that the construct definition for a writing or speaking test, or the writing or speaking portion of a test, will normally include more than one component. What would you say are the components of the construct definitions in the following examples?
   a The holistic rating scale in Figure 7.1
   b The analytic rating scale in Figure 7.2
   c The holistic rating scale in Figure 7.3

2 Look back at the analytic rating scale example in Figure 7.2, and review the descriptors for the content and organization subscales. Composition raters using these scales often had difficulty differentiating these two subscales, which was one of the reasons the analytic rating scale was adopted.

    a Do you see any ways in which these two subscales could be revised to make them more distinct from each other? Give specific suggestions for how to revise the band descriptors.

    b Assume that a decision was made to combine content and organization to form one subscale (language will be left alone). How would you word the new combined band descriptors, making as few changes in the existing criteria as possible.

3 Look back at the holistic rating scale example in Figure 7.1. Imagine that you have been asked to convert it to an analytic rating scale. The revised scale will still only address accuracy of language use, but will do so using multiple subscales.

    a How many subscales would you use? Which ones would you use?

    b How would you word the descriptors for this revised rating scale? *(Use the same number of levels as in the original scale.)*

4 Look at one of the holistic speaking or writing rating scales listed in the "Further Reading" section of this chapter.

    a What would you say are the components of the construct definitions in that example?

    b If you were asked to convert it to an analytic rating scale, how many subscales would you use? What would they be?

    c How would you word the descriptors for this revised scale? *(Use the same number of levels as in the original scale.)*

5 Choose one of the rating scale examples in this chapter. Based on your reading of this chapter, are there any changes, adjustments, or refinements you would recommend?

8 VALIDATION

Introduction

Previous chapters have focused on planning and writing tests. We now move to a process that should begin before the test is administered—perhaps even before the pilot testing stage (see Chapter 9)—but which should continue even after the test has entered operational use. Previously, we have been concerned with planning and creating a test that will be as useful as possible for its intended purpose; now, we look at the question of how successful we have been in this regard. Note, however, that this process is not actually as linear as it might sound; the test development process is actually iterative, recursive, or even cyclical. Decisions or findings at one stage may prompt us to revisit earlier stages, such as when we revise specifications as a result of problems during the test writing process, or when we go back and rewrite questions as a result of pilot testing results. Similarly, by the time we evaluate the validity of a test, will probably have some idea as to what we will find, while our findings may lead to changes in the test as well.

In this chapter we shall explore the meaning of the term *validity* in educational testing and measurement, and how the technical meaning of the term has developed to become synonymous with *construct validity*. We shall also consider how validation procedures have been expanded to include consideration of both construct validity and the consequences of test use in an **assessment use argument (AUA)** and discuss what sorts of evidence are appropriate for the various parts of an AUA.

Previous Conceptions of Validity

In everyday lay language, "valid" often means that something is true, logically correct, or appropriate. In language assessment, and in the broader field of educational testing, however, it has a somewhat different meaning. It is often referred to as whether a test actually assesses the things it claims to assess, although we will shortly learn that this is in fact something of an oversimplification. Furthermore, current views of validity are rather changed from those of only a few decades ago. I will therefore start by discussing earlier conceptions of validity, because these are still encountered in the testing literature from time to time. It is also useful to consider these earlier conceptualizations of validity because many of the types of evidence previously used to demonstrate validity are still used today. Finally, by learning about how thinking on this topic has evolved, readers are less likely to fall prey to persuasive writers who argue for "new" approaches that were in fact tried and abandoned years ago.

Cronbach and Meehl (1955) outline the mid-20th century view of multiple types of validity. These were construct validity, concurrent validity, predictive validity, and content validity. Construct validity *at that time* referred to the degree to which "a test could be interpreted as a measure of some attribute or quality which is not 'operationally defined'" (Cronbach and Meehl (1955: 282). *Concurrent validity* was the degree of relationship between test scores and scores on a different test that was intended to assess the same construct(s). *Predictive validity* was the correlation between test scores and later performance on something, such as overall academic success. Concurrent and predictive validity were eventually combined to form *criterion-related validity*. Finally, *content validity* was defined as the adequacy with which the test items sampled the "universe" (i.e. domain) to which the test developer wanted scores to generalize. In other words, it asked how well the test sampled the subject matter or curriculum on which the test was based.

Eventually, treating these as separate types of validity was deemed unsatisfactory, and the "trinitarian doctrine" (Shepard 1993) of three validity types—construct validity, criterion-related validity, and content validity—was rejected in favor of a unitary view of validity as being entirely construct validity. (Recall that Chapter 1 defined construct validity as the degree to which it is appropriate to interpret a test score as an indicator of the construct of interest.) Content representativeness and relevance (Messick 1989b), while important, came to be seen as inadequate by itself, in part Shepard notes, because of the potential for other factors (for example, test taker gender) to affect scores. Another problem was that, as Messick points out, explanations of content validity often included mention of ability, essentially conflating this with construct validity.

Similarly, "criterion-related validity" proved unsatisfactory as a separate type of validity. Thorndike and Hagen (1969) note practical issues in choosing an appropriate criterion. On a more conceptual level, Shepard raises several other issues, particularly the point that while correlation with other measures is an important form of support for validity, we must ask "both why a test predicts something and why that relationship should be relied upon in making decisions" (Shepard 1993: 411). In my thinking, this is a critical conceptual problem with the notion of criterion-related validity. If a test correlates highly with future performance or some other measure, it is probably because they are measuring essentially the same things—that is, the same construct(s). Another issue with the notion of criterion-related validity involved something called "validity coefficients"; even today, one may still come across references to this term from time to time. These coefficients were estimates of criterion-related validity, that is, correlations between scores on a test and some other measure, often another test. As correlation with other measures has become accepted as a form of evidence for construct validity, not a type of validity in and of itself, the term has largely fallen into disrepute and disuse. What made the term especially problematic, I would argue, is that the term itself seems to suggest a stronger claim of validity than one would expect to be associated with a single piece of supporting evidence. Construct validity can be *supported* using statistical approaches, but unlike reliability, it cannot really be *expressed* statistically, or measured precisely.

More Recent Views of Validity

As was just explained, it turns out to be difficult to discuss a validity "type" without returning to the notion of the construct, which is largely why validity is now seen as being construct validity. Thus, the former validity "types" are now treated as *types of evidence* supporting the construct validity of a test—that is, supporting the argument that score-based inferences and interpretations regarding examinee ability are appropriate. The "trinitarian doctrine" of validity theory has therefore been superseded by a focus on construct validity and validity arguments, a concern for the consequences of test use, and a resultant interest in critical language testing and test fairness.

Construct Validity and Validity Arguments

Shepard (1993) notes that when it was first discussed in the 1950s, construct validity was the poorer, weaker sister to the other validity types, and was something only used when criterion-referenced validity could not be employed. This is hardly the case today, as the "weak sister" has since risen to greater prominence, now being seen as the essence of validity, with the other two types merely serving as types of support for construct validity, rather than types of validity in their own right. As early as 1988, Cronbach noted that "most validity theorists have been saying that content and criterion validities are no more than strands within a cable of validity argument" (Cronbach 1988: 4). Shortly thereafter, Messick noted that the field of educational and psychological testing was "moving toward recognition of validity as a unitary concept, in the sense that score meaning as embodied in construct validity underlies all score-based inferences" (Messick 1989b: 19). Only a few years later, Shepard referred to construct validity as being "the whole of validity theory" Shepard (1993: 418). The broader field of educational and psychological measurement and testing has since then made this view official. The current *Standards for Educational and Psychological Testing* define validity as construct validity, calling it "the degree to which evidence and theory support the interpretation of test scores entailed by proposed uses of tests" (American Educational Research Association, American Psychological Association, and National Council on Measurement in Education 1999: 9).

This reference to evidence is consistent with the view that validity must be supported by evidence, which is used to construct an argument that ties together supporting facts or data to make a case justifying the score based inferences and the intended uses of the test (Messick 1989b). This **validity argument** or *validation argument* (both terms are in common use) is rather like a court case—it should contain a clear, coherent interpretive argument, which is based on plausible assumptions. Just as a courtroom argument ultimately boils down into "guilty" or "not guilty," a validation argument will try to make the case for a test's construct validity, and the appropriacy of the test's use for its specified purpose. The validation argument begins with an interpretive argument, and then presents evidence supporting this argument (Kane 1992, 2001), which pertains to one or more specific "score-based inferences and uses of tests" (Chapelle 1999: 263). Because it applies to both inferences *and* use, this "argument must link concepts, evidence, social and personal consequences, and values" (Cronbach 1998: 4). Any argument, of course, is more convincing if it has multiple sources of support. Messick (1988) points out that relying entirely on one type of validity evidence is not appropriate, regardless of the nature of the test. Thus, content-related evidence for achievement tests, or predictive utility for selection testing, is not sufficient.

Consequences of Test Use, Critical Approaches, and Test Fairness

As Chapelle (1999) points out, in validation we need to consider support for *how* the test will be used, not only for interpretations regarding the meanings of the scores. This follows Messick's argument for taking into consideration both *meaning* and *values* in arguing for or making decisions about test interpretation and test use, and his resultant concern that a validation argument should provide evidence for score interpretations as well as for the consequences of those interpretations (Messick 1989a, 1989b). Shepard (1993) takes essentially the same position in arguing that while the traditional definition of validity dealt with the extent to which a test measures what it purports to measure, validation should also examine whether the test *does* what it claims to do. Similarly, Bachman and Palmer (1996) include construct validity and impact among their qualities of test usefulness, separating interpretation and justification of test use, respectively.

This concern over the uses of language tests helped pave the way for later developments such as critical language testing. Lynch (2001) and Shohamy (2001) both take critical perspectives on the use of tests, viewing them as a means of exercising power. From this perspective, each of them then derives a model of or framework for test use. Lynch proposes a validity framework composed of five categories: fairness, ontological authenticity, cross-referential authenticity, impact/consequential validity, and evolved power relations. On the other hand, Shohamy's model addresses the intentions and effects of using tests, the exercise of power involved in the use of tests, the consequences resulting from test use, and the symbolic functions portrayed by tests, which embody a particular educational ideology. She additionally outlines a set of principles which make up critical testing, as well as the responsibilities of language testers and several rights of test takers.

Coming at matters from a slightly different perspective, Kunnan (2004) has proposed a framework for evaluating the fairness of a test. This framework, which is summarized in Table 8.1, consists of five qualities: validity, absence of bias, access, administration, and social consequences. The qualities, in turn, are rooted in the principles of justice and beneficence (i.e. being beneficial for others, or doing good). More recently, he has added a complementary test context framework, which is intended to evaluate tests and test use at the macro level of "the traditions, histories, customs, and academic and professional practices, and social and political institutions of a community" (Kunnan 2008: 241). He does this by breaking down the various contexts in which testing takes place, dividing them into the political and economic context; the educational, social, and cultural context; the technology and infrastructure context; and the legal and ethical context.

Main quality	Main focus of analysis
1 Validity	
Content representativeness and relevance	Representativeness of items, tasks, topics
Construct or theory-based validity	Construct/underlying trait
Criterion-related validity	Score comparison with external criteria
Reliability	Internal consistency, inter-rater, and alternate forms
2 Absence of bias	
Offensive content or language	Content and language of population groups
Test language	Dialect, register and style use
Disparate impact	Differential item functioning
Standard setting	Standard setting and selection decisions
3 Access	
Educational	Opportunity to learn
Financial	Cost and affordability
Geographical	Location and distance
Personal	Accommodations
Equipment and conditions	Familiarity of equipment and conditions
4 Administration	
Physical setting	Physical settings
Uniformity and security	Administration and security procedures
5 Social consequences	
Washback	Impact on instruction and learning
Remedies	Re-scoring/evaluation

Table 8.1 Kunnan's 2004 Fairness Framework (as summarized in Kunnan 2008: 237)

Taken together, all of the perspectives and frameworks above point to a consensus that we need to consider the appropriacy of two things: the interpretation of test scores, and the ways that a test is used. It is difficult to argue against either of these ideas. After all, who wants to claim that test scores do not really need to mean anything, or that tests do not need to be fair, and used fairly? It is the need to consider both of these aspects of test scores—their meaning, and the effects of their use—that has led to a recent expansion in how we evaluate test validity.

An Expansion of Validity Arguments

Bachman (2005) builds upon the notion of validity arguments, as well as upon Bachman and Palmer's (1996) approach of attempting to maximize test usefulness, with his introduction of the *assessment use argument* (AUA). In its conceptualization, the AUA seems to be a natural development from previous approaches, in that it combines the arguments for inferences and test use (Chapelle 1999; Cronbach 1988; Kane 1992; Messick 1989a, 1989b; Shepard 1993). Bachman makes this explicit by explaining that the AUA consists of both a validity argument and a test utilization argument. The AUA appears at first glance to be quite different from previous approaches, however, because Bachman's model includes the use of formal argument structure (following Toulmin 2003), which organizes and presents arguments using formal logic. Besides this greater level of formalism, however, it also expands upon the notion of validity arguments by calling for the argument to include evidence for each link in the chain of inferences from examinee performance to score interpretation (see Figure 8.1).

The formal aspects of the AUA—warrants, rebuttals, backing, and so forth—are beyond the scope of an introductory text such as this one, and for supporting the use of a test for a particular purpose at the classroom, language program, or school level, they probably represent an unnecessary level of detail. Large-scale and/or high-stakes testing, however, will require a more extensive, detailed AUA. Thus, the greater level of detail involved in formal argument structure might be more appropriate in such cases, in that it helps lay out explicitly all the points that need to be addressed in the AUA.

Regardless of the size or stakes involved in a testing situation, however, Bachman's notion of providing support for each link in the logic chain is extremely helpful to anyone attempting to validate a test, as it gives specific guidance on how to collect and present information supporting score-based inferences and test use. (Note that while technically, we should speak of validating particular uses of a test, rather than validating tests themselves, this reduced wording is quite common. What really matters, though, is that we keep firmly in mind that a test must be validated for specific uses, not as some sort of isolated entity.)

Students perform tasks on a test

↓

Students get scores for how well they perform those tasks

↓

Based on those scores, we make inferences about each student's
ability to use the target language

↓

Based on these beliefs about their ability levels, we make decisions

Figure 8.1 How Tests Are Used to Make Decisions

In practical terms, an AUA is essentially a report arguing that test scores really are indicators of the construct(s) of interest, and that the test should therefore be used for its intended purpose. If we consider Figure 8.1, showing how tests are used to make decisions, we can see that for each arrow, we are making an assumption or drawing an inference, connecting the steps in this process. Each of these assumptions or inferences is supported by information about reliability, construct validity and authenticity, and impact, respectively. As another way of looking at all this, Kane, Crooks, and Cohen (1999) use the metaphor of bridges rather than arrows, and we can therefore view supporting information—information about the qualities of usefulness—as supporting those bridges. Furthermore, much like a bridge, the relationship works both ways, which is why Bachman (2005) uses double-headed arrows. I have used unidirectional arrows in Figure 8.1, however, to help visually clarify the direction that should be followed in preparing an AUA for a test.

Note that this discussion of AUAs simplifies the presentation in Bachman (2005) and Kane, Crooks, and Cohen (1999). The second arrow in Figure 8.1, the link between scores and the drawing of inferences on the basis of those scores, is treated as two separate steps in their descriptions. In an introductory text such as this one, however, it does not seem appropriate to delve into the distinctions between universe scores and target scores, or between generalization and extrapolation.

To elaborate upon Figure 8.1 somewhat, the tasks that students perform on a test will, presumably, provide information about the students' language ability (i.e. the construct(s) of interest). We assume that scores accurately reflect how well students performed the test tasks (i.e. how well they comprehended listening or reading passages, answered questions, or responded to speaking or writing prompts). In turn, we assume that those scores really do tell us something about how well students can use the target language, in the context of the TLU domain. These are, of course, inferences about constructs, as contextualized in the TLU domain. Finally, once we have drawn these inferences, and believe we know something about their language ability in the context of interest, we make some sort of decision, which was the whole point of giving the test or assessment in the first place.

Each of these links in the chain of inferences and assumptions (i.e. the arrows, or the bridges) corresponds to one or more of Bachman and Palmer's (1996) qualities of usefulness. Thus, if we claim that students' scores really reflect their performance on a test, as opposed to random chance and luck, we need to be able to demonstrate that those scores are consistent—that is, that they have adequate levels of reliability or dependability (as discussed in Chapters 6, 18, and 19). Appropriate evidence to support these claims for an NRT would be Cronbach's alpha and the standard error of measurement (SEM); for a CRT, they would include the dependability coefficient Φ, the CRT confidence interval (CI_{CRT}), and dependability classification estimates such as $\Phi(\lambda)$. For rated tests, an estimate of inter-rater reliability would also be appropriate.

We also need to make the argument that those scores actually are useful for telling us about learners' ability to use the target language, and to do so in the context of the TLU domain to which we wish to generalize. If the scores are not useful for doing that, then obviously, there is not much point in using the test! We support this claim by providing evidence of the test's authenticity and construct validity, two related but distinct concepts (as discussed in Chapters 1 and 3). We can use this evidence to support our arguments that the score-based inferences (about each learner's ability to use the target language) which we are making are sufficiently justified. Evidence for authenticity can be provided by comparing the test tasks with the relevant TLU domain tasks; language testing experts Lyle Bachman and Adrian Palmer recommend using a framework describing task characteristics, which makes possible a point-by-point comparison between the tasks of the TLU domain and test (Bachman 1990; Bachman and Palmer 1996). For construct validity, there are a great many types of evidence that can be provided, including a comparison of test content with course content (in school-related testing, of course), and correlations between the test and other indicators of language ability (for example, other test scores, teacher evaluations, or overall performance in a language course). Other forms of evidence used in validation can involve the use of corpus-based tools, discourse analysis, conversational analysis, and verbal protocol analysis, methodologies which will be addressed in Chapter 10.

At this point, we must make the case that the decisions we will make on the basis of the score-based inferences are appropriate. This can be done by providing evidence about the test's impact, including its fairness, and about its authenticity as well. As noted in Chapter 3, we should evaluate impact in terms of how large it is, and how positive it is; thus, we should provide evidence that the impact has been sufficiently large (or small), and sufficiently positive. This might include looking at impact in terms of the test's effects on how students are studying or learning, its influence on what and how teachers are teaching, the impact on students and teachers personally, and effects on the program or school in general. We should also provide any evidence we can muster to show that the test is fair in terms of absence of bias, access, administration, and social consequences (Kunnan 2004). For example, do different groups do differently well on the test, or does the test have different types of impact for different groups (in terms of age, gender, class, ethnicity, etc.)? Finally, in addition to impact and fairness, authenticity can also be useful in helping support the use of a test as well, by helping justify the claim that our score interpretations are relevant to the decisions we are making (Bachman 2005).

In Chapter 3, setting minimum levels for each of the qualities of usefulness was explained as part of writing the test context and purpose specifications. Presumably, when those requirements were set before the test was even written, it was deemed that if the minimum levels were reached, then the test would be adequate for its intended purpose. In writing the AUA, then, we can use the information about qualities of usefulness as was just described and in Figure 8.1, and for each of them, discuss the extent to which the minimum acceptable level was met or exceeded. This illustrates once again the importance of planning the test before it is written—not only do the context and purpose specifications inform the writing of the specifications of the test structure and individual tasks, they also play an important role in defending the use of the test.

Unfortunately, things do not always go according to plan, and sometimes a test, particularly during pilot testing (see Chapter 9), will not achieve all the targeted levels for the qualities of usefulness. If the minimum acceptable level was *not* reached for one or more of them, the AUA must do one of two things. Occasionally, it will be reasonable to argue that the minimum acceptable level was actually set higher than was necessary. If this claim is made, though, *it must be supported*. Just saying that "the test was not as authentic as we said it needed to be, but that's OK" does not make it acceptable, any more so than lying about my height, weight, and age will actually make me taller, thinner, and younger.

More often, the most appropriate course will be to note in what ways the test did not achieve the minimum acceptable levels, identify the cause(s) to which this can be attributed, and outline plans for improvement. For example, if a test had an unacceptably low level of reliability, the Spearman-Brown prophecy formula (in an NRT; see Chapters 6 and 18) might be used to provide an indication of how many items to add, and item analysis might be used to suggest which existing test questions need revision. Distractor analysis and patterns in the poorly functioning items might also help identify patterns leading to problematic questions, which could then be used to help revise the task specifications. Any additional items, then, would be less likely to share in those problems.

It may be a natural question to ask where the focus of effort should be in putting together an AUA. Clearly, claims about the qualities of usefulness need to be supported with some sort of backing, but as Cronbach (1988: 13–14) points out, "Validation cannot proceed along all lines at once." Instead, it should focus on the *plausible* arguments likely to be made by someone unfriendly to the use of the test. Clauser, Kane, and Swanson (2002: 419) add that "Evidence that provides further support for a highly plausible assumption does not add much to the overall plausibility of the argument. Evidence relevant to the most questionable inferences in the interpretative argument provides the most effective contribution to the validity argument." In addition, any likely uses of the test should be addressed in the utilization argument (for example, expanding the use of a placement test to also provide diagnostic feedback for students). Inappropriate uses that might plausibly be proposed (for example, using an achievement test for the purposes of certifying general proficiency) should also be addressed, or at least warned against.

Finally, readers may also be wondering what sorts of evidence an AUA should try to provide. Messick (1996: 253) points out that just as "validity cannot *rely* on any one of the complementary forms of evidence,… neither does validity *require* any one form." What it does require "is a compelling argument that the available evidence justifies the test interpretation and use" (Messick 1995: 744). On the other hand, merely relying on communicative tasks and saying that they are authentic and therefore inherently valid has long been viewed as inadequate (see, for example, Stevenson 1985). This inadequate approach is closely related to face validity, which refers to whether a test *looks* valid to the untrained eye. It is usually strongly associated with authenticity and *perceived* fairness, and works roughly as well as judging a book by its cover—that is, quite poorly. As a result, merely claiming high face validity and substituting that for actual validity has also been deemed professionally unacceptable for decades (see, for example, Bachman 1990; Mosier 1947). Nevertheless, administrators or other teachers may occasionally suggest settling for face validity alone, or attempt to rely on the mere fact that authentic-looking tasks are being used. These suggestions should be rejected firmly, and not accepted as a substitute for actually compiling evidence to support the appropriacy of test-based inferences and their use for a given purpose.

Setting Realistic Expectations

Some readers, at this point, may still be wondering how much of this they actually need for their own tests. At the classroom level, for example, some will probably say that there is no way and no need to write an AUA for every quiz, test, or other assessment that is used. Indeed, they are correct that this would be impractical. However, if generic specifications are being used for quizzes or tests, a very brief AUA, even if only in outline form, can be a handy thing to have if students or administrators ever raise any challenges. Many teachers will already be doing a fair amount of the reasoning for an AUA mentally, anyway, but writing everything down makes it less likely that something will be missed, and more likely that weak areas will be improved. Furthermore, tests are frequently recycled in most programs, regardless of their quality; therefore, because they may be used so many times over the years, their quality is more important than it might be for a test that was used once and then discarded forever.

For tests that are used beyond the classroom level, however, the AUA is even more important. Even if the students do not question the test, that does not necessarily mean everything is fine. Students often do not know enough to have any idea whether a test is appropriate, but that does not free teachers and administrators from a professional responsibility to use tests properly. Thus, when teachers are involved in tests used at the program or school level, such as placement tests for incoming students, they need to make sure that at least some sort of AUA is put forward. Of course, the higher the stakes and larger the scale of the testing, the more breadth and depth should be expected in the AUA; but having even a relatively brief outline-format report will be enough to show the school or program that the test is producing valid scores and is appropriate for its intended use(s).

As a final note, the need to provide evidence supporting test use—both inferences and their utilization to make decisions—is strongly supported by standards of professional ethics and practice. These include the *Guidelines for Practice* and *Code of Ethics* of the International Language Testing Association (International Language Testing Association 2000, 2007), the *Principles of Good Practice for ALTE Examinations* and *Minimum Standards for Establishing Quality Profiles in ALTE Examinations* (Association of Language Testers in Europe 2001, 2007), the EALTA Guidelines for Good Practice (European Association for Language Testing and Assessment 2006), and the AERA/APA/NCME *Standards for Educational and Psychological Testing* (American Educational Research Association, American Psychological Association, and National Council on Measurement in Education 1999).

In fairness, it must be admitted that these sets of guidelines and standards were principally developed for application to large-scale and high-stakes testing, with the exception of the EALTA Guidelines, which include a section specifically focusing on classroom testing and assessment. While it is true that we can never expect to hold a school testing committee and a large professional testing organization to the same level of expectations, these documents do point out the types of things that should be done in order to ensure fair, valid, and appropriate test use. Regardless of the level at which we are working, I doubt many teachers will want to argue that it is acceptable to use unfair, invalid, or inappropriate tests, or to use tests in an unfair or inappropriate manner. So, while we may *believe* that a test is "good enough" for its intended purpose, we will not *know* that it is until we can provide some sort of evidence. I hope that the simplified AUA framework I have discussed in this chapter has shown to teachers that test validation *is* feasible, even at the local level, and does not actually require extensive professional expertise or the use of arcane skills. I further hope they will find the framework useful in showing them where to provide evidence, making the process less threatening and more approachable.

Summary

In Chapter 8, we have examined test validity and validation. We began by considering the development of validity theory and emergence of construct validity as the essence of validity, with other previous types of validity reduced to types of evidence used in validation arguments. We also discussed how concerns over the use and impact of tests, particularly in terms of consequences and fairness, has led to an expansion of validity arguments, and the emergence of the assessment use argument (AUA) as a way to structure those arguments. We looked at how different types of information can be used as support in an AUA, particularly information about the qualities of usefulness, but also evidence about the fairness of the test. Finally, we concluded by discussing the level of detail needed in an AUA for different testing situations, highlighting the need for some sort of evidence supporting test use in all cases. In Chapter 9 we will change pace somewhat, moving from a focus on planning and analysis to consideration of how to prepare for a test administration itself, how to carry it out, and what to do once the tests have been collected.

Further Reading

Alderson, J. C., C. Clapham, and **D. Wall.** 1995. Chapter 8 'Validation'. *Language Test Construction and Evaluation.* Cambridge: Cambridge University Press.

Bachman, L. F. 1990. Chapter 5 'Test method' for a system for systematically describing test task characteristics and TLU domain characteristics, as a way of demonstrating authenticity; Chapter 7 'Validation'. *Fundamental Considerations in Language Testing.* Oxford: Oxford University Press.

Bachman, L. F. and **A. S. Palmer.** 1996. Chapter 3 'Describing tasks: Language use in language tests' for a system for systematically describing test task characteristics and TLU domain characteristics, as a way of demonstrating authenticity; Chapter 7 'Developing a plan for the evaluation of usefulness' for procedures for evaluating test usefulness. *Language Testing in Practice.* Oxford: Oxford University Press.

Bachman, L. F., and **A. S. Palmer.** 2010. Chapter 4 'Justifying the use of language assessments'. *Language Assessment in Practice.* Oxford: Oxford University Press.

European Association for Language Testing and Assessment. 2006. *EALTA Guidelines for Good Practice in Language Testing and Assessment.* Retrieved June 25 2010, from
http://www.ealta.eu.org/guidelines.htm.

International Language Testing Association. 2000. *Code of Ethics for ILTA.* Retrieved July 10 2009, from
http://www.iltaonline.com/index.php?option=com_content&view=article&id=57&Itemid=47.

International Language Testing Association. 2007. *International Language Testing Association Guidelines for Practice.* Retrieved July 10 2009, from
http://www.iltaonline.com/index.php?option=com_content&view=article&id=122&Itemid=133.

Discussion Questions

For the following questions, consider a language test that you have taken, administered, or are otherwise familiar with (preferably an important test, such as an end-of-course final exam or a placement test).

1 *Briefly* describe the test in terms of:
   a purpose
   b construct(s) to be assessed
   c interpretive framework (NRT or CRT)
   d intended test takers
   e minimal acceptable levels for each of these qualities of usefulness: reliability, authenticity, construct validity, and impact.

2 If you needed to prepare an AUA for the test, what sort of information would you want to gather or present to support claims that the test had acceptable levels of:
   a reliability or dependability
   b authenticity
   c construct validity.

3 Think of at least one type of evidence you could collect to investigate the impact of the test on each of the following areas *(remember that impact should be evaluated in terms of both the size of the impact and how positive it is)*:
   a How students will study or learn
   b What teachers will teach (i.e. course content)
   c How teachers will teach (i.e. teaching and class activity methods, etc.)
   d The impact on students personally
   e The impact on teachers personally
   f Effects on the program or school in general

4 Think of at least one type of evidence you could collect to evaluate the fairness of the test in each of the following areas:
   a Absence of bias
   b Access
   c Administration
   d Social consequences

9 TEST ADMINISTRATION

Introduction

Previous chapters have dealt with the planning and writing of language tests, and with scoring, reliability analyses, and validation work which is performed after testing. Until now, however, we have not considered procedures for actually administering tests. After clarifying the aims of this chapter, we will discuss the following issues: pilot testing; the steps involved in preparing for a "live" administration, i.e. planning ahead, assembling and copying the test, scheduling facilities and equipment, and planning tests with a speaking component; the test registration process; procedures for admitting and seating the students; proctoring/invigilating the test; scoring the tests, entering the data, and reporting the results; and archiving and destroying tests and data. We shall also consider the important area of test accommodations for examinees with disabilities.

Purpose and Goals of This Chapter

Most of the advice in this chapter is oriented towards tests being administered at the school or program level. Most teachers do not need much advice about how to administer tests in class, although a large amount of this chapter's content will still be relevant to that setting. On the other hand, though, most teachers do not have much expertise at or experience with handling larger testing situations involving dozens or even hundreds of students taking a test. Those who have helped proctor (*proctor* is the most common term in American English, and means the same thing as the British *invigilate* or *invigilator*) or score tests in those situations will have *some* idea of what is going on and how to organize similar efforts, but they often know less than their supervisors might think they do, since being involved in something is not the same as being in charge of it.

The goal of this chapter, therefore, is to help provide a roadmap for teachers to follow who are dropped into the situation of having to coordinate a medium or large institutional test. Note that in this chapter, the term "large" will be used in the sense of large at the local or institutional level. This is not quite what is usually meant by large-scale testing, however, which normally refers to programs involving thousands of test takers *or more* per year. In the grand scheme of things, most of these examples are actually more along the lines of medium- (involving hundreds of test takers) or even small-scale (involving a few dozen examinees) testing.

It is thus important for readers to distinguish between what needs to be done for any test, even at the classroom level, and what is necessary for larger tests at the school or program level. After all, although both situations share a number of similarities, testing 20 people and testing 200 (or even 2,000) are far from the same. Throughout this chapter, the example of placement testing will be used when discussing tests used at the school or language program level. This is because placement tests are usually the largest single test given at a particular institution, and they often involve new students who do not know the procedures (or even layout) of the institution. Of course, similar-sized tests used for any other purpose will probably follow similar procedures, and have similar requirements for planning, facilities, personnel, and procedures.

Pilot Testing

The first step before a test should be used for making decisions about students is to conduct **pilot testing**. Also referred to as *pre-testing* or *trialing*, this is when a new test or a new test form is given to a sample of learners who are similar to those who will take the actual test once it becomes operational. It is very important for several reasons. First, it helps to ensure sure that constructed response tasks elicit the types of responses expected, and that directions are clear enough for students to understand what they are supposed to be doing. It also makes it possible to estimate the reliability or dependability of the test, so it will be clear whether the minimum acceptable level has been reached. If it has not, the pilot test data can be used to estimate how much longer the test should be made, and what items should be revised in order to improve score consistency. Similarly, in rated tests, pilot testing makes it possible to see how well the rating scale is working, and whether adjustments might be necessary. These adjustments may be as minor as, for example, making a few small wording changes in the descriptors, or as major as combining two subscales in an analytic rating scale.

Furthermore, in cases where new procedures are being tried out—particularly computer-based testing, but potentially in other situations, such as new interview protocols—pilot testing, rather than testing with one or two people individually, can be essential. Without it, problems will not become apparent until it is too late. For example, if a listening comprehension test includes the use of streaming audio or video, it may not be possible to tell whether there will be problems with server load until 20 or 50 people attempt to access the same file simultaneously.

At the classroom level, it may not be possible to perform pilot testing, of course. It is therefore important that teachers review their tests in advance, to make sure that the coverage of course material is sufficiently broad and even, and that nothing is being assessed that has not been taught. Any task formats or procedures which will be new to the students need to be scrutinized carefully, and teachers need to consider the ways that things could go wrong, or be misunderstood. Once the test is administered, anything that discriminates negatively (see Chapters 6, 15, and 16) should be removed and not included in calculating students' grades.

Preparing For a "Live" Administration

Once the pilot testing has been completed, the results taken into account, and any necessary changes made to the test or procedures, we are ready to begin preparing for a "live" administration of the test; that is, an administration in which the test is being used for its intended purpose. This requires a significant amount of preparation and planning, much more than might be expected. Smooth test administrations do not simply happen on their own!

Planning Ahead

A number of things have to be worked out before the day of the test. The more people who will be taking the test, and the more proctors, interviewers, composition raters, and clerical staff will be needed, the more careful and detailed the planning must be. The nature of the institution comes into play here as well: If all of the new students at a language school are taking placement tests, there is probably no competing use for classrooms, equipment, and teachers to help administer and score the test. On the other hand, if incoming language students at a college or university are being tested, there may be dozens of other activities going on at the same time, some of which might interfere with the smooth administration of the test. The more complicated the situation, and the more competing demands there will be for classroom space and other resources, the earlier plans must be made.

One important area of planning involves timelines. It is important to think about how long it will take to write the test, print and copy it (or take care of the equivalent steps, if it is a computer- or web-based test), register students, seat them, go over directions, administer the tests, collect them, score them, do data entry and compile results, and report the results. Realism and expecting unexpected problems are important here—consider how long it *really* takes to do something (for example, typing in one student's registration information), multiply it by the number of times it will need to be done, and then add a safety margin. It also helps to think about when results must be reported, and when teachers will be required to be present, and to use those dates to help plan when to administer the test.

Another important part of the planning process is to schedule the necessary personnel early enough. In some cases, it may be necessary to make these plans almost a year in advance—if there is a test administered two to four times per year, for example, and each teacher is required to help out a certain number of times, the coordinator should decide how many people will be needed to proctor, score writing tasks, administer interviews, etc. on each of those occasions. The numbers may not be consistent, especially in a college or university setting, where the largest numbers will probably be at the beginning of the academic year, and smaller numbers of students are likely to need testing at the beginning of other semesters or quarters. In intensive language programs, on the other hand, the largest groups might be at the beginning of summer, when these schools often see their largest enrollments. Whatever the case, it is important to make sure that everyone has it on their schedule well in advance.

As an illustration, when I was the administrative coordinator for the ESL Placement Examination at the University of California, Los Angeles (the UCLA ESLPE), each graduate teaching assistant (TA) had to help twice with either proctoring or composition rating for each quarter that they were teaching ESL. I therefore had to assign people before the start of classes in September, since a particular TA was not required to help with every test administration. This meant getting the roster of TAs for that academic year, usually in early August, and asking if anyone wanted to request to *not* work the first week of January, third week of March, or fourth week of June: the dates for the winter, spring, and summer test administrations. Everyone had to help with the fall testing dates, as there were 500–800 test takers in three sessions on two days. Only TAs were allowed to be composition raters, but other graduate students were eligible to serve as proctors. For reasons involving US student visa regulations, proctoring was one of the few chances for many non-TA international graduate students to work in the US legally. Thus, there was almost always a ready supply of extra people for proctoring.

All of the assignments, except for some of the proctoring slots, needed to be made by mid-August, and communicated to the TAs, so they knew which day(s) they would be needed the week before classes started. Some of them questioned the need to plan something as simple as proctoring and rating ten months in advance; I would have as well before taking the job myself. What seems on the outside to be hyper-organization, though, may turn out to be merely necessary to make things work. Thus, if you find yourself in a similar situation, with skilled personnel (for example, teachers) who can rate or interview and others (for example, administrative staff, or teachers from other programs) who can proctor, assign the raters and interviewers first. Then, if there are remaining teachers to put in the proctor slots, do so; otherwise, fill the remaining proctor slots with people who could not be used as raters or interviewers.

As mentioned earlier, sometimes there will be uneven numbers of students taking a test at different times of the year. Therefore, if significant changes are being made in the test or testing procedures, and it is administered more than once a year, it is a good idea to make them during a smaller test administration, not during the largest one. Certainly, it is important to think through all the opportunities for something to go wrong with the new setup, but—at the risk of sounding too dramatic—inevitably something will not have been anticipated such as power failures, server failures, or malfunctioning sound equipment. Trying out new things when there are fewer people taking the test makes it much easier to deal with problems, and limits the potential damage that can occur.

Another thing to plan for is whether it will be necessary to provide food and drinks for the proctors, interviewers, raters, administrative help, or students. Often, large tests may be held after regular class hours, or outside the regular school term, as it will be easier to find vacant classrooms in which to administer the test. At these times, however, it may be more difficult for the people running the test (not to mention the students!) to find someplace to eat, or even to get something to drink. At the very least, even if there is no budget for providing food or drinks for the proctors and interviewers, warn them so they will know to make preparations for themselves. After all, when a proctor finally gets a break in the middle of a five-hour evening shift (setting up for registration, conducting registration, and administering the test), few things are more depressing than standing in front of a closed coffee shop.

Another possibility to consider is that if students *are* being fed, it might be sensible to take advantage of the opportunity to hold an orientation for them as well. ELS Language Centers in Oklahoma Center did this every four weeks following placement testing (usually 30–60 students), when I was a teacher there. Pizza and soda were relatively inexpensive, and the students and teachers found it very convenient not to have to worry about lunch. Teachers were able to focus instead on finishing up with the testing and putting materials away, and students did not mind staying for new student orientation.

Assembling and Copying the Test

In this section, I am deliberately omitting discussion of the "packaging" of a computer-based test (CBT). Because of the greater range of possibilities and choices, as well as the technical aspects involved, this is a topic more appropriately discussed elsewhere, although a very brief introduction to the topic and suggestions for additional introductory readings are provided in Chapter 10. This section will therefore focus on the more traditional paper-and-pencil testing format, which in any case is still in far more common use than CBT. Note that with the exception of collating and numbering test booklets, the issues of pagination, printing, and copying that are discussed here will apply to classroom tests no less than they do to program- or school-wide tests.

Before printing out the test, it is important to check the pagination and spacing. Whenever possible, a reading passage should be entirely on one page, the only exception being when the passage is longer than one page. If comprehension questions cannot be put on the same page as the passage, they should at least be put together so that moving between the questions and the passage will be as convenient as possible. There should be no "orphan" items by themselves on a page—for example, one question at the bottom of the page after the reading passage, with the rest of the items on the next page. The reason that such items are so problematic is that they are often missed by students. If students are using separate answer sheets, this is particularly dangerous, since they may put all their answers on the wrong lines as a result.

Another issue often ignored by novice test constructors is that *questions should never be split across page breaks*. For example, a multiple-choice item stem should never be at the bottom of one page, with the options at the top of the next one.

Similarly, all of the matching items for a given section should be on the same page. Generally speaking, in fact, it is good for each section of the test to be as distinct as possible, and for sections using different task formats to be separated from each other. Ideally, sections will be arranged so that they are *not* split onto separate pages, as splitting them may prove confusing or distracting.

One way to help squeeze things into a smaller space is to "cheat" on the spacing. While consistent formatting is important, so test takers are not distracted or confused, minor adjustments will often go unnoticed. The font size of the writing on the test should not be reduced, so that all parts remain equally clear. On the other hand, the size of the spaces between items, or between item stems and options, can often be reduced without it being noticeable to anyone not already looking for it.

If the test includes pictures (for example, for vocabulary tasks), and the test will be copied in black and white, there may be problems with the copying if the pictures are still colored. Rather than letting the copy machine or computer printer handle the conversion to black and white, it is better to change the picture properties first. In Microsoft Word for Windows, this is done by right-clicking the picture, selecting "Format Picture…," and changing the color or color mode (depending on the version of Word being used) to "grayscale." Grayscale converts various colors to different shades of gray, producing clearer pictures than simple black and white. It may be tedious to do this individually for each picture, but the result will be much clearer when copied.

Another point worth noting is that the order of the test sections is important. In particular, unless very specific time limits are being given for each section, listening comprehension questions should be put before anything else. In this way, all of the students can do the listening at the same time, and then can continue the test at their own pace. One important exception to this rule, however, is with CBT, if students are listening to passages using headphones. In fact, if the listening passages are being delivered via the Web or an internal network (i.e. they are not on individual computers or storage media), it makes excellent sense to put the listening later in the test, so that test takers will start at different times, thus staggering the "hits" on the server. While it might sound unimportant, this is not a minor issue. As few as 20 simultaneous server hits can dramatically slow or even crash a server, particularly if it is streaming a video file. Therefore, if students will be starting a computer-based listening section at the same time, it is probably a good idea to have only a few at a time click "play."

Once the test is arranged and paginated, page numbers added, item numbers checked, and everything proofread and spell-checked, a master copy should be printed out. This should be done on a good printer, one that will make a very clear product without blemishes, lines, distortions, etc. This should be reviewed again, since sometimes problems can be missed on the computer screen. At this point, a sample copy should be made and examined, to make sure the copier is not leaving random lines or marks. A decision between single- and double-sided copies must be made, too. Double-sided copies can save paper and money, but they may also be harder to flip back and forth if students are taking a reading test, unless they are printed in booklet form. They take longer to make than single-sided copies, which may be a factor if the copying is being done at the last minute. In humid conditions, or with older copy machines, they are also far more likely to cause paper jams. These factors need to be taken into consideration, and decisions made appropriately. The test booklets should be stapled together as well.

If the test contains more than one booklet or paper, these will have to be collated. In large testing situations, it may also be necessary to number each test booklet. Rather than hand-writing the numbers, it is probably preferable to buy a number stamp. These can be set to increase by one every time something is stamped (i.e. 001, 002, 003, etc.) or to increase only after every two stamps (i.e. 001, 001, 002, 002, 003, 003, etc.), or even more (triplicate, quadruplicate, etc.). If separate answer sheets are to be used, they need to be included in the test packets as well; if they are optical scan sheets (i.e. special sheets in which students write their answers by filling in circles or boxes with a pencil), however, it may be a bad idea to number them, as this might confuse the scanner which will electronically "read" the sheets to process the scores. In that case, it may be simpler to hand them out separately at the start of the test, since such sheets normally have a space on which to write the test booklet number.

The steps described above are summarized in Table 9.1, as a reference.

- Are reading passages on one page apiece, unless longer than one page?
- Are reading comprehension questions on the same page as each other, or at least put together?
- Are there any "orphan" items?
- Are any questions (or matching sections) split across page breaks?
- If the test includes pictures, are they all in grayscale?
- If there is a listening comprehension section (on a paper-based test), is it first?
- Are the pages all numbered correctly?
- Are item numbers all correct?
- Has the test been spell-checked and proofread?
- Is the master copy of suitable quality?
- Will double-sided copying put passages and their items back-to-back?
- For multiple-booklet tests, are booklets all numbered and collated correctly?

Table 9.1 Questions to Answer When Proofing a Test

Once the tests have been collated and numbered, they need to be counted and boxed. If testing will go on in more than one room, separate boxes must be prepared for each location. The simplest solution, of course, is to use the boxes that the copy paper came in, assuming there are enough boxes to go around. Each box needs to be labeled clearly with its contents, and a checklist should be put inside with an inventory of all the materials that need to go to the testing room. If cassette tapes or CDs are being used for listening comprehension, they should be put in the box, along with pencils, any necessary signs (for example, "QUIET PLEASE—TEST IN PROGRESS," "DO NOT ENTER—TESTING IN PROGRESS," or "PLACEMENT TEST →") and tape for attaching them to walls, doors, or even trees. Each box also needs to contain a script for the head proctor to read, giving an outline of the procedures, directions for the test, and clear statements of how much time is to be provided for each portion of the test. If exit slips will be given to the students telling them how and when to get their test results, bundles of these should also be put in each box.

Naturally, as part of the planning process, decisions need to be made about who is going to do all of this, when will they do it, and where the tests be will stored securely until the day of the test. The word "securely" is particularly important here, as the reliability (and validity) of the test can be compromised if some examinees gain access to test questions and answers before the test. How much of a danger this is depends in part on the stakes of the test—the more important the test in the eyes of the test takers, the more incentive some of them will feel to cheat. The wisest approach, of course, is to deny any of them that opportunity.

Scheduling Facilities and Equipment

Of course, it will not be much use to have all the tests properly prepared but not have anywhere to administer them. Someone must be in charge of reserving enough rooms, and large enough rooms, to handle the anticipated number of examinees. As a rule, if it is unclear how many students will be taking the test on a given day, it is a good idea to reserve extra rooms, or larger rooms. On the other hand, scheduling too many rooms can mean that too many proctors are scheduled, since someone will have to be scheduled to do the testing in those rooms. In the case of interview testing, of course, a number of *smaller* rooms are probably more desirable. Failing that, however, it may be acceptable to have two or three interviews going on simultaneously in a larger room, *as long as* they are not taking place so close together as to be distracting to the students and interviewers.

Arrangements must also be made for sound equipment for listening tests—either reserving equipment, or if it is built into the rooms, making sure that proctors can get access to it and know how to use it—and for recording equipment for speaking tests. The equipment all needs to be tested a few days before the day of the exam, so that arrangements can be made if there is a problem, and then it needs to be tested once again *on the day of the actual test*. For recording, the test needs to include playing back the recording, of course.

If computer labs are being used, the organizational model may have to be quite different. There may not be enough computers available for everyone to take the test at the same time, meaning that an entire computer lab might need to be reserved for one or more days—even an entire week—so that students can take the test in smaller groups. When scheduling computer labs, therefore, it is important to think through how many hours of lab time will be needed to test the anticipated number of students. It should also be assumed that at least one computer in any given lab will be down at any given time, so it is not always prudent to schedule exactly as many students as work stations, unless it is definite that they are all working that day.

In general, when reserving space for testing, if possible, arrangements should be made to ensure that the area outside the testing location(s) will be designated as quiet zones—that is, no movie filming involving loud noises going on outside, no construction work, and no nearby events involving large numbers of attendees. (Note that none of these are hypothetical examples!)

As was pointed out earlier, program- or school-level tests may be administered outside the regular school term, or outside regular class hours. As a result, doors that would normally be unlocked may be locked instead. It is therefore important to have keys to all the necessary rooms and buildings. It is also prudent in some cases to make custodians aware of what will be happening, so they are not taken by surprise when asked to open doors and so forth. It is also a good idea to make sure that the restrooms near the testing rooms will not be locked.

Planning Tests With a Speaking Component

If a test only consists of written components (including listening comprehension), the testing process is somewhat more straightforward, only requiring a given student to go to one room. When a test includes a speaking component in addition to the written portions, however, it will probably be necessary to rotate students through one or more separate rooms where they will take the speaking portion of the test. Obviously, it is impossible to do the speaking portion for all of the students simultaneously; it therefore becomes necessary to divide the test takers into groups, each of which takes portions of the test at different times. The limiting factor here is mainly the length of time that it takes to conclude the speaking section for a given group of test takers. Once that length of time has been determined, the order of testing for each group can be worked out, with one group interviewing first, a second group taking the writing section first and then being interviewed, and so on. (Note that I am using the term "interview" as a sort of shorthand here, even though the speaking section of the test may not necessarily be an actual interview.)

Registration

In some cases, students will have already registered for the test in advance, and the testing coordinator will know almost exactly how many examinees to expect. In other situations, though, there may only be a vague notion of the likely number, and registration must all take place on site, shortly before the test begins. Of course, registration in advance is preferable, but it is not always possible, for a variety of reasons. This second, more difficult situation will therefore be the focus of this section, but much of what is contained here will apply to contexts where test takers have preregistered—after all, these students will still have to check in for the test, and may need to be directed from some central location to multiple testing rooms.

One very important thing to do is to plan the registration process. If several hundred people are expected, it is probably a bad idea to have them line up outside an office. Weather permitting, it is better to set up outside. Whatever the location, signs saying "TEST REGISTRATION" with directional arrows should be posted nearby. Tables and chairs for the proctors helping with registration are also important. This will speed up the process immensely. If test takers are registering on site for the first time, or even if they are only checking in, examinees should be given some sort of pre-printed registration slip or admission ticket. Test takers should provide photo identification as well. The student's name can be hand-written on the slip (or pre-printed in the case of advance registration), but the slip should already state which room the student should report to for the test. Since the students will often be new at this school, it is helpful if the back of the slip includes a map giving directions from the registration site to the testing room—especially if they are in different buildings. In addition, when the test is in a different building from registration, it is a very good idea for proctors to go over the directions verbally with each student, pointing at the map as they explain. This is especially true with students being given instructions in their second language. As a practical matter, it is also helpful to remind students (even adults) to stop at the restroom on the way.

If multiple testing rooms will be used, it is a good idea to have a separate stack of registration or admission slips for each room, with that room pre-printed on the slips. Obviously, there should not be more slips for a room than there are seats for test takers. Of course, "seats" does not refer to the number of chairs, but to the number of chairs that can be *used*, because with important tests, it is a good idea to maintain a certain amount of distance between students to discourage cheating. Within the stack for a given room, it may also be helpful to separate them into smaller bundles, each bundle paper-clipped together. This makes it easier to keep track of how many students have been sent to that room, without having to count the remaining slips one by one.

Finally, it may prove necessary in some situations to verify that each person registering for the test is actually a student, and is actually a student who is supposed to take the test. One way this can be a problem is if an educational institution issues student identification cards, but not all new students have received one yet at the time of the test. Another potential issue is that if all incoming students at a university are required to take a test, it may be necessary to verify that all the students showing up really are *incoming* students, not returning ones. The reason it may be important to verify that someone really is supposed to take the test is that some people might take the test with the sole purpose of finding out about the content, memorizing parts of it, or even covertly copying (using cameras, pen scanners, or other devices) or recording the test. There are a variety of different ways that this verification can be done, and what works in a given institution will depend on a wide variety of factors, although in some cases a little creative planning or coordination with school administrators who know the local scene well may be necessary.

Admitting and Seating the Students

In large-scale testing situations, it is a good idea to keep students outside the testing room until it is time for them to come in, shortly before the test. Once the proctors have checked the contents of the boxes and set up the sound system (assuming there is a listening component), they can begin admitting the students, collecting the registration or admission slips as they enter the room one by one. It may be necessary to check photo identification again at this stage, of course; if this is done, it is important that proctors actually *look* at the photo on the ID; I know of one case, when I was an undergraduate student, of a Caucasian and Chinese Malaysian student trading places on a final exam! As students are admitted to the testing room by the door proctor(s), they should be asked to turn off their mobile phones, pagers, and other similar communications devices, and maybe even to hand these items in. This purpose of this is not only to minimize interruptions during the test, but also as part of the test security policy to prevent cheating, including both receiving outside help and passing on test content.

Before the seating begins, the proctors should be familiarized with the seating plan for the room. For example, they need to be told whether to leave one or two empty seats between test takers, and whether to leave empty rows between them as well. Usually, it is a good idea to have examinees seated directly behind each other, so it will be harder for them to see each other's tests. When practical, proctors should leave every third row empty, so that proctors can move to any student's seat during the test. This is especially useful if a student needs to ask a question about the test, although it is also handy for deterring cheating and helping watch for its occurrence.

One or more proctors also need to be assigned the role of seating proctors. Their job is to direct students to specific seats, breaking up groups of friends, for example. This is easily done by sending one student to the left, the next to the right, and so on, or if there is only one section of seats, putting the students who enter together in different rows. Besides directing traffic, a seating proctor also needs to ensure that students sit where they are directed. Those who sit in the wrong place may be doing so through an innocent mistake, but they still need to be moved elsewhere. This will make copying and the use of hand signals harder, and will help frustrate efforts such as using pre-positioned crib notes. Students who insist that they do not want to sit somewhere else have always seemed suspicious to me. Such cases are fortunately rare, but when they arise, I have always found it sufficient to calmly and politely explain that they must either move or leave the room, and that they will certainly not be allowed to take the test in their current seat. A policy on purses, bags, and the like also needs to be set—if bags are not to be permitted near students' seats, they should be directed to place them near the front of the room in a secure and supervised space.

Proctoring the Test

Once everyone is seated, the head proctor should begin to read the directions from the script. Other proctors will help pass out test booklets and answer sheets, pencils, and so on. One or two may also be put in charge of counting registration slips, to make sure that everyone who entered the room was supposed to. It is important that proctors try to avoid being intimidating or making the students uncomfortable. It is, of course, important to keep an eye out for cheating, but most of the students are not planning to engage in any sort of misconduct, and they should not be treated as "guilty until proven innocent." Instead, proctors should maintain a positive demeanor, and be as friendly as possible within local cultural boundaries, while keeping their eyes open at the same time.

When selecting a head proctor, it is good to pick someone with a voice that carries well, and who will come across to the examinees as being in charge. This is not really the same thing as being tall, broad-shouldered, and deep-voiced; the attitude and self-confidence is more important. Other important qualities are the ability to remain calm and apply common sense when problems arise, as they often will, and to be able to handle a room with a large number of students.

Scoring the Tests and Entering the Data

One important point about scoring in interview tests, which was partially addressed in Chapter 7, is that the scoring should be done *during* the interview, not afterwards. Occasionally, an inexperienced tester will intend to go back and write down the scores later. This is inevitably a mistake, however, unless the test is being recorded. Even then, there is little point in doing it later. It is better to take a few extra seconds to write the scores down during the interview, than to have to sit through the entire thing a second time. Furthermore, sometimes the scores are not as definite as they seemed, when the moment comes to actually write them down. As it turns out, "I have a pretty good idea of the score" and "I am ready to write down a number" are rather different levels of certainty. If the interviewer is not yet ready to assign a score to each subscale (assuming an analytic scale is being used), then they probably need to continue the interview a little longer.

For tests involving either speaking or writing assessment, plans must be made for rater or interviewer training and norming. These plans need to include who will do the training, where it will be done, and how long it will last. If norming is to be done with samples from the current test administration (which is more likely with writing assessment), then plans also need to be made for how and when to identify appropriate tests. Plans also need to be made for where and when the actual rating will take place. The best arrangement is probably a room with enough tables for each rater to have space to spread out a little. Typically, a rater needs to have room for the rating scale, stacks of rated and unrated tests, space to read the test currently being scored, and perhaps a cup of coffee.

If some of the student information must be typed into a computer manually, it is often helpful to have two people doing the job: one to read the information, and the other to type it. This allows the typist to see the computer screen while typing, and makes it easier to catch mistakes. The process is also much faster than solo data entry.

Reporting the Results

What needs to be reported will depend on the purpose of the test, and on the context in which it is being used. For example, the results of a classroom quiz and a placement test used by an entire language program will not be reported in the same fashion, or with the same level of detail. The larger the context, the more formal the reporting will need to be. At the same time, however, unless used test items and forms are publicly disclosed after every examination, the larger test will probably be reported with a lesser level of detail.

For example, when reporting results to the students in a single class (such as on a quiz, midterm exam, or unit test), most teachers let the students see the actual papers. One effective strategy is to go over the individual questions, not only providing the correct answers or eliciting them from students, but also explaining what needed to be done in order to answer correctly. When reporting the results for a placement exam, however, students may only be given the level into which they are placed, or they may be given their score band for each area assessed by the test (reading, writing, listening, etc.). Alternatively, the students may not be told their scores on various sections of the test, but the teachers into whose classes they are placed might be given this information.

If the test takers are children, then they and their parents may be given results with different levels of detail and explanation. Students with more formal education may want more detailed descriptions than those with little formal education, and so on. Depending on the situation, however, the level of information to be provided to test takers and other stakeholders is not necessarily always the same. Band descriptors for students' performance may be somewhat simpler than those used in rating scales for speaking or writing, for example, or might be written with a different orientation (for example, in terms of what the learner can do, rather than in more abstract descriptive terms). Whatever the case may be, though, decisions should be made in advance as to what level of information will be provided to the test takers after the scoring process is complete.

If results are provided to students in hard copy format, one way to simplify the process is to use pre-printed results sheets. If only part of a page is needed, perforated forms can be ordered, so two to four reports can be printed on one sheet of paper. The pre-printed results sheets should contain boxes for reporting scores and/or percentiles, and perhaps for boilerplate comments (i.e. sets of standardized descriptive comments) about what students can do at that level, or describing their current level of language ability. These could be overall descriptions for various levels of ability, or could be subdivided into as many categories as there are sections on the test. If results are reported electronically, similar forms can be used, whether in e-mail messages or on secure web pages.

Finally, some thought must also be given to where and when the results will be given to students. If they will only be given to students in person, a suitable location needs to be chosen ahead of time, and students should be told where it is before they leave the testing room. There need to be enough people available to help distribute—and explain, if necessary—the results to students. Some language programs strongly prefer in-person delivery of results, as this gives them a chance to also tell examinees about elective courses that are available to them, and potentially boost enrollment. Other programs, on the other hand, are not as concerned with promoting their courses, or do not have the personnel available to do so, and thus try to get the results out to students with as little interaction as possible—either simply handing out results slips without comment, or delivering results electronically or by mail.

Archiving and Destroying Tests and Data

Once the test is administered and scored, and the results have been reported, it might seem that the experience is concluded and it is time to relax. Unfortunately, before the testing coordinator starts planning for the next administration, there is one remaining duty: archiving and/or destroying the test. Tests often need to be stored for a certain amount of time. This may be because of legal or institutional requirements for retaining student work, or it may just be out of caution, in case there are questions later on about a student's results. Having the tests on hand can be particularly useful if test takers or their parents wish to complain about or contest the test results. In addition, when the stakes of the test will seem high to the students or their families, it is probably a good idea to have in place at least a basic plan for how appeals or challenges of results will be handled, how test results will be reviewed when questions are asked, etc. Such procedures can be especially important in more litigious countries, and can help catch any mistakes that might have been made, and bolster the credibility of the test results if the original results are confirmed following review.

Writing tests and recordings of speaking tests may also be kept for the purposes of creating rater training materials, or for subsequent research. Note, of course, that secondary uses may be subject to certain restrictions. For one thing, there may be legal requirements or regulations covering the use of examinee materials (i.e. writing samples, recorded speech, background information, and even responses to individual test questions). In the United States, for example, every university has a board or committee that must approve *in advance* any use of such data, or must approve a project as being benign enough that it is exempt from such approval. A very important element in this approval process is the degree of anonymity of the test takers. If the researcher is able to identify them individually, the project automatically triggers a higher level of scrutiny (usually a full review by the board), although this is often close to a formality when existing datasets are being used.

Another important issue here is the notion of *informed test taker consent*. That is, did examinees give permission for their testing materials to be used for other purposes? Even if this is not mandated by law, this is an important ethical consideration (International Language Testing Association 2000, 2007). What makes the question rather tricky in some cases is that the idea to use test data for research may only occur to someone *after* the test has been administered, when it is no longer practical to obtain consent from the test takers. In such cases it is important to consider what level of anonymity the test takers will enjoy, and whether there are any potential adverse effects that they could suffer as a result of the project. One thing that can simplify all these considerations, of course, is if we assume from the beginning that a test might be used for secondary purposes such as research, test development, and so on, and we therefore ask test takers to consent to the anonymous use of their responses for these purposes. This can be included on the registration form, for example. Note, however, that if examinees are not being asked for this consent in their native languages, clear and simple language must be used, or the consent form needs to be translated into their mother tongues.

How long to keep tests and testing materials can also depend on the amount of *secure* storage space available. However long things are to be kept, they need to be boxed and labeled clearly, with something more descriptive than "PLACEMENT TESTS." The date of the test should therefore be included on the box, probably on more than one side. A good practice is to remove old tests on an annual basis, and have them shredded securely.

On the other hand, some things do not need to be kept once the test results have been announced. For example, if students do not write in their test booklets, and the booklets are not reused, they can be destroyed immediately, as long as the master copy and all the student answer sheets are kept. Writing tests, however, and recordings of interviews or other speaking performances do need to be kept. As digitization becomes simpler, however, it may become increasingly common (and accepted) to scan writing tests and digitize any analog recordings. Kept on long-term storage media such as DVDs or high-capacity hard drives, there may not be any reason to destroy them, *if* they are likely to serve some useful purpose. Note, however, that DVD copies made on a personal computer have a probable lifespan of several years. The expected lifespan of the particular products being used should therefore be investigated, and if it is important to keep copies indefinitely, then they should be recopied every few years.

The question of what constitutes a useful purpose is an important one. Keeping old student materials for too many years without any need is inappropriate—if nothing else, it increases the possibility of the privacy of their records being violated. On the other hand, if (a) there are legal or institutional requirements to keep permanent records of important tests, (b) they are likely to be used in examining the usefulness of the test, or (c) they are likely to be useful for research purposes, it makes sense to keep them. Apart from a compelling reason such as these, however, such records should eventually be securely destroyed.

Test Accommodations

A final area to consider when preparing for test administration involves offering reasonable accommodations to examinees with disabilities, whether permanent or temporary. The key in these cases is to ensure that the playing field is leveled to the extent possible—that is, that any accommodations should aim to make it possible for a test taker to demonstrate his or her level of language ability without interference from their disability, by "removing construct-irrelevant barriers" (Sireci, Scarpati, and Li 2005) to its assessment. At the same time, it is important to avoid giving that person an unfair advantage over others who are taking the test; thus, providing appropriate accommodations can be something of a balancing act.

A few of the issues most likely to require some sort of accommodation include visual impairment or blindness, hearing impairment or deafness, mobility or movement issues (including arthritis), learning disabilities (for example, dyslexia or attention deficit disorder), psychological or emotional problems (for example, severe anxiety or depression), and sometimes even pregnancy. Whether the problem is temporary or permanent does not usually matter, unless there is some flexibility in when the test can be taken.

Researchers Sireci, Scarpati, and Li note that research on the effectiveness of different types of accommodations is difficult, because of the number of different types of accommodations, differences in how the same type of accommodations are implemented, and different needs of the students. However, that being said, increased time does seem to consistently help students' scores (Sireci, Scarpati, and Li 2005). Increased time is far from the only type of accommodation possible, of course. What follows is a combination of my own first- and second-hand experience with these issues, and published descriptions of accommodation practices in large-scale language assessment (Gutteridge 2003; Khalifa 2005; Khalifa and Weir 2009; Shaw and Weir 2007; Taylor and Gutteridge 2003); note that in almost every one of the following situations, additional testing time may also be appropriate.

For example, test takers who are blind or otherwise visually impaired may need large print tests, Braille tests, someone to read reading passages and questions aloud, additional lighting, magnifying lenses, additional time, or some combination of these. Much to the surprise of most sighted people, it also turns out that there are three versions of Braille within English alone (representing different levels of contractions), so it is important to make sure that a Braille test (whether on paper or using screen reading software) is in a version that the test taker is comfortable with, particularly if his or her native language uses a different version of Braille. For writing tests, it may be necessary to allow the test taker to type in Braille, or to type a normally hand-written test. Other approaches such as dictation by the examinee, or the use of voice recognition software, may be necessary as well.

Learners who are hearing impaired may need a louder delivery than normal, perhaps in a location with less background noise than in a normal testing room, or they may need to be able to lip-read. For listening comprehension passages or interviews, test takers who are entirely or almost entirely deaf may need sign language interpretation—although there is the issue here of having to learn a different language's sign language conventions. There is also the question of the extent to which such a test will be comparable to the standard version.

Mobility and movement issues include more than special seating, and extend to such things as difficulty sitting for the length of the entire test, arthritis or other problems making it difficult to write (or even type), and even partial or full paralysis. Accommodations for these sorts of problems might include the use of special writing implements (especially for those with arthritis), the opportunity to type instead of handwriting one's responses, the use of voice recognition software, and even additional breaks in some cases.

Test takers with learning disabilities may need other types of accommodations besides additional time, including being allowed to use a scribe or voice recognition software. They may also need special consideration during the scoring of their tests, especially on writing tests; for example, spelling and other mechanics issues may be ignored in such situations, when they would not normally be. Serious psychological issues may necessitate being allowed to take the test in a quiet room free of distractions, as well as additional time to reduce anxiety.

Finally, any accommodations need to be tailored to the needs of specific individuals—that is, although a certain accommodation may be appropriate for most test takers with a particular disability, it may not be appropriate for *all* of them. This recommendation also appears to be true for accommodations aimed at non-native speakers of a language who must take content area tests (for example, in math and science) written in the second language (see, for example, Abedi, Hofstetter, and Lord 2004; Albus, Bielinski, and Thurlow 2005; Kopriva, Emick, Hipolito-Delgado, and Cameron 2007). Usually, issues such as this can be resolved with little or no acrimony, particularly if the institution has an office dedicated to assisting disabled students. Such offices can also be an invaluable resource in *providing* accommodations, not merely advising on them.

Summary

In this chapter, we have considered a variety of topics that are important to proper test administration. The process begins with pilot testing, and after any necessary revisions have been made to the test, preparation for "live" administration of the test begins, including planning ahead, assembling and copying the test, scheduling facilities and equipment, and additional logistical issues related to speaking assessment. The discussion then moved on to a focus on medium- and large-scale testing, including the test registration process, procedures for admitting students to the testing room and seating them, and for proctoring the test. This was followed by suggestions on how best to score tests and enter data, as well as what results should be reported to test users. We next considered the topics of archiving and securely destroying tests and test data, including the legal and ethical issues involved. The chapter then concluded with a discussion of test accommodations for test takers with disabilities. In the final chapter of Part I, we will discuss a number of topics that deserve book-length treatment of their own, but which go beyond the scope of an introductory course in language testing. The goal of that chapter will be to familiarize readers with the topics and provide suggestions for further reading, for those interested in learning more about them.

Further Reading

Bachman, L. F. and **A. S. Palmer.** 1996. Chapter 12 'Language test administration'. *Language Testing in Practice.* Oxford: Oxford University Press.

Gutteridge, M. 2003. 'Assistive technology for candidates with special needs'. *Research Notes* 12, 15. Retrieved June 27 2010, from http://www.cambridgeesol.org/rs_notes/offprints/pdfs/RN12p15.pdf.

Khalifa, H. 2005. 'Are test taker characteristics accounted for in Main Suite reading papers?' *Research Notes* 21: 7–10. Retrieved June 27 2010, from http://www.cambridgeesol.org/rs_notes/offprints/pdfs/RN21p7-10.pdf.

Khalifa, H. and **C. J. Weir.** 2009. Chapter 2 'Test-taker characteristics'. *Examining Reading: Research and Practice in Assessing Second Language Reading.* Cambridge: UCLES/Cambridge University Press.

International Language Testing Association. 2000. *Code of Ethics for ILTA.* Retrieved July 10 2009, from http://www.iltaonline.com/index.php?option=com_content&view=article&id=57&Itemid=47.

International Language Testing Association. 2007. *International Language Testing Association Guidelines for Practice.* Retrieved July 10 2009, from http://www.iltaonline.com/index.php?option=com_content&view=article&id=122&Itemid=133.

Shaw, S. D. and **C. J. Weir.** 2007. Chapter 2 'Test-taker characteristics'. *Examining Writing: Research and Practice in Assessing Second Language Writing.* Cambridge: UCLES/Cambridge University Press.

Taylor, L. and **M. Gutteridge.** 2003. 'Responding to diversity: Providing tests for language learners with disabilities'. *Research Notes* 11: 2–4. Retrieved June 27 2010, from http://www.cambridgeesol.org/rs_notes/offprints/pdfs/RN11p2-4.pdf.

Discussion Questions

For the following questions, consider a language test that you have taken, administered, or are otherwise familiar with (preferably an important test, such as an end-of-course final exam, a placement test, or a nationally or internationally administered test).

1 *Briefly* describe the test in terms of its purpose and intended test takers.

2 Are you aware of any pilot testing that was done for this test?
   a If so, how would you describe it?
   b If you do not know anything about this test being piloted, or know that it was not, how would you have recommended that pilot testing be done for it?

3 What can you recall, good or bad, about:
   a How the test was planned for?
   b The physical layout of the test—how it was assembled and copied, numbered, etc.?
   c The facilities and equipment used in administering the test?
   d How speaking was handled, if the test included speaking?

4 What do you know or remember about each of the following, and how would you suggest improving them?
   a Registering for the test
   b Admitting and seating the students
   c Proctoring the test
   d Reporting the results
   e Archiving and destroying tests and data

5 What types of disabilities are you aware of (or do you think might be common) among the people who take this test? What sorts of accommodations would you recommend for dealing with them?

10 OTHER IMPORTANT TOPICS IN TESTING

Introduction

In this concluding chapter of Part I, I want to discuss a few topics that are important, but which will not fit into this book, whether for reasons of length or because they go beyond what should be covered in an introductory level book. My goal is to provide a brief introduction to each topic, so that readers are aware of it, and will be at least glancingly familiar with it. We shall take a brief look at the areas of: *computer-based testing (CBT)*; quantitative research approaches in language testing such as *item response theory (IRT)*, *generalizability theory* and standard setting; special considerations involved in *assessing young learners (AYL)* and assessing *language for specific purposes (LSP)*; qualitative research methods such as *verbal protocol analysis (VPA)* and *discourse analysis*; and *corpus-based research* approaches. The references cited here will also serve to provide a starting point for those who are interested in learning more about any of these subjects.

Computer-Based Testing

Computer-based testing (CBT) has been an important concern in language testing since the mid-1980s (Chalhoub-Deville 2001). Nevertheless, there seems to be agreement that although it offers a great deal of promise, it can be argued that thus far it has still largely failed to bring about much change in language assessment (Carr 2006a; Douglas and Hegelheimer 2007; Jamieson 2005; Ockey 2009a). Carr describes a number of advantages and potential advantages of CBT over paper and pencil (P&P) testing, including more attractive looking tests, more engaging and authentic tasks, and improved test delivery, scoring, and efficiency. However, these features alone are probably not enough to justify converting from P&P testing to CBT. CBT requires a computer for each test taker, potentially tying up computer labs for extended periods of time if large numbers of students need to be assessed under secure conditions. Therefore, because of cost and scheduling issues, switching to CBT is probably only justified if it will be a value-added change in some way (Buck 2001).

One area that *can* be a source of added value in CBT, but remains difficult to apply widely, is **computer-adaptive testing (CAT)**. CAT works by selecting an item of average difficulty, and presenting it to a student. If the student answers correctly, a slightly more difficult item is selected next; if the student answers this item incorrectly, a slightly easier one is presented to the student instead. The test continues in this fashion, estimating the student's ability level after each response. It makes these calculations by taking into consideration the difficulty level of each item, and whether it was answered correctly or incorrectly. This method allows the CAT system to estimate each student's score very precisely, but using only a relatively small number of items. This makes the testing not only accurate, but also very efficient.

Naturally, there are drawbacks to CAT as well, or it would be used much more widely. Perhaps the largest issue is that it requires a large item pool, since the test needs to have a reasonable number of questions at a wide range of difficulty levels. Furthermore, all of these items must have been precalibrated—that is, their difficulty and discrimination already estimated, almost always using **item response theory** (see the next section of this chapter). In combination, these two factors often serve as insurmountable obstacles to using CAT, except for very large testing programs. (As will be explained below, item response theory requires responses from *at least* several hundred students to calibrate item parameters, although some purists will insist that the minimum number is actually several thousand.) Another drawback is that because each item must be scored immediately, this has almost always limited CAT to multiple-choice questions. Admittedly, however, most of the institutions with the resources needed to develop a CAT are so large, and have such large testing programs, that they have probably been using multiple-choice anyway.

After reading all this talk of drawbacks and difficulties, some readers might wonder why the topic is even being discussed. CBT still remains promising, however. One of the features that makes it so promising is **computer-automated scoring (CAS)**, which has the potential to enable meaningful changes in the types of task formats used in tests. Much of the CAS research thus far has focused on the scoring of essays (for overviews, see Carr 2006; Douglas and Hegelheimer 2007; Jamieson 2005; Ockey 2009a; Weigle 2002), although there is a small but growing body of research into the use of CAS for assessing speaking as well (see Ockey 2009a, for an overview of this topic and related controversy; see Yang, Buckendahl, Juszkeiwicz, and Bhola 2002, for a useful discussion of the types of strategies that can be employed to validate CAS systems; and see Xi 2008, for one of the few published accounts thus far of validation research into CAS and speaking assessment).

At present, CAS of extended response tasks requires the development or licensing of expensive software, making it beyond the reach of most programs. As with all technology, however, prices will eventually become more affordable. At some point, therefore, language programs will be forced to consider the pros and cons of this approach to scoring, which raises certain concerns, but can also offer great advantages in terms of how quickly responses are scored, and how cheaply (see Carr 2010, for a discussion of these issues). As a general rule, the more spoken or written responses that are scored at a given institution using CAS, and the longer the responses are that are being scored, the more competitive the price will be compared to paying human raters.

Another area of promise for CBT is the development of **web-based testing (WBT)**. As Carr (2006) notes, this offers a number of advantages, including ease and flexibility of delivery, simplified test construction and delivery via a familiar interface (i.e. a web browser), and reduced costs over other forms of CBT. Beyond these, however, is a factor that combines with CAS to offer a chance for more fundamental changes in testing practice. Many large- and medium-scale tests include a writing component, and some a speaking component as well. At present, though, short-answer and other limited-production tasks are generally restricted to use in classroom assessment in US contexts, although this is not always the case elsewhere, as most of the tests from Cambridge ESOL demonstrate. Using such tasks on a larger scale requires human scoring, and is why the multiple-choice test has dominated large-scale assessment (particularly of reading, listening, grammar, and vocabulary) for decades, at least in the United States. WBT, however, makes it possible to capture short-answer responses on tests, allowing them to be reviewed by a CAS system. These CAS systems can be much less expensive—and can even be developed locally if someone is available with a basic knowledge of programming—as they do not need to use scoring procedures as complex as those required for rating writing or speaking (Carr 2008a; Carr and Xi 2010). I believe that the potential to make the use of limited production tasks feasible in medium-, large-, or even relatively small-scale testing is one of the most promising areas of CBT.

Item Response Theory

At the conceptual level, **item response theory (IRT)** is rather simple. Mathematically, it is rather complex, but the underlying concepts have a certain degree of elegance. This section provides a somewhat simplified conceptual overview of the topic; readers interested in learning more might do well to start by reading *Fundamentals of Item Response Theory* (Hambleton, Swaminathan, and Rogers 1991).

IRT is a statistical approach to performing item and reliability analysis, and is probably more easily understood by contrasting it to *classical test theory*, the approach to item analysis and reliability generally followed elsewhere in this book. As explained in Chapters 15 and 16 in Part 2 of this book, classical test theory views item difficulty in terms of how many students answered a question correctly. Discrimination is treated in terms of either (a) the difference in difficulty for two groups (high- and low-performing students for NRT, masters and non-masters for CRT), or (b) how well performance on the item correlates with total test score (NRT) or passing or failing the test (CRT). The likelihood of guessing is not really addressed in classical theory, aside from the occasional use of the correction for guessing formula, the use of which is questionable. This formula works by penalizing incorrect answers, but not blank ones; the effect is that if someone guesses randomly on all the questions, their score will be reduced to 0, or *slightly* higher if they are lucky. The problem with this is that students with a greater preference for risk-taking are likely to receive different (lower) scores than students who are more cautious. Thus, scores are influenced by something other than the construct of interest, introducing construct irrelevant variance (Messick 1989a, 1989b) into the test scores, and thus undermining construct validity.

IRT, on the other hand, is a *probabilistic* model. In other words, it assumes that for an item with a given level of difficulty, the probability that a test taker will answer correctly depends on their level of ability. If their ability level is very low, they still have a small chance to answer a difficult item correctly. Likewise, a high ability student may occasionally answer even an easy item incorrectly. This concept is illustrated in Figure 10.1, which shows that at low levels of ability, a student has a very low chance of answering this particular question correctly. Similarly, if a student has a high level of ability, they have a very good chance of answering the item correctly. Furthermore, while the figure is too small to see this, the probability never *actually* reaches 0% or 100% (0.0 or 1.0 in the graph); instead, it just comes infinitely close to those values. An average level of ability is denoted by 0.0; it may help to view the ability scale in terms of the number of standard deviations above or below the mean (with 0 being the mean).

Also, note that in the example in Figure 10.1, if a student has an average level of ability (0.0), they have a 50% chance of giving a correct answer. Dotted lines have been added to the figure to help clarify this point. The point at which examinees have a 50% chance of answering an item correctly is important, and is how the difficulty level of an item, abbreviated b_i (and therefore referred to as an **IRT b parameter**), is defined. (Exactly why the difficulty parameter in a one-parameter model is abbreviated b instead of a is unclear. This can be confusing to those learning IRT for the first time, but eventually becomes second nature.) In other words, the difficulty of an item is equal to the ability level at which examinees would have a 50% chance of answering it correctly.

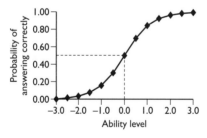

Figure 10.1 The Item Characteristic Curve For an Item ($b_i = 0.0$)

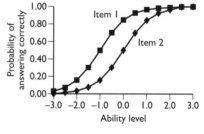

Figure 10.2 The Item Characteristic Curves For Two Items With Different Difficulty Levels ($b_1 = -1.0$, $b_2 = 0.0$)

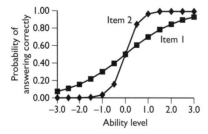

Figure 10.3 The Item Characteristic Curves For Two Items With Difficulty 0.0, but Differing Discrimination Values ($a_1 = 0.5$, $a_2 = 2.0$)

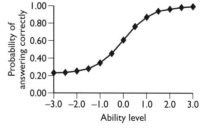

Figure 10.4 The Item Characteristic Curve For an Item Being Described by a Three-Parameter Model ($a_i = 1.0$, $b_i = 0.0$, $c_i = 0.23$)

As shown in Figure 10.1, for this particular item, the difficulty level is 0, which means that a student with an average level of ability has an even chance (i.e. a 50% chance) of answering this question correctly. A student with an ability level one standard deviation below the mean would have a roughly 15% chance to answer correctly, whereas a student one standard deviation above the mean would have a roughly 85% chance. A graph such as the one in Figure 10.1 is known as an item characteristic curve, since it shows the probability for one item; that is, an item with a different difficulty level would have a different curve. An example of two items differing only in terms of difficulty can be seen in Figure 10.2. The difficulty level for Item 1 is −1.0, since this is the ability level at which test takers have a 50% chance of answering correctly. Similarly, the difficulty level for Item 2 is 0.0. An IRT model that only includes difficulty is known as a **one-parameter model**; note that the two items in Figure 10.2 only differ in terms of this one parameter, i.e. their difficulty level.

Item discrimination in IRT is taken as the slope of the line at its difficulty level. The steeper the slope, the better job the item does of separating students below that level from students above it. Figure 10.3 illustrates this by showing two items with differing levels of discrimination. Both items have equal difficulty levels, so students have a 50% chance of getting either item correct if their ability level is average (i.e. equal to 0). However, on item 1, which has a rather low discrimination of 0.5, the probability of answering correctly does not change that much for students a little lower or higher in ability. In contrast, item 2 has a high discrimination value, so even a minor change in ability has a large impact on an examinee's likelihood of answering correctly. For both items, it may be instructive to look at the graph and estimate the probability of a correct answer for students with ability levels of −0.5 and 0.5. The discrimination, or slope, parameter is abbreviated a_i (and therefore referred to as an **IRT a parameter**), and an IRT model that includes both difficulty and discrimination is known as a **two-parameter model**. An item provides the most information about a test taker's ability if the student's ability level is close to the item's difficulty level, and items with higher discrimination provide more information than those with low values for the discrimination parameter.

As hinted earlier, IRT models can also take guessing into account, as is illustrated in Figure 10.4. The *guessing parameter*, abbreviated c_i (and therefore referred to as an **IRT c parameter**), is based on the probability of answering the item correctly if randomly guessing. It is slightly lower than that, however, because professional item writers are usually good at writing attractive distractors; therefore, since it does not represent the likelihood of guessing correctly, but is based on that likelihood, it is sometimes called the *pseudo-chance parameter*. For example, in Figure 10.4, the item probably has four options, but c_i is 0.23 rather than 0.25. If test takers were only guessing randomly, we would expect that they would have a 25% chance of getting a given item correct. Truly random guessing is rare, however, as test takers will read the options, and many will be led astray by attractive distractors. In the case of this particular item, attractive distractors have reduced the pseudo-chance parameter to slightly below 0.25; thus, even at the lowest ability levels, examinees have a 23% chance of answering the question correctly, rather than the 25% chance we might expect for a four-item multiple-choice question. An IRT model that includes the c parameter is known as a **three-parameter model**.

An important concept in IRT is **model fit**, that is, how well the actual responses of test takers match what we would expect based on the item parameters. In the examples in Figures 10.1–10.4, we see idealized cases. In the real world, however, rather than all the dots falling on a single S-shaped line, we might see a cloud of dots (which represent individual test takers) scattered around the line. In cases of items with good model fit, the dots would all be close to the line, meaning that the IRT model predicts test taker responses well. In an item with poor fit, the cloud would be spread out more, with many dots far away from the line.

Model fit is particularly important when considering which IRT model to use, although whether to use a one-, two-, or three-parameter model is often a judgment call. Normally, adding more parameters will make the model fit the data better; however, using more parameters also requires the use of more items and more test takers. In addition, sometimes the difference in model fit is not large enough to matter, making the use of additional parameters unnecessary in those situations.

IRT is a large-sample statistical approach, meaning it requires responses from at least several hundred test takers to get stable parameter estimates (Embretson and Reise 2000). This, along with its need for specialized software and mathematical complexity, explains why it is not widely used outside professional testing organizations. Large-scale tests, on the other hand, such as the TOEFL and IELTS (see, for example, Marshall 2006), almost always make use of IRT to calibrate their item pools—that is, to ensure there are enough items of appropriate difficulty levels, with sufficient discrimination, and also to provide an estimate of the overall reliability of the test. IRT is also used for calibrating CAT item pools, and this need for large numbers of test takers adds another level of difficulty (no pun intended!) to setting up adaptive testing programs.

There are actually a large number of IRT models besides the three already described. However, the only additional one that needs to be discussed here is the **Rasch model**. In its basic form, the Rasch model is equivalent to the *one-parameter model* (Hambleton and Swaminathan 1985). In particular, the **many-facet Rasch**, or *FACETS model* (Linacre 1989) is worth noting. This model views item difficulty as being a function of the various facets of the measurement process: differences among students, differences in rater severity, differences in task difficulty, and so on. It provides estimates of how much each facet contributes to task difficulty, and thus to task scores, and can be used to identify raters who need additional training, tasks that are too difficult or easy in comparison to others, and estimates of student ability. The many-facet Rasch model is particularly popular in estimating reliability and diagnosing individual rater problems in tests of speaking and writing, and has been used in a number of studies in language assessment (for example, Bonk and Ockey 2003; O'Sullivan 2002; Van Moere 2006; Weigle 1998).

Generalizability Theory

Generalizability (G) theory is another statistical approach that has developed as something of an expansion upon classical test theory. Like the many-facet Rasch model, G theory is also concerned with the various facets of the measurement process, but unlike that model, test takers are not referred to as another facet, but rather as the "object of measurement." As was stated previously in Chapter 6, G theory is important because it is the means by which dependability coefficients such as Φ and $\Phi(\lambda)$ and the CRT confidence interval are calculated directly, rather than approximated by plugging NRT reliability estimates into shortcut formulas. When a composite score is used for a test composed of several sections, and an overall reliability or dependability coefficient is desired, **multivariate generalizability theory** (see Brennan 2001) provides a solution. In cases where a test includes more than just one group of items or tasks, such as when the items are grouped into several sections, or when there are multiple raters for multiple tasks, G theory also provides a more accurate model for computing reliability than does Cronbach's alpha. In simple situations, however, where students have answered an undifferentiated set of questions (i.e. not divided into groups, all coming from the same content area), been rated once on several separate tasks, or been rated several times on a single task, Cronbach's alpha will be equal to the **generalizability coefficient** (Shavelson and Webb 1991).

These would seem to be enough to recommend G theory by themselves, but in fact, they are only indirectly relevant to another important contribution that G theory makes to the field of measurement. Of equal or greater importance is the point that it can also be used to determine how much **score variance** (essentially, differences in scores across items and students) stems from each facet of the assessment process, such as differences in rater severity, differences in task or item difficulty, or occasions on which the test might be taken. It can also examine the effects of interactions among these facets and the object of measurement—for example, not only consistent differences in rater severity, but whether certain raters are more stringent with some test takers and more lenient with others, or whether some raters give more "hawkish" or "dovish" (more severe or more lenient, respectively) ratings on certain tasks than on others. By calculating the proportion of variance accounted for by each facet, as well as by the object of measurement (i.e. differences among students in terms of their ability levels), we can compare the relative sizes of these effects, and identify which areas are contributing most to unreliability. We can also estimate, for example, the effects of increasing the number of raters and/or tasks on a speaking or writing test, without having to collect additional data.

Since both are concerned with the effects on scores of various facets of the measurement process, it should come as no surprise that several language assessment studies have combined G theory with many-facet Rasch measurement. These have included Bachman, Lynch, and Mason (1995), Kozaki (2004), and Lynch and McNamara (1998).

For those desiring to learn more about this approach to measurement theory, the best place to start is probably Shavelson and Webb's quite readable *Generalizability Theory: A Primer* (1991). Those wanting additional information on the topic can move on to Brennan's comprehensive 2001 book on the subject, entitled *Generalizability Theory*. His earlier, less comprehensive 1992 work, on the other hand, is primarily useful as a reference, and contains little that is not covered in the later book.

Standard Setting

Brown and Hudson (2002) provide a summary of a number of approaches to the topic of how and where to set cut scores in criterion-referenced tests. Their treatment, which follows Jaeger's (1989) classification scheme, serves as a valuable primer on the topic, including clear tables and charts helping illustrate and summarize the various procedures. Jaeger classifies approaches to standard setting into two families of approaches or models. Both groups of approaches include the use of expert judgments, but differ in terms of what is being judged. **Test-centered continuum models** involve expert judgments being made about the content of the test itself. In contrast, **examinee-centered continuum models** are based on expert judgments made about test takers' performances.

Berk (1986) provides an even more comprehensive description of approaches to standard setting, reviewing 38 different methods and classifying them in three dimensions, of which he then selects 23 for inclusion in a "consumer's guide." After describing these approaches, he provides separate recommendations for several groups: classroom teachers, testing specialists working in the schools, licensure and certification boards, and test publishers and testing contractors.

Skorupski and Hambleton (2005) advise that when conducting a standard-setting exercise, it is vital to make sure that the judges or panelists understand the purpose of what they are doing. They emphasize that raters must be trained sufficiently to have a shared understanding of the rating instruments and procedures, and (in test-centered continuum models) a clear understanding of the tasks being judged. They also caution that judges' levels of confidence in and understanding of the rating task may not be as high as they will claim when simply asked—that is, if asked whether they are confident and understand, they will agree, but if asked to express reservations about their ratings, the vast majority do have some. As a result, they recommend against rushing the judging process, whether because rushing will contribute to additional rater uncertainty, or because hurrying was a contributing factor to it. Finally, they caution that judges seem to find polytomously scored constructed response tasks more difficult to rate than dichotomously scored selected response tasks.

This discussion of standard setting would seem incomplete without a few examples from the language assessment research literature. One interesting study is Kozaki's (2004) study on the setting of cut scores for a medical translation test, which used expert judges' ratings of performances, and included the application of both generalizability theory and many-facet Rasch measurement. Another study using generalizability theory is Shin's (2005) comparison of three approaches to setting cut scores for a placement test used in an advanced academic ESL program, which also examined the consistency of rater decisions regarding minimally acceptable student performance. Bechger, Kuijper, and Maris (2009) report an interesting two-part study in which cut scores were set for a government-sponsored test of Dutch as a second language. Finally, a study by Davis, Buckendahl, and Plake (2008) describes a project to set cut scores on high school reading tests in two languages, with the objective of requiring the same level of expectations for students regardless of the language in which they were tested.

Assessing Young Learners

Just as teaching language to children cannot use entirely the same methodology as teaching adults (see, for example, Brown 2007; Peck 2001), assessment must also be adapted to fit this audience. The assessment of young learners' language ability is becoming increasingly widespread (see McKay 2006), and mirrors the increasing importance internationally of language education for children, and beginning at ever earlier ages, especially in English (see Graddol 2006). While generally speaking the principles presented in this book are applicable to this population, it is particularly important to use age-appropriate tasks, as well as to assess young learners on the types of language ability they will have. For example, just as it is a mistake to teach very young children formal grammatical rules, they should not be assessed on their declarative knowledge of L2 grammar. Their ability to use those patterns correctly, on the other hand, can be an appropriate topic for assessment. Of course, as children age and develop cognitively, they become increasingly able to handle abstract concepts such as formal grammatical rules, as well as to handle more adult-like task formats on tests.

When assessing young learners, it is not so much that fundamentally different task formats need to be used, as it is that the ones used for adults need to be planned appropriately, particularly in terms of topic and length. It is important to consider, too, the learners' level of cognitive development, as well as the sorts of things that they can do in their first language. Thus, when writing specifications for reading or listening comprehension passages (see Table 4.3 on page 75), we should restrict ourselves to lengths and topics that are reasonable not just in terms of the children's language ability, but their familiarity (topics) and level of patience (length). The same is true for genre and rhetorical mode in reading passages, and in listening, the type of speech act, register, and communicative functions should be similarly controlled. For example, it might be questionable to ask eight-year-old children to listen to a passage about making an airline reservation, as this topic might not be particularly accessible in their *first* language. Similarly, a reading passage for eight-year-olds about a trip to Las Vegas should focus on vacationing with family, not attending conventions or trade shows, and ought to emphasize hotel swimming pools, rather than casinos.

In terms of whether to use selected response, limited production, deletion-based, or extended production tasks, again, the ability of the students to do these things in their first language needs to be considered as well. If a child has not learned how to write letters in their own language, having them write a letter in a second language is probably out of the question, and therefore not possible as a test task. Age appropriacy also comes into play in item-based tasks in terms of the length of each question, the length of responses to limited production tasks, and how many items there are—indeed, test length will tend to be more important, the younger the intended test takers are.

As for extended response tasks, as noted earlier, we need to keep in mind what the learners would be able to do in their first language. In speaking tests, interviews should be about topics familiar to children, something that will vary somewhat from country to country, but which usually will include family, play, and other things from the children's daily lives. Similarly, role-plays may also be feasible, if framed so they seem more like a "Let's pretend" game than a formal language elicitation tool, and include roles with which the children are likely to be familiar. Presentations for which children prepare in advance *may* be appropriate, assuming their language ability is adequate to the task, especially as children grow older and gain experience delivering class presentations in their first language. As for writing tasks, these will probably be even more restricted, given that even the first language writing tasks to which they are accustomed will probably be limited in length and type.

Assessing Language For Specific Purposes

Another topic of considerable importance is the assessment of **language for specific purposes (LSP)**. LSP is the teaching or learning of a language with a focus on a specific professional area, such as medicine, engineering, or potentially (but less commonly) on even more narrowly focused areas such as specific types of engineering, medical specialties, etc. The goal of LSP programs is not to improve language ability in the general sense (although this will probably happen to some extent anyway), but rather to focus predominantly on the elements of language ability (for example, vocabulary, language functions) needed in that particular job or career field. LSP is quite similar to language for vocational purposes, and is often seen as subsuming that category; when a distinction is made between them, it is based on the level of education required of people working in that field, with vocational language programs being intended for jobs that do not require a university degree, and LSP programs being intended for those that do. It may be useful in many cases to make this distinction, given the differences in task types for which students must be prepared, and in the levels of academic preparation that students can be assumed to have.

The central problem with planning LSP tests, as opposed to planning other types of language assessments, involves the role of topical knowledge within the construct definition. By its very nature, LSP assessment will require the use of topical knowledge specific to the field being assessed. As Bachman and Palmer note, there are three ways in which to handle the question of topical knowledge and its relationship with the construct definition. One option is to exclude topical knowledge from the construct definition, basing it entirely on language ability. A second approach is to include both areas in the construct definition—that is, to assess both language ability *and* topical knowledge. The third choice is to include both topical knowledge and language ability, but to define them as separate constructs (Bachman and Palmer 1996: 121ff.).

However we choose to address topical knowledge in our construct definition, the test must then be written with this in mind. The first option (i.e. not to include topical knowledge in the construct definition) is what is seen in most language assessment situations; in LSP testing, though, this is unlikely to be appropriate. Using this option would effectively strip away the LSP aspect, making it no longer an LSP test. It is worth noting, however, that there are cases in which a non-LSP test is used to certify adequate proficiency levels for the purposes of employment and so on, with no intention of using the test to assess topical knowledge or the ability to process topical knowledge in the second language (see, for example, O'Neill, Buckendahl, Plake, and Taylor 2007; Xi 2007).

The second option, including topical knowledge in the construct definition, gives us a hybrid construct, meaning that we are not assessing purely language ability, but rather something along the lines of the ability to comprehend and/or produce language in order to communicate about topical content, or to use language to perform a particular job. This approach can be appropriate when we have reason to believe that prospective test takers all share a certain level of topical knowledge. It may also be appropriate when we want to require a certain level of topical knowledge in order to pass—for example, in some employment testing, when test takers must have certain levels of both language ability and professional expertise to be qualified for the job.

The third approach, defining language ability and topical knowledge as separate constructs, can also work with LSP assessment. As Bachman and Palmer point out, however, while the inferences may be simpler than with the second option, this third option requires assessing the two constructs separately, with separate test tasks, or requires the use of separate rating scales to assess the levels of language ability and content knowledge displayed on the test. In spite of this complication, they recommend this approach in situations where we do not know much about the likely level of test takers' content knowledge.

Verbal Protocol Analysis

Verbal protocol analysis (see Green 1998) is a tool for studying the processes involved in different parts of the testing process. For test takers, examples might include reading a passage and answering questions (for example, Vongpumivitch 2004), writing an essay (for example, van Weijen, van den Bergh, Rijlaarsdam, and Sanders 2009), or taking an integrated reading and writing test (for example,

Plakans 2009). Verbal protocol analysis is not confined to examinees, however; it can also be used to investigate the processes by which interviews are conducted and scored, or compositions are rated (for example, Barkaoui 2010; Weigle 1998). The person whose mental processes are being studied talks through or otherwise describes what they do and think during the task being analyzed. This is normally done in one of two ways: in a **think-aloud protocol**, or a **recall protocol** (or *retrospective protocol*). Both are typically recorded (preferably with video, so that later on statements about "this" or "that" are clear) and later transcribed in full or in part. They may be done in the target language, the person's first language, or a combination of the two. When the person giving the verbal report is a test taker, the choice is usually left up to them; in contrast, it is more likely that the target language will be used when the subject is a rater or interviewer, as they will *probably* be thinking in the target language anyway.

A *think-aloud protocol* (for example, Barkaoui 2010; Vongpumivitch 2004; Weigle 1998; van Weijen et al. 2009) involves performing the task of interest but, as the name suggests, thinking out loud—that is, talking about what is going through one's mind as the task is performed. Criticisms of this method focus on ways in which the procedure might interfere with the very processes being studied, and thus threaten the validity of the results. These sources of potential interference include the points that thinking aloud can render the process of task performance somewhat self-conscious and artificial; the act of thinking aloud may slow down mental processing and thus alter the person's thought processes; and the procedure may be distracting, interfering with normal processing. Despite these issues, however, there are no other ways available to directly access the mental processes of test takers or raters while they are actually engaged in the process of taking the test (or rating it, as the case may be).

In contrast, a *recall protocol* (or *retrospective protocol*) (for example, Schmitt 1999) does not take place during the task itself, but afterwards. As the name suggests, a test taker, rater, etc., is interviewed after completing the task of interest. As with think-aloud protocols, the idea is to identify the processes and procedures in which the person engaged. Typically, the person is guided through this process by an interviewer who prompts them to recall what they thought or did during specific portions of the process. The effectiveness of the procedure is often enhanced by including a video recording of the procedure being studied, which the person views during the recall as an aid to memory, pausing the recording as necessary. While recall protocols have the advantage of not interfering with natural processing as think-aloud protocols do, they do rely on fallible memory, and thus are not as direct a means of accessing processes of interest. This is particularly true if the protocol does not take place very close to the time the activity actually took place. Another potential source of complication is the practical matter that the longer the amount of time between the task and the recall, the more likely it is that the person will not only forget, but may even lose interest in the procedure or become unavailable for other reasons, thus wasting the effort of recruiting and recording them.

Because of the limitations of each approach, it is possible to use both think-aloud and recall protocols (for example, Plakans 2009) in the same study, although this may not be possible in every case. When it can be done, though, this probably provides the strongest insights into the processes being studied.

Discourse Analysis

Discourse analysis is an important research area in applied linguistics, and can be described in several ways, but perhaps the clearest definition is that discourse analysis is the study of "patternings of language in use and the circumstances (participants, situations, purposes, outcomes) with which these are typically associated" (Trappes-Lomax 2004: 133). It can be viewed as subsuming the areas of conversational analysis (CA; see, for example, Gardner 2004) and grammatical analysis (see, for example, Celce-Murcia and Larsen-Freeman 1999). Unlike CA, however, discourse analysis does not always focus on spoken interaction; and unlike grammatical analysis, it is not limited to a single aspect of the language. Discourse analytic studies may focus on one or more of a wide range of phenomena, such as the instrumentalities of language (for example, the communicative code, register, or genre), communicative functions, the context in which the interaction takes place (in terms of culture, institutions, and knowledge or expectations held in common by speakers), or the spoken or written texts themselves (Trappes-Lomax 2004).

Discourse analysis can be useful for defining constructs for speaking or writing, as well as for writing test specifications. In particular, this relates to specifying the sorts of discourse features that should be elicited in speaking and writing tests, as well as which features should be included in listening or reading comprehension texts (particularly including genres, rhetorical modes, types of speech acts, registers, and communicative functions; see Table 4.3). Discourse analysis can also be helpful in identifying features to include in rating scales (for example, Galaczi 2008), as well as to better understand what is going on in interview tests (for example, Lazaraton 1996; Lazaraton and Davis 2008). Furthermore, it can be used in evaluating the construct validity (for example, Luk 2010) or authenticity of a test (He and Young 1998), or as a way of building in greater authenticity from the beginning (for example, Enright 2004).

Discourse analysis feeds naturally into corpus-based approaches (see below) as well. I personally find that discourse analytic studies of one sort or another can be highly useful in terms of laying the foundation for quantitative studies, by identifying what to look for, and then following the quantitative studies as a way of helping interpret the results, provide examples of what has been found, and contextualize the findings. In fact, studies which merge both qualitative and quantitative approaches, often referred to as "mixed method" approaches (for example, Carr 2006b; Wigglesworth and Elder 2010), allow us to take advantage of the strengths of both paradigms: the rich description of qualitative methods, and the ability to make generalizations and extrapolations in quantitative studies.

Corpus-Based Research Approaches

A *corpus* is a large body of text that has been stored on a computer and is designed for linguistic analysis (Stubbs 2004). Although earlier corpora (the plural form of *corpus*) were often as small as one million words, they tend to be much larger today, sometimes running to the hundreds of millions of words. Once a corpus has been designed—in particular, in order to sample an appropriate TLU domain—assembled, and tagged so as to mark linguistic features such as parts of speech (i.e. word class), it can be searched for things such as grammatical patterns, collocation patterns, and vocabulary frequency. Two particular types of corpora are of importance here: native speaker corpora, and learner corpora drawn from learner language. For many years, corpora were mostly limited to samples of written language, but there is increasing use of spoken corpora today, although such corpora must first be transcribed, which can present additional complications (see Rietveld, van Hout, and Ernestus 2004).

Since the late 1990s, corpora have been seeing increasing use with regards to language assessment research and test development (Taylor and Barker 2008). There are several important ways in which they have been applied to language testing. Perhaps the simplest and most obvious has been as a way of empirically describing the TLU domain, rather than relying solely on test designers' and writers' intuitions.

When describing the TLU domain, corpora are particularly valuable in that they can provide empirical descriptions of language use, such as the frequency with which vocabulary is used, including descriptions of the lexical features of different language contexts, genres, registers, and so on (Read 2007). This is important, as native speakers are often unable to estimate word frequency correctly (see Alderson 2007, and to a lesser extent, Schmitt and Dunham 1999). By extension, we may also wonder about the extent to which native speakers can accurately estimate the frequency of various grammatical structures as well, something of concern if we do not wish to over- or under-represent a given structure on our tests. We can also apply corpus findings to test design in other ways, such as basing test tasks on the TLU domain, through the use of both native speaker and learner corpora. One way in which this can be done is by basing test task specifications on the findings of corpus studies of the TLU domain (for example, Jaén 2007).

A second way to apply corpus-based approaches to language testing is to use a learner corpus to identify typical errors at a given proficiency level. This can help inform test focus in terms of, for example, the structures that should receive emphasis at a given proficiency level (especially in grammar tests). In addition, it can also be used to help in the development of rating scales by providing empirical descriptions of the language used at various levels. Common learner errors can also be used as a source of distractors for multiple-choice items (Taylor 2004; Taylor and Barker 2008).

A third category in which corpus approaches can be used in language assessment is validation research. One example of this would be investigating the authenticity of reading and listening comprehension passages, by comparing their vocabulary or grammatical content to that of the TLU domain—or, more precisely, to a corpus which is believed to be *representative* of the TLU domain (for example, Li and MacGregor 2010; Sawaki and Nissan 2009). Another corpus-based approach to validation would be to use corpora created from test taker responses on a test, and examine whether the performances actually elicited on the test contain the key features called for by the test specifications. This might be used, for example, to confirm whether particular language functions that are supposed to be elicited in a speaking task are in fact being produced, or to examine the degree of peer-to-peer interaction in a group oral interview setting (for example, He and Dai 2006).

Summary

This chapter has covered a number of different topics, each of which is important in its own right, but which cannot be addressed in any detail in an introductory book of reasonable length. We began by considering issues involved in computer-based testing (CBT), as well as several approaches to implementing it. We continued by taking up item response theory (IRT), a powerful statistical approach that is best suited to larger-scale testing, and generalizability (G) theory, which is particularly useful for rated performances, but which can be applied to item-based tests as well. The chapter then moved on to standard setting, and a brief discussion of the issues involved there. We next considered the assessment of young learners, and assessing language for specific purposes. We then concluded with several additional research paradigms: verbal protocol analysis (including think-aloud and recall interviews), discourse analysis (under which I have subsumed both conversation analysis and grammatical analysis), and corpus-based research approaches.

This concludes the first portion of this book; the following nine chapters will be devoted to explaining quantitative concepts and practicing their application, primarily using Microsoft Excel.

Further Reading

Computer-Based Testing

Carr, N. T. 2006a. 'Computer-based testing: Prospects for innovative assessment' in L. Ducate and N. Arnold (eds.). *Calling on CALL: From Theory and Research to New Directions in Foreign Language Teaching* (CALICO Monograph Series Vol. 5: 289–312). San Marcos, TX: CALICO.

Douglas, D. and **V. Hegelheimer.** 2007. 'Assessing language using computer technology'. *Annual Review of Applied Linguistics* 27: 115–132.

Jamieson, J. 2005. 'Trends in computer-based second language assessment'. *Annual Review of Applied Linguistics* 25: 228–242.

Ockey, G. J. 2009b. 'Developments and challenges in the use of computer-based testing (CBT) for assessing second language ability'. *Modern Language Journal* 93 (s1): 836–847.

Item Response Theory

Brown, J. D. and **T. Hudson.** 2002. *Criterion-Referenced Language Testing.* Cambridge: Cambridge University Press, pp. 128–148, and 199–211.

Embretson, S. E. and **S. P. Reise.** 2000. *Item Response Theory for Psychologists.* Mahwah, NJ: Lawrence Erlbaum Associates.

Hambleton, R. K., H. Swaminathan, and **H. J. Rogers.** 1991. *Fundamentals of Item Response Theory.* Newbury Park, CA: Sage Publications.

Generalizability Theory

Brown, J. D. and **T. Hudson.** 2002. *Criterion-Referenced Language Testing.* Cambridge: Cambridge University Press, pp. 175–199.

Shavelson, R. J. and **N. M. Webb.** 1991. *Generalizability Theory: A Primer.* Newbury Park, CA: Sage.

Standard Setting

Berk, R. A. 1986. 'A consumer's guide to setting performance standards on criterion-referenced tests'. *Review of Educational Research:* 56 (1): 137–172.

Brown, J. D. and **T. Hudson.** 2002. *Criterion-Referenced Language Testing.* Cambridge: Cambridge University Press, pp. 248–268.

Skorupski, W. P. and **R. K. Hambleton.** 2005. 'What are panelists thinking when they participate in standard-setting studies?' *Applied Measurement in Education* 18 (3): 233–256.

Assessing Young Learners

McKay, P. 2006. *Assessing Young Language Learners.* Cambridge: Cambridge University Press.

Peck, S. 2001. 'Developing children's listening and speaking in ESL' in M. Celce-Murcia (ed.). *Teaching English as a Second or Foreign Language* (3rd ed.). Boston: Heinle and Heinle, pp. 139–149.

Assessing Language for Specific Purposes

Bachman, L. F. and **A. S. Palmer.** 1996. *Language Testing in Practice.* Oxford: Oxford University Press, pp. 120–129.

Douglas, D. 2000. *Assessing Language for Specific Purposes.* Cambridge: Cambridge University Press.

Verbal Protocol Analysis

Green, A. 1998. *Verbal Protocol Analysis in Language Testing Research: A Handbook.* Cambridge: UCLES/Cambridge University Press.

Plakans, L. 2009. 'Discourse synthesis in integrated second language writing assessment'. *Language Testing* 26 (4): 561–587.

Discourse Analysis

Celce-Murcia, M. and **D. Larsen-Freeman.** 1999. *The Grammar Book: An ESL/ EFL Teacher's Course* (2nd ed.). Boston: Heinle and Heinle.

Gardner, R. 2004. 'Conversation analysis' in A. Davies and C. Elder (eds.). *The Handbook of Applied Linguistics.* Malden, MA: Blackwell Publishing, pp. 262–284.

Trappes-Lomax, H. 2004. 'Discourse analysis' in A. Davies and C. Elder (eds.). *The Handbook of Applied Linguistics.* Malden, MA: Blackwell Publishing, pp. 133–164.

He, A. W. and **R. Young.** 1998. 'Language proficiency interviews: A discourse approach' in R. Young and A. W. He (eds.). *Talking and Testing: Discourse Approaches to the Assessment of Oral Proficiency.* Amsterdam: John Benjamins Publishing Company.

Corpus-Based Research Approaches

Biber, D., S. Conrad, and **R. Reppen.** 1998. *Corpus Linguistics: Investigating Language Structure and Use.* Cambridge: Cambridge University Press.

Kennedy, G. 1998. *An Introduction to Corpus Linguistics.* Harlow, England: Addison Wesley Longman.

Stubbs, M. 2004. 'Language Corpora' in A. Davies and C. Elder (eds.). *The Handbook of Applied Linguistics.* Malden, MA: Blackwell Publishing, pp. 106–132.

Taylor, L. and **F. Barker.** 2008. 'Using corpora for language assessment' in E. Shohamy and N. H. Hornberger (eds.). *Encyclopedia of Language and Education* (2nd ed.). Heidelberg, Germany: Springer Science + Business Media, pp. 1–14.

Discussion Questions

For Questions 1–6, consider a language test that you have taken, administered, or are otherwise familiar with (preferably an important test, such as an end-of-course final exam or a placement test). Discuss the advantages and disadvantages of the following points, and make a recommendation in each case.

In some cases, you may not know what the current practice actually is with the test. If you do not, base your answers on your best guess about the test.

1 Is this administered in paper-based format (P&P), or computer-based format (CBT)?

    a What would be the advantages and disadvantages of converting it from P&P to CBT, or from CBT to P&P?

    b If CBT were to be used, what would be the advantages and disadvantages of using web-based testing (WBT)?

    c What would be the advantages and disadvantages of using CAT for this test (assuming it is item-based)?

    d What would be the advantages and disadvantages of using computer-automated scoring for extended production tasks, or for limited production tasks (assuming these task formats apply in this case)?

2 Does this test use item response theory (IRT), or the classical approach that we have dealt with in this book (for reliability and item analysis)?

    a What would be the advantages and disadvantages of converting to IRT (or moving away from IRT, if that is what is being used at present)?

    b Is there a large enough group of test takers to make IRT appropriate?

    c Would many-facet Rasch measurement be appropriate for any parts of this tests, and if so, which one(s)? Why or why not?

3 Does this test use generalizability theory for estimating reliability or dependability?

    a What would be the advantages of converting to G theory for all or part of the test (or moving from G theory to classical approaches discussed in Chapter 6)?

    b Which part(s) of the test might use G theory most appropriately, and which parts would it probably be least appropriate for?

4 For setting cut scores on this test, would you be more likely to use a test-centered continuum model, or an examinee-centered continuum model?

5 How might you recommend using verbal protocol analysis as part of your validation work?

    a Would you recommend using it to examine test taking processes, or rater or interviewer processes?

    b Would you recommend using a think-aloud protocol, recall protocol, or both?

6 How might you recommend using discourse analysis to help validate this test?

7 How would you recommend using corpus-based approaches to improve and/or validate the test?

    a Would you suggest revising the test specifications, using corpus research findings to help?

    b Would you recommend using information from a learner corpus about typical errors at various proficiency levels? If so, how would you use this information?

    c How might you use corpus-based approaches in doing the research for a validity argument for the test?

Questions 8–9 are separate from 1–7, and do not refer to the same test.

8 Imagine a context in which you might need to create a test for children. The test will include reading, writing, speaking, and listening. What task format(s) would you choose for each of these four areas?

9 Imagine a context in which you might need to create a test of language for a specific purpose.
   a What areas or "skills" would the test include, and why?
   b What task formats would you choose for each area or skill?
   c How would you address the question of content knowledge in your construct definition?

PART II

INTRODUCTION

Part II contains the quantitatively-oriented chapters of the book. Each chapter consists of an explanation of the topic being covered, followed by step-by-step instructions detailing how to complete the related worksheet, and discussion of the results. The files for the Excel worksheets can be found on the disk included with this book. They are read-only files, however, so they will need to be saved with new filenames (e.g., with the user's initials added to the original filename) on the user's computer. The completed versions of the worksheets are also on the disk, and are also read-only.

Readers using Microsoft Office for Macintosh computers (e.g., Excel 2004 or 2008) will find that the formulas and functions are the same as in the Windows versions, but sometimes the menus and dialog boxes may differ a little. They should not be extremely difficult, however, and Mac users who are using Office are probably already somewhat used to this sort of thing anyway.

The chapters move from an introduction to using Excel by means of creating a course gradebook, to descriptive statistics and visual representations of data. The book then proceeds to correlation, the relationship between two sets of scores, before covering how to identify problematic test questions and problematic distractors (incorrect options) on multiple-choice questions. It then explains how to calculate the overall scoring consistency of a test.

Excel is used in all but the last two worksheets, 18.2 and 19.1. While it would be possible to use Excel for these worksheets, I believe it is actually simpler to do them using paper, pencil, and a scientific calculator. Interested readers can, of course, enter the formulas into Excel if they so desire.

Regarding the arrangement of this part of the book, the reader will note that the scoring of multiple-choice items is dealt with relatively late, not until Chapter 17. This avoids the earlier chapters becoming too content-heavy but, more importantly, it allows us to address correlation first in Chapter 14 and to touch upon the point-biserial coefficient for individual options. Delaying multiple-choice scoring until Chapter 17 also means that readers have already had three Excel worksheets to help them become familiar with using Pearsonian correlations, and the scoring is logically connected with the distractor analysis.

11 ORGANIZING DATA IN MICROSOFT EXCEL

Introduction

Before beginning a discussion of *how* to use Microsoft Excel, it might be a good idea to first address *why* we might wish to use Excel. The answer is that we have to do certain things involving math to make sure our tests and other assessments are working properly, and to help us identify areas in need of improvement. The grudging response to that is often "Well, OK, but I hate math. Can't we use something that will do the math for us instead?" My response to this is always, "Yes, that's why we're using Excel." Excel is not a program for people who are great at math, but rather a program that does math *for* you. It is also available almost anywhere in the world where there are computers, and is a very convenient way to enter data even if they will be analyzed later in an actual statistics package. Besides its broad availability, the important features are easy to learn, and it is able to do all of the analyses covered in this second part of the volume, aside from Worksheets 18.2 and 19.1, which are better done with pencil, paper, and a calculator.

Recognizing that not all readers will be familiar with Excel—in my experience, some will even have been actively avoiding it—I will begin with a bit of familiarization with Excel, before proceeding to the first worksheet. First, though, I would be remiss if I did not point out that Excel is not really a statistics program, and should probably be avoided for most inferential statistics (including several statistical operations it is *supposed* to be able to handle). But for the sorts of analyses covered in this book, expensive statistics packages are not really necessary, and in any case, such programs cannot easily do certain analyses, especially for CRT. For that matter, my personal favorite program for reliability and item analysis software, Lertap 5 (Nelson 2008; see Carr 2004 for a review), actually runs *within* Excel.

Objectives

By the end of this chapter, readers will know or understand:
- The layout of Microsoft Excel
- The labeling system for columns, rows, and cells

- How to move around a worksheet and select groups of cells using both keyboard shortcuts and the mouse
- How to insert additional rows, columns, or empty cells, and how to delete and move around rows, columns, or groups of cells
- Several ways of getting data into Excel: by typing it in manually, opening text files, or copying and pasting tables from Microsoft Word
- The basics of formatting cells, columns, and worksheets
- How to perform basic mathematical operations (addition, subtraction, multiplication, and division), use exponents, and insert Excel functions (for example, the **AVERAGE** and **SUM** functions)
- Relative and absolute cell references
- The concept of curving course grades
- How to create a class gradebook in Excel, rather than using paper, pencil, and a calculator

Getting to Know the Layout of Excel

The terminology used for Excel is based on pre-computer accounting. In the past, accountants and bookkeepers kept all records on paper. A single large piece of paper with columns and rows of numbers was called a **spreadsheet** or **worksheet**. Several related worksheets kept together (perhaps even attached or bound together) were called a **workbook**. When Excel was created, this terminology was carried over. A single Excel file is called a workbook, and normally ends in the file extension .xls (for versions through 2003) or .xlsx (for Excel 2007). Figure 11.1 shows a screenshot of an Excel 2007 workbook, and Figure 11.2 shows a screenshot of an Excel 2003 workbook. In Figure 11.1, the workbook consists of three worksheets (Box 1 and Box 2); the second workbook only consists of one worksheet.

As can be seen from both figures, each vertical column on the spreadsheet is assigned a letter, and each horizontal row is assigned a number. Each row or column has a button at its top or left side. These buttons are used to select the row or column—that is, to "make them turn blue," and to tell Excel that something (usually formatting or deleting) is going to be done to all the cells in that column or row.

Each "box" in the spreadsheet is called a *cell*. A cell's address is given by its column and row. For example, the cell in the top left corner of the spreadsheet is **A1**. The cell below it is **A2**, and the cell to its right is **B1**. The *active* cell (the cell that has been clicked on, and that typing will edit) is indicated in the Name Box; anything that is typed will go in the Formula Bar, including formulas, but also text and numbers. (N.B. The adjacent Insert Function Button will be discussed below.) When it comes time to enter data, each student will occupy *one row* in the spreadsheet, and each test question, rating, test score, etc. will occupy *one column*. Putting people in rows and questions in columns is an arbitrary rule, but it is one followed almost universally. Among other things, reversing the columns and rows would make it difficult to move the data to any other program for analysis. Even more important, however, is that each test taker's results should go in *one* row, not several; anything else will make the results almost impossible to analyze, because the data for a given question, rating, etc. will not be contiguous.

For those unfamiliar with Office 2007, the Ribbon (Box 3 and Box 4 in Figure 11.1) may look confusing. The menus in earlier versions (Box 1 in Figure 11.2) have all been replaced with toolbars, which are located on various tabs. This row of tabs is called the Ribbon. The Office Button, in the top left corner of the window (Box 12 in Figure 11.1), is not a decoration, but actually opens a menu similar to the old **File** menu, albeit somewhat different.

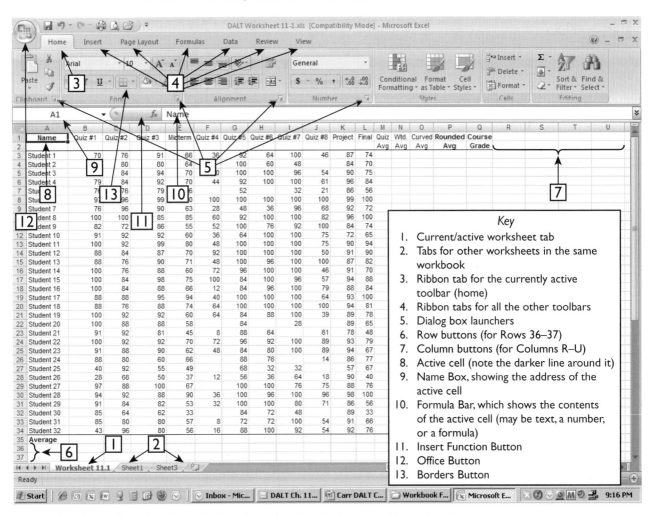

Figure 11.1 Screenshot of a Microsoft Excel 2007 Workbook Containing Three Worksheets

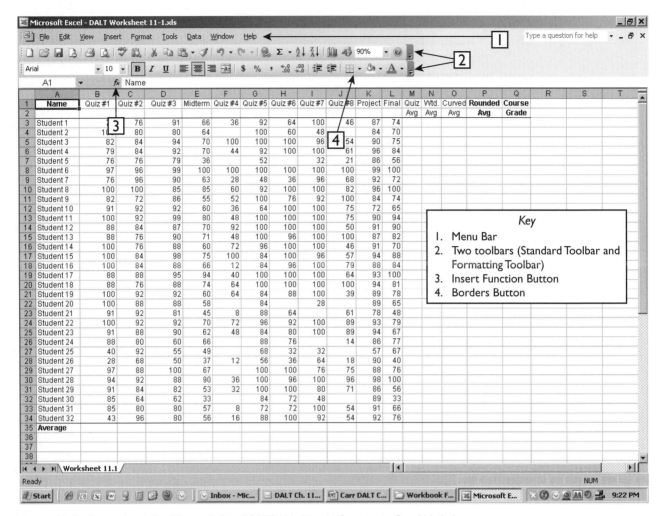

Figure 11.2 Screenshot of a Microsoft Excel 2003 Workbook Containing One Worksheet

Moving Around and Selecting Cells

There are several ways to move around the worksheet and select the desired cell—that is, to make it the active cell (see Box 8 in Figure 11.1). The simplest way is to use the mouse, and click on the desired cell. This is not always very efficient, however, especially if the cell you are trying to select is not very close to the currently active cell. In many cases, it is much faster to use the keyboard to move around: the arrow keys (←→↑↓), and the `Page Up` and `Page Down` keys. An additional feature that makes this way of navigating around the worksheet even faster is to use `Ctrl` with an arrow. This moves the cursor in the direction of the arrow, to one of two places. If the active cell (the cell that is currently selected, and thus surrounded with a heavy line) contains something—a number, text, or a formula—the cursor will move to the next edge of a group of cells with contents.

For example, in Figure 11.2, the active cell is **A1**. If Ctrl + → is selected, the cursor will move to **Q1**. (N.B. When keyboard shortcuts are presented, a plus sign means that two keys are pressed simultaneously. A comma means that they are pressed in sequence. The comma and plus sign are *not* actually typed!) If Ctrl + ↓ is pressed once, the cursor will move to **Q2**. If Ctrl + ↓ is pressed a second time, the cursor will go to **Q65536** (in a .xls file), at the very bottom of the spreadsheet, but still in Column Q. From there, Ctrl + ↓ will move the cursor to **A65536**, at the bottom left corner of the spreadsheet. Ctrl + ↑ will make **A48** *(not visible in the figure; see Worksheet 11.1)* the active cell, and pressing Ctrl + ↑ once more will make **A47** the active cell. Pressing Ctrl + ↑ a third time will move the active cell to **A45**, and so on to **A41**, **A35**, **A3**, and then back to **A1**. This may seem confusing to some new users, but it is worth taking a little time to practice. People who are used to only using the mouse are usually amazed at how fast someone can work who uses the keyboard, and when working with large datasets, the mouse becomes very slow and difficult to control.

Very frequently, it will be important to select more than one cell at a time. For example, when using formulas (introduced below), such as for averaging together a group of numbers, it is necessary to specify which numbers are to be averaged. A group of contiguous cells is called a **range**. In the spreadsheet in Figure 1.2, if we decide to compute an average for Quiz 1, we will probably put that average in cell **B35**. The range we will select will be all the cells from **B3** to **B34**, which is written **B3:B34**.

As with moving around the spreadsheet, there are a variety of ways to select a range of cells. The easiest-looking one is probably to click and drag with the mouse. In Figure 11.2, to select the **B3:B34** range, a user would select **B3**, click and hold down the left mouse button, drag the mouse down to **B34**, and then release the mouse button. An alternative approach would be to select **B3**, then hold down the Shift key and left-click on cell **B34**.

Even faster, of course, would be to use the keyboard. When selecting large ranges of vertical text, Shift + Page Up or Shift + Page Down will work. I find that this offers less control, however, than using Shift with an arrow key, or Ctrl + Shift with an arrow key. Continuing the same example, if **B3** is the active cell, a user could hold down the Shift key and press the ↓ button 31 times. A better way, of course, would be to hold down Shift + Ctrl, and press ↓ once.

Inserting, Deleting, and Moving

Sometimes when we are working in Excel we realize that we need an extra column or row someplace. In other cases, we may need to shift part of one row over to the right, or shift part of a column down. There are several ways to insert a row or column. One way is to right-click on a cell, and select **Insert** from the context menu. This will open the **Insert** dialog box. **Shift cells right** or **Shift cells down** will do just as it says. **Entire row** will insert a new row above the current one, and

Entire column will insert a new column to the left of the current one. Inserting a row or column will cause Excel to relabel all the columns being moved right or the rows being moved down. Fortunately, if any formulas (see below) include references to the moved cells, they will be automatically updated by Excel.

Another way to open the **Insert** dialog box in Excel 2003 is to click on the **Insert** menu in Excel 2003, and select **Cells**, **Rows**, or **Columns**. This can also be done in either Excel 2003 or 2007 by typing Alt + i, and either e, r, or c, respectively. In Excel 2007, insertions can also be made by clicking on the triangle in the bottom (or left, on some computers) half of the **Insert** button, on the **Home** toolbar, and then making the appropriate choice from the menu that appears.

A row, column, or cell can also be deleted, and the contents shifted up or to the left. As with inserting, the **Delete** dialog box can be opened by right-clicking a cell and selecting **Delete**. Shifting cells up or to the left will move the contents of the active cell's row or column. Deleting the entire row or column erases it. As with insertion, if cell addresses change, Excel will automatically correct the formulas. If a formula referred to one or more cells that were deleted, however, it may produce an error, whether immediately apparent or not. In Excel 2003, the **Delete** dialog box can be opened by clicking on the **Edit** menu. In both Excel 2003 and 2007 this can also be done using the keyboard by typing Alt + e, and then d. In Excel 2007, clicking on the triangle in the bottom half (or right side) of the **Delete** button, on the **Home** toolbar, will also work.

Moving a cell, row or column, or range can be done using the mouse, or by cutting and pasting. If the mouse is used, the cell(s), row(s), or column(s) should be selected, and then the cursor must be positioned exactly over the edge of the selected range. A four-headed arrow will appear, and while that arrow is visible, hold down the left mouse button, and drag the selection to the new location. (If the cursor moves slightly before the mouse is clicked, and the four-headed arrow disappears, the range will have to be selected again.) Unless the new location is empty, releasing the button ("dropping" the selection) will produce a dialog box asking **Do you want to replace the contents of the destination cells?** If **OK** is selected, the previous contents will be overwritten and replaced. Canceling the operation will return the selection to its previous location.

If the selection is moved by cutting and pasting, blank cells will be left in the original location, and there will be no confirmation request before the contents of the new location are replaced. For those unfamiliar with these processes, cutting, copying, and pasting have toolbar buttons, are contained in the **Edit** menu of Excel 2003, and use the keyboard shortcuts Ctrl + x, Ctrl + c, and Ctrl + v, respectively.

Getting Data Into Excel

When text or numbers need to be typed in a spreadsheet, click on the first cell to be filled. Whatever is being entered can then be typed; it is not necessary to click on the formula bar to begin typing, although this will work as well. Clicking on the formula bar is necessary, however, if the cell's contents are being edited, not replaced.

After the contents of a cell have been typed, it is possible to move on to the next cell by using an arrow key. Hitting Tab will move to the next cell on the right. Hitting Enter will move down, *except* that if a row of data is entered using Tab, and Enter is hit after typing in the last cell, the active cell will be in the next row, but it will be in the first column in which data was typed. For example, in Figures 11.1 and 11.2, imagine if the teacher typed the name for Student 1, and then all of Student 1's grades, before moving on to Student 2, when entering the data. If Tab was used to move across the row, and then Enter was hit after finishing **L3**, the active cell would then become **A4**.

When typing in a cell, if it is necessary to undo what was typed, before Enter, Tab, or an arrow key has been hit, Esc will erase what was typed. If the change has been made, though, and a new cell has become the active cell, the **Undo** button, or Ctrl + z, can be used to undo the changes. Undo will not work, though, on any changes made before a document was last saved.

It is also possible to open text files in Excel. This is easiest with *delimited* data—that is, when the columns are separated, normally by tabs or commas. The most common extensions for these files will be .txt and .csv, although others are possible. Excel spreadsheets can also be saved as delimited text files, although this will remove all formatting and formulas (leaving only the results of the formulas), and only the active worksheet will be saved when this is done. Fixed width files can also be opened in Excel—in such files, every cell in a given column has the same number of characters. Users of this book are less likely to have to deal with these files, but if it proves necessary, it is easy to figure out, although tedious, since the columns must be manually separated.

Data can also be pasted into Excel from tables in Microsoft Word. Any borders in the original table will be copied into Excel, and will need to be removed manually if they are unwanted. Additionally, cells often need to be reformatted, if they are to remain the normal height. This requires turning off the text wrapping feature, which Excel automatically applies to the table cells when they are pasted in. This is done with the **Format Cells** dialog box. Once the cells in question are selected, it can be activated by right-clicking somewhere in the range, by clicking the triangle on the **Format** button (**Home** toolbar) in Excel 2007, by opening the **Format** menu in Excel 2003 and selecting **Cells**, or on the keyboard by typing Alt, o, e. Once the dialog box is open, click on the **Alignment** tab, and uncheck (or switch off) the **Wrap text** checkbox.

Tab-delimited text can be pasted directly from Word into Excel. Pasting in any other type of text, however, will lead to each paragraph taking up one cell, with the cells forming a column.

Some Tips For Formatting

Sometimes it is desirable to wrap text in headings—that is, if the text is wider than the cell, it continues onto a second or third line, displaying all of the text and making the cell taller in the process. Doing this involves opening the **Format Cells** dialog box (see above), and checking (or switching on) the **Wrap text** checkbox. Two other useful options that are found in the same dialog box are changing the orientation of text, and changing the formatting of numbers. Text alignment is found under the **Alignment** tab. In particular, it may be desirable to make heading text run vertically, so that the heading row is taller than normal, but columns do not become too wide. This can be done by specifying the number of degrees to rotate the text, or by clicking and dragging the red diamond. Date formatting, unsurprisingly, is found under the **Number** tab, by selecting **Date** from the list on the left side of the dialog box. This can be important when weird or mysterious things happen to dates, such as "6/09" becoming 9-Jun, or "6/9/09" becoming "6/9/2009," as soon as the date is entered. Adjusting the number of decimal places displayed is also done in the **Number** tab, by selecting **Number** from the list on the left side of the dialog box. Alternatively, the number of decimal places to display can also be adjusted using the **Increase Decimal** and **Decrease Decimal** buttons on the **Home** toolbar.

Changing the page orientation between landscape and portrait in Excel 2007 is done by clicking on the **Orientation** button of the **Page Layout** toolbar. In Excel 2003, it is done by opening the **File** menu, selecting **Page Setup**, clicking the appropriate radio button under the **Page** tab. Changing the orientation is especially useful if the spreadsheet will be printed out. Note that the **Page Setup** dialog box can also be launched in Excel 2007 from the **Page Setup** portion of the **Page Layout** toolbar.

Several other important formatting options are included in the **Page Setup** dialog box and **Page Layout** tab. These include displaying gridlines during printing, and adjusting margins. The **Page Setup** dialog box also controls inserting headers and footers, and changing the page order for printing. In Excel 2007, gridlines can be controlled using the **Page Layout** toolbar, but page order requires the **Page Setup** dialog box.

Although there are a number of other formatting options, the only one both important and unobvious enough to need coverage here is adjusting column width. This can be done automatically by double clicking on the line between two column buttons, which will AutoFit the left-hand column. If the entire column is selected, it will make the change based on the widest cell. If a specific cell is selected when the change is made, the adjustment for the entire column will be based on the width of that particular cell. Alternatively, column widths can be manually adjusted by clicking and dragging the line between column buttons. **Column** width can also be specified using the **Format** menu in Excel 2003, and the **Format** button on the **Home** toolbar in Excel 2007.

Basic Mathematical Operations and Functions

A formula is entered into a cell by starting with **=**, followed by the rest of it. Addition uses the **+** sign, subtraction uses the hyphen **–**, multiplication uses an asterisk *****, and division uses the forward-leaning slash **/**. Thus, 2 + 2 would be entered **= 2 + 2**. The spaces are optional. If this formula is entered, the cell will display **4**. The formula will only be visible if that cell is selected, in which case the formula will appear in the formula bar.

Adding the contents of two or more cells is quite easy. Imagine, for example, that in Figure 11.2, we wanted to add together Student 1's scores for Quiz 1 and Quiz 2. We decide to put this formula in S3, which is safely out of our way. Click on S3, type **=**, and then move the cursor (using either arrow keys or clicking on the cell with the mouse) to B3. Next, type **+**, select C3, and hit Enter. The result should be **146**, displayed in S3.

Exponents are handled using the carat **^**. For example, 2^2 would be typed **= 2^2**.

Since it is impossible to write fractions, as such, parentheses are used. For example, $\frac{1+2}{3+1}$ would be entered **= (1 + 2)/(3 + 1)**, and the cell would display **.75**.

Many mathematical operations, particularly complex ones, can be performed automatically using Excel functions. Two of the simplest are **SUM** and **AVERAGE**. **SUM** computes the total for a group of numbers, and **AVERAGE** calculates their mean (i.e. the sum of all the values in a group of numbers, divided by the number of numbers). The **SUM** function is entered by typing **=SUM*(RANGE)***, where *RANGE* is the group of cells being totaled. **AVERAGE** is entered the same way: **=AVERAGE*(RANGE)***. For example, let us say we want to find the class average for Quiz 1 from Figure 11.2. These scores are in the range **B3:B34**, so we would select **B35**, type **=AVERAGE(**, select the range (using the mouse or the arrow keys), then type **)**, and press Enter. The result would read **=AVERAGE(B3:B34)**, and cell **B35** would display **85.6**. The formula, including the range, can also be typed in manually, but this is usually a bad idea, since it can be very easy to make a mistake when typing the range.

Some functions will be difficult to enter manually, or may be hard to remember. When we do not remember the function, or its syntax, we can use the **Insert Function** dialog box. There are several easy ways to open this. The easiest in both Excel 2003 and 2007 is to click on the **Insert Function** button (shown in Figure 11.1, and again in Figure 11.2 for greater clarity), or to type Alt, i, f. Alternatively, using the **Insert** menu and selecting **Function** in Excel 2003 (Figure 11.2, Box 3), or clicking on the **Insert Function** button on the **Formulas** toolbar in Excel 2007. Excel 2007 also has eight additional buttons for various categories of functions, but whether these are helpful or inconvenient is a matter of individual preference.

Once the **Insert Function** dialog box is open, the list of available functions can be searched through in its entirety, or grouped into categories. Once a function is selected, the **Function Arguments** dialog box will appear; if the directions for a given function are not clear, **Help** will usually do much to clear things up.

Relative and Absolute Cell References

In the previous example for calculating **AVERAGE**, the range used was **B3:B34**. If we wanted to calculate a class average for every grade from the course, we would simply copy **B35**, select the range **B35:L35** (or **C35:L35**; it does not matter if we paste the formula in on top of itself). We do not need to change the formula, because Excel does not actually believe us when we say **B3:B34** in the **AVERAGE** formula. Excel uses **relative cell references** in most cases. This means that when **B35** is selected, and the formula is entered containing **B3:B34**, Excel does not *interpret* that as meaning that particular group of cells, *per se*. Rather, the program interprets it as meaning "the range of cells from 31 rows above the active cell, in the same column, down to 1 row above the active cell." This explains why, when the formula is pasted into **C35**, it averages the numbers in Column C, not Column B.

There are times, however, when a particular cell or range needs to be used in several formulas. One example of this is when a weighted average is computed for each student in a class, as shown in Figures 11.1 and 11.2, and as will be demonstrated in Worksheet 11.1. Another example from the same worksheet is if we wish to use a lookup table to enter course grades (A+, A, A-, etc.), rather than entering them manually. When a specific cell or range is used in every case, rather than relative reference, the address of the cell or range inserts a dollar sign $ before the row and column labels. Continuing our earlier example, then, if we used the formula **=AVERAGE($B$3:$B$34)**, and pasted that formula in under every assignment on the spreadsheet, we would have the same number in every column! Procedures for using **absolute cell references** are explained in the instructions for Worksheet 11.1, since a concrete presentation will probably be easier to understand.

Worksheet 11.1: Creating a Class Gradebook in Excel

Introduction

The purpose of this worksheet is to create a gradebook in Excel—that is, a record of every student's grade on every test, quiz, or assignment in the course, and their end-of-course course grade. Doing this in Excel is faster and more convenient than using paper records and a calculator, and reduces the likelihood of error in performing the calculation. The course grades are based on the average quiz grade (30%), the course project (30%), the midterm exam (20%), and the final exam (20%).

Sometimes, instructors discover at the end of the term that the grades in their courses are lower than they would expect, and an undesirably large number of students will be receiving lower grades than the teachers might like. It may be desirable, in such cases, to adjust the grades at the end of the course—perhaps teachers are concerned that they graded more strictly than they should have, or extenuating circumstances hindered the students' performance. While it is true that carefully calibrated tests and assignments may reduce the likelihood of this happening, no measure is perfect, and the problem may not become apparent until all the grades are averaged together. In cases where this problem of low grades arises, we can **curve** the grades, that is, adjust the course grades so that students receive higher grades than they would have otherwise. There are many approaches to this, but I will outline one here that I believe is fairly simple to implement, and adjusts the grades on the basis of overall class performance.

In this example, grades will be curved, in that if the class average is below 85% (a mid-range B, in the American grading system), points will be added to every student's final score in order to raise the average to this target. For example, if the class average is 81.3%, we will add 3.7% to each student's final score, but if the class average is already 85% or higher, there will be no change. The resulting "curved" average will then be rounded to the nearest whole number, and Excel will look up what letter grade each student should receive for the course based on the rounded average. Readers can, of course, use any value they want in real life; 85% is simply what I am using here. A decision must also be made about the blanks in the worksheet. Will they be changed to zero, or will they be left blank (and thus ignored in the averaging)?

Procedures

1 Open the file **DALT Worksheet 11-1.xls**.

2 Choose how to treat missing quiz grades. Leaving them blank means Excel will ignore these cells when computing the average quiz grade for each student. Changing the blanks to 0 (by typing in the number in each blank cell) will lower several students' grades dramatically. In the tutorial, the quiz grades will be left blank, but readers can experiment with using 0 as well.

3 We will use the assignment weights discussed previously (quizzes 30%, midterm exam 20%, final project 30%, final exam 20%). These need to be entered into the worksheet, in cells **B42:B45**. They can be entered either as decimals or as percentages (for example, .30 vs. 30%).

4 Similarly, we will stick with the earlier decision to curve grades, and to use 85% as the target for the class average. 85 should therefore be typed in **B47**.

5 The first thing to calculate is the quiz average (each student's average score on eight quizzes):

a Select **M3**, and type **=AVERAGE(**

b Select **B3:D3**, by either clicking on **B3**, or using the arrow keys to move there.

c Type **,** (a comma).

d Select **F3:J3**.

e Type **)** (a right parenthesis) and press Enter.

f Use the **Format Cells** dialog box to round **M3** to one decimal place (**71.9**). Doing this now means that the same formatting will be applied when the formula is pasted in below.

g Copy **M3**. Select **M3:M34**, and paste.

6 Next, compute the weighted average, using a combination of relative and absolute cell references:

a Select **N3**, and type **=**

b Using the mouse or arrow keys, select **M3** (the quiz average), and type *****

c Scroll down the screen and select **B42**.

d Press the F4 key once. (Readers using Excel for Mac should press Command + t instead of F4.) This is essential, as it converts **B42** to **$B$42**, making it an absolute reference. A very common place to go wrong is to forget this step. Forgetting to use the absolute reference will *not* affect the result in **M3** (which makes it easier to make this error and not realize it), but all the results in **M4:M34** will be incorrect. *If the* F4 *key is accidentally hit twice, do not panic.* Simply press it three more times, and the cell reference will cycle through **B$42**, **$B42**, **B42**, and then back to **$B$42**.

When reading this reference, it helps to think of the dollar sign as meaning "always." Thus, **$B$42** means "This cell will always be in Column B, and will always be in Row 42." Without the dollar signs, a (relative) reference to **B42** from **N3** would be equivalent to "12 columns to the right of the active cell, and 39 rows below the active cell."

e Type **+**

f Select **E3** (the midterm score), and type *****

g Select **B43**, press F4 once, and type **+**

h Select **K3** (the project grade), and type *****

i Select **B44**, press F4 once, and type **+**

j Select **L3** (the final exam grade), and type *****

k Select **B45**, press F4 once, and press Enter.

l The result in **N3** should now read **75.66**. Use the **Format Cells** dialog box to change the number format to one decimal place.

m Copy **N3**, select **N3:N34**, and paste.

7 Before the curved average can be computed, we need to have the class average for the weighted average, to know how much to adjust scores by.

a Select **B35**.

b Type **=AVERAGE(**

c Select **B3:B34**, and type **)**

d Press Enter. This will result in an average of **85.56**.

   e Format **B35** so that it only has one decimal place.

   f Copy **B35**, select **B35:N35**, and paste. We can now see that the class average for the overall course (the average of the weighted averages) is **78.0**.

8 Next, before we calculate the curved average, we still must compute how much to curve course grades *by*.

   a Select **B48**, type **=**, and select **B47**.

   b Type **–**, select **N35**, and press Enter. The result (**7**) will be the number of points added to each student's course grade.

9 Now, compute the curved average.

   a Select **O3**, type **=**, select **N3**, and type **+**

   b Select **B48**, press F4, and press Enter. The result should be **82.63**.

   c Reformat **B48** so there is only one decimal place.

   d Copy **O3**, select **O3:O34**, and paste.

10 The next step is to round the curved average. (If you do not curve grades in your own class, you should apply this procedure to the weighted average instead.) This step uses the **INT** function, which "integerizes" any number it is applied to. That is, it drops all decimals. For example, Student 1 has a curved average of **82.6**; **INT(82.6)** would equal **82**.

The problem is that in rounding, we normally want fractions of .5 and above to round up to the next highest number, so 82.6 should round up to 83. This can be handled quite easily, though, by adding .5 to the function *argument* (i.e. the part inside the parentheses). Thus, **INT(82.6 + .5)** will give us 83, which is obviously correct. This little trick always works, as can be seen by playing with a variety of values (for example, 82.0, 82.1, 82.499, 82.5, or 82.9). Anything with a decimal of .5 or greater will round up, and anything less will round down.

There is one important caveat to keep in mind about rounding: Sometimes, a cell will display a number ending in .5, but it will not round up. This is almost certainly a sign that the .5 has already been rounded up from .45 or .49 or something similar. Excel uses 15 decimal places; whether it *displays* all of them—or even none of them—they are still there. Even experienced users sometimes forget this, and can become confused and frustrated when the correct formula seems to be giving the wrong number. To confirm whether this is happening in your case, check by increasing the number of decimals being displayed. You can reduce them again once you have confirmed that this is, in fact, the problem.

Why do we need Excel to do the rounding for us, if rounding is so easy? It *is* easy, but doing it manually for each student probably takes longer than doing it automatically. Using Excel also reduces the chances for manual rounding errors.

   a Select **P3**. Type **=INT(** and select **O3**.

   b Type **+ .5)** and press Enter. The cell should now display **83.00**.

c Reformat **P3** (using the **Format Cells** dialog box, or the **Decrease Decimal** button) to remove all decimals, making it **83**. Since this is the final score in the course, we should make it more obvious, so make it **bold**.

d Copy **P3**, select the range **P3:P34**, and paste.

11 The next step involves automatically assigning letter grades based on the rounded average. The range **B51:C64** contains a vertical lookup table for this—that is, the table is arranged vertically, and we will use the vertical lookup function (**VLOOKUP**) to find the correct letter grade to assign for each student. This table can be simplified to remove plus/minus grading. Note that the scores in the table are in ascending order, and that there are two values for F (0 and 59).

a Select **Q3**.

b Press the **Insert Function** button, located next to the formula bar. Select the category **Lookup & Reference**, select **VLOOKUP**, and click **OK**.

c Select the **Lookup_value** argument. Click on the button with a red arrow next to this text box. The dialog box will mostly disappear. Use the mouse to select **P3**, and click on the button with the red arrow again, *or* press Enter.

d Select the **Table_array** argument. Click the button next to this text box, and select the range **B51:C64**. We want to use the same range (i.e. the same table) for every student, so we need an absolute reference. Press F4 once, and then click the button with the red arrow again, *or* press Enter.

e Add the **Col_index_num** (column index number) argument. The letter grades are in the second column of the lookup table, so type **2**. Beneath the fourth text box and to the right, you should now see **= "B"** displayed. Since an 83 is supposed to be a B, not a B- or B+, the formula seems to be correct.

f We can ignore the **Range_lookup** argument, since it is only needed when we want an exact match, which we do *not* want here.

g Click **OK**, or press Enter.

h Select **Q3**, make it **bold**, copy, select **Q3:Q34**, and paste. If you see **#N/A** in many of the lower cells, you have probably forgotten to use an absolute reference for **B51:C64** (i.e. the range used in the formula should be **$B$51:$C$64**, not simply **B51:C64**).

Note that this example uses the American system of "A+" denoting the highest grade possible, and "F" the lowest. Plus/minus grading (A+, A, A-, etc.) was used here, although "straight" letter grading (A, B, C, D, and F with no plus or minus grades) can be used by simply deleting the plus/minus grades and using a smaller lookup table. Similarly, other grading systems could be used, such as assigning numbers from 1 to 4 or 1 to 5, as long as they are put in the proper order.

12 Select **N35**, copy, select **N35:P35**, and paste. This will add class averages for the curved and rounded averages.

13 Next, we want to replace the border between Rows 34 and 35.

   a Select **M34:Q34**.

   b Click the triangle at the side of the **Borders** button (see Figures 11.1 and 11.2), and select **Bottom Border**.

14 Finally, it may be interesting to see how many students earned each grade. Rather than counting this ourselves with a piece of paper, however, we will let Excel do the counting for us, using the **COUNTIF** function.

   a Select **D52** (ignore **D51**), and click on the **Insert Function** button. Select the **Statistical** category.

   b Scroll down the list to **COUNTIF**, and click on **OK**. Note that there are several similar counting functions, so make sure you do not accidentally choose the wrong one.

   c Select the **Range** argument. Click on the button with the red arrow next to the **Range** textbox. Scroll up the screen, select **Q3:Q34**, and press F4, since we want to use this same range for all our counting. This will give us the range **$Q$3:$Q$34**. Click the button with the red arrow again, or press Enter.

   d Select the **Criteria** argument. Click on the button with the red arrow next to the **Criteria** textbox, and select **C52**. Click the button with the red arrow again, or press Enter.

   e Click **OK** or press Enter to finish creating the function. Cell **D52** should now display **0**, since none of the students received an F.

   f Copy **D52**, select the range **D52:D64**, and paste. The number of grades should total 32, and tallies for individual letter grades can be compared with Column Q.

15 You may check your answers by comparing them to the file **DALT Worksheet 11-1 COMPLETED.xls**.

Discussion

The spreadsheet is finished, but we are now able to examine the effects of changing the "curve to" score, entering 0 for missing quiz grades, or changing the weighting of different assignments. Because of the way this worksheet has been set up, changes in these will be automatically reflected in the rounded averages, course grades, and tallies of how many students received each grade. For example, if you are unhappy with the grade distribution, because it is too high, experiment with changing **B47** to 75 or 80. Note, however, that if the "curve to" score is below the class average, the curving formula will produce disastrous results. There is a more complicated formula that will automatically address this issue, although it is more complicated than I would like to explain at this point in the book. The formula, which could be entered in **O3** during Step 9, is **=IF($N$35>=$B$47,N3,N3+$B$48)**. It should then be copied and pasted into **O3:O34**.

I should add that I strongly recommend against curving grades on each individual assignment; besides adding extra columns to the spreadsheet, and complicating the process of averaging the grades, there is also the risk that students will surprise the teacher and do very well on the final exam or final project, thus raising the course average to an undesirably *high* level.

Finally, besides adjusting the "curve to" score, different weighting schemes can be experimented with as well. Of course, it should go without saying that if the weighting of assignments and the class curve policy have been announced already, making changes at the end of the course is hardly fair, unless the changes are in the direction of greater leniency.

Summary

In this chapter, we have become familiar with the layout of Microsoft Excel and its labeling system for columns (denoted by letters), rows (denoted by numbers), and cells (denoted by their column and row designations, in that order). An important rule was also introduced. That each person in a dataset must be put in his or her own row, and each test question, assignment grade, etc. in its own column.

We have seen that using keyboard shortcuts (CTRL + arrow), instead of relying entirely on the mouse, can be a faster and more efficient way to move about in a worksheet, and to select (Shift + arrow, Shift + CTRL + arrow) groups of cells. We have learned how to insert, delete, and move rows, columns, or groups of cells, as well as some strategies for manually typing data into Excel, opening text files, and copying and pasting tables from Microsoft Word. We have covered the basics of how to format cells, columns, and worksheets so that the display (on the screen or when printed out) will present the information we want in a way that seems clear.

We then moved onto using Excel to actually *do* things, starting with how to perform mathematical operations in Excel and how to insert Excel functions that automate some of those mathematical operations (for example, summing and averaging, using the **SUM** and **AVERAGE** functions). We explored the concept of relative and absolute references to cells and ranges, and how to use the F4 key to cycle through the various combinations of dollar signs and cell addresses. The explanatory portion of the chapter concluded with an overview of the concept of curving course grades. Worksheet 11.1 provided practice with the points that had been explained.

Readers should now feel more comfortable moving around and selecting text in Excel worksheets, and should be somewhat accustomed now to column, row, and cell references; performing mathematical operations; and using simple Excel functions. The concept of relative and absolute references should also be clear, although when to use one or the other will probably take some time to become intuitive. Finally, readers should now be able to use Excel to calculate grades for their own classes, to assign grades automatically using lookup tables, and to curve the grades if they find it advisable to do so.

12 DESCRIPTIVE STATISTICS AND STANDARD SCORES

Introduction

This chapter provides more practice with basic functions in Excel. It begins with an overview of **descriptive statistics**, which are quantitative measures that describe how a group of scores are distributed, particularly how much they are clustered together, how much they are spread out from each other, and how the distribution of scores is shaped. This is followed by Worksheet 12.1, which provides practice calculating these statistics, and a brief discussion of the worksheet results. There is then a brief discussion of **standard scores**, followed by Worksheet 12.2, which provides practice calculating two types of standard scores (*z* **scores** and *T* **scores**).

Objectives

By the end of this chapter, readers will know or understand:

- **Frequency distributions, histograms**, and **frequency polygons**, and how they illustrate the way in which a set of scores is distributed
- The **normal distribution**, and how to describe the shape of a distribution statistically
- **Measures of central tendency** and **dispersion**
- Expected or preferred values for descriptive statistics in various types of situations
- How to calculate descriptive statistics in Excel
- Standard scores, including *z* and *T* scores
- How to calculate standard scores in Excel
- The interpretation of standard scores

Overview of Descriptive Statistics

We can divide descriptive statistics into three groups: *measures of central tendency, measures of dispersion*, and descriptions of the shape of the score distribution.

The Normal Distribution, and Describing the Shape of a Distribution

The two indicators of the shape of the score distribution are skewness and kurtosis. Before explaining these two concepts, however, it may be helpful to describe the *normal distribution* first. Figure 12.1 shows the *histogram* of a set of scores, which is a bar chart showing the *frequency distribution*, or how many students received each score. These scores have a distribution extremely close to perfect normality—which is rare or nonexistent in most real-life data—with skewness exactly equal to zero, meaning the pattern of the bars in the chart is perfectly symmetrical. The kurtosis shown in the histogram is also extremely close to zero. This level of perfection (i.e. skewness and kurtosis both exactly or almost exactly zero) is something highly unlikely to happen outside a textbook, unless we have a very large number of test takers.

Of course, if a perfectly normal distribution is not something we "normally" see, the natural question is why it is *called* a normal distribution, and why statisticians are so concerned with how normal their datasets are (or are not). That is because it is an ideal that real data will actually begin resemble as the number of people (or *cases*) in the dataset increases. Usually, if some ability has a normal distribution in the population at large, we begin see a particular group of examinees' scores begin *approaching* normality somewhere around roughly 35 cases. The larger the number of cases, the more normal the data will become. It is still rare for even relatively normal datasets to be *perfectly* normal, though—skewness and kurtosis will probably not be exactly zero, but will usually be very close, at least in norm-referenced tests. (See the section below entitled "What Are Good Values For Descriptive Statistics?" for a discussion of the distributions expected for norm- and criterion-referenced tests.) As the sample size moves up to several hundred or several thousand examinees, they will get even closer to zero, that is, to having a textbook-perfect normal distribution.

As noted above, a bar chart showing a frequency distribution is known as a histogram, as illustrated in Figure 12.1. The same distribution is reproduced as a *frequency polygon* (a line graph showing the frequency distribution) in Figure 12.2, so that it can be compared to an ideal normal distribution, which can be seen in Figure 12.3. The shape of the normal distribution is, of course, the famous bell curve. (Note that creating histograms and frequency polygons in Excel is the subject of Chapter 13.)

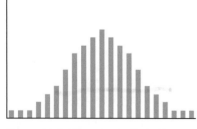

Figure 12.1 Histogram of an Almost Perfectly Normal Distribution of Scores (skewness = .000, kurtosis = .009)

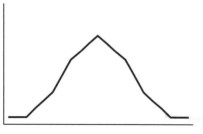

Figure 12.2 The Same Distribution as in Figure 12.1, as a Frequency Polygon (without data markers)

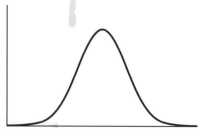

Figure 12.3 The Normal Distribution, For Purposes of Comparison

Skewness tells how far off to the left or right the "hump" is in a distribution—that is, how off-center or asymmetrical the distribution is. Figure 12.4 shows a *positively* skewed distribution—the low number of cases far to the right will skew the mean in that direction. Likewise, the distribution in Figure 12.5 is negatively skewed. With skewness, a useful mnemonic is that *the tail tells the tale.* That is, the direction in which the *tail* points (*not* the side with the "hump") is the direction of the skewness. If there is zero skewness, the distribution is by definition not skewed to the left or right, and it is symmetrical, as in the normal distribution.

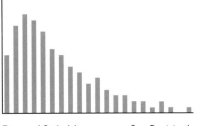

Figure 12.4 Histogram of a Positively Skewed Distribution

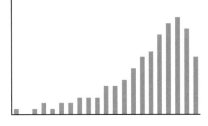

Figure 12.5 Histogram of a Negatively Skewed Distribution

The other descriptive statistic that describes distributional shapes is **kurtosis**, the degree to which the distribution is peaked or flattened. As with skewness, a perfectly normal distribution has a kurtosis of exactly zero, although these are seldom seen in real life, especially with the smaller sample sizes that most teachers work with. In fact, the example in Figure 12.1 has a kurtosis of 0.009, which means it is *very* slightly peaked in comparison to a perfectly normal distribution. Furthermore, since it is usually enough to report kurtosis (and skewness, too) to one decimal place, this nearly textbook-perfect case would normally be reported as 0.0 anyway—in other words, it would look perfectly normal, because of rounding, even though it deviates from true normality by a tiny amount.

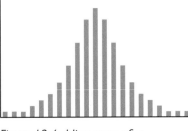

Figure 12.6 Histogram of a Distribution With Positive Kurtosis

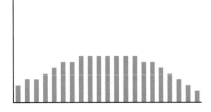

Figure 12.7 Histogram of a Distribution With Negative Kurtosis

Any time the skewness or kurtosis of a set of scores is not zero, by definition it is *somewhat* skewed or kurtotic. In real life, though, we almost never encounter perfect normality in data; the question is whether a dataset is normal *enough*. As for how to tell whether a distribution is highly skewed or kurtotic, simply from the skewness and kurtosis statistics, this is somewhat difficult. Bachman (2004: 74) recommends as a rule of thumb that if the skewness or kurtosis has an absolute value of less than two (i.e. from –2 to 2), the distribution is "reasonably normal."

Another approach is to calculate the standard error of the skewness (SES), and the standard error of the kurtosis (SEK). The skewness is divided by the SES, and if the absolute value is greater than two, the skewness is judged to be significant. In the same fashion, if the kurtosis divided by the SEK has an absolute value greater than 2, the distribution is significantly kurtotic. The formulas for calculating the SES and SEK are:

$$SES = \sqrt{\frac{6n\,(n-1)}{(n-2)(n+1)(n+3)}} \quad \text{and} \quad SEK = \sqrt{\frac{4\,(n^2-1)SES^2}{(n-3)(n+5)}}, \text{ where } n \text{ is the sample size.}$$

Finally, the degree of skewness or kurtosis can be evaluated by inspecting a histogram (a bar chart showing the distribution) or frequency polygon (a line chart showing the distribution) of the scores. Chapter 13 will address how to create these graphs in Excel.

Measures of Central Tendency

Measures of central tendency describe where most of the scores are in the distribution—that is, did students mostly receive high scores, low scores, or scores in the middle? There are three measures of central tendency. The **mean (M)** is the same as the average, the total of all the scores divided by the number of scores. The **median (Mdn)** is the middle score. Half the scores are below this point, and half are above it. It is equal to the 50th percentile, and is especially important when there are small sample sizes (below 30–35 cases, or students), or when the distribution is noticeably skewed. If there are an even number of scores, and the middle two are not equal, these two scores are averaged together to compute the median. In such cases, a fractional score is possible; in all other cases, the median is a whole number.

The median is important for low sample sizes because even if the sample is drawn from a larger population with a normal distribution (for example, all the students in a given country that are studying English at a particular level or in a particular type of program), a small sample may not be representative enough to be normal itself. For skewed data, it matters because the mean will be lowered or raised in the direction of the tail, and not as close to the center of the "hump" as might be expected. This is especially important at the classroom level, since this will almost always involve a small number of students, and scores that may not be normally distributed.

Finally, the **mode (Mo)** is the most common score. It is the peak of the "hump" of the distribution. Distributions in which there are two modes are said to be **bimodal**, as illustrated in Figure 12.8. The mode is also especially important for small samples and skewed data, and it is crucial when we are describing categorical data (for example, students' nationalities, genders, or course sections—things that cannot be ranked, only counted).

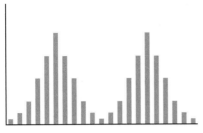

Figure 12.8 A Bimodal Distribution

Measures of Dispersion

Measures of dispersion indicate how spread out the scores are. The **standard deviation** (*s*, or SD) is analogous to the average difference between individual scores and the mean. After all, very few examinees will actually have an average score (i.e. equal to the mean). Each score will therefore be some distance from the mean, and the standard deviation gives us an idea of how far, in general, that distance is. There are two formulas for calculating the standard deviation. The *sample* formula is used when we are generalizing from one group of test takers to a larger one. The *population* formula is used when the entire group of interest is the group that took the test, and we do not wish to generalize to some larger population. By convention, the population formula is used in most classical testing estimates of reliability (see Chapter 18). The sample and population standard deviation formulas are:

$$\text{Sample: } s = \sqrt{\frac{\sum (X - M)^2}{(n\text{-}1)}} \qquad \text{Population: } s = \sqrt{\frac{\sum (X - M)^2}{N}}$$

where *s*   = the standard deviation,

   X   = each individual test score,

   M   = the mean of the test scores,

   n   = the sample size, and

   N   = the population size.

Note that both *n* and *N* refer to the number of cases being analyzed. The difference, again, is whether the standard deviation is being calculated for a sample, or a population.

Figure 12.9 illustrates the relationship between the standard deviation and the normal distribution. If a set of scores is normally distributed, roughly 68% of test takers will have scores within one standard deviation of the mean, and about 95% will have scores that are no more than two standard deviations above or below the mean. All but a fraction of a percent (0.26%) of the test takers will be within three standard deviations of the mean, when scores are normally distributed.

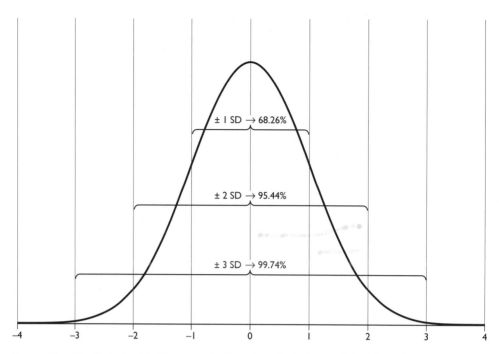

Figure 12.9 The Relationship Between the Standard Deviation and the Normal Distribution

A measure of dispersion closely related to the standard deviation is the *variance*, which is the square of the standard deviation (i.e. s^2). It is neither very useful nor easily interpretable by itself, but it is important because it is used in a number of formulas. Like the standard deviation, it has both sample and population formulas.

Another indicator of dispersion is the **semi-interquartile range**, or Q. Just as the standard deviation is related to the mean, Q is related to the median, and just as the median is especially important in skewed data or small samples, so is Q. It is therefore most regrettable that many studies ignore it. The median is the 50th percentile, or the second quartile (Q_2). The third quartile (Q_3) is the 75th percentile, and the first quartile (Q_1) is the 25th percentile. Q is equal to half the difference between the third and first quartiles: $Q = \dfrac{Q_3 - Q_1}{2}$. Note that the *semi-interquartile range* should not be confused with the interquartile range, which is simply $Q_3 - Q_1$.

The final measure of dispersion that we will discuss is the *range*, which measures the difference between the highest and lowest scores. This does not give us much information about the overall shape of the distribution, of course, since the range only tells us about the two most extreme scores, not about any of the people in between. It is still worth reporting, however, as the distance between those two end points can be important at times. Its formula is Range $= X_{high} - X_{low} + 1$, where X_{high} and X_{low} are the highest and lowest scores on the test.

What Are Good Values For Descriptive Statistics?

The short answer to this question is that it depends on what is expected or needed for a particular type of test. A norm-referenced test is expected to have a relatively normal distribution, with skewness and kurtosis relatively close to zero (as discussed above), and the measures of central tendency close together. In a sample with a perfectly normal distribution, skewness and kurtosis will be zero, and the mean, median, and mode will actually be equal. This is illustrated in Figure 12.10, an example with a perfect normal distribution. The shape of the distribution, if it is graphed in a histogram or frequency polygon, should resemble that of the normal distribution—that is, it should be shaped like the bell curve. We also expect to see the relationship between the standard deviation and percentages of test takers break out as shown in Figure 12.9—that is, that roughly 68% of the examinees will be within one standard deviation of the mean, 95% will be within two standard deviations, and nearly 100% will be within three standard deviations of the mean.

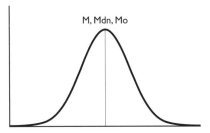

Figure 12.10 A Normal Distribution, With the Mean, Median, and Mode Equal

On the other hand, normal distributions are *not* necessarily expected for criterion-referenced tests. In fact, they are not usually expected. A CRT pre-test, administered when students are not expected to have learned the material yet, will normally have a strongly positive skewness. A CRT post-test, given when students should have mastered the content covered by the test, can be expected to have a negative skewness. In each of these cases, *how* skewed the distribution will be depends on how many **outliers** there are: students who do much better or worse than most, usually defined as those who score more than three standard deviations above or below the mean. In these cases, we may also find small standard deviations (Brown 1990).

The only times we should expect to see a normal distribution in a CRT are in cases where students at many different levels of ability will be taking the same test, particularly in placement and proficiency testing. Even then, however, this is not guaranteed; if most of the people taking a placement test have little or no background in the language, for example, they will mostly receive low scores, and we could expect to see a positively skewed distribution. Likewise, if most are at a relatively high level, but a few are at a low level, we would expect to see a negatively skewed distribution. If there are two large groups taking the test, one with mostly high-level students and the other with mostly low-level students, we should expect a bimodal distribution, unless the two groups are fairly close together.

As for whether a mean (or median, or mode) is too high or too low, this also depends on the type of test. If we expect a normal distribution, the three measures of central tendency should be close together; in fact, as mentioned in an earlier paragraph, this is often used as an indication of how normally distributed a set of scores is. If scores are negatively skewed, the mean will be somewhat lower than the median, and the median will be a bit lower than the mode (which will, of course, be at the peak of the distribution). Likewise, if scores are positively skewed, we can expect the mean to be greater than the median, and the median will be greater than the mode (again, at the peak of the "hump"). This is illustrated in Figures 12.11 and 12.12.

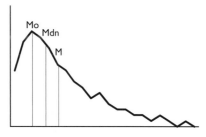   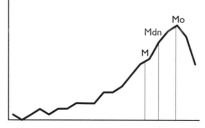

Figure 12.11 Relationships Among the Measures of Central Tendency For a Positively Skewed Set of Scores

Figure 12.12 Relationships Among the Measures of Central Tendency For a Negatively Skewed Set of Scores

Finally, if a homogeneous group is taking a test, we expect only one mode, at least if we are grouping scores into **bins** (for example, rounding scores to the nearest 5, as with 100, 95, 90, 85, etc.), which will help smooth out a certain amount of natural variability, especially in small samples. If we see multiple modes in a histogram or frequency polygon—that is, more than one "hump" in the distribution—we may have more than one group of test takers taking the same test, whether we realized they were different or not. Note, however, that by groups, I do not necessarily mean clearly recognizable groups. The students may not realize they belong to one group or the other, or may think of the groups in terms having nothing to do with the test or language ability—for example, students who study hard vs. those who do not, students who have lived in the target language country vs. those who have not, or 10th vs. 11th grade students.

Worksheet 12.1: Calculating Descriptive Statistics in Excel

Introduction

The purpose of this worksheet is to compute the total score for each student and his or her percentage correct score, and then to calculate the various descriptive statistics discussed in the first portion of this chapter.

Procedures

1 Open the file **DALT Worksheet 12-1.xls**.

2 Compute the total score for Student 1 using the **SUM** function:

   a Select cell **W2**.

   b Type **=SUM(**

   c Using the mouse or cursor (arrow) keys, select the range **B2:U2**.

   d Type **)** and press Enter.

   e **W2** should now display the number **7**.

3 Compute the percentage correct score for Student 1:

   a We could use the Excel function **COUNT** to determine how many questions there are in the test, but since the dataset is labeled clearly, it is obvious there are 20, and we will simply use that number.

   b Select cell **X2**.

   c Type **=** and select **W2**.

   d Type **/20** and press Enter.

   e **X2** should now display the value **0.35**.

   f Select **X2**, and open the **Format Cells** dialog box (go to the **Home** toolbar on the ribbon and click **Format**, then **Cells**). Click on the **Number** tab, select **Percentage**, and adjust the number of decimal places to two. Click **OK**. (Alternatively, use the **Percent Style** button on the **Home** toolbar, and the **Decrease Decimal** or **Increase Decimal** button located to the right of the **Percent Style** button, to change the formatting).

   Note that in this worksheet, all of the scores are whole numbers. This will not be the case on every test, however, which is why Step 3f is included here.

   g **X2** should now display the value **35.0%**.

4 Paste these two formulas in for all the other students:

   a Select the range **W2:X2**.

   b Copy the selection, and select the range **W2:X31**.

    c Paste

5 Compute the mean for total score:

    a Select **W33** and type **=AVERAGE(**

    b Select the range **W2:W31**.

    c Type **)** and press Enter. The answer should be **10.833**.

    d Use the **Decrease Decimal** button to make the result only show one decimal place (i.e. **10.8**).

6 Compute the median for total score:

    a Select **W34** and type **=MEDIAN(**

    b Select the range **W2:W31**.

    c Type **)** and press Enter.

    d **W34** should now display the number **11**.

7 Compute the mode for total score:

    a Select **W35** and type **=MODE(**

    b Select the range **W2:W31**, type **)**, and press Enter.

    c **W35** should now display the number **7**.

Note: At this point, the procedure for using a function and inserting a range should be relatively straightforward. Any lingering uncertainty can be addressed by consulting the worksheet file with the answers already computed (**DALT Worksheet 12-1 COMPLETED.xls**) or by viewing the tutorials on the accompanying disk. From this point on, therefore, when a function is to be inserted, directions will take the form of "Select **W33** and insert the function **=AVERAGE(W2:W31)**" for specific examples. General discussion of how to use a function will take the form of "Use the function **=AVERAGE(Range)**," where "**Range**" is the range to be selected. Formulas involving division or algebraic operations, however, will of course be explained in greater detail. As a reminder, functions can be typed in directly, or can be inserted using the **Insert Function** dialog box (covered in Chapter 11). Furthermore, recall that if functions are typed, they are not case-sensitive: Excel will automatically capitalize them for you.

8 To calculate the highest score received on this test, select **W36**, insert the function **=MAX(W2:W31)**, and press Enter. The answer should be **19**.

9 To calculate the lowest score received on this test, select **W37**, insert the function **=MIN(W2:W31)**, and press Enter. The answer should be **3**.

10 Next, to calculate the range:

    a Select **W38** and type **=**

    b Select **W36** and type **−**

    c Select **W37**, type **+1**, and press Enter.

    d The correct answer will be **17** (19 − 3 + 1 = 17).

11 To calculate the standard deviation, treating the dataset as a population:

    a Select **W39**, insert the function **=STDEVP(W2:W31)**, and press Enter. The answer should be **3.5785**.

    b Select **W39** again, and decrease the number of decimal places to one (using either the **Format Cells** dialog box or the **Decrease Decimal** button). Note how the first decimal place changes due to rounding—the spreadsheet will display **3.6**, but the additional decimals, and more, are still available if the format is changed again.

12 To calculate the standard deviation, treating the dataset as a sample taken from a larger population of interest:

    a Select **W40**, insert the function **=STDEV(W2:W31)**, and press Enter.

    b Select **W40** again, and decrease the number of decimal places to one. Note that (at three decimal places) the two estimates are quite close, differing by only .06 points. Because the difference between the formulas is whether to divide by $n - 1$ or by N, the larger the sample size, the closer the two formulas become. Conversely, the smaller the sample, the greater the difference will be between results from the two formulas.

13 To calculate the population variance, select **W41**, insert the function **=VARP(W2:W31)**, and press Enter. The answer is **12.806**. (Note that the formula for the sample variance would be **=VAR(W2:W31)**. Either formula could also be calculated by squaring the appropriate standard deviation.)

14 The 75th percentile is also the 3rd quartile. We will use the **QUARTILE** function for this, which is a two-argument function. That is, it takes the form **=QUARTILE(Range, quart)**, where **quart** is the quartile number (i.e. 1, 2, or 3). (Note that calculating the 0th quartile will return the lowest score that anyone received on the test, and calculating the 4th quartile will return the highest score on the test.) To calculate this:

    a Select **W42**.

    b Insert the function **=QUARTILE(W2:W31,3)**, and press Enter. The answer is **13**.

15 The 25th percentile is the 1st quartile. To calculate this, select **W43**, insert the function **=QUARTILE(W2:W31,1)**, and press Enter. The answer is **8**.

16 Q, the semi-interquartile range, is the difference between Q_3 and Q_1, divided by 2. To calculate this:

    a Select **W44**.

    b Type **=(**

    c Select **W42**, type **−**, and select **W43**.

    d Type **)/2** and press Enter.

    e The answer should be **2.5** ($\frac{13\text{-}8}{2} = \frac{5}{2} = 2.5$).

17 To calculate the number of test takers, select **W45**, type **=COUNT(W2:W31)**, and press Enter. The answer is **30**.

18 To calculate the skewness, select **W46**, insert the function **=SKEW(W2:W31)**, and press Enter. Normal practice is to report skewness to either one decimal place or three; I suggest reporting it to one decimal place, but formatting it to show three for the moment. The correct answer is **0.070**.

19 To calculate the standard error of the skewness (SES), we will use the square root function **=SQRT(number)**:

   a Select **W47**, and type **=SQRT((6***

   b Select **W45**, and type ***(**

   c Select **W45**, and type **−1))/((**

   d Select **W45**, and type **−2)*(**

   e Select **W45**, and type **+1)*(**

   f Select **W45**, and type **+3)))**

   g Complete formula: **=SQRT((6*W45*(W45−1))/((W45−2)*(W45+1)*(W45+3)))**

   h Press Enter. The answer is **0.4269**.

20 To test for significant skewness, divide the skewness by the SES:

   a Select **W48**, and type **=**

   b Select **W46**, and type **/**

   c Select **W47**, and press Enter. The answer is **0.1637**.

21 To calculate the kurtosis, select **W49**, insert the function **=KURT(W2:W31)**, and press Enter. The answer is **−0.1935**. As with kurtosis, we will format **W49** to show three decimal places, but will probably only report one in the end. (Note that when rounded to three decimal places, **W49** will show **−0.193**; this is because the four-digit value is actually rounded up from −0.193496.)

22 To calculate the standard error of the kurtosis (SEK):

   a Select **W50**, and type **=SQRT((4*(**

   b Select **W45**, and type **^2−1)***

   c Select **W47**, and type **^2)/((**

   d Select **W45**, and type **−3)*(**

   e Select **W45**, and type **+5)))**

   f Complete formula: **=SQRT((4*(W45^2−1)*W47^2)/((W45−3)*(W45+5)))**

   g Press Enter. The answer is **−0.8327**.

23 To test for significant kurtosis, divide the kurtosis by the SEK:

   a Select **W51**, and type **=**

   b Select **W49**, and type **/**

    c Select **W50**, and press Enter. The answer is **–0.2324**.

24 Next, we will copy the formulas we have just done, and paste them into the next column, so we have descriptive statistics for the percentage correct scores as well:

    a Select the range **W33:W51**, and copy it.

    b Select **X33**, and paste.

25 Finally, much of the second set of descriptives needs to be reformatted:

    a Select the range **X33:X44**, and open the **Format Cells** dialog box (see Chapter 11).

    b Change the number category to **Percentage**.

    c Change the number of decimal places displayed to **1**.

    d Click **OK**.

    e The range is clearly incorrect (**180.0%**). Select **X38**, and use the left mouse button to click inside the Formula Bar, at the far right side of the equation. Press Backspace once, type **.01**, and press Enter. The range will change to **81.0%**.

    f The skewness, kurtosis, and related figures will not change, but we might as well format them so that they are consistent with the adjacent values. Select **X46:X51**, open the **Format Cells** dialog box, and under the **Number** category, format the cells to display three decimal places and click **OK**.

26 You may check your answers by comparing them to the file **DALT Worksheet 12-1 COMPLETED.xls**.

Note: For ease of reference while doing future worksheets. Table 12.1 provides a summary of the formulas used in the worksheet.

Discussion

Now that the descriptives have been calculated, we should review the results briefly. The first question is how normal our data are (which is not the same thing as how good our results are!). The mean and median are close together, as we would expect in a normal distribution, and the skewness and kurtosis are both small, in terms of their sizes, and their values divided by their standard errors. Based on this, the data appear to be fairly normally distributed. The standard deviation, range, and semi-interquartile range do not really inform us much as to the normality of the score distribution; they do, however, show us that the scores are moderately spread out.

Statistic	Excel function
Total	=SUM(Range)
Mean	=AVERAGE(Range)
Median	=MEDIAN(Range)
Mode	=MODE(Range)
High score	=MAX(Range)
Low score	=MIN(Range)
Range	=MAX(Range)-MIN(Range)+1
Standard deviation (population)	=STDEVP(Range)
Standard deviation (sample)	=STDEV(Range)
Variance (population)	=VARP(Range)
Quartile (Q_1, Q_2, Q_3)	=QUARTILE(Range,Quart)
Semi-interquartile range (Q)	=(QUARTILE(Range,3)-QUARTILE(Range,1))/2
n	=COUNT(Range)
Skewness	=SKEW(Range)
SES	=SQRT((6*n*($n-1$))/(($n-2$)*($n+1$)*($n+3$)))
Kurtosis	=KURT(Range)
SEK	=SQRT((4*(n^2-1)*SES^2)/(($n-3$)*($n+5$)))

Table 12.1 Summary of Excel Functions Used in Worksheet 12.1

The mode, however, is not where we would expect it to be; with a very minor amount of positive skewness, it would be likely to be slightly lower than the median and mean, but it is not. The truth is, however, that Excel has ignored the fact that there are three modes in this dataset. There are four students each who scored 7, 8, or 10 on this test. Assumptions about distributional shapes tend to break down when there is a bimodal or trimodal distribution, as in this case. Thus, we should not be worried by the mode result, but *should* report all three modes. The fact that there are three modes would not be immediately obvious to someone reading these results, of course, which serves as an object lesson for why viewing some sort of graphical representation of the data (covered in Chapter 13), as in Figure 12.13, can be a vital step in identifying the true nature of the distribution.

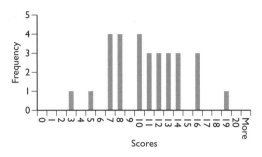

Figure 12.13 Histogram of Total Scores From Worksheet 12.1

Readers with access to a dataset of their own should try to calculate these descriptive statistics with that real-world dataset, and consider how closely the findings match what their initial impressions of the results had been. The statistics may confirm what was already suspected, but may also highlight some unexpected results as well.

Overview of Standard Scores

Standard scores are a relatively simple subject, and while this book would be incomplete without them, they are simple and straightforward enough not to need their own separate chapter. A standard score shows how far above or below the mean a test taker scored. Since this involves a comparison of each student with the rest of the test takers, they are clearly associated with NRT. A **z score** (also sometimes *z*-score, *Z* score, or *Z*-score) expresses the distance from the mean in terms of standard deviations. In other words, it tells how many standard deviations above or below the mean a student scored. A group of *z* scores will have a mean of 0 and a standard deviation of 1. Recalling Figure 12.9, then, in a normally distributed group of scores, we can expect that about 68% of the test takers will have *z* scores between 1 and –1. About 95% will have *z* scores between 2 and –2, and *nearly* 100% of the examinees will have *z* scores between 3 and –3.

While *z* scores are a useful way of comparing individuals' scores to those of the rest of the group, they are far from transparent to most people. They are therefore not, as a rule, useful for reporting scores to test users, including students, parents, and even most administrators and teachers. Any time that they *are* reported to test users, though, the scores must be accompanied by an explanation of what the scores mean—that is, that they are useful primarily as a way of comparing a test taker's score to the rest of the group's scores.

The related ***T* score** simply rescales the *z* score, so that there are fewer fractions (or none, depending on rounding) and no negative scores. One reason for using *T* scores is because receiving a below-average score can be traumatic enough for some students, and giving them negative scores might be too embarrassing or upsetting. The other reason is that they do not involve as many fractions or decimals as *z* scores, which some score users may find harder to interpret. Nevertheless, *T* scores are still not transparent, so if they are ever reported to score users, it must be explained clearly that their value lies in comparing the performance of an individual test taker with the performance of the rest of the examinees. The formulas for *z* and *T* scores are:

$$z = \frac{X - M}{s} \qquad \text{and} \qquad T = 10z + 50,$$

where   *X*   = an individual student's test score,

          M   = the mean test score, and

          s   = the standard deviation of the test scores.

Worksheet 12.2: Calculating Standard Scores in Excel

Introduction

The purpose of this worksheet is to calculate the standard scores (*z* and *T*) for the test that was analyzed previously in Worksheet 12.1.

Procedures

1   Open the file **DALT Worksheet 12-2.xls**.

2   If you feel you need to review how to calculate descriptive statistics, delete the total score, percentage correct score, and descriptive statistics from Columns W and X, and redo the steps covered in Worksheet 12.1.

3   Compute the *z* score for Student 1:

    a   Select cell **Z2**.

    b   Type **=(**, and select **W2**.

    c   Type **−**, and select **W33**.

    d   Press F4 once, type **)/**, and select **W39**.

    e   Press F4 once, and press Enter. **Z2** should display **−1.07122**.

    f   Complete formula: **=(W2−$W$33)/$W$39**

4   Select **Z2** again, and use the **Decrease Decimal** button until only one decimal place is showing (i.e. **−1.1**).

5   Compute the *T* score for Student 1:

    a   Select cell **AA2**.

    b   Type **=**, and select **Z2**.

    c   Type ***10+50**, and press Enter. **AA2** should display **39.28783**.

    d   Complete formula: **=Z2*10+50**

6 Select **AA2** again, and use the **Decrease Decimal** button until no decimals are showing (i.e. **39**).

7 Paste the two formulas in for all 30 students:

   a Select **Z2:AA2**, and copy.

   b Select **Z2:AA31**, and paste.

8 Compute selected descriptives for the two sets of standard scores:

   a Select **W33** and copy. Select **Z33:AA33** and paste.

   b Select **W39** and copy. Select **Z39:AA39** and paste.

   c Select **W45:W51** and copy. Select **Z45:AA45** and paste.

   d Reformat all the pasted cells (or select **Z33:AA51** and reformat) so that three decimal places are showing.

Discussion

Note that the means for the z and T scores are 0 and 50, and the standard deviations are 1 and 10, respectively. Note also that the skewness and kurtosis, and their standard errors, are the same. Thus, this rescaling changes the scores, but maintains the shape of the distribution.

By comparing the z scores to the mean and standard deviation, we can see that a z score of 0 indicates a student with a score equal to the mean. Examples of this are Students 16, 17, and 29, although these students' z scores have actually been rounded down from 0.047; their raw scores are 0.2 points above the mean). We can note a similar relationship with students who have raw scores of 10 points; they are 0.2 standard deviations below the mean, and they therefore have z scores of -0.2, as with Students 14, 19, 20, and 21.

The same pattern holds true for T scores as well, of course, although the relationship is less transparent than for z scores, which actually are expressed in terms of standard deviations above or below the mean.

If you have a set of actual test scores, you might try calculating z and T scores for them, and then comparing students' standard scores to their raw scores (as calculated in Worksheet 12.1). Seeing these relationships with an additional set of data may help make the relationships even clearer.

Summary

In this chapter, we have explored frequency distributions, as well as two means of representing them visually: histograms and frequency polygons. (How to create histograms and frequency polygons will be covered in Chapter 13.) We then discussed ways of describing the shape of a distribution statistically, using skewness and kurtosis. This was followed by measures of central tendency (the mean, median, and mode), and of dispersion (the standard deviation, variance, range, and semi-interquartile range). The values that are considered "good" for descriptives in various situations were also explained, with the answer depending on the testing paradigm (NRT vs. CRT) and the purpose(s) for which the test is administered. The first section of the chapter then concluded by demonstrating how to calculate descriptive statistics using Excel.

The second portion of the chapter then explained standard scores, which show how far above or below the mean a test taker's score is, in terms of standard deviations. We then learned how to calculate standard scores, and received a little practice in interpreting them.

Readers should now be able to calculate and interpret the descriptive statistics for their own testing results, and to calculate and interpret standard scores as well.

13 CREATING GRAPHS OR CHARTS IN EXCEL

Introduction

This chapter discusses two important, parallel ways to represent data visually, histograms and frequency polygons. It starts with the notion of the frequency distribution table, and then discusses several points that need to be kept in mind when creating these figures. It explains how to install the Analysis ToolPak in Excel, and then presents instructions for and practice in creating histograms and frequency polygons for a set of scores.

Objectives

By the end of this chapter, readers will know or understand:

- how scores can be grouped at regular intervals (bins, or score intervals) for greater manageability
- the ways in which histograms and frequency polygons (whether with or without data markers) provide similar but different views of the distribution
- how to install the Analysis ToolPak in Excel, if it is not already installed
- how to create a histogram in Excel, and then reformat and resize it
- how to convert a histogram to a frequency polygon in Excel.

Overview of Visual Representations of Data

As we saw in Worksheet 12.1, sometimes descriptive statistics do not present the entire picture, and we must see a graph of the score distribution to gain a full understanding of the pattern of results on a test. The first step in doing this is to create a frequency distribution, a table showing how many test takers received each score. This can be done manually with paper and pencil, using tally marks, or it can be done using the Excel function **COUNTIF**, as in Worksheet 11.1, when we counted the number of students receiving each grade. A third approach is to let Excel do the counting automatically, as part of the **Histogram** add-in, as will be explained below. Table 13.1 provides an example of a frequency distribution, one which may be familiar to readers.

Score	Frequency	Score	Frequency	Score	Frequency
0	0	7	4	14	3
1	0	8	4	15	0
2	0	9	0	16	3
3	1	10	4	17	0
4	0	11	3	18	0
5	1	12	3	19	1
6	0	13	3	20	0

Table 13.1 Example of a Frequency Distribution

The frequency distribution in Table 13.1 lists all the possible scores on this test, from 0 to 20; of course. Sometimes, however, we need to group scores together, rather than reporting them for each individual score. This is particularly true when scores are reported on a scale of 0–100. Unless we want to have a 100-column table, we should group the scores at regular intervals, which will make them more manageable. It will also make any graphs that are based on the frequency distribution clearer and easier to read. These groupings are sometimes called *score intervals*, but Excel calls them *bins*, which will be the term I use here for the sake of clarity and consistency. If the term is confusing, just keep in mind that we are sorting the scores, just as we might sort apples or shoes by their sizes.

What size to use for the bins depends in part on how many different scores were possible, and also on keeping the number of bins reasonable. Guilford and Fruchter (1978) recommend that in general, 10–20 bins is most appropriate, with 10–15 probably the most common range. On a 10-item quiz, 11 bins are probably best, as the scale is already compact. That is, with only 11 possible scores (0–10), there are not many bins to begin with; therefore, if reduced the number (to, say, five bins), too many scores might be lumped together, and we might lose important detail. If a group of scores ranges from 0 to 100, ten-point bins might be too large, but two points might be too small; I would therefore tend to use five-point bins (i.e. 21 bins of five points apiece) in that situation.

Once the frequency distribution has been added up, it is possible to graph it. A histogram is a bar chart (usually with vertical bars) of the frequency distribution. A frequency polygon is a line graph of the frequency distribution—often with data markers, but not always. Figure 13.1 provides an example of a histogram, and Figures 13.2 and 13.3 illustrate a frequency polygon for the same distribution, both with and without data markers (respectively). When there are gaps in the distribution, as in this case, a histogram may be easier to interpret.

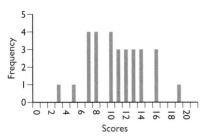

Figure 13.1 Example of a Histogram

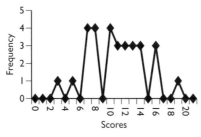

Figure 13.2 Example of a Frequency Polygon, With Data Markers

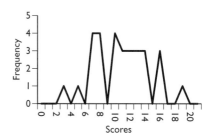

Figure 13.3 Example of a Frequency Polygon Without Data Markers

When the distribution is relatively smooth, however, with no "gaps", a frequency polygon can provide a very clear view of the data (see Figure 13.4). Whether to use data markers is a subjective choice, but in general, the closer together the data points or bins, the more crowded and distracting they become, unless the markers are resized. Figures 13.4–13.6 contrast a "frequency polygon-friendly" distribution: without markers, with markers at the Excel default size, and with smaller markers, respectively.

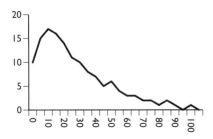

Figure 13.4 Example of a Frequency Polygon For a Relatively Smooth Distribution, No Data Markers

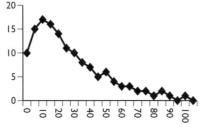

Figure 13.5 Example of a Frequency Polygon For a Relatively Smooth Distribution, Data Markers at Default Size

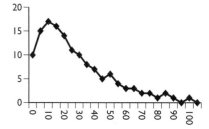

Figure 13.6 Example of a Frequency Polygon For a Relatively Smooth Distribution, Data Markers 20% Smaller Than Default Size

As was already mentioned, it is important to select an appropriate bin size for histograms (and frequency polygons). The effect that bin size can have on the usability of the graph becomes truly apparent, though, when different sizes are compared side by side. Figures 13.7–13.11 show the same distribution as Figures 13.1–13.3, but converted to percentage correct metric. They illustrate the effects of having bins at 1, 2, 5, and 10 percentage point intervals. Note, however, that the horizontal axis in each histogram uses the same scale, making these comparisons easy to evaluate. The histogram with five-point bins (Figures 13.9 and 13.11), seems the best. Unlike Figure 13.10, it has the same shape as the ones with smaller bins, but is easier to read than Figures 13.7 and 13.8, given that the bars do not need to be so thin in order to squeeze in room for up to 101 of them (from 0 to 100). (Admittedly, this is in part because the scores are all in 5% increments. Nevertheless, even if they were not, the degree of consolidation from one- to five-point bins would be less than that from one to ten.) Keep in mind, however, that with a smaller distribution, ten points might prove more appropriate, and with a larger sample and larger view of the histogram, one- or two-point bin sizes *might* prove optimal.

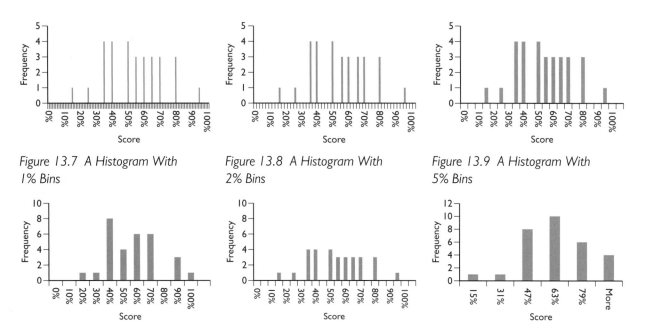

Figure 13.7 A Histogram With 1% Bins

Figure 13.8 A Histogram With 2% Bins

Figure 13.9 A Histogram With 5% Bins

Figure 13.10 A Histogram With 10% Bins

Figure 13.11 A Histogram With 5% Bins, Vertical Axis Rescaled to 0–10 For Comparison with Figure 13.10

Figure 13.12 A Histogram With Bins Generated Automatically by Excel, and Reformatted to Percentages

Figure 13.12 shows the effect for the same dataset of not selecting bins in advance, but allowing Excel to assign them automatically instead. As we can see, having bins that are only 1 or 2% percent "wide" is not very practical, especially with this small sample. With a very large sample it might be more productive, but we would need the histogram to be rather large for that level of detail to be clear enough to be useful. Allowing Excel to automatically create the bins does not seem like a very good idea, as 16-point intervals are not very intuitive. Furthermore, we lose all indication that no students had scores close to either end of the distribution, and the very shape of the histogram is markedly different, even when compared to one using ten-point bins. It should be pointed out that the histogram in Figure 13.12 has "More" as its last category on the horizontal axis. This is actually the default setting in Excel, although there will never be any cases in the "More" bin if there are no scores in the dataset that are larger than the top bin. The procedure for deleting "More" will be discussed below in the directions for Worksheet 13.1.

Finally, taken together, Figures 13.9–13.11 illustrate another important point. The vertical axis must be kept constant if two histograms are to be compared. For example, it may not be obvious at first glance that Figures 13.9 and 13.10 are *not* comparable—but in fact, the bars in 3.9 should only be half the height of those in 13.10. This becomes apparent when the five- and ten-point bin histograms use the same scale for the vertical axis, as in Figures 13.10 and 13.11. This error when comparing histograms, or even when reporting histograms together, can obscure the actual patterns of the data. Doing it deliberately is a form of lying with statistics.

Preparing Excel For Histogram Analyses

To create a histogram in Excel, we can manually create a frequency distribution, and then manually create the chart from scratch. This is much more complicated than simply using the Excel **Histogram** tool. This is not usually available in Excel, however, when it is first installed, but it is a free component that comes with Excel, as part of the Data Analysis ToolPak. If the Data Analysis ToolPak has not been installed or unpacked yet, it must be before continuing any further. This may require the program disk that came with Microsoft Office, or it may not—it is very difficult to predict. Whether you will need the disk does not seem to depend on your version of Excel or Windows, or on which computer you are using. If the disk is required, follow the instructions, which are fairly minimal and straightforward. Note, however, that the procedures are somewhat different, for installing the Analysis ToolPak in Excel 2007 and 2003.

Installing the Analysis ToolPak in Excel 2007

1   Click on the **Office** Button (see Figure 11.1), and then click on **Excel Options**, near the bottom right of the menu. This will open the **Excel Options** dialog box.

2   Click on **Add-Ins**, in the list on the left side of the dialog box.

3   At the bottom of the dialog box, there will be a pull-down menu next to the word **Manage**. Select **Excel Add-Ins**, and click **Go**.

4   A new dialog box will appear with a list of the add-ins that are available. Click the check box next to **Analysis ToolPak**, and then click **OK**.

5   A dialog box may pop up saying that it is not installed, and asking if you would like to install it now. Click **Yes**.

6   Shortly after, you may be prompted to insert the program disk for Microsoft Office. Follow the directions on the screen if you are.

7   Once it is installed, a new section labeled **Analysis**, with one wide button (**Data Analysis**), should appear at the right end of the **Data** toolbar. If it is *not* visible, close all copies of Excel, restart the program, and it should be there. If it is not, try installing it again.

Installing the Analysis ToolPak in Excel 2003

The procedure for Excel 2003 is slightly simpler than for 2007.

1   Click on the **Tools** menu, select **Add-Ins**, and a dialog box will appear.

2   Click the check box next to **Analysis ToolPak**, and then click **OK**.

3   A dialog box may pop up saying that it is not installed, and asking if you would like to install it now. Click **Yes**.

4   Shortly after, you may be prompted to insert the program disk for Microsoft Office. Follow the directions on the screen if you are.

Installing the Analysis ToolPak in Excel for the Macintosh

Note that Excel 2008 for Macintosh does not include the Analysis ToolPak, but that free software is available—and recommended by Microsoft—that can create histograms (see Microsoft Corporation, n. d.).

1   Depending on the version of Excel being used, open either the **File** menu and select **Options** → **Add-Ins**, or the **Tools** menu and select **Add-Ins**.

2   Click the check box next to **Analysis ToolPak**, and then click **OK**.

3   A dialog box may pop up saying that it is not installed, and asking if you would like to install it now. Click **Yes**.

4   Shortly after, you may be prompted to insert the program disk for Microsoft Office. Follow the directions on the screen if you are.

Worksheet 13.1: Creating a Histogram and a Frequency Polygon in Excel

Introduction

Once it is installed, the **Histogram** tool is fairly simple in Excel, and requires only a small amount of preparation. In fact, formatting the resulting graphs (the "chart output," in Excel terminology) so that they are more easily read, and will print and photocopy more clearly, is in reality far more complicated than actually creating the histogram. This worksheet will consist of three phases: setting up the bins and creating the histogram, reformatting the histogram, and copying the histogram and converting that copy to a frequency polygon.

Procedures

Setting up the Bins and Creating the Histogram

1   Open the file **DALT Worksheet 13-1.xls**.

2   Decide on the appropriate bin size for the variable(s) for which you wish to create a histogram. If you think you will need to compare several different sizes of bins, prepare them in columns next to each other before beginning; when creating multiple histograms, a worksheet tends to fill up rather quickly, and not being systematic from the start is virtually *guaranteed* to lead to confusion

over which histogram is which. Here, however, we will only need one set of bins, running from 0–20 in one-point increments:

a Select **AC1**, type **Bins**, and press Enter.

b Select **AC2**, type **0**, and press Enter.

c Select **AC3**, type **=**, and select **AC2**.

d Type **+1**, and press Enter.

e Select and copy **AC3**.

f Select **AC3:AC22**, and paste.

3 Select **AF2**. You will have to re-select this cell in a few moments (in Step 8), but it will be outlined when you are looking for it, making it less likely that you will accidentally misplace your new frequency distribution table and histogram on top of something you did not want to delete.

4 Save the file now, in case you skip Step 8. This will allow you to close and reopen the file, undoing any damage that resulted.

5 Open the **Histogram** dialog box:

a To open the **Histogram** dialog box in Excel 2007, click on the **Data** tab of the Ribbon, and at the right end of the toolbar, click on the button labeled **Data Analysis**. Select **Histogram**, and click **OK**.

b To open the **Histogram** dialog box in Excel 2003, click on the **Tools** menu, select **Data Analysis**, select **Histogram**, and click **OK**.

6 The **Input Range** text box should be selected; whether it is or not, however, click on the gray button with a red arrow that is next to it. Select **W2:W31**, which will automatically appear as **$W$2:$W$31**, without your having to press F4. Click the button with the red arrow again, and the dialog box will reappear.

7 Click on the gray button with the red arrow that is next to the **Bin Range** text box. Select **AC2:AC22**, which, like the previous range, will automatically be formatted as **$AC$2:$AC$22**. Click the button with the red arrow again, and the dialog box will reappear.

8 This step is easy to skip, but doing so can wreak havoc on your spreadsheet. Skipping it will often result in overwriting the last histogram created, and/or rendering the previous one useless. Select whether to have the histogram and its accompanying frequency distribution table appear in a new workbook (i.e. a new Excel file), a new worksheet within the current workbook, or somewhere in the current worksheet. We will proceed on the assumption that it is wanted in the current worksheet. The address we specify is where the top left corner of our output (i.e. the frequency distribution table and histogram) will appear.

a Click the **Output Range** radio button.

b Click the gray button with the red arrow next to the **Output Range** text box.

c Find the cell that is highlighted—in this case, it should be **AF2**. This seems like a good place to put the new output, so click on it, *even though it already has the heavy black line around it*. After you do, it should have both the heavy black line and the dancing dashed line. As before, the selection should be automatically changed to **$AF$2**. If you decide you want the top left corner of the output to go somewhere else, select that other cell instead. It will only have the dancing dashed line, but it will be selected.

d Click the gray button with the red arrow, and the dialog box will reappear. If something long or strange (for example, a backwards range selection) appears in the text box, try this step again. The text box should only contain the address of a single cell.

9 Click the checkbox next to **Chart Output**; otherwise, you will only get a frequency distribution table, *with no histogram*.

10 Click **OK**. Your frequency distribution table and histogram should now appear. The entire frequency distribution table will be selected; deselect it by clicking an empty cell before typing anything. (Note that if the dataset changes, the frequency distribution table will *not* automatically update. You must use the **Histogram** tool again, although doing so *without* chart output and selecting the same output range will let you preserve any formatting changes you have already made to the chart itself, assuming the bins do not change.)

Reformatting the Histogram

The histogram that Excel creates is not really quite what we want to paste into a report, and in fact, wastes space within the chart with unnecessary components. This can be fixed, though. The process is not difficult, but it does require an annoying number of steps. These steps are not exactly the same in the 2003 and 2007 versions of Excel.

11 We do not need the **Histogram** title inside this graph. Most style guides require separate figure captions. It is also a very poor caption (A better caption might be "Histogram of Total Scores on an Imaginary Test," or something along those lines), and it takes up extra space that could be occupied by the graph. Therefore, delete the title:

a Move your mouse cursor over the word **Histogram**, and when you see a four-headed arrow, left-click one time, and press the `Delete` button.

b Alternatively, right-click the text, and in the context menu, click **Delete**.

12 If there are multiple datasets in the same graph, it is important to have a legend with which to tell them apart. This is not the case here, so delete the legend (the box to the right of the histogram, with a blue box and the word **Frequency**), following the same method as in Step 11.

13 Change the color of the bars, so they will print and copy more clearly.

a Right-click the bars in the graph. If you have successfully clicked the right place, the context menu will include the option **Format Data Series**. (If you see **Format Plot Area** or **Format Chart Area**, you have clicked the wrong spot, and need to try again.)

b Left-click on **Format Data Series**, which opens the **Format Data Series** dialog box.

c Change the color of the bars:

    i *In Excel 2007:* select the **Fill** option on the left side of the dialog box. Select **Solid fill**, click on the **Color** button (the one with a paint bucket), and select a shade of gray or black. Click on **OK**. (Note that the examples in this chapter all use Black, Text 1, Lighter 50%, the second option of the second column under Theme Colors.)

    ii *In Excel 2003:* select the **Patterns** tab at the top of the dialog box. Select a shade of gray or black, and click on **OK**.

14 Resize the histogram, so it is as small or large as you want it to appear in its final form.

a Click on the outside border of the chart. In each corner, and in the middle of each side, there will be a group of dots (Excel 2007) or a black square (Excel 2003). It is possible to manually resize by clicking and dragging one of these locations, but this risks changing the proportions (height vs. width) of the histogram unintentionally, making it more difficult to keep consistent dimensions if several histograms are going to be used. If you resize in this way, make sure you are happy with the aspect ratio—although you can correct it exactly later on, if you use Excel 2007.

b *In Excel 2007:* Lock the aspect ratio (i.e. ratio of height to width) of the chart, to prevent accidentally changing it:

    i Click on the chart, and then on the **Format** tab of the Ribbon.

    ii On the far right side of the **Format** toolbar, use the height and width text boxes to adjust the size of the histogram to 1.57″ x 2.57″ (3.99 cm x 6.53 cm).

    iii Click on the **Size and Properties** dialog box launcher (at the far right end of the toolbar).

    iv In the **Size and Properties** dialog box, on the **Size** tab, find the **Lock aspect ratio** checkbox. If it is in dark type, proceed to Step 14.b.v. If it is in gray type, click **Close**, click the outer border of the chart once (while the four-headed arrow is visible), and reopen the **Size and Properties** dialog box. The **Lock aspect ratio** checkbox should now be in dark type, not gray.

    v Once the **Lock aspect ratio** checkbox is visible in dark type, click the checkbox, and click **Close**. The proportions of the chart will now remain the same when it is shrunk or enlarged.

vi   Note that once the chart is pasted into Word or PowerPoint, the aspect ratio will come unlocked. The procedure for locking it again will be the same as in Excel.

vii   You can now change the size of the histogram either by clicking and dragging a corner, or by changing the height and width numbers on the **Format** toolbar. (Note that this toolbar is *only* visible when you have selected the chart.) Using the actual numbers can be very handy if you are attempting to make two or more histograms exactly the same size, as in Figures 13.1–13.12.

viii   If you have specific dimensions you decide to apply later, you may have to unlock the aspect ratio temporarily. Go back into the **Size and Properties** dialog box, unlock the aspect ratio, and then adjust the size the way you want. Then re-lock it.

c   *In Excel 2003:* it is not possible to lock the aspect ratio Excel 2003, so any changes in size must be made carefully. On the other hand, once they are pasted into Word, Excel 2003 charts do have their aspect ratios locked if resizing is done with the corner squares (*not* with the ones in the middle of each side). In another difference between versions, Excel 2003 charts cannot be edited—only resized as a whole—once pasted into Word, since in effect they are then treated as pictures. This is not the case for Excel 2007 charts pasted into Word, though, as these can be edited in either program.

15 Reformat the horizontal axis title, and change it from **Bin** to something more graceful.

a   Position the mouse cursor over the axis title. A four-headed arrow should appear. Left-click the text once, and the outline of a text box will appear.

b   Select the word **Bin**, either by double-clicking it, or by clicking and dragging across it.

c   Change the formatting so it is not **bold** anymore, and type something more descriptive, such as **Score**. Change the font if you do not like it (**Arial**, Calibri, and similar sans serif fonts are best)

d   If the axis title is too large or too small now that you have resized the chart, adjust the font size accordingly. Do not go below 8-point font, however, because anything smaller will be illegible. For this activity, practice by resizing the font to 8 points. Open the context menu by right-clicking the axis title:

i   *In Excel 2007:* choose **Font**, which will open the **Font** dialog box, where all changes except the content of the text can be made.

ii   *In Excel 2003:* choose **Format Axis Title** from the context menu, click on the **Font** tab, and then make the changes.

e   You can also change the font formatting a different way, using a dialog box. This is particularly important when using Excel 2003:

In Excel 2007:

i Right-click the axis title, and select **Font** from the context menu. This will open the **Font** dialog box.

ii Adjust the font, font style, and size using this dialog box, and click on **OK**.

In Excel 2003:

i Right-click the axis title, and select **Format Axis Title** from the context menu.

ii Click on the **Font** tab, and adjust the font, font style, and size as in Excel 2007.

iii Make sure the **Auto scale** checkbox (bottom left of the dialog box) is unchecked. If it is turned on, this feature will automatically adjust the size of the axis label when you enlarge or reduce the histogram; if you already know how large you want a label to be, this is undesirable. (Note: You will not *always* adjust chart size before reformatting axis labels, so **Auto scale** *can* undo your formatting changes if you do not turn it off. Whether it will turn on automatically can be unpredictable.)

f If you accidentally delete the axis title, you can use **Undo**, or if you notice too late and need to reinsert it, you can recreate it:

In Excel 2007:

i Click anywhere on the chart, and then select the **Layout** tab of the Ribbon.

ii Click the **Axis Titles** button, and select **Primary Horizontal Axis Title**.

iii Click on **Title Below Axis**.

iv Start again from Step 15a.

In Excel 2003:

i Right-click a clear spot near the bottom of the chart, and select **Chart Options** from the context menu.

ii Select the **Titles** tab of the **Chart Options** dialog box.

iii Type the axis title in the textbox for **Category (X) axis**, and click **OK**.

16 To reformat the vertical axis title, repeat Step 15 for that axis title as well, except for changing the wording of the title, which does not need to be changed. Adjust the axis title to 8-point regular font.

17 The procedure for formatting the font used on the horizontal axis is the same as for the axis title (i.e. follow Step 15), but there are additional things to format on the axis itself:

a   If the label "More" appears at the end of the horizontal axis, it can be deleted by deleting the word from the frequency distribution table. (If there are no scores higher than the highest bin, after all, it is hardly necessary to keep this category.) To see an example with "More" in the histogram, see Figure 13.12.

b   Right-click the horizontal axis labels, and select **Format Axis** from the context menu. This will open the **Format Axis** dialog box. Note that the Excel 2003 version of the **Format Axis** dialog box is less powerful, but is also simpler. The 2007 version has a list of formatting categories on the left side; the 2003 version has a group of tabs at the top. In the change to 2007, besides adding shadow and 3D effects (which should only be used if they will not interfere with clarity!), the various functions were regrouped. Most notably, the tick mark options moved from **Patterns** to **Axis Options**, and (in a step away from usability), editing the font was moved to a separate dialog box (as discussed in Step 15 above).

c   It is usually best to leave the tick mark options (**Axis Options** in 2007, **Scale** in 2003) largely alone, except for their scaling—that is, the distances between the tick marks. An important detail is that the intervals or interval units, or number of categories between tick marks or tick mark labels, are in terms of *bins*. In other words, "one" does not mean one *point*, necessarily; it means one *bin*. If the bins are each five points "wide," then an interval or category distance of one means five points. What values to use in setting these tick marks and labels depends on how crowded the axis labels will be. (See, for example, Figures 13.7–13.10, which use the same axis labels for varying numbers of tick marks and bin sizes.)

   i   Experiment with adjusting the interval unit (Excel 2007) or number of categories (Excel 2003) between labels to **1**.

   ii   One interval unit or category between labels is too crowded to be easily read, so reverse the change, so that there are two units or categories between labels (i.e. there are labeled tick marks for all even numbers and zero, and unlabeled tick marks for all odd numbers).

d   The axis labels will look better if they are rotated 180°:

   i   Click on **Alignment**.

   ii   *In Excel 2007*, change the text direction to **Rotate all text 90°**.

   In Excel 2003, click on the red diamond and drag it down to **−90°**.

e   If the number of decimal places needs to be changed:

   i   Click on the **Number** tab or section.

   ii   Select the appropriate choice under **Category** (usually **Number** or **Percentage**).

   iii   Adjust the number of decimal places, and click **OK**.

f No further reformatting of the horizontal axis seems necessary right now, so click **Close** (Excel 2007) or **OK** (Excel 2003).

18 Essentially the same procedures are followed in reformatting the vertical axis, except that the text alignment does not need changing, and there are more options for the tick marks and labels on the vertical axis. (The greater number of options is because the units on the horizontal axis have already been specified by the bins.)

a Open the **Format Axis** dialog box, and click on **Axis Options** (Excel 2007) or the **Scale** tab (Excel 2003). In these sections, we can set the values for the minimum value on the axis, the maximum value displayed, the major unit, and the minor unit.

b If, for some reason, we have gotten decimals, this needs to be corrected. (This is a rare problem, but it does seem to happen occasionally.) Some charts might be allowed to have fractions on the vertical axis, but in a histogram, this is not possible (i.e. there can be no half students!). We should also set an appropriate maximum value—we will use 10 in this example.

In Excel 2007:

i Click on the **Fixed** radio button for **Maximum**, and type **10** in the text box. This will make the top of the scale stop at 10.

ii Click on the **Fixed** radio button for **Major unit**, and type **2** in the text box. This will give us labels and tick marks at 0, 2, 4, 6, 8, and 10.

iii Click on the **Fixed** ratio button for **Minor unit**, and type **1** in the text box. Then click on the pull-down menu next to **Minor tick mark type** and select **Outside**. This will give us unlabeled tick marks between each of the labeled ones.

iv Click on **Close**.

In Excel 2003:

i *Un*check the checkbox next to **Maximum**, and type **10** in the text box.

ii Uncheck the checkbox next to **Major unit**, and type **2** in the text box. This will give us labels and tick marks at 0, 2, 4, 6, 8, and 10.

iii Uncheck the checkbox next to **Minor unit**, and type **1** in the text box.

iv Click on the **Patterns** tab, and click on the **Outside** radio button under **Minor tick mark type**. This will give us unlabeled tick marks between each of the labeled ones.

v Click on **OK**.

Copying a Histogram and Converting the Copy to a Frequency Polygon

Now that we have created and reformatted the histogram, we will make a matching frequency polygon, which will be scaled in the same way as the histogram.

19 Select the chart, copy it, select cell **AI12**, and paste. A new histogram should appear, identical to the first one. (Note that any empty cell just below the histogram would do; **AI12** was an arbitrary choice.)

20 Right-click the new histogram, but not on the bars, and select **Change Chart Type** (Excel 2007) or **Chart Type** (Excel 2003) from the context menu.

21 Select **Line with Markers**, and click on **OK**.

22 Next, we will change the color of the line and data markers:

In Excel 2007:

a Right-click the line and data markers, and select **Format Data Series**.

b Click on **Line Color**, and select the **Solid line** radio button.

c Click on the **Color** button (the one with the paint bucket), and select the same color as for the histogram earlier (**Black, Text 1, Lighter 50%**, which looks like dark gray; the second color in the second column).

d Click on **Marker Fill**, and select the **Solid fill** radio button.

e Click on the **Color** button, and select the same color as in 22.c.

f Click on **Marker Line Color** (this is the color of the line that surrounds the marker—not changing this will give us gray markers with tiny blue borders), and select the **Solid line** radio button.

g Click on the **Color** button, and select the same color as in Steps 22.c. and 22.e.

h If the marker size needs to be changed, click **Marker Options**, select the **Built-in** radio button, and adjust the size as necessary. For practice, reduce the size to 5 points. (**Marker Type**, or shape, can be changed here as well, if desired, using the pull-down menu.)

i Click **Close**.

In Excel 2003:

a Right-click the line and data markers, and select **Format Data Series**.

b Click on the **Patterns** tab.

c Under **Line**, select the **Custom** radio button.

d Use the **Color** pull-down menu to change the line color to dark gray.

e Under **Marker**, select the **Custom** radio button.

f Use the **Foreground** and **Background** pull-down menus to select dark gray. (**Marker Style**, or shape, can be changed here as well, if desired, using the pull-down menu.)

g If the marker size needs to be changed, change the number next to **Size**. For practice, reduce the size to 5 points.

h Click **OK**.

Discussion

As noted earlier, creating histograms is actually fairly simple. It is the formatting that is tricky, but only because of the number of small details, not because any one of the features is actually difficult. Once the histograms have been created, they can be copied and pasted into Word or PowerPoint for use in reports or presentations.

One final point to keep in mind when using Office 2007 is that often, even after pasting into a different application, if the frequency distribution table changes in Excel, the histogram or frequency polygon in Word or PowerPoint will be updated to match the revised data.

As with Chapter 12, if you have access to some real test data, you may find it further instructive to compare the descriptive statistics and standard scores with a histogram and/or frequency polygon of the scores.

Summary

In this chapter, we began by looking at how to group scores at regular intervals, with the size of the bins (or score intervals) depending largely on the number of points possible. We also saw how histograms and frequency polygons provide similar but different views of a given distribution. Following this, we covered how to install the Analysis ToolPak in Excel, if it was not already installed. We then learned how to create histograms in Excel, as well as how to reformat and resize them, and how to convert histograms to frequency polygons.

14 CORRELATION

Introduction

This chapter discusses the concept of correlation. It begins with a brief explanation of the levels of data, or types of variables, and then discusses which **correlation coefficients** are appropriate to use with each type of variable. The relationship between correlation and item discrimination (see Chapters 5, 15, and 16 for detailed coverage of item discrimination) for both norm- and criterion-referenced testing will be introduced, and then Worksheet 14.1 will provide instructions for and practice in using Excel to calculate two different correlation coefficients.

Objectives

By the end of this chapter, readers will know or understand:

- what **correlation** is
- what the various **levels of data** are, and how they relate to correlation
- **Pearsonian correlation coefficients**
- how to calculate two types of correlation coefficients (*Pearson* r and *Spearman* ρ) in Excel.

Overview of Correlation

Correlation is the degree of relationship between two sets of numbers. For example, if two sets of test scores are highly correlated, then students with high scores on one test will have high scores on the other test as well. Similarly, students with low scores on one test will have low scores on the other. A negative correlation indicates an inverse relationship. In other words, when one set of scores is high, the other is low. Obviously, if two tests are supposed to measure the same thing and have a negative correlation, there is something very wrong. (Of course, if they have no correlation at all, something is wrong as well.)

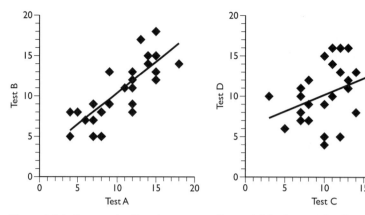

Figure 14.1 Scatterplot Showing a Strong Correlation (r = .799) Between Two Sets of Test Scores, With Trendline

Figure 14.2 Scatterplot Showing a Moderate Correlation (r = .436) Between Two Sets of Scores, With Trendline

Correlation can be examined by looking at a scatterplot, the type of graph shown in Figures 14.1 and 14.2, but the interpretation of such graphs is naturally rather subjective. For example, in looking at Figure 14.1 we can obviously see that Test A and Test B are measuring similar things; in fact, they may be intended to measure the same construct, and could even be parallel forms of the same test. For Test C and Test D in Figure 14.2, however, we might miss the relationship entirely if not for the trendline helping illustrate it; even so, the data points do not adhere to the trendline very closely, which is of course why the correlation coefficient is barely half the size of that between Tests A and B. Rather than depend upon human eyes and judgment alone, then, we also need to calculate a *correlation coefficient*, a mathematical estimate of the strength of relationship between two sets of numbers. A correlation coefficient of 0.0 means there is no relationship at all, and a correlation of 1.0 means there is a perfect relationship between the scores. A correlation of –1.0 means there is a perfect *inverse* relationship. A correlation of .436, as in Figure 14.2, indicates that the two sets of scores are probably measures of related or similar abilities, but are also assessing rather different things. (Note that poor reliability for one or both tests will also depress a correlation coefficient; see Thorndike and Hagen 1969.) If Tests C and D are intended to be assessing the same abilities, they were likely written with rather different specifications, assuming there were no major issues with the quality of the tests. Alternatively, there may have been other intervening factors that influenced scores on one of the tests, such as half the class sitting in bad chairs during one test, and the other half sitting in the bad chairs during the other test.

Levels of Data

There are a number of different correlation coefficients, each with its own formula. In order to know which one is most appropriate, we must first determine what level of data we are working with. The term **levels of data** refers to the types of variables we are correlating.

The lowest level of data is **categorical variables**, sometimes called *nominal* variables. These are variables that can be grouped into categories, but the categories cannot be put in any sort of meaningful order. Examples include gender, native language, country of origin, and favorite color. All we can do is to count the number of people in each category.

When two dichotomous categorical variables are correlated with each other, we should use the **tetrachoric correlation coefficient**, or the ϕ (phi, pronounced *fee*) *coefficient*. In this book, we will deal with ϕ, among other reasons because it is much simpler to calculate than the tetrachoric.

Two polytomous categorical variables can be correlated using polychoric correlation coefficients. However, this book will only be concerned with dichotomous categorical variables, which are important in estimating item discrimination for criterion-referenced tests.

The next level of data is **ordinal variables**. These are variables where different levels—*ordered* categories essentially—can be observed, and put in some sort of order, or ranked. In fact, ordinal variables are often assumed to be rankings, although this is not always the case. We do not assume that the distances between different levels of an ordinal variable are the same. For example, if we are ranking students based on how well they did on a test, the difference between the students with the highest and second-highest scores may not be the same as between the second- and third-highest-scoring students. Besides class standings, other examples of ordinal data are percentiles (a form of ranking), and most ratings on speaking or writing tests, since there are usually not many levels on the scale and the distances between the score bands are not always the same in terms of amount of ability.

When we correlate two ordinal variables, we can use **Kendall's τ (tau)**, or more commonly, the **Spearman rank-order correlation coefficient**, or **Spearman ρ (rho)**. Worksheet 14.1 includes practice calculating the Spearman ρ. Its formula is $\rho = 1 - \dfrac{6 \times \sum D^2}{n(n^2 - 1)}$, where D is the difference between a student's rankings on two different tests, and n is the sample size.

The third level of data is **interval variables**. These are variables which are arranged in order, as with ordinal data, but there are equal distances between each point on the scale. These variables take their name from the fact that they tell us how wide the interval is between score points (Brown 1988), and the difference between each pair of score points is equal (for example, the distance from 99% to 98% is the same as from 98% to 97%). In virtually every case, an interval variable is also a **continuous variable**, that is, a variable that can have any value within a particular range, with the range typically fairly large (Allen and Yen 1979; Bachman 2004). Considering the number of levels of the variable is therefore one way to help separate them from ordinal variables.

It is *not* the number of potential values alone that makes the variable interval, though. For example, as noted previously, percentile scores are ordinal, in spite of having a large number of gradations, since they are a form of ranking. Similarly, there are hundreds of native languages in the world, but a student's L1 is still a categorical variable, since languages cannot be rank-ordered. On the other hand, test scores that are reported in terms of the number of questions answered correctly, or percentage correct, are generally examples of interval data. Also, although a single rating (for speaking or writing) is almost always an ordinal variable, if enough of them are added (or averaged) together, the resulting variable may qualify as an interval variable.

To correlate two interval variables, we use the **Pearson product-moment correlation coefficient**, or **Pearson *r***. For *r* to be truly appropriate, however, both variables need to have relatively normal distributions (see Chapter 12). In the case of severe non-normality, ρ should be calculated instead. (See Allen and Yen 1978; Bachman 2004; and Brown 1988 for discussions of other requirements for correlational studies, including factors that can cause results to be meaningless or uninterpretable.)

The final, and highest, level of data is **ratio variables**. Ratio variables are like interval variables, in that there is an equal distance between each pair of points on the scale, but a ratio variable also includes a true zero point. For that reason, ratio variables are somewhat rare in language learning research and testing. For instance, if a student gets zero points on a proficiency test, that does not necessarily mean that he has absolutely zero mastery of the language, any more than scoring 100% makes a learner 100% proficient in the language. Age can be a ratio variable, as can age of arrival in a country (a variable of interest in some second language acquisition research). There are few other examples in language teaching and learning, though. Ratio variables are also correlated using Pearson *r*.

Pearsonian Correlation Coefficients

The term **Pearsonian correlation coefficients** is used from time to time in describing several coefficients: the Pearson *r*, ϕ, and the point-biserial. We have already noted that the Pearson *r* is used to correlate two interval or continuous variables, and that ϕ is for correlating two dichotomous variables. The *point-biserial* correlation coefficient is used to correlate a dichotomous variable with a continuous variable, as when we want to measure the relationship between how students performed on one test question (scored dichotomously) and on the overall test (a continuous, interval-scale variable).

What is interesting about these three correlation coefficients is that they are really the same one, masquerading under three different names. The reason that three terms are used is that, because ϕ and the point-biserial are special cases of the Pearson *r* (two dichotomies, or one dichotomy and a continuous variable), it is possible to use shortcut formulas to calculate them. In the time when computers were rare, slow, expensive, and required great expertise to operate, statistics was a slow and painful field, which made these shortcuts important.

The general equation for the Pearson product-moment correlation coefficient is:

$$r_{xy} = \frac{\sum (X - M_x)(Y - M_y)}{nS_xS_y},$$ where X and Y are a student's scores on Tests X and Y, M_x

and M_y are the means for Tests X and Y, n = the sample size, and S_x and S_y are the (population) standard deviations for Tests X and Y.

One nice feature about any Pearsonian coefficient—even if it is generally only used with the Pearson r, and not generally with the point-biserial or ϕ—is that if we square the correlation, it provides an estimate of the proportion of variance shared by the two tests. For example, using the example in Figure 14.1, r_{AB} = .799, and r_{AB}^2 = .639, meaning that the two tests are measuring common factors, to the extent of 63.9%. Conversely, 36.1% of each test is measuring something distinct, a combination of specific factors and error (Thorndike and Hagen 1969). This is illustrated using a Venn diagram in Figure 14.3, with the common factors labeled "overlap" and the remainder for each test labeled "uniqueness." A similar pattern can be seen for Tests C and D in Figure 14.2: r_{CD} = .436, and r_{CD}^2 = .190, indicating common variance (the amount of score variation that is explained by common factors) for the two tests is 19.0%, as illustrated in Figure 14.4. Finally, while this property of r is very useful, it is crucial to remember that this squaring procedure *cannot* be done with Spearman ρ.

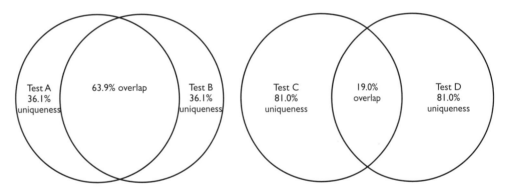

Figure 14.3 Venn Diagram For Tests A and B

Figure 14.4 Venn Diagram For Tests C and D

Worksheet 14.1: Calculating Pearson *r* and Spearman ρ in Excel

Introduction

The purpose of this worksheet is to calculate the Pearson *r* for two tests, and then to calculate the Spearman ρ for the same pair of tests. For the Pearson *r*, we will use the **PEARSON** function, and compare it with **CORREL**. We will then use Excel to manually calculate ρ.

Procedures: Calculating Pearson r

1   Open the file **Carr DALT Worksheet 14-1.xls**. (Note: Readers who want additional practice calculating descriptive statistics could delete the ones at the bottom of the spreadsheet, and recalculate them, before beginning this chapter's activities.)

2   Select **K1**, type **Pearson *r***, and press Enter.

3   The **PEARSON** function takes the form **=PEARSON(RANGE1, RANGE2)**:

   a   In **K2**, type **=PEARSON(**, and select **B2:B31**.

   b   Type **,** and select **C2:C31**.

   c   Type **)** and press Enter.

4   Select **K3**, and repeat the process in Step 3, but using **=CORREL(RANGE1, RANGE2)** instead.

5   After comparing the two results, format them to show three decimal places.

The two functions produce exactly the same result. The reason there are two formulas that do the very same thing probably has to do with backwards compatibility with a very early version of Excel. I recommend using **PEARSON**, so that it always remains clear to you what formula you are using.

6   Select **L1** and type **r^2**. Press Enter.

7   Calculate r^2:

   a   Select **L2**, and type **=**.

   b   Select **K2** and type **^2**.

   c   Press Enter, and reformat to show three decimal places. The result should be .575.

Procedures: Calculating Spearman ρ

8   Select **E1**, and type **X Rank**. Select **F1**, and type **Y Rank**. Center and **bold** these two headings.

9   First, we need to rank the students according to their scores on Test X. We will get a head start using the **RANK** function, but we cannot trust it entirely, and will have to manually adjust its results later:

   a   Select **E2**, type **=RANK(**, and select **B2**.

   b   Type **,** and select **B2:B31**.

   c   Press F4, type **)**, and press Enter.

   d   Select **E2**, copy, select **E2:E31**, and paste.

10 We need to sort the students from highest ranking to lowest ranking on Test X:

   a   Select **A1:E31**.

   b   Open the **Sort** dialog box, and sort by **X Rank**:

In Excel 2007:

i   On the **Home** toolbar, click the large **Sort & Filter** button, and click on **Custom Sort**.

ii   Make sure the checkbox is checked that says **My data has headers**.

iii   Using the pull-down menu under **Column**, sort by **X Rank**.

iv   Under **Order**, use the pull-down menu to select **Smallest to Largest**.

v   Click **OK**.

In Excel 2003:

i   Click on the **Data** menu, and click on **Sort**.

ii   Make sure the radio button is selected that says **My list has Header row**.

iii   Using the **Sort by** pull-down menu, sort by **X Rank**.

iv   Select the **Ascending** radio button.

v   Click **OK**.

11 Now we need to adjust the tied rankings. *Spearman ρ requires tied rankings to be averaged together.* Excel does not handle ties this way, so we must make the adjustments manually:

   a   The first two students, Students 10 and 15, are tied for first place. The average of 1 and 2 is 1.5, so type **1.5** in both **E2** and **E3**.

   b   Three students are tied for fourth place. The average of 4, 5, and 6 is 5, so type **5** in **E5**, **E6**, and **E7**.

   c   Four students are tied for eighth place. The average of 8, 9, 10, and 11 is **9.5**, so type this into these cells.

   d   Three students tied for 12th place, so type **13** for all three of them.

   e   Similarly, type **18.5** for the students who tied for 17th place; **21.5** for the two that tied for 21st place; **23.5** for the pair that tied for 23rd place; **26** for the three tied for 25th place; and **29** for the last three students.

12 Next, we need to rank the students according to their scores on Test Y. Select **F2**, and use the function **=RANK(C2,$C$2:$C$31)**:

   a   Type **=RANK(** and select **C2**.

   b   Type **,** and select **C2:C31**.

   c   Press F4, type **)**, and press Enter.

   d   Select and copy **F2**.

   e   Select **F2:F31**, and paste.

13 Now we need to sort the students from highest ranking to lowest ranking on Test Y:

a   Select **A1:F31**.

b   Open the **Sort** dialog box, and sort by **Y Rank**, following the same five-step procedure as in Step 10.b. above.

14 The next step is to adjust the tied rankings for Test Y, using the same averaging procedure as in Step 11. The ties will be changed to **5.5**, **12**, **16**, **19.5**, **22.5**, **24.5**, and **26.5**.

15 Select **H1** and type **D**. Select **I1** and type **D^2**. Make these headings **bold**.

16 Select **H2**, and calculate D, the difference between the first student's ranks (Student 13) on Test X and Test Y:

a   Type **=** and select **E2**.

b   Type **–** and select **F2**.

c   Press Enter. The result should be **8.5**.

17 We now need to calculate D^2 for the first student:

a   Select **I2**, type **=**, and select **H2**.

b   Type **^2** and press Enter. The result should be **72.25**.

18 Select **H2:I2**, copy, select **H2:I31**, and paste.

19 Next, calculate ΣD^2:

a   We will be leaving **Row 32** blank, as in previous worksheets, to separate the different parts of the worksheet.

b   Select **H33** and type **Sum**. Press Enter.

c   Select **I33** and use the **SUM** function to total **I2:I31**. The result should be **998.5**.

20 Select **H34** and type **n^2**. Press Enter.

21 Calculate n^2: Select **I34**. Type **=** and select **B45**. Type **^2** and press Enter. The result should be **900**.

22 Select **H35** and type **rho**. Press Enter.

23 Calculate ρ: Select **I35**. Type the formula **=1– (6*I33)/(B45*(I34–1))** and press Enter.

24 Reformat the result to show three decimal places. The result should equal **.778**.

Discussion

In this dataset, both sets of test scores are continuous variables, interval-level data, and rather normally distributed, so it is appropriate to use r. A value of .758 is rather high, and the r^2 of .575 indicates that 57.5% of the score variance for each test is common variance (see Figures 14.3 and 14.4). The Spearman ρ coefficient is actually slightly higher, but we should not bother reporting it, unless our focus is on students' *rankings* on the tests, not their scores.

Readers who wish to practice with their own data might consider first which correlation coefficient would really be more appropriate, based on the descriptive statistics and on the nature of the data. For example, ratings for speaking or writing might be more appropriately treated as ordinal data (and therefore suggest the use of Spearman ρ), although the degree of normality is probably more important. On the other hand, normally distributed interval data would call for the use of the Pearson r.

Summary

This chapter began with an overview of the concept of correlation, followed by a discussion of the levels of data, or types of variables (nominal or categorical, ordinal, interval, and ratio), and how the variable type effects the correlation coefficient that can be used. This was followed by an explanation of how the three Pearsonian correlation coefficients (ϕ, the point-biserial, and Pearson r) are in fact the same one, along with discussion of the squaring the Pearson r. The chapter then addressed how to calculate Pearson r and Spearman ρ in Excel.

15 ITEM ANALYSIS FOR NORM-REFERENCED TESTING

Introduction

This chapter explains the concepts of test question difficulty and discrimination for norm-referenced tests, topics which are also discussed in Chapter 5, and which lay the groundwork for Chapter 16 as well. This chapter begins by explaining how difficulty is calculated and what it means, and proceeds to do the same for item discrimination. Worksheet 15.1 will demonstrate how to perform and interpret an NRT item analysis with dichotomous data, and Worksheet 15.2 will demonstrate the slightly different procedures used to analyze dichotomous test questions.

Objectives

By the end of this chapter, readers will know or understand:

- **item facility (IF)**, an estimate of item difficulty
- two item discrimination indices (**point-biserial** and ID_{UL}), which are estimates of how well an item separates high- and low-ability test takers
- how to interpret norm-referenced item analysis results
- how to calculate norm-referenced item analysis estimates using Excel
- **IF***, **ID***$_{UL}$, and $r_{item\text{-}total}$, item analysis indices for polytomous data
- how to use Excel to calculate item analysis indices for polytomous data
- how to interpret norm-referenced polytomous item analysis results.

Overview of Item Analysis

Item Difficulty

Item difficulty is typically expressed in terms of *item facility (IF)*, the proportion of test takers who answered a given question correctly. (Some sources may refer to it as *p*, but this can be easily confused with the *p* in significance testing, which is not related. To avoid that element of potential confusion, therefore, this book will use IF.) IF can also be viewed as an index of item easiness, although that *term* is not ever used. Values can range from 0.0, which means none of the students answered correctly, to 1.0, which means everyone answered it right. For dichotomous items, the IF is simply the average of the individual scores (all equal to 0 or 1) on that item.

When an item is scored polytomously, IF must be replaced with IF* (see Bachman 2004), which is interpreted the same way, but requires a small additional step to calculate. (Specifically, IF* is equal to IF divided by the number of points possible for that item. This keeps IF and IF* on the same 0–1 scale.) Ideally, an item's difficulty should be at the level that provides the most information possible about examinee ability. This translates to half of the students answering correctly and half incorrectly *at the ability level that is of the greatest interest—not* half of the overall group taking the test.

For norm-referenced tests (NRTs), the goal is to differentiate among students, ranking them from high to low in a bell-shaped curve (i.e. with a statistically normal distribution), so the ideal target level for IF in a norm-referenced test is around .50 (Bachman 2004). If this is achieved, the item will provide the maximum information for the largest group of test takers, that is, those in the middle of the distribution. In practice, however, a range of .30 to .70 is normally used (Allen and Yen 1978). A question with an IF below .30 is usually deemed too difficult, and one with IF above .70 is considered too easy.

It bears pointing out that in most classroom grading, the norm-referenced framework is not appropriate. In curriculum-related testing, its primary use would be in placement tests, or perhaps diagnostic tests, although both types of testing might more appropriately use a criterion-referenced framework. Therefore, in most classroom testing contexts—and even most curriculum-related testing contexts—too much focus on IF is probably inappropriate. The role of IF in CRT item analysis will be discussed in Chapter 16.

Discrimination

Item discrimination is how well a given item separates (i.e. discriminates between) examinees with high and low ability. In NRT, it is often viewed as the relationship between how students did on an item, and their overall scores on the test containing that item. Regardless of whether the NRT or CRT framework is being used, though, there are two basic approaches to calculating discrimination: correlational and subtractive, which Nelson (2000) refers to as the correlation and upper-lower methods. Oddly enough, the calculations are essentially the same, within a given approach, for CRT and NRT, the only difference being what is subtracted or correlated.

In the **correlational approach to estimating item discrimination**, a correlation coefficient is calculated between scores on individual items, and something else. For NRT, the correlation is between the item and total score. The most common NRT correlational discrimination index is called the *point-biserial*, which is abbreviated $r_{\text{p-bis}}$, r_{pbis}, $r(pb)$, and sometimes even $pb(r)$. The point-biserial is a Pearsonian correlation coefficient, meaning it is a shortcut formula for the Pearson product-moment correlation coefficient, or "Pearson *r*" (as was explained in Chapter 14). The shortcut formula, which is for correlating a continuous variable (for example, total test score) with a dichotomous variable (for example, an item score) is not actually very important anymore, as the full-fledged Pearson *r* formula is easy to calculate with a computer, and most spreadsheet software includes the Pearson *r* formula already anyway. In the days when calculations were done with pencils, paper, slide rules, and adding machines, or punch-card computing, however, the shortcut was a valuable time-saver. The point-biserial is the correlation between an item score (how well each student did on that particular test question) and total test score. (Note that if polytomous items are used, the correlation is not technically a point-biserial anymore, but an actual Pearson *r*, the $r_{\text{item-total}}$. As we will be using the Pearson *r* formula anyway, though, this does not really matter.) However, if there are multiple sections (for example, reading and listening), discrimination should be based on total *section* scores. For example, listening scores should not figure into estimating the discrimination of reading items, and vice versa.

In the **subtractive approach to estimating discrimination**, the IF of a low-scoring group is subtracted from the IF of a high-scoring group. In NRT, this is usually done with the students who scored in the top and bottom groups on the overall test, or at least in the top and bottom groups on that *section* of the overall test. Typical recommendations for how large the groups should be are the top and bottom 25%, 27%, or one third. (One of the best ways to choose the group size, sometimes, is to find a point between 25% and 33% that will give an even number of test takers.) The problem with using too large a percentage of the students is that the groups may then not be different enough in ability, artificially depressing the discrimination estimates for items. The problem with using groups that are too small, on the other hand, is that this may artificially inflate the discrimination estimates. The NRT subtractive discrimination index is referred to as ID_{UL} (upper-lower discrimination), or sometimes simply ID. (For polytomous data, ID^*_{UL} is used.) Its formula is simple:

$$ID_{UL} = IF_{upper} - IF_{lower}.$$

Whether the correlational or subtractive approach is better in a particular situation depends in large part on the number of students taking the test. If the group is large enough to have a relatively normal distribution, then the point-biserial may be a little superior—not only because it does not pose the problem of deciding where to draw the lines for the upper and lower groups, but also because it includes test takers from the middle of the group in the estimate as well.

Interpreting Item Analysis Results

Table 15.1 presents the rule-of-thumb cut-off values for NRT item analysis statistics. The purpose of these values is to help ensure reliability will be satisfactory. Reliability is affected by the number of items on a test, but the quality of the items plays a crucial role as well. Long tests full of poorly discriminating items, in particular, can still have very low reliability levels.

Approach	Guideline
Difficulty	$.30 \leq IF \leq .70$
Discrimination	
Correlational approach $r_{\text{p-bis}}$	$r_{\text{p-bis}} \geq .30$
Subtractive approach (ID_{UL})	$ID_{UL} \geq .40$

Table 15.1 Rules of Thumb For Interpreting NRT Item Analyses

It should be pointed out that the values in Table 15.1 are mainly intended for use in high-stakes testing. Teacher-made tests intended for classroom use can often get by with somewhat lower discrimination values, and difficulty estimates even farther from .50. The question, of course, is what levels *are* acceptable for classroom test item analysis? The answer, unfortunately, depends in part on whom one asks. Nelson (2001) summarizes the findings of the measurement literature on the topic. For the ID_{UL}, he reports that most experts seem to find .20 and above acceptable for teacher-made tests, and perhaps even a bit lower (even .10), although others argue that an item with a discrimination of .20 needs to be revised or discarded. For point-biserial coefficients, Nelson suggests that in light of the literature, it may be reasonable for teacher-made classroom tests to have values even as low as .15. On the other hand, he summarizes his findings with respect to IF as being in the .3 to .7 range, the same as in Table 15.1.

Regardless of all these semi-official rules of thumb, guidelines, and so on, practically speaking, for a teacher doing item analysis after a test he has made himself, the most important thing to do is to consider the reliability level of the test, or the reliability of each section (see Chapter 18). The closer the test is to the minimum level set in the test context and purpose specifications, the less item revision is necessary. Item statistics, then, can be seen as indicators of where efforts to improve items need to be focused. Looked at as a group, they can also help indicate whether the cause of unsatisfactory reliability is a test that is too short, or a test that has weak items (and which *may* also be too short as well).

Item discrimination seems to be particularly tricky for a number of new test developers and analysts. One point that needs to be emphasized is that there is no maximum value listed for item discrimination in any of these rules. ID_{UL} and $r_{\text{p-bis}}$ cannot go above 1.00 (perfect discrimination), but the closer they get to that, the better the item. *There is no such thing* as having too high a discrimination value. A common mistake for novice item analysts is to confuse the IF rule of thumb with the rules for the point-biserial or ID_{UL}. Items may be too hard or too easy, but "The discrimination for Item 17 was too high" is something that should never be said in polite company.

Two interrelated issues have to do with item discrimination near or below zero. If the point-biserial or upper-lower discrimination is near zero, or even *slightly* below zero, this indicates that the item is effectively contributing nothing to the reliability of the test. Near-zero discrimination is often the result of extremely easy (IF near 1.00) or extremely difficult (IF near zero) items. Negative discrimination, on the other hand, means an item is actively harming the reliability level. Normally, the first thing to do in such a case is to check the scoring key. If the key is correct, the item needs to be reviewed to see whether it has two correct options, is ambiguous, or is deceptive in some way. The negative discrimination means that low-scoring students did better on that question than high-scoring students. Such items should be the top priority for revision.

Note that I am not necessarily recommending deleting these items, even though they are harming our test. If it is possible, weak or bad items should be salvaged—presumably, they were included in the test because the person who wrote it thought that question covered some portion of the construct being assessed. Furthermore, it is *usually* easier to fix bad items than it is to write new ones from scratch.

Worksheet 15.1: Performing Item Analysis For an NRT

Introduction

The purpose of this worksheet is to calculate the IF, ID_{UL}, and $r_{p\text{-bis}}$ for an NRT with dichotomous items, and then to interpret the results. Note that readers who want additional practice calculating descriptive statistics could delete those at the bottom of the spreadsheet, and recalculate them, before beginning this chapter's activities.

Procedures

1   Open the file **DALT Worksheet 15-1.xls**.

2   Select **V1**, and insert a new column (using the **Insert** button on the **Home** toolbar in Excel 2007, or the **Insert** menu in Excel 2003).

3   Select **A33**, and type **IF**. Make it **bold**.

4   Select **A35**, and type **IF(upper)**. Select **A36**, and type **IF(lower)**.

5   Select **A38**, and type **ID(UL)**. Make it **bold**.

6   Select **A40**, and type **r(p-bis)**. Make it **bold**.

7   Now that we have set up the headings on the worksheet, we need to sort the students by total score. Otherwise, we will not be able to separate them into upper and lower groups.

   a   Select **A1:Y31**.

   b   Sort the selection by the Total Score column:

In Excel 2007:

i   On the **Home** toolbar, click the **Sort & Filter** button, and select **Custom Sort**.

ii   Click on the checkbox **My data has headers**.

iii   Using the **Sort by** pull-down menu under **Column**, select **Total**.

iv   Use the pull-down menu under **Order** to select **Largest to Smallest**.

v   Click **OK**.

In Excel 2003:

i   Open the **Data** menu, and select **Sort**.

ii   Click on the **My list has header row** radio button.

iii   Use the **Sort by** pull-down menu to select **Total**.

iv   Click the **Descending** radio button.

v   Click **OK**.

8 We are now ready to calculate IF for Item 1. For dichotomous items, IF is the average of the (0, 1) item scores.

   a Select **B33**.

   b Enter the formula **=AVERAGE(RANGE)**, selecting **B2:B31** as the range.

   c Format the result to show three decimal places (**.533**)

9 Now we can calculate IF_{upper} and IF_{lower} for Item 1.

   a Decide how large the upper and lower groups should be. We will use 10 in each group, since this divides evenly. (Note that this also follows Bachman's advice to use thirds in smaller groups, and 27% in larger ones, defined as $n \geq 100$.)

   b Select **B35**.

   c Enter the formula **=AVERAGE(RANGE)**, selecting **B2:B11** as the range.

   d Select **B36**, and enter the same formula, but using **B22:B31** as the range.

   e Format the results for both numbers to show three decimal places (**.800** and **.100**).

10 Now calculate ID_{UL} for Item 1.

   a Select **B38**, and type **=**

   b Select **B35**, type **−** and select **B36**.

   c Complete formula: **=B35−B36**.

   d Press Enter. Format the result to three decimals (**.700**), if it is not so already.

11 Calculate the $r_{p\text{-bis}}$ for Item 1.

   a Select **B40**. Type **=PEARSON(** and select **B2:B31**.

   b Type **,** and select **X2**.

   c Press F4, and then type **:**.

   d Type **X31**, press F4, and type **)**. Press Enter.

   e Complete formula: **=PEARSON(B2:B31, $X$2:$X$31)**. Note the need for an absolute reference for the total score, so that this same column of numbers is used in every one of the item-total correlations.)

   f Format the result to three decimals (**.610**).

12 Select **B33:B40** and copy. Select **B33:U40** and paste.

13 Reformat column widths as necessary so that all results will display. When you reformat the cells containing hash signs (**####**), they will show the items with a negative discrimination value.

Note that while we will not discuss **Conditional Formatting** (in Excel 2007) in this book, readers interested in using it could apply it now.

Discussion

As can be seen from Table 15.2, most of those items flagged for low discrimination by one approach were also flagged by the other (based on the cut-off values in Table 15.1). Surprisingly, only two items had IF values that were out of the desired range, both of which were easier than desirable. Of those, Item 17 might be best left alone, given its extremely high discrimination values, and the fact that it is only slightly outside the target range.

Of particular concern are Items 10 and 20, which had strong negative discrimination values, regardless of the approach being used. These should be the top priority for review. Of nearly as much concern is Item 18, which has a near-zero point-biserial value (negative, but of a trivial size), and a somewhat larger negative discrimination—small, but less trivial. It too needs prompt examination and revision. Following this, if the reliability is a bit low, Items 6, 12, 19, and possibly 16 might be considered for revision, at least if this is a high-stakes test. For a teacher-made test, however, 16 (and perhaps even 19) may be acceptable.

Item	IF	ID$_{UL}$	$r_{p\text{-bis}}$
Q01	0.533	0.700	0.610
Q02	0.533	0.600	0.498
Q03	0.433	0.600	0.529
Q04	0.633	0.900	0.699
Q05	0.500	1.000	0.717
Q06	0.567	0.100	0.185
Q07	0.433	0.400	0.398
Q08	0.400	0.400	0.399
Q09	0.500	0.800	0.624
Q10	0.633	−0.400	−0.287
Q11	0.567	0.400	0.429
Q12	0.633	0.200	0.158
Q13	0.700	0.500	0.457
Q14	0.333	0.700	0.645
Q15	0.633	0.500	0.506
Q16	0.200	0.300	0.396
Q17	0.733	0.700	0.688
Q18	0.567	−0.100	−0.060
Q19	0.800	0.200	0.256
Q20	0.500	−0.500	−0.345

Table 15.2 Results of Worksheet 15.1, NRT Item Analyses

Worksheet 15.2: Performing Item Analysis For an NRT With Polytomous Data

Introduction

The purpose of this worksheet is to calculate the IF*, ID*$_{UL}$, and $r_{\text{item-total}}$ for an NRT with polytomous items, and then to interpret the results.

Procedures

1   Open the file **DALT Worksheet 15-2.xls**. Note the similarities of the headings to those in Worksheet 15.1. IF and ID have been replaced with IF* and ID*$_{UL}$, $r_{p\text{-bis}}$ with $r_{\text{item-total}}$, and a new row of values, MAX POSS., has been added. (Presumably, anyone giving a test will already know how many points each question is worth. Thus, this set of values is already filled in.)

2   Sort the students by total test score:

    a Select **A1:X31**, and open the **Sort** dialog box (*Excel 2007:* **Home** toolbar → **Sort & Filter** button → **Custom Sort**; *Excel 2003:* **Data** menu → **Sort**)

    b Specify that the data has a header row/headers, and sort by **Total Largest to Smallest** (*Excel 2007*)/ in **Descending** order (*Excel 2003*). Click **OK**.

3 Calculate IF* using the formula IF* = IF÷MAX POSS.

    a Select **B35**, and insert the formula **=AVERAGE(B2:B31)/B33**.

    b Press Enter, reformat the result to display three decimal places (**.533**), and adjust column width.

4 IF*$_{upper}$ is calculated the same way as IF*, but only includes the top 10 students. Select **B37** and insert the formula **=AVERAGE(B2:B11)/B33**.

5 To calculate IF*$_{lower}$, select **B38** and insert the formula **=AVERAGE(B22:B31)/B33**.

6 Reformat **B37** and **B38** so that they display three decimal places.

7 To calculate ID*$_{UL}$, select **B40** and insert the formula **=B37−B38**. Format the result to display three decimal places (**.400**).

8 Select **B42**. Insert the formula **=PEARSON(B2:B31,$X$2:$X$31)**. (Remember to select **X2:X31** and then press F4 in order to create the absolute reference **$X$2:$X$31**. Alternatively, you could press F4 separately for **X2** and again for **X31** to get **$X$2** and **$X$31**.)

9 Format the result to show three decimal places (**.520**).

10 Select **B35:B42**. Copy, select **B35:U42**, and paste. Adjust column widths as necessary.

Item	IF*	ID*$_{UL}$	$r_{item-total}$
Q01	0.533	0.400	0.520
Q02	0.400	0.450	0.438
Q03	0.378	0.433	0.517
Q04	0.483	0.500	0.534
Q05	0.517	0.500	0.709
Q06	0.533	0.333	0.339
Q07	0.433	0.400	0.341
Q08	0.367	0.200	0.293
Q09	0.456	0.533	0.586
Q10	0.467	−0.100	−0.126
Q11	0.533	0.050	0.045
Q12	0.544	0.167	0.215
Q13	0.467	0.250	0.421
Q14	0.333	0.500	0.556
Q15	0.450	0.350	0.507
Q16	0.300	0.400	0.529
Q17	0.583	0.475	0.615
Q18	0.567	−0.100	−0.070
Q19	0.617	0.100	0.147
Q20	0.467	−0.067	−0.114

Table 15.3 Results of Worksheet 15.2, NRT Polytomous Item Analyses

Discussion

The results of this item analysis exercise are summarized in Table 15.3. Surprisingly, there are more problematic items than in the previous group of dichotomous questions; on the other hand, none of the items have IF* values outside the desired range of .3 to .7. The three negatively discriminating items need to be reviewed as early as possible, even though these estimates are all *relatively* small in absolute value. Item 11 is essentially contributing nothing, as both its discrimination estimates are very close to zero. Items 8, 12, and 19 are not contributing much to reliability, and probably need review; Items 13 and 6 might also be examined, depending on which discrimination index is used. Of course, aside from Items 10, 18, 20, and perhaps 11, the importance of item review and revision will depend on the current reliability level (see Chapter 18).

As a final note, although this worksheet illustrated how to perform these analyses for an NRT, they could easily be adapted to polytomous CRT data by replacing all use of IF with IF*, as was done here for calculating both difficulty and discrimination.

Summary

In this chapter, we began by discussing item facility (IF), which is used to estimate item difficulty. We then moved on to item discrimination indices, which in norm-referenced testing are intended to separate high- and low-ability examinees. Norm-referenced discrimination was classified based on whether it is calculated using correlation (point-biserial) or subtraction (ID_{UL}). Rules of thumb were presented for interpreting difficulty and discrimination, before the first section concluded by explaining how to calculate these estimates using Excel.

The second portion of the chapter dealt with the equivalents of IF, ID_{UL}, and the point-biserial when we are working with polytomous norm-referenced data: IF^*, ID^*_{UL}, and $r_{item-total}$. The chapter showed how to calculate these estimates using Excel, and concluded with brief coverage of how to interpret the results of such analyses.

16 ITEM ANALYSIS FOR CRITERION-REFERENCED TESTING

Introduction

This chapter continues the discussion of item analysis, extending it to the case of criterion-referenced testing (CRT). It begins by discussing the more limited role of item difficulty in CRT analyses, and then proceeds to discuss subtractive and correlational estimates of CRT item discrimination. It concludes with Worksheet 16.1, which demonstrates how to perform and interpret a CRT item analysis.

Objectives

By the end of this chapter, readers will know or understand:
- the role of item difficulty (IF) in criterion-referenced testing
- three item discrimination indices (*item φ* and, the *difference index*, and *B-index*), which are estimates of how well an item separates test takers at the mastery and non-mastery levels
- how to interpret criterion-referenced item analysis results
- how to calculate criterion-referenced item analysis estimates using Excel.

Overview of CRT Item Analysis

Item Difficulty in CRT

As explained in Chapter 15, in norm-referenced testing (NRT) we target the .50 level for item facility (IF). This is because an NRT attempts to spread test takers out along a continuum, spreading them out as much as possible, and because the largest number of test takers will be in the middle. CRT involves a different goal— separating masters from non-masters (i.e. those who are above some criterion level, or cut score, from those who are not). Nevertheless, a similar sort of logic applies in terms of item difficulty. For CRT, ideally, we want items that 50% of the test takers *who were at the cut score* will answer correctly—that is, at the cut-off line between passing and failing, between one grade and another (for example, A vs. B), or between one level and another (as in the case of placement exams).

In practice, this is an extremely difficult thing to estimate; as a result, in CRT, we normally report IF (or IF*, for polytomous data), but only use it to help interpret the other results. IF is not used by itself to keep or reject items; after all, on an achievement test, we *hope* that most of the students get most of the questions right! Similarly, on a diagnostic pre-test, we would not expect students to answer many questions correctly on things they had not studied yet. There is therefore no rule of thumb to apply to IF when doing CRT item analysis. This issue is intimately related to the discussion in Chapter 12 of the shape of score distributions expected for a CRT: positively skewed, negatively skewed, or essentially normal.

Item Discrimination in CRT

As noted in Chapter 15, *item discrimination* is how well a given item separates (i.e. discriminates between) examinees with high and low ability. In NRT, it is the relationship between how students did on an item, and their overall scores on the test. In contrast, in CRT, it is the relationship between item performance and mastery/non-mastery. Note that when a CRT has multiple cut scores (for example, a placement test, or a test on which letter grades such as A, B, and C are assigned), that means there are multiple decision points where we classify students as masters/non-masters. Thus, since each cut score represents a separate decision point, CRT discrimination must be calculated separately for each cut score. For example, if a placement test is used to place students into one of six levels in a program, it will have five cut scores, and each item must have five discrimination estimates (one for each cut score).

As with NRT, in the CRT framework, item discrimination can be calculated using two basic approaches: *correlational* and *subtractive*. In the *correlational approach to estimating item discrimination*, a correlation coefficient is calculated between scores on individual items, and something else. For NRT, the correlation is between the item and total score. For CRT, the correlation is between the item and mastery/non-mastery. The mastery decision is dichotomous (master/non-master, pass/fail, etc.); for a dichotomous test item, then, the ϕ coefficient, or *item ϕ*, is the CRT correlational index of discrimination. When there are multiple sections to a test (for example, a test with grammar, listening, and reading sections), of course, the discrimination should be calculated based on the performance on each section, not performance on the test overall. Thus, the discrimination for listening items should be based on who was above or below a particular cut score on the listening comprehension section, not on the test as a whole.

To return to a point raised in Chapter 5, in cases where the cut scores have not been set yet, or are not trusted very well, it may make sense to report the point-biserial in CRT as a supplementary index of discrimination. This is *not* something that is normally done, but as a temporary measure, it at least provides some information. Presumably, wherever the cut score(s) is (are) eventually set, mastery decisions will be related in some fashion to total test score. Another interim measure might be to examine the effects on item discrimination of a wide variety of potential cut scores, and see which cut score(s) will offer the best results, keeping those and discarding the others.

Moving on to the *subtractive approach* to *estimating discrimination*, when following this approach the IF of a low-scoring group is subtracted from the IF of a high-scoring group. In CRT, the two groups are defined as *masters* and *non-masters*, rather than the *upper* and *lower* groups (as in NRT). There are two types of subtractive discrimination indices for CRT. The first, the **difference index (DI)**, requires giving the test twice, once to masters and once to non-masters. Its formula is $DI = IF_{masters} - IF_{non-masters}$. Brown and Hudson (2002) describe two different ways in which the DI can be calculated: **differential groups studies** and **intervention studies**. In a *differential groups study*, two existing groups are identified. One group is deemed to be at the mastery level in whatever ability is being assessed, and the other group is judged to still be non-masters. The IF value for each group is then calculated, with the DI equaling the difference between them. An example of this would be using students from two consecutive levels in a language program to investigate how well test questions discriminated between students at those two levels. This would be most appropriate if comparisons were also made between other pairs of levels as well, as part of an analysis of items used in a placement test.

The other way to calculate the DI is through an *intervention study*. The test is still administered to two groups, but the two groups are actually one group of students at different times—before and after they have received instruction in whatever material is being assessed. This is essentially a pre-test/post-test model.

It is not always feasible to administer a test twice, however, or to two different groups. Furthermore, if a test has multiple cut scores, calculating the DI would mean more than two groups. These factors help to make the **B-index** popular, as it only requires a single test administration. The mastery and non-mastery groups are defined whether a student's total score on the test (or section of the test) was above or below the cut score. As with any CRT discrimination index, it must be calculated separately for each cut score, as changing the cut score changes who gets counted as a master or a non-master. Its formula is given as $B = IF_{masters} - IF_{non-masters}$, or $B = IF_{pass} - IF_{fail}$.

As noted in the preceding chapter, these discrimination estimates can be adapted to polytomous data by using IF* instead of IF. Thus, B* or DI* would be calculated by using $IF^*_{masters}$ and $IF^*_{non-masters}$. Similarly, rather than item ϕ, we would calculate $r_{item-mastery}$ (much as we calculate $r_{item-total}$ with polytomous NRT items), although it would still be a Pearson r.

Interpreting Item Analysis Results in CRT

Table 16.1 provides a summary of the rules of thumb for interpreting CRT item analysis results. As the table notes, IF is *not* generally used as a criterion for item selection, retention, rejection, revision, and so on. In the absence of being able to calculate the IF of items for people near the cut scores, we merely report it to assist us in making sense of our discrimination estimates. For example, if an item has a very low discrimination, that could be because it is extremely easy or extremely difficult.

Approach	Guideline
Difficulty	N/A*
Discrimination	
Correlational approach φ	φ ≥ .30
Subtractive approach (DI, B-index)	DI ≥ .40
	B ≥ .40

*Generally, IF is only reported in CRT analyses to help in interpreting the discrimination estimates.

Table 16.1 Rules of Thumb For Interpreting NRT Item Analyses

Worksheet 16.1: Performing Item Analysis For a CRT

Introduction

The purpose of this worksheet is to calculate the IF, B-index, and φ indices for a CRT with dichotomous items. We will assume that there is only one cut score for this test, and we will use 70%. Of course, it would be equally possible to choose some other score instead.

Note that if multiple cut scores were used for this test, it would be necessary to recalculate the B-index and φ for each cut score.

Procedures

1 Open the file **DALT Worksheet 16-1.xls**.

2 Sort the students by total test score:

    a Select **A1:Y31**, and open the **Sort** dialog box (*Excel 2007:* **Home** toolbar → **Sort & Filter** button → **Custom Sort**; *Excel 2003:* **Data** menu → **Sort**)

    b Specify that the data has header row/headers, and sort by **Total** in descending order/largest to smallest. Click **OK**.

3 Classify the students as masters or non-masters:

    a Select **Z1**. Type **Mastery?** and make it **bold**.

    b Type **1** next to each student whose score was 70% or above. Type **0** next to each student whose score was below 70%.

        i. **Z2:Z8** will all contain **1**.

        ii. **Z9:Z31** will all contain **0**.

4 Calculate IF:

    a Select **B33**, and insert the formula **=AVERAGE(B2:B31)**.

    b Press Enter. If necessary, reformat the result to display three decimal places (**.533**), and adjust column width.

5 Calculate IF_{pass}:

    a Select **B35**, and insert the formula **=AVERAGE(B2:B8)**. This group is all the students who scored 70% or higher on the test.

    b Press Enter. If necessary, reformat the result to display three decimal places (**.857**), and adjust column width.

6 Calculate IF_{fail}:

    c Select **B36**, and insert the formula **=AVERAGE(B9:B31)**. This group is all the students who scored below 70% on the test.

    d Press Enter. If necessary, reformat the result to display three decimal places (**.435**), and adjust column width.

7 Calculate the B-index:

Select **B38** and insert the formula **=B35–B36**. If necessary, format the result to display three decimal places (**.422**) and adjust column width.

8 Calculate φ:

    a Select **B40**. Insert the formula **=PEARSON(B2:B31,$Z$2:$Z$31)**.

        i If you are selecting the range **Z2:Z31**, rather than typing the cell references, remember to press F4 to create the absolute reference **$Z$2:$Z$31**. *(N.B. I recommend this approach.)*

        ii If you are typing the cell references, rather than selecting them, remember to press F4 twice: once after typing **Z2**, and again after typing **Z31**. *(N.B. The problem with typing the cell references, rather than selecting them, is that you do not get any experience that you can apply to working to work with your own data later.)*

    b Format the result to show three decimal places (**.358**), and adjust the column width if necessary.

9 Select **B33:B40**. Copy, select **B33:U40**, and paste. Adjust column widths as necessary.

Discussion

The results of the item analyses are summarized in Table 16.2. Obviously, the most worrisome items are Questions 10 and 20, both of which have large negative discrimination values regardless of the estimation procedure used. As was explained in Chapter 15, the key should be checked first; if the items were scored correctly, they need to be reviewed for the possibility of having two correct answers, being ambiguous, or being tricky in some fashion. After all, if these were *positive* discrimination estimates of the same magnitude (i.e. the same absolute value), they would probably be large enough for the items to be acceptable on a teacher-made classroom test.

Following these, Items 7, 12, 13, 15, 18, and 19 may need revision, especially if this is a high-stakes test, or if the current dependability estimate is low. They are not actively harming the dependability of the test, though, unlike 10 and 20.

In some cases, the two discrimination indices provide conflicting information on the quality of the items. In these cases (6, 11, 16, and 17), what to do will depend on the items themselves, and is something of a judgment call. In actual testing practice, it is probably more common to report a single discrimination index; however, if two are being used, as in this exercise, and if they provide different results for the same item, we can probably consider such an item to be borderline in its acceptability.

Item	IF	B-index	ϕ
Q01	0.533	0.422	0.358
Q02	0.533	0.422	0.358
Q03	0.433	0.739	0.631
Q04	0.633	0.478	0.420
Q05	0.500	0.652	0.552
Q06	0.567	0.379	0.323
Q07	0.433	0.180	0.154
Q08	0.400	0.410	0.354
Q09	0.500	0.466	0.394
Q10	0.633	−0.267	−0.234
Q11	0.567	0.379	0.323
Q12	0.633	0.106	0.093
Q13	0.700	0.205	0.189
Q14	0.333	0.683	0.613
Q15	0.633	0.106	0.093
Q16	0.200	0.298	0.315
Q17	0.733	0.348	0.333
Q18	0.567	0.193	0.164
Q19	0.800	0.261	0.276
Q20	0.500	−0.280	−0.236

Table 16.2 Results of Worksheet 16.1 (CRT Item Analyses)

In conclusion, it should be emphasized once more that if there are multiple cut scores, the B-index, ϕ, or DI must be recalculated for *each* of them. In the example above, if we decided to add cut scores at 60%, 80%, and 90%, for instance, we would need to redo the worksheet three more times, and report the B-index and/or

ϕ at each of the cut scores. One important point is that an item that discriminates well at a certain cut score may do poorly at one or more other cut scores. That does not necessarily mean it is a bad item, but rather that additional items may be needed that discriminate well at those other cut scores.

Summary

In this chapter, we began by discussing item facility (IF), which is used to estimate item difficulty, but which is not used in criterion-referenced item analysis other than as an aid to interpretation of other things. We then moved on to item discrimination indices, which in criterion-referenced testing are intended to differentiate test takers above the mastery level from those below it. Criterion-referenced discrimination indices were classified on the basis of whether they are calculated using the correlational (point-biserial ϕ) or subtractive (interpreting discrimination) approach. Rules of thumb were presented for interpreting discrimination, before the chapter ended by explaining how to calculate these estimates using Excel.

17 DISTRACTOR ANALYSIS AND SCORING MULTIPLE-CHOICE ITEMS IN EXCEL

Introduction

This chapter discusses **distractor analysis** for multiple-choice questions. The instructions for Worksheet 17.1 then show how to calculate the number of students selecting each response, as well as how to convert raw response data (A, B, C, etc.) into dichotomous item scores (0, 1).

Objectives

By the end of this chapter, readers will know or understand:

- how to score multiple-choice response data using Excel
- the purpose of distractor analysis
- common distractor analysis tools, including response frequency and the point-biserial for each *option* (as opposed to each item)
- how to interpret distractor analysis results and use them to identify problematic options in need of revision
- how to perform distractor analysis using Excel.

Overview of Scoring and Distractor Analysis

At the classroom level, responses to tests will often be handwritten and hand-scored. Unless a teacher is planning to perform distractor analysis, any item or reliability analyses will probably be performed by just entering the scores for the individual items. For teachers who want to analyze the distractors on a multiple-choice test, though, it is much more convenient to enter just one set of responses—the student responses (A, B, C, etc.)—and score those in Excel, rather than to type in item scores and the raw responses separately. In situations where optically scanned test answer sheets are used to collect student responses, the scanning software may or may not include a way to score the responses, meaning that a large number of letters needs to be converted to scores. Regardless of why we may need to do this, it will be seen in Worksheet 17.1 that scoring the raw responses in Excel is not very difficult.

As for **distractor analysis**, the process of statistically identifying which options on a selected response task did their jobs well, it might be best to explain why we would ever need to bother with it in the first place. As Chapter 5 noted, it is easy to write poor multiple-choice questions, and even the most experienced and conscientious test writers will find themselves needing to revise some of their questions from time to time. Chapters 15 and 16 showed how to identify items in need of revision, but this does not do anything to suggest where we might start revising a particular item. Sometimes we may want or even need a hint, and one good source of ideas is to look at how well each of the distractors is performing.

One of the most important things to look at in distractor analysis, and one of the easiest, is to examine how attractive each option is on a given question. One rule of thumb is that at least 10% of the examinees should choose each distractor; any distractor that has a lower response frequency is not really pulling its own weight (Bachman 2004). After all, if no—or almost no—test takers find a distractor plausible enough to choose it, then it is not really serving any purpose.

Another possibility when doing distractor analysis is to calculate the point biserial for each option on an item. This procedure is explained in Worksheet 17.1, and involves calculating the point-biserial coefficient as many times as there are options (for example, for a four-option multiple-choice question, the point-biserial is calculated four times). This is done by treating A as correct and correlating that item with total test score, then treating B as correct and correlating the item with total test score, and so on. (Note that the correct answer will, of course, have the same point-biserial as would be found during ordinary item analysis.) Any distractor should have a negative point-biserial coefficient—that is, people who choose a wrong answer should tend to have lower test scores, and vice versa. A distractor point-biserial score close to zero is an indication that that distractor is not really helping attract the low-scoring test takers any more than the high-scoring ones, and that it might be a candidate for revision. A distractor with a non-trivial positive point-biserial ("trivial" is a subjective term, but for these purposes, we might treat it as including anything greater than .05 or .10) is truly problematic, as it means that students who selected that option tended to have higher scores on the overall test, and vice versa. Such distractors need to be reviewed, to see whether they might be deceptive, correct, ambiguous, or otherwise tricky or confusing.

One final approach to distractor analysis is to calculate the mean z score (see Chapter 12) of all students choosing a particular option (Nelson 2001). Any distractor with a positive z score is considered problematic, since that means above-average students tended to select that option. Similarly, if the correct answer has a negative z score, that would be similarly problematic, as it would mean that below-average students are the ones tending to answer correctly. The problem with using this approach is that practically speaking, it really requires the use of test analysis software that includes these calculations. Doing these calculations manually in Excel requires such extensive manipulation of the data and so many steps as to render it impractical, save for the most enthusiastic Excel users.

Example of How to Apply Distractor Analysis to an Item

An example of how to apply distractor analysis can be seen in the item in Figure 17.1. This reading comprehension item, which was based on a passage about a Vietnamese legend, had an item facility of 0.15, and a point-biserial of −0.29. We therefore know that it was problematic: if it was taken from a norm-referenced test, it was too difficult and had negative discrimination, and if it was on a criterion-referenced test, it would almost certainly have a negative item ϕ or B-index. It is only by using distractor analysis, however, that can we find where the problem(s) may have arisen that caused the poor item performance.

Why did the king want his sons to find new dishes?
A because of his love of good food
B for use in worshipping their ancestors
C to prove which one loved him the most
D to test whether they would obey his orders

Figure 17.1 Example of an Item With Problematic Distractors

Option	Response %	$r_{\text{p-bis}}$
A	15%	−0.29
B	81%	0.50
C	2%	−0.46
D	2%	−0.42

Table 17.1 Distractor Analysis Results For the Example Item

By looking at the response frequencies alone, we might surmise that options C and D were problematic because very few students picked them. We would see that option B was more attractive than option A (the correct answer), but we would not be sure that this was necessarily problematic based on the response frequencies alone, particularly given that the item was difficult. Furthermore, the problematic nature of the options and correct answer is probably not discernable merely by reading the item.

When we consider the point-biserial as well, though, the picture becomes more complex, but also shows us important details. Things become more complex in that we see that options C and D have strongly negative point-biserial values, which is a desirable state of affairs. In spite of their unpopularity, then, we *might* consider leaving them alone and focus more attention on options A and B. Option A, the correct answer, has a high negative point-biserial, indicating that it was more attractive to low-ability test takers than to high-ability ones, something that is highly problematic. On the other hand, option B was attractive to higher-ability test takers.

We should therefore first confirm that option A was correct, and that B was *not* correct. If there has been no error, we need to revise both options, and perhaps even the stem as well. We might also try modifying C and D, although it could be that correcting the issues with A and B will make C and D more popular without any additional changes.

Worksheet 17.1: Distractor Analysis and Multiple-Choice Scoring in Excel

Introduction

This worksheet will explain how to find the percentage of test takers selecting each response to a multiple-choice test. It will then show how to score multiple-choice response data. It will conclude by showing how to calculate the point-biserial coefficient for each option.

Procedures: Computing Response Frequencies

Open the file **DALT Worksheet 17-1.xls**.

1 Use the **COUNTIF(RANGE, CRITERIA)** function to count the number of students who chose A as the answer for Question 1:

   a Select **B35**. Type **=COUNTIF(**.

   b Select **B3:B32** *(not **B2**!)*, type **,"A")**, and press Enter.

   c Complete formula: **=COUNTIF(B3:B32, "A")**

   d Alternate formula: **=COUNTIF(B$3:B$32,$A35)**

Note that the range **B$3:B$32** is a **mixed cell reference** (a combination of absolute and relative cell references) and tells Excel to count the number of instances of "A" in rows 3–32 of whatever the current column is—that is, the same column as the cell in which this formula is being used. The last argument (**$A35**) also tells Excel to use whatever is in the current row—the same row as the cell in which this formula is being used—from Column A.

2 Count the number of students who chose B, C, or D for Question 1, repeating the process in Step 2 (in cells **B36:B38**):

   a If you used the formula in 1.c, re-enter it (do not copy and paste!) in cells **B36:B38**, but substituting "B," "C," or "D" for the **CRITERIA** (sic), as appropriate.

   b If you used the alternate formula from Step 1.d, simply copy **B35**, select **B35:B38**, and paste.

3 Select and copy **B35:B38**. Select **B35:U38** and paste.

4 Select **B38:U38**. Using the **Borders** button on the toolbar, reapply a bottom border if it disappeared during Steps 2 and 3.

5   Confirm the number of responses for each item. This should equal *n*, the number of students, but if there has been a formula error, or if there is something wrong with the data (blanks, misread or mistyped responses, etc.), this will help us spot that fact:

   a   Select **B39**.

   b   Use the **SUM** function to total **B35:B38**.

   c   Complete formula: **=SUM(B35:B38)**.

   d   Select and copy **B39**. Select **B39:U39**, and paste. (All 20 items should show 30.)

6   Calculate the percentage that selected each option:

   a   Select **B42**.

   b   Type **=** and select **B35**.

   c   Type **/** and select **B39**. Press F4 twice, so that **B39** becomes **B$39**, and press `Enter`.

   d   Complete formula: **=B35/B$39**.

   e   Click the **Percent Style** button. No decimals are necessary.

   f   Select and copy **B42**. Select **B42:B45** and paste.

   g   Using the **Borders** button on the toolbar, reapply a bottom border to **B45**.

   h   Select **B42:B45** and copy. Select **B42:U45** and paste.

Procedures: Scoring Multiple-Choice Responses

This next set of steps uses the **IF** function, which takes the form of **=IF(logical_ test, value_if_true, value_if_false)**.

7   Score Student 1 on Question 1:

   a   Select **W3**.

   b   Type **=IF(** and select **B3**.

   c   Type **=** and select **B2**.

   d   Press F4 twice, so **B2** becomes **B$2**.

   e   Type **,1,0)** and press `Enter`.

   f   Complete formula: **=IF(B3=B$2,1,0)**.

8   Select and copy **W3**. Select **W3:AP32** and paste.

9   Calculate total score for Student 1:

   a   Select **AS3**.

   b   Use the **SUM** function to total **W3:AP3**.

   c   Select and copy **AS3**. Select **AS3:AS32**, and paste.

10 Those interested in additional practice can compute the descriptive statistics indicated in **AS34:AS48**.

Procedures: Calculating the Point-Biserial For Each Option

The following steps start by making copies of the response data, which we will then work with. We will leave the original data (in **B3:U32**) undisturbed after it is copied.

11 Make a copy of the response data and total scores:

    a Select **B3:U32** and copy. Select **AV3** and paste.

    b Select **AS3:AS32** and copy. Select **BP3**.

    c Right-click **BP3**, choose **Paste Special** from the context menu, click the **Values** radio button, and click **OK**. (Note that pasting only the values, not the formulas, prevents Excel from trying to total A + B + C etc., which of course will not work.)

12 Make three more copies of the response data and total scores:

    a Select and copy **AV3:BP32**.

    b Select **BS3** and paste.

    c Select **CP3** and paste.

    d Select **DM3** and paste. We now have four identical copies of the student responses and total scores.

13 Next, we will convert all instances of A to 1 in the first copy of the student responses

    a Select **AV3:BO32**.

    b Press Ctrl + h to open the **Find and Replace** dialog box.

    c In the **Find what** textbox, type **A**, and in the **Replace with** textbox, type **1**.

    d Click the **Replace All** button. A message box will tell you how many replacements were made; click **OK**.

14 Now, we will convert all instances of B, C, and D to 0 (in the first copy of the student responses, i.e. **AV3:BO32**):

    a Use **Find and Replace** again to replace B with 0.

    b Replace C with 0.

    c Replace D with 0.

    d All the responses should now be zeroes and ones, with no letters remaining.

15 Now we need to repeat the process in Steps 14–15 for the second copy of the student responses (**BS3:CL32**):

    a Close the **Find and Replace** dialog box, and select **BS3:CL32**, the second copy of the response data.

   b Reopen the **Find and Replace** dialog box (Ctrl + h), and replace B with 1.

   c Replace A, C, and D with 0.

16 Repeat this process with **CP3:DI32** (C → 1; A, B, D → 0) and **DM3:EF32** (D → 1; A, B, C → 0).

17 Now that we have converted the letters to dichotomous variables, we can calculate the point-biserial for option A on every item:

   a Select **AU34**, type **A pb(*r*) =**, and press Enter.

   b Select **AV34**. Type **=PEARSON(**, and select **AV3:AV32**.

   c Type **,** and select **BP3:BP32**.

   d Press F4, and press Enter.

   e Complete formula: **=PEARSON(AV3:AV32,$BP$3:$BP$32)**

   f Select **AV34**. Reformat to display three decimal places, and copy.

   g Select **AV34:BO34** and paste.

18 Repeat the process for Options B, C, and D:

   a Select **BR34**, type **B pb(*r*) =**, and press Enter.

   b Select **BS34** and enter the formula **=PEARSON(BS3:BS32,$CM$3:CM 32)**.

   c Reformat **BS34** to three decimal places, copy, and paste into **BS34:CL34**.

   d Calculate C pb(*r*) and D pb(*r*) in the same way.

19 Now that we have calculated the option point-biserial values, we should paste the values below the option frequency percentages:

   a Select **AU34:BO34**, and copy.

   b Select **A48**. Right-click **A48**, select **Paste Special** from the context menu, and click on the **Values** radio button. Click **OK**.

   c Repeat this procedure for the B, C, and D point-biserial values, pasting them immediately below the A pb(*r*) row (i.e. **A48:U51** will display all of the option point-biserial results for the test).

   d Select **B48:U51**, and reformat to display three decimal places. Reformat column width as necessary.

Discussion

Table 17.1 summarizes the distractor analysis results that we just computed. If we are strictly applying Bachman's (2004) recommendation of at least 10% response frequency per distractor, and if we flag any distractor with a positive or even near-zero point-biserial value, 16 out of 20 items will be flagged as having at least one option in need of revision. The situation may not actually be quite as dire as these numbers suggest, however. As we shall see in just a moment, most of these items are only slightly problematic, and are not exactly in urgent need of revision. Assuming we do have the time and the resources to consider revising all 16 items, however, in all but five cases we will only need to revisit one or two options per question—not necessarily the entire item.

Response frequencies					Option point-biserials			
	% A	% B	% C	% D	A pb(r)	B pb(r)	C pb(r)	D pb(r)
Q01	53%	13%	3%	30%	0.610	0.018	0.061	−0.701
Q02	13%	53%	17%	17%	−0.311	0.498	−0.229	−0.154
Q03	17%	17%	43%	23%	−0.279	−0.054	0.529	−0.327
Q04	7%	20%	10%	63%	−0.249	−0.512	−0.233	0.699
Q05	20%	50%	13%	17%	−0.279	0.717	−0.228	−0.454
Q06	57%	13%	13%	17%	0.185	0.155	−0.228	−0.179
Q07	33%	43%	13%	10%	−0.066	0.398	−0.201	−0.326
Q08	10%	30%	20%	40%	0.047	−0.315	−0.163	0.399
Q09	50%	27%	13%	10%	0.624	−0.435	−0.228	−0.140
Q10	13%	3%	63%	20%	−0.009	0.112	−0.287	0.303
Q11	17%	20%	7%	57%	−0.104	−0.396	−0.062	0.429
Q12	7%	63%	13%	17%	0.050	0.158	0.046	−0.279
Q13	13%	10%	70%	7%	−0.037	−0.450	0.457	−0.249
Q14	33%	10%	33%	23%	−0.263	−0.047	0.645	−0.393
Q15	10%	10%	17%	63%	−0.264	−0.047	−0.404	0.506
Q16	23%	30%	20%	27%	−0.062	−0.254	0.396	−0.035
Q17	73%	20%	3%	3%	0.688	−0.582	−0.199	−0.199
Q18	17%	23%	57%	3%	−0.154	0.180	−0.060	0.061
Q19	80%	3%	3%	13%	0.256	−0.199	−0.199	−0.091
Q20	7%	50%	30%	13%	−0.025	−0.345	0.234	0.210

Note: Correct answers are underlined and problematic distractors are shaded.

Table 17.2 Distractor Analysis Results For Worksheet 17.1

In particular, if an item's only problem is that one option is at 7% (as with Item 4) with the current sample size ($n = 30$), that is only one student below the 10% threshold, and probably is not a very big problem. A similar group of only slightly problematic items in this example consists of Items 7, 11, 13, 14, and 15. The point-biserials for one or two of their distractors may be small, but they are all still negative. Furthermore, their distractors were all chosen by at least *nearly* 10% of the students—which, again, is probably not much of a concern in a small sample such as this one.

The process of revising the test should begin with those items that had poor discrimination values, or (in NRT) which were too easy or too difficult. Once items with problematic difficulty or discrimination levels have been improved upon, we can then attempt to improve problematic distractors from other items, as time permits. (Note that the point-biserial for an item's correct answer is the same as the *item's* point-biserial. Similarly, the response frequency for the correct answer is the same as the IF, converted from a proportion to a percentage.) Based on their negative item point-biserials, our top candidates for revision are Items 10, 18, and 20, particularly 10 and 20 in light of their magnitudes (i.e. large absolute values).

Item 10 Option B needs revision, since few test takers chose it, but its positive point-biserial suggests that that option *may* be partially correct or tricky. Given that Option D has a strong positive point-biserial, D may in fact be the correct answer, and the scoring key could be wrong—if so, then Option C would be good as it is currently written, since it has a negative point-biserial. If the key is correct, though, C needs revision. Similarly, if D is in fact the correct answer, its positive point-biserial of .303 indicates it would be acceptable as currently written.

Item 20 is also highly problematic, in light of its negative discrimination. The fact that only 7% of the test takers (one short of the 10% mark) chose Option A is not the primary cause for concern, however. Rather, the point on which to focus is that Option B, the theoretically correct answer, has a strong negative point-biserial, indicating that students who did well on the test tended to do worse on this item than students who did poorly overall. Unlike Item 10, we have *two* distractors with positive point-biserials. Unless two of the distractors are correct and the "officially" correct answer is wrong, this item will need extensive revision of its options (and perhaps even its stem). If there *are* two correct distractors and an incorrect "answer," though, Option B should be left alone, and one or both of Options C and D will need revising, and the key should be changed accordingly.

Item 18 is slightly less problematic than the first two, because while it has a negative discrimination value, it is close to zero, indicating that it is only harming reliability slightly. Like Item 20, it too has a pair of distractors with positive point-biserial estimates, one of which was only chosen by 3% of the examinees (one student). All the options except Option A need to be examined and probably revised. With so many problematic options, the stem may also be contributing to the situation, so it should be reviewed as well.

After this group of three highly problematic items, we should review Items 6, 12, 16, 17, and 19. Items 6, 12, and 19 have weak discrimination values; Items 16, 17, and 19 are outside of the .30–.70 range for IF, meaning they would be problematic in an NRT, but not necessarily in a CRT. By looking at which options were selected by too few students (Options 17C, 17D, 19B, and 19C; possibly 12A), or have problematic point-biserial values (Options 6A, 6B, 12A, 12B, 12C, 16A, 16D, 19A, and 19D), we can know where to focus our revision efforts on these items. As a clarification, note that that 17C and 17D are not actively *hurting* reliability, and in fact do have adequately large negative point-biserials. Making these two distractors more attractive should increase item difficulty enough to move it into the targeted range, assuming this is an NRT. Note further that the issues with 6A and 6B could be interrelated, but it is impossible to be sure without reading the question.

A last, slightly problematic group of items, for which we should consider revising specific options, is Items 1 and 8. Option C on Item 1 was not attractive to enough test takers, and had a weak positive point-biserial. (A weak positive point-biserial indicates that high-scoring test takers did slightly more poorly on that item than low-scoring test takers, but the pattern is so weak as to suggest there may not be much relationship at all between that item and total score.) Option B should also be examined, since it too had a weak positive point-biserial. On Item 8, the only problem is that Option A had a weak positive point-biserial, so this option should be revisited. Note, however, that since both these items had satisfactory difficulty and discrimination values, they are not *very* high priorities if resources (time and/or item writers) are stretched thin.

Finally, it should be pointed out that these analyses have all used the point-biserial correlation, which is normally used for item discrimination in NRT. In CRT, however, readers might consider performing these analyses using ϕ instead, although the point-biserial will provide some useful information in a CRT as well (see Chapter 16).

Summary

In this chapter, we began by discussing the purpose of distractor analysis as a means of improving item quality—that is, the results tell us where we should focus our efforts in revising items. We focused on two particular tools for this, the response frequency for each option, and the individual option's point-biserial correlation with total test score. This was followed by an example of how to interpret these results to identify problematic options in need of revision. The chapter then presented how to score multiple-choice data using Excel, as well as how to perform distractor analyses in Excel. It concluded with additional practice interpreting the results of distractor analyses.

18 RELIABILITY: SCORING CONSISTENCY FOR NORM-REFERENCED TESTS

Introduction

This chapter discusses reliability. It begins by briefly reviewing the concepts of reliability and the standard error of measurement (SEM), topics which are covered more extensively in Chapter 6, with a focus on internal consistency reliability. It moves then to discussion of the Spearman-Brown prophecy formula and the two different ways in which it can be applied. Worksheet 18.1, the last one to use Excel, will demonstrate how to calculate Cronbach's alpha (an internal consistency reliability estimate) and the SEM. Worksheet 18.2 will then cover how to apply the Spearman-Brown prophecy formula using paper, pencil, and a calculator. While it would be possible to use Excel to apply this formula, it is actually easier and faster to do it by hand (with the help of a calculator) than to enter the formula.

Objectives

By the end of this chapter, readers will know or understand:

- approaches to estimating *reliability*, particularly *internal-consistency reliability*
- the effect of test length on reliability, and the *Spearman-Brown prophecy formula*
- how to calculate *Cronbach's alpha* and the *standard error of measurement (SEM)* using Excel
- how to apply the Spearman-Brown prophecy formula using paper, pencil, and a calculator.

Overview of Reliability

As explained in Chapter 6, reliability is the consistency of scoring in norm-referenced testing. When a student receives a score on a test, that number (the *observed score*) is the product of his *true score*, or ability if the test had no measurement error, combined with *measurement error*. We use reliability formulas to estimate how much of that observed score is attributable to the true score, not to error.

Some approaches to estimating reliability involve administering tests twice—either the same test twice (*test-retest reliability*), or two equivalent forms of the test (*parallel forms reliability*)—and then correlating the results.

Other approaches to reliability, known as *internal consistency reliability*, only require administering a test once. As the name suggests, they look at the extent to which different parts of the test are measuring the same thing, or the degree to which they are measuring it in the same way. These different parts may be two halves of the test (*split-half reliability*), in which case we must use the Spearman-Brown prophecy formula to correct for the fact that each half is, naturally, only half as long as the overall test, and therefore less reliable than the two halves together. Alternatively, we may use a formula such as Cronbach's alpha to estimate internal consistency reliability. Cronbach's alpha is equivalent to averaging together the results of all the possible split halves (Wainer and Thissen 2001), with the Spearman-Brown length correction already accounted for by the formula. The formula for Cronbach's alpha is:

$$\alpha = \frac{k}{k-1}\left(1 - \frac{\sum s_i^2}{s_x^2}\right)$$

where k = the number of items on the test,

s_i^2 = the *population* variance for an individual item on the test,

$\sum s_i^2$ = the sum, or total, of all these item variances, and

s_x^2 = the *population* variance of the total test score—that is, after the total score is calculated for each student, the variance of those scores is calculated.

Besides giving us an estimate of the amount of measurement error involved in a score, alpha (or any other reliability coefficient) is also an important factor when correlating scores on two tests. Simply correlating two tests means that the correlation will be affected by unreliability in each test. If we apply the **correction for attenuation**, however, we are effectively providing the correlation between the true scores on the two tests (Allen and Yen 1979; Bachman 2004; Thorndike and Hagen 1969). The formula for this correction is:

$$r_{T1T2} = \frac{r_{12}}{\sqrt{\alpha_1 \alpha_2}}$$

where r_{T1T2} = the corrected correlation between Test 1 and Test 2, that is, the estimated correlation between their true scores,

r_{12} = the correlation between the observed scores for Test 1 and Test 2,

α_1 = the reliability of Test 1, and

α_2 = the reliability of Test 2. (Note that although Cronbach's alpha, abbreviated α, is used here, any other reliability estimate is also allowed in this formula.)

Besides being concerned with the overall consistency (and accuracy) of our test scores, we also need to be concerned about the effects of measurement error on individual students. After all, if we know there is measurement error involved in a test (as there is), we recognize that a student's observed score is not the same as their true score. We expect it to be somewhat close to their true score, though. Presumably, the more reliable the test, the closer together the true score and observed score will be. Likewise, the more measurement error there is, the farther apart they might be expected to lie. The standard error of measurement (SEM) serves as a confidence interval for us. Because of the properties of the normal distribution, we can be 68% sure that a student's true score will be within one standard error of measurement of their observed score. We can be 95% confident that their true score is within two SEMs of their observed score, and over 99% that they will be no more than three SEMs apart. The formula for the SEM is

$SEM = s_x \sqrt{1 - \alpha}$, where s_x is the standard deviation for total test scores, and α is

reliability. (Note that although Cronbach's alpha, abbreviated α, is used here, any other reliability estimate is also allowed in this formula.)

Reliability—and the SEM, as a result—is influenced by the quality of items, as well as the number of items. Item quality here refers especially to discrimination— if the questions on a test are all measuring the same thing, they should be highly correlated with each other, and therefore they should correlate highly with total test score. This item-total correlation is, of course, expressed by the point-biserial correlation coefficient, which is used as an NRT discrimination index. Furthermore, adding additional items to a test will tend to improve its reliability, assuming they are of comparable quality to the ones already included. When reliability is lower than the target level set in the test context and purpose specifications (see Chapter 3), we need to revise problematic items, add additional items, or both. Chapters 15–17 have dealt with item analysis, and how to identify items that need revision. When it comes to adding items, however, how many do we need? To answer this question, at least in NRT, we can use the Spearman-Brown prophecy formula:

$$r_{\text{new}} = \frac{mr_{\text{old}}}{1 + (m - 1)r_{\text{old}}}$$

where r_{new} = the reliability after changing the length of the test,

          r_{old} = reliability before changing the length of the test, and

          m = the factor by which the length of the test will be changed. (N.B. As pointed out in Chapter 6, m is not the number of items on the test, and it is not the number of items the test needs to add.)

Thus, if we want to increase the length of the test by 50%, m will equal 1.5, because the revised test will be 150% of the original length of the test. If we double the number of items, m will equal 2. On the other hand, if we cut the number of items by 30% for some reason, *m* will equal .7, because the new test will only be 70% as long as the original.

The formula above is the one used when calculating the effect on reliability of a particular change in test length. We can also use it, however, if we want to know how much to change the length in order to reach some target reliability level. In that case, we solve for *m*, rather than for r_{new}. We can use the formula above to do this, or we can transform it for greater convenience, making the math a little simpler, as below.

$$m = \frac{r_{new}(1 - r_{old})}{r_{old}(1 - r_{new})}$$

Worksheet 18.1: Calculating Cronbach's Alpha and the SEM in Excel

Introduction

This worksheet will explain how to calculate Cronbach's alpha and the standard error of measurement (SEM) in Excel. It will then demonstrate the effect on reliability and the SEM of deleting several negatively discriminating items from the test.

Procedures

1 Open the file **DALT Worksheet 18-1.xls**.

2 Calculate the population variance for Item 1:

    a Select **B42**.

    b Type **=VARP(** and select **B2:B31**.

    c Type **)** and press Enter.

    d Complete formula: **=VARP(B2:B31)**

    e Make sure the result is formatted to show three decimal places (**.249**).

3 Select and copy **B42**. Select **B42:U42** and paste.

4 Use the **COUNTA** function to calculate *k*. **COUNTA** counts the number of cells that are not empty, whereas **COUNT** only counts the number of cells containing numbers, or formulas that return numbers. (Note that if we manually type in 20 for *k*, and if we delete any items later to see what the effect is on reliability, we will have to update *k* separately.)

    a Select **B44**.

    b Type **=COUNTA(** and select **B1:U1**.

    c Type **)** and press Enter.

   d Complete formula: **=COUNTA(B1:U1)**

   e Do not display any decimal places.

5 Add together all the item variances using **SUM**. The complete formula is **=SUM(B42:U42)**. Make sure the result is formatted to show three decimal places (**4.592**).

6 Use the formula $\alpha = \dfrac{k}{k-1}(1 - \dfrac{\sum s_i^2}{s_x^2})$ to calculate alpha:

   a Select **B46**.

   b Type **=(** and select **B44**.

   c Type **/(** and select **B44**.

   d Type **−1))*(1−** and select **B45**.

   e Type **/** and select **X41**.

   f Type **)** and press Enter.

   g Complete formula. **=(B44/(B44−1))*(1−B45/X41)**

   h Make sure the result is formatted to display three decimal places (**.675**).

7 Use the formula $SEM = s_x \sqrt{1 - \alpha}$ to calculate the SEM:

   a Select **B47**.

   b Type **=** and select **X39**.

   c Type ***SQRT(1−** and select **B46**.

   d Type **)** and press Enter.

   e Complete formula: **=X39*SQRT(1−B46)**

   f Make sure the result is formatted to display one decimal place (**2.0**).

Based on both the point-biserial and ID_{UL} estimates, Items 10, 18, and 20 all have varying degrees of negative discrimination. Ideally, we will review these items and try to improve them; however, let us take a few moments right now to see what the effect would be on reliability of simply deleting these problematic questions.

8 Now, we will examine the effect of deleting items with negative discrimination:

   a Click on the button for **Column K**, and press Delete. This will delete Item 10.

   b Click on the button for **Column S**, and press Delete. This will delete Item 18.

   c Click on the button for **Column U**, and press Delete. This will delete Item 20.

   d Because of the way we have set up the worksheet, the total score variance, sum of the item variances, and k have all automatically updated. We now see that the revised value for alpha is .810, and the revised SEM is 1.8 points (10.6% of 17 points).

   e Undo the three deletions.

9 Reformat **B46** to show five decimal places (**.67515**). Write this number down, and then return it to its previous three figures.

Discussion

The rule of thumb for a high stakes test, as noted in Chapters 3 and 5, is that alpha should be .800 or greater. For a lower-stakes test the level to target is somewhat subjective, but for any significant grade in a course, I would be reluctant to use anything below .700. At that point, 30% of the score is attributable to measurement error; much lower, and it is over a third. Making decisions that will affect students usually calls for a higher level of confidence in the information being used to make those decisions. As a way of determining whether a certain reliability is acceptable or insufficient, the SEM can be used to show what the confidence level is for the test.

In the current example, when including all 20 items, at .675, our reliability is slightly below the borderline of acceptability for a classroom test. With an SEM of 2.0 points (10%), we can be 68% confident that a student's observed score is within two points of their true score. We can be 95% confident that their observed score and true score are no more than four points (20%) apart. The confidence interval represented by the SEM is fairly wide, and might be deemed unacceptably large, although this is something of a judgment call. (Recall that the implications of confidence intervals for students near cut scores—i.e. decision points—apply only in criterion-referenced testing, and this issue was discussed in Chapter 6.)

If we eliminate the three items with negative discrimination values, rather than attempting to revise them as we normally would, we find that alpha increases to .810, which would be satisfactory even for a high-stakes test. The SEM decreases slightly, to 1.8 points, or 10.6% (because the entire test is now worth only 17 points). We now have 68% and 95% confidence intervals of 1.8 points and 3.6 points, respectively (10.6% and 21.2%).

Worksheet 18.2: Applying the Spearman-Brown Prophecy Formula

Introduction

In this worksheet, we will use the Spearman-Brown prophecy formula to examine first the effect of increasing the length of the test we analyzed in Worksheet 18.1 by 50%, and then to calculate a value for *m* that should allow us to achieve a reliability of .800. In both parts of the worksheet, we will work from the reliability estimate for all 20 items, taken to five decimal (i.e. .67515) places for greater accuracy and fewer rounding errors.

As noted in the introduction, this worksheet does not use Excel. Using paper, pencil, and calculator is probably easier and faster than using Excel would be.

Readers therefore should get out a blank piece of paper, a pencil or pen, and a calculator before starting.

Procedures

1 We will use the formula $r_{new} = \dfrac{mr_{old}}{1 + (m-1)r_{old}}$ to calculate r_{new}, given the following:

> m = 1.5 (i.e. we will increase the length of the test by 50%, from 20 to 30 items, so it is 1.5 times its original length)

r_{old} = .67515

a Write the formula on your paper, and then rewrite it with the correct values plugged in for the variables: $r_{new} = \dfrac{mr_{old}}{1 + (m-1)r_{old}} = \dfrac{(1.5)(.67515)}{1 + (1.5-1)(.67515)}$

b Solve the formula by multiplying, dividing, adding, and subtracting, as appropriate:

$$r_{new} = \frac{(1.5)(.67515)}{1 + (1.5-1)(.67515)} = \frac{1.012725}{1 + (.5)(.67515)} = \frac{1.012725}{1 + .337575} = \frac{1.012725}{1.337575}$$

c $r_{new} = .75714 \cong .757$

2 Next, we will use the revised version of the formula, $m = \dfrac{r_{new}(1 - r_{old})}{r_{old}(1 - r_{new})}$,

to find what new test length would give us a reliability of .800:

a Write the formula on your paper, and then rewrite it with the correct values plugged in for the variables: $m = \dfrac{r_{new}(1 - r_{old})}{r_{old}(1 - r_{new})} = \dfrac{(.800)(1-.67515)}{(.67515)(1-.800)}$

b Solve the formula by multiplying, dividing, adding, and subtracting, as appropriate: $m = \dfrac{(.800)(1-.67515)}{(.67515)(1-.800)} = \dfrac{(.800)(.32485)}{(.67515)(.200)} = \dfrac{.25988}{.13503}$

c $m = 1.925 \cong 1.9$

d We can confirm this answer by using the first version of the formula:

i. $r_{new} = \dfrac{mr_{old}}{1 + (m-1)r_{old}} = \dfrac{(1.9)(.67515)}{1 + (1.9-1)(.67515)} = \dfrac{(1.9)(.67515)}{1 + (.9)(.67515)} = \dfrac{1.28279}{1 + .60764} = \dfrac{1.28279}{1.60764}$

ii. $r_{new} = .79793 \cong .798$

Discussion

190% (i.e. 1.9) of 20 items is 38, which brings us within a hair's breadth of .800. On the other hand, if we use the three-place estimate for m of 1.925 (not shown above), the new reliability is estimated at .800. 192.5% of 20 items rounds to 39 items, illustrating a handy suggestion to keep in mind: if a rounded value of m (rounded downwards, that is) is checked and r_{new} is a fraction below the target reliability level, add one extra item to the number of new ones to be written. In the case of this 20-item test, we can see that it will require 19 more items of comparable quality to bring our reliability up from .675 to .800. On the other hand, in Worksheet 17.1 we also saw the importance of having positively discriminating items, a point that was illustrated when dropping three poor items actually boosted reliability above .800.

Summary

In this chapter, we began with a brief review of the concepts of reliability and the SEM, which had been introduced in Chapter 6. We then discussed the Spearman-Brown prophecy formula, and two ways in which it could be applied. This was followed by two worksheets, one using Excel to calculate Cronbach's alpha and the SEM, and the other using paper, pencil, and a calculator to practice using the Spearman-Brown prophecy formula.

19 DEPENDABILITY: SCORING OR CLASSIFICATION CONSISTENCY FOR CRITERION-REFERENCED TESTS

Introduction

This chapter deals with dependability, the CRT analog of reliability. It begins with a brief review of estimates of dependability for scores and the criterion-referenced confidence interval, before moving on to the dependability of classification decisions. Worksheet 19.1 will provide practice estimating Φ, the CI_{CRT}, and $\Phi(\lambda)$.

Objectives

By the end of this chapter, readers will know or understand:

- how *dependability* contrasts with *reliability* in terms of the decisions being made
- how to apply shortcut formulas to estimate Φ, CI_{CRT}, and $\Phi(\lambda)$ using norm-referenced reliability statistics and a paper, pencil, and calculator.

Overview of Dependability

Dependability, which is covered in greater conceptual detail in Chapter 6, is consistency of measurement in the context of criterion-referenced testing. It can be divided into *consistency of scoring*, which is similar to reliability for an NRT, and *consistency of classification* (i.e. classification of students as masters or non-masters).

Dependability of scoring differs from reliability in that while norm-referenced tests are concerned with *relative* decisions—ranking students consistently—criterion-referenced tests are used to make *absolute* decisions. Deciding how one student's performance on a test compares to that of other students is a relative decision—the sort for which an NRT is used. In contrast, if we attempt to decide how much ability a student demonstrates on the test, without reference to the performance of any other student(s) or group of students, we are making an absolute decision. Of course, ranking people is somewhat easier to do accurately than obtaining a measure of ability. This is even true when making judgments about visible characteristics, such as height, or even age. If we are asked to put a group of people in order by age, we will probably make fewer mistakes than we will if we have to estimate each person's age. This difference between absolute and relative decisions is why a test's dependability is always at least slightly lower than its reliability would be. However, in a CRT situation, we are limited to using dependability, rather than reliability, because of the interpretive framework—the question of whether we are making relative (NRT) or absolute (CRT) decisions.

The best way to estimate dependability is using generalizability theory, a statistical methodology that is too advanced to cover in an introductory testing book. Fortunately, there is a formula available that allows us to estimate Φ, the CRT dependability index, using Cronbach's alpha and a few other statistics (Brown 1990). Unfortunately, *this formula only works with dichotomous data*:

$$\Phi = \frac{\dfrac{ns^2}{n-1}(KR20)}{\dfrac{ns^2}{n-1}(KR20) + \dfrac{M(1-M)-s^2}{k-1}}$$

where n = the number of people who took the test,

s^2 = the variance (using the *population* formula) of test scores, in **proportion-correct metric** (i.e. the decimal equivalent of the percentage of questions that were answered correctly; for example, a proportion-correct score of .80 means that the student answered 80% of the questions correctly),

KR-20 = the reliability of the test, using Cronbach's alpha or the K-R20 formula (Note that K-R20 is used here, rather than alpha or $r_{xx'}$, in order to emphasize that this shortcut only works with dichotomous data. It does not really matter whether alpha or KR-20 is used, as the result will be the same. The hyphen is omitted from K-R20 because it looks like K − R20, which could be mistaken for "K minus R20."),

M = the mean of the *proportion* scores, and

k = the number of items on the test.

In Chapter 18, the standard error of measurement (SEM) was discussed as an estimate of the confidence interval showing the likely distance between a student's observed score and their true score. It can also be viewed as an estimate of the accuracy of individual test scores. In CRT, the equivalent estimate is the *CRT confidence interval*, or CI_{CRT}, which also can be approximated (Brown and Hudson 2002) using the formula $CI_{CRT} = \sqrt{\dfrac{M(1-M)-s^2}{k-1}}$. As with the Φ shortcut

formula, *this formula also requires proportion-correct metric*. The CI_{CRT} is interpreted analogously to the SEM, in terms of 68% and 95% confidence intervals about observed scores. It differs from the SEM, of course, in that the CI_{CRT} is used for absolute score decisions, not relative ones. (See Chapter 6 as well for a discussion of the use of the CI_{CRT} with students who are near cut scores.)

Finally, besides being used to assign scores, CRTs are also often used to make classification decisions about students—that is, classifying them as masters or non-masters, as being above or below a certain level of ability, and so on. Common examples of this type of decision include pass-fail decisions, the assigning of letter grades, or the placement of new students into one level of a program or another.

Just as scoring consistency needs to be estimated, classification consistency does as well. As noted in Chapter 6, estimates of classification consistency can be categorized on the basis of whether they treat all classification errors as being equally important or severe (*threshold loss error indices*), or they view small errors as being less serious than large errors (*squared error loss agreement indices*). In curriculum-related testing, squared error loss agreement estimates tend to be more useful; the most popular of these is probably $\Phi(\lambda)$. Like the other dependability estimates discussed in this chapter, it is ideally estimated using generalizability theory, but *with dichotomous data* it can be approximated through a shortcut formula (Brennan 1992) that employs NRT reliability results:

$$\Phi(\lambda) = 1 - \frac{1}{k-1}\left[\frac{M(1-M) - s^2}{(M-\lambda)^2 + s^2}\right]$$

where k = the number of items on the test,

M = the mean of the *proportion* scores,

s^2 = the population variance of the *proportion* scores, and

λ = the cut score.

Brennan (1980) points out that $\Phi(\lambda)$ is at its lowest value, and equal to Φ, when the cut score is equal to the mean. Because $\Phi(\lambda)$ includes the cut score within its formula, its value will change if the cut score changes—in other words, it is cut-score dependent. In fact, this dependence is signaled by its very name, since λ is the symbol for the cut score. Thus, if a test has multiple cut scores, $\Phi(\lambda)$ must be recalculated separately for each of them, just as the CRT item discrimination indices must be as well.

Worksheet 19.1: Estimating Φ, the CI$_{CRT}$, and $\Phi(\lambda)$ From NRT Reliability Statistics

Introduction

In this worksheet, we will use shortcut formulas to estimate three dependability indices using descriptive statistics and the results of NRT reliability analyses. The indices to be calculated are Φ, the CI$_{CRT}$, and $\Phi(\lambda)$. When doing calculations such as these, particularly when they are approximations of the actual formulas, not the exact formulas themselves, it is a good idea to keep as many decimal places as possible from step to step, to minimize errors from repeated rounding. In the following examples, we will work with five significant digits or five decimal places, whichever is greater.

As with Worksheet 18.2, this worksheet does not use Excel, since using paper, pencil, and calculator is probably easier and faster than using Excel would be. Readers therefore should get out one or more blank pieces of paper, a pencil or pen, and a calculator before starting.

Procedures

1 We will start by using the formula $\Phi = \dfrac{\dfrac{ns^2}{n-1}(KR20)}{\dfrac{ns^2}{n-1}(KR20) + \dfrac{M(1-M)-s^2}{k-1}}$, using

the reliability estimate and descriptive statistics from Worksheet 18.1. Recall the following results, converted to proportion-correct metric and expanded to five significant digits: $n = 30$, $s^2 = .032014$, K-R20 = α = .67515, $M = .54167$, and $k = 20$.

a Write the formula on your paper: $\Phi = \dfrac{\dfrac{ns^2}{n-1}(KR20)}{\dfrac{ns^2}{n-1}(KR20) + \dfrac{M(1-M)-s^2}{k-1}}$

b Rewrite it, plugging in the correct values for the variables:

$$\Phi = \dfrac{\dfrac{(30)(.032014)}{30-1}(.67515)}{\dfrac{(30)(.032014)}{30-1}(.67515) + \dfrac{.54167(1-.54167)-.032014}{20-1}}$$

c Solve the formula by multiplying, dividing, adding, and subtracting, as appropriate:

$$\Phi = \dfrac{\dfrac{(30)(.032014)(.67515)}{29}}{\dfrac{(30)(.032014)(.67515)}{29} + \dfrac{.54167(.45833)-.032014}{19}}$$

d $\Phi = \dfrac{\dfrac{.64843}{29}}{\dfrac{.64843}{29} + \dfrac{.24826-.032014}{19}} = \dfrac{\dfrac{.64843}{29}}{\dfrac{.64843}{29} + \dfrac{.21625}{19}}$

e $\Phi = \dfrac{\dfrac{.64843}{29}}{\dfrac{.64843}{29} + \dfrac{.24826-.032014}{19}} = \dfrac{\dfrac{.64843}{29}}{\dfrac{.64843}{29} + \dfrac{.21625}{19}}$

f $\Phi = \dfrac{.022360}{.022360+.011382} = \dfrac{.022360}{.033742} = .66268 \cong .663$

2 Next, we estimate the CI$_{CRT}$ using the formula $\quad CI_{CRT} = \sqrt{\dfrac{M(1-M)-s^2}{k-1}}$

and the following results from Worksheet 18.1: $M = .54167$, $s^2 = .032014$, and $k = 20$.

a Write the formula on your paper, and then rewrite it with the correct values plugged in for the variables:

$$CI_{CRT} = \sqrt{\frac{M(1-M)-s^2}{k-1}} = \sqrt{\frac{(.54167)(1-.54167)-.032014}{20-1}}$$

b Solve the formula by multiplying, dividing, adding, and subtracting, as appropriate:

$$CI_{CRT} = \sqrt{\frac{(.54167)(.45833)-.032014}{19}} = \sqrt{\frac{.24826-.032014}{19}} = \sqrt{\frac{.216246}{19}}$$

c $\quad CI_{CRT} = \sqrt{\dfrac{.216246}{19}} = \sqrt{.011381} = .10668 \cong .107 = 10.7\%$

3 Finally, we estimate $\Phi(\lambda)$ for a cut score of 70%, which can also be written as $\Phi(\lambda=.70)$. This is the same cut score as was used in Worksheet 16.1. The

formula is $\Phi(\lambda) = 1 - \dfrac{1}{k-1}\left[\dfrac{M(1-M)-s^2}{(M-\lambda)^2+s^2}\right]$, and as with the other two

estimates, we will use the results of Worksheet 18.1. Therefore, $k = 20$, $M = .54167$, and $s^2 = .032014$.

a Write the formula on your paper: $\Phi(\lambda) = 1 - \dfrac{1}{k-1}\left[\dfrac{M(1-M)-s^2}{(M-\lambda)^2+s^2}\right]$

b Rewrite the formula with the correct values plugged in for the variables:

$$\Phi(\lambda) = 1 - \frac{1}{20-1}\left[\frac{(.54167)(1-.54167)-.032014}{(.54167-.70)^2+.032014}\right]$$

c Solve the formula by multiplying, dividing, adding, and subtracting, as appropriate:

$$\Phi(\lambda) = 1 - \frac{1}{19}\left[\frac{(.54167)(.45833)-.032014}{(.15833)^2+.032014}\right] = 1 - \frac{1}{19}\left[\frac{(.54167)(.45833)-.032014}{.025068+.032014}\right]$$

d $\Phi(\lambda) = 1 - \dfrac{1}{19}\left[\dfrac{.24826-.032014}{.057082}\right] = 1 - \dfrac{1}{19}\left[\dfrac{.216246}{.057082}\right]$

e $\Phi(\lambda) = 1 - \dfrac{1}{19}\left[\dfrac{.216246}{.057082}\right] = 1 - \left(\dfrac{1}{19}\right)(3.78834) = 1 - .19939 = .80061 \cong .800$

Discussion

A dependability of .663 is clearly unsatisfactory, although it is only marginally lower than the reliability estimate of .675. Of course, if we recalculated these results with the three negatively discriminating items removed (see Worksheet 18.1), the result for Φ would probably be much closer to .800. (Note that those readers interested in calculating the effects on Φ, the CI_{CRT}, and $\Phi(\lambda)$ of dropping those three items should repeat this exercise using the following values: $n = 30$, $s^2 = .056225$, $\alpha = .80981$, $M = .53725$, and $k = 17$.)

The poor dependability estimate no doubt plays a role in the large confidence interval. This result of 10.7%, or 2.1 points out of 20, means that a test taker's true score is 68% likely to be within 10.7% of their observed score, and 95% likely to be within 21.4% of their observed score. This is rather a large range, and indicates that scores are not terribly accurate. For example, if a test taker has an average score of 54.2%, we are 95% confident that their true score lies somewhere between 32.8% and 75.6%. For a tighter confidence interval, we are only 65% sure that their true score is somewhere between 43.5% and 64.9%. This is an important finding. Although the dependability of .663 is not precipitously low, and is probably close to acceptable for low-stakes purposes such as classroom testing, we only become aware of the high variability in individual scores when we consider the CI_{CRT}. With confidence intervals of over 10%, large numbers of students may be at risk of being misclassified, a fact we would otherwise have remained ignorant of.

The classification dependability index $\Phi(\lambda)$ offers the most hopeful bit of news in these results. It indicates an acceptably high degree of consistency in how students are classified as masters or non-masters at the $\lambda = 70\%$ cut score. Although it was not calculated for other cut scores, we know that if decisions are made at 80% or 90%, for example, $\Phi(\lambda)$ will be even higher, given that they are further away from the mean. By the same token, a cut score closer to the mean (for example, at 60%) would have a lower $\Phi(\lambda)$ value than the one calculated here.

Summary

In this chapter, we reviewed the notion of dependability, contrasting it with reliability in terms of whether test scores are to be used for relative or absolute decisions. Shortcut formulas were presented for estimating indices of score dependability, CRT confidence intervals, and classification dependability. Worksheet 19.1 then provided an opportunity to practice applying those formulas and interpreting the results.

GLOSSARY

λ: See cut score.

φ: A correlational estimate of item discrimination for CRT, it is the correlation between item performance and mastery-non-mastery. Also a correlation coefficient used to correlate two dichotomous variables. As a rule of thumb, item φ should be ≥ .30 when used for item discrimination.

Φ: See *CRT dependability index*.

Φ(λ): Commonly used squared error loss agreement index (i.e. index of CRT classification consistency). Calculated using generalizability theory, but can be estimated for dichotomous data using a shortcut formula. As a rule of thumb, Ψ(λ) should be ≥ .80.

ρ: See *Spearman ρ*.

absolute cell reference: Referring to a cell or range in a spreadsheet in terms of exactly where it is, not in relation to the active cell. Performed in Excel using F4 button.

absolute decisions: Assigning scores to students, as in CRT.

acceptable response scoring: Cloze scoring method that counts any reasonable response as correct; may include partial credit for incorrect answers that are partially correct.

achievement test: Test used to identify how well students have met course objectives or mastered course content.

admission test: Test used to decide whether a student should be admitted to the program.

alternate forms reliability: See *parallel forms reliability*.

alternate forms: See *parallel forms*.

alternatives: The possible answers on a multiple-choice or matching task, from which the test taker must choose. (See *options*.)

analytic scoring: Use of a rating scale or rubric in which each category of concern is rated separately (e.g., grammatical accuracy, content, organization, etc.).

answer choices: The possible answers on a multiple-choice or matching task, from which the test taker must choose. (See *options*.)

assessment use argument (AUA): Bachman's expansion of validity arguments using formal argument structure. Includes evidence for each link in the chain of inferences from examinee performance to score interpretation.

authenticity: Degree to which test tasks resemble target language use (TLU) tasks.

B*: Polytomous CRT subtractive item discrimination index, equivalent to the B-index.

B-index: Subtractive estimate of item discrimination for CRT, equal to the difference in item facility between masters and non-masters. As a rule of thumb, B should be $\geq$ .40.

bimodal distribution: A distribution with two modes.

bins: Score intervals, or groupings of scores used in graphing a score distribution or creating a frequency distribution table; each score is rounded off (e.g., to the nearest 5 or 10 points).

CAS: See *computer-automated scoring*.

CAT: See *computer-adaptive testing*.

categorical variables: Variables that can be grouped into categories, but the categories cannot be put in any sort of meaningful order (e.g. gender, native language, country of origin, and favorite color). All we can do is to count the number of people in each category.

cell: A single "box" in a spreadsheet.

CI$_{CRT}$: See *CRT confidence interval*.

classical test theory: Model underlying traditional approaches to calculating reliability, which assumes that observed test scores are the result of test takers' true scores combined with measurement error. Also referred to as *classical true-score theory*.

classical true-score theory: See *classical test theory*.

classification dependability: Consistency with which test takers are classified as masters or non-masters. Estimated using threshold loss and squared error loss agreement indices.

cloze test: Single words throughout a passage are replaced with blanks, and students must write the missing words in the blanks, or select the correct word in the case of multiple-choice cloze. Normally, the first two sentences or two will be left intact, so readers can gain a sense of the passage.

column: A vertical line of cells in a spreadsheet.

completion: See *fill-in-the-blank*.

computer-adaptive testing (CAT): Type of computer-based testing in which the computer selects which item to present to a test taker based on their previous responses. Because the items all target the individual test taker's ability level, testing is both efficient and accurate.

computer-automated scoring (CAS): Using a computer to automatically score written or spoken constructed response tasks, including both limited production and extended production responses.

concurrent validity: The degree of relationship between test scores and scores on a different test intended to assess the same construct(s). Later subsumed under criterion-related validity, but now viewed as a type of evidence (correlation with other measures) supporting construct validity, not a separate type of validity in its own right.

Conditional Formatting: Function in Excel 2007 and later versions that automatically changes the highlighting of cells, columns, or rows based on user-defined criteria, such as whether values are above or below some particular level.

conditional SEM (CSEM): Estimate of the standard error of measurement (SEM) calculated for a specific score level.

construct: The ability that we want to assess. Not directly observable.

construct-based test development: Approach to planning tests that starts out by considering the construct that is being assessed, and selecting or creating test tasks that will tap into it (that is, that will elicit evidence showing how much of the construct each examinee has).

construct definition: Statement of what specific aspects of language ability a construct is regarded as including (see Table 3.1).

construct validity: Degree to which it is appropriate to interpret a test score as an indicator of the construct of interest.

constructed response task: Test task calling for the examinee to write or say something in response. Constructed response tasks can be further subdivided into limited production and extended production tasks.

content validity: The adequacy with which test items sample the universe to which the test developer wants scores to generalize; that is, how well the test samples the subject matter or curriculum on which the test is based. Now viewed as a type of evidence (content representativeness and relevance) supporting construct validity, not as a separate type of validity in its own right.

continuous variable: A variable that can have any value within a particular range, with the range typically being fairly large.

corpus: A large body of text that has been stored on a computer and is designed for linguistic analysis.

correction for attenuation: Adjustment that adjusts the correlation between two tests so that it is not reduced by measurement error; in effect, it provides the correlation between the true scores on the two tests by adjusting for their reliabilities.

correlation: The degree of relationship between two sets of numbers.

correlation coefficient: A mathematical estimate of the strength of relationship between two sets of numbers.

correlational approach to estimating item discrimination: In order to estimate item discrimination, a correlation coefficient is calculated between scores on individual items, and on something else. In NRT, scores are correlated with total test score (point-biserial); in CRT, they are correlated with passing/failing or mastery/non-mastery (ϕ).

criterion-referenced test (CRT): Test on which results are interpreted in terms of how much a learner knows in "absolute" terms, that is, in relation to one or more standards, objectives, or other criteria, and not with respect to how much other learners know. CRT scores are generally reported in terms of the percentage correct, not percentile.

criterion-related validity: Umbrella term that included both concurrent validity and predictive validity. Now viewed as a type of evidence (criterion-relatedness) supporting construct validity, not as a separate type of validity in its own right.

Cronbach's alpha: Internal consistency reliability estimate (NRT); probably the most commonly used. Equivalent to computing all the possible split-half reliability estimates and averaging them together. As a rule of thumb, alpha should be $\geq .80$.

CRT: See *criterion-referenced test.*

CRT confidence interval (CI_{CRT}, CRT CI): Confidence interval for a test taker's observed score on a CRT, telling us how likely it is that their true score is within a certain range around (i.e., a certain distance from) their observed score. Calculated using generalizability theory, but can be estimated for dichotomous data using a shortcut formula.

CRT dependability index (Φ): Estimate of score dependability for CRT. Calculated using generalizability theory, but can be estimated for dichotomous data using a shortcut formula. As a rule of thumb, Φ should be $\geq .80$.

CSEM: See *conditional SEM.*

C-test: Task format similar to a cloze test, but with the second half of every other word deleted. C-tests are most commonly used as measures of general written language proficiency, and in particular, seem to assess both vocabulary knowledge and grammar.

curve grades: To adjust the course grades so that students receive higher grades than they would have otherwise.

cut score (λ): Score used to separate masters from non-masters, passing from failing, or to separate two levels on a placement exam. CRT item discrimination (the B-index or item ϕ) and classification consistency (e.g., $\Phi(\lambda)$) must be estimated separately for each cut score being used on a given test.

deletion-based tasks: Task formats in which a words, phrases, or portions of words are deleted in a written passage and replaced with blank spaces. Test takers must then fill in these blanks, either by writing in the empty space or by selecting from a range of options. They are most commonly a subset of limited production items, but they can also be written using selected response formats.

dependability: Consistency of scoring for a criterion-referenced test. Estimated statistically. (Compare *reliability*.)

descriptive statistics: Quantitative measures that describe how a group of scores are distributed, particularly how much they are clustered together, how much they are spread out from each other, and how the distribution of scores is shaped.

descriptors: In a rating scale, the descriptions of performance within a particular score band, which are based on the construct definition.

DI: See *difference index*.

DI*: Polytomous CRT subtractive item discrimination index, equivalent to the difference index.

diagnostic test: Test used to identify learners' areas of strength and weakness. Some language programs also use diagnostic tests to confirm that students were placed accurately.

dichotomous: Scored as correct or incorrect, receiving 0 or 1 point.

difference index (DI): Subtractive CRT discrimination index that requires giving the test twice, once to masters and once to non-masters. Can be calculated as part of a differential group study or intervention study. As a rule of thumb, the DI should be ≥ .40.

differential groups study: Approach to calculating the DI in which two existing groups are identified. One group is deemed to be at the mastery level in whatever ability is being assessed, and the other group is judged to still be non-masters.

direct test: Test that requires examinees to use the ability that is supposed to be being assessed; for example, a writing test that requires test takers to write something, or a speaking test that requires examinees to speak.

discourse analysis: The study of patternings of language in use and the circumstances (participants, situations, purposes, outcomes) with which they are typically associated.

discrete-point test: Test that uses a series of separate, unrelated tasks (usually test questions) to assess one "bit" of language ability at a time. This is typically done with multiple-choice questions.

discrimination indices: Measures of item discrimination.

dispersion: See *measures of dispersion*.

distractor analysis: Process of statistically identifying which options on a selected response task did their jobs well. It may involve response frequency, and/or correlation between selecting the item and total score (NRT) or mastery/non-mastery (CRT).

distractors: Incorrect options on a multiple-choice or matching item.

empirical rating scale development: Constructing a rating scale by looking at a sample of actual learner performances, dividing them into groups based on the level of performance, and then describing the characteristics of the written or spoken responses at each level.

exact word scoring: Cloze scoring method that requires that test takers supply the word that was in the original passage; any other word, regardless of how well it might fit in the blank, is counted wrong.

examinee-centered continuum models: Standard setting approaches that are based on expert judgments made about test takers' performances.

extended production task: Test task requiring responses that are longer than one sentence or utterance. They may only be two sentences or utterances long, or they might be much more extensive.

FACETS model: See *many-facet Rasch model.*

field dependence: Cognitive style associated with analytic processing.

field independence: Cognitive style associated with holistic processing.

fill-in-the-blank: Limited production task format in which test takers write a short response (normally one word) to complete a short bit of text, usually one sentence long.

Fisher's *Z*-transformation: Statistical transformation that allows a set of correlation coefficients to be averaged together.

fixed-deletion cloze: Type of cloze in which the words are deleted randomly—that is, every nth word is deleted, where *n* is some number chosen in advance. Also known as *nth-word deletion cloze, fixed ratio,* or *random deletion cloze,* since the deletions are at evenly-spaced intervals, which makes it effectively random which words (and which *types* of words) will be deleted: *n* is usually at least five (Alderson 1983), but often 10 or more.

form: a version of a test that is written to the same specifications as others. It uses the same task formats, assesses the same constructs, and so forth, but contains different tasks (prompts, questions, passages, etc.).

formative assessment: Test or other assessment that takes place while students are still in the process of learning something, and that is used to monitor how well that learning is progressing (see, e.g. Leung 2004). Closely related to progress assessment, and to the extent that the results of an assessment are used to guide the subsequent teaching and learning process, such assessment is formative.

frequency distribution: A table listing how many students received each score.

frequency polygon: A line graph showing how many test takers received each score.

G theory: See *generalizability theory*.

gap-fill: See *fill-in-the-blank and rational-deletion cloze.*.

generalizability coefficient: Estimate of (NRT) reliability obtained using generalizability theory. Equal to Cronbach's alpha when one group a test takers has a single undifferentiated set of scores.

generalizability (G) theory: A statistical approach that has developed as something of an expansion upon classical test theory. It attempts to model the effect on score variance of differences among test takers, and relevant facets of the measurement process (e.g. tasks or raters). It is also used to calculate Φ, the CI_{CRT}, and $\Phi(\lambda)$, as well as reliability estimates.

group oral interview: Task format in which pairs or small groups of students discuss one or more specific topics; these may be a list of questions or topics, or a reading or listening passage.

guessing parameter: See *IRT c parameter*.

high-stakes test: Tests with serious or important consequences for test takers or other stakeholders, e.g. tests used for immigration purposes or for entry to higher education.

histogram: A bar chart showing how many test takers received each score.

holistic scoring: Use of a rating scale or rubric in which the performance is given just one overall rating, which is based on the various categories of concern taken together as a whole.

ID$_{UL}$: See *upper-lower item discrimination*.

ID*$_{UL}$: Polytomous NRT subtractive item discrimination index. Equivalent to the upper-lower item discrimination.

IF: see *item facility*.

IF*: Polytomous item facility (difficulty) index.

impact: Effects of the test on people and institutions. This includes, but is not limited to, washback.

incomplete graphic organizer: Limited production task format in which test takers fill in empty spaces in a blank or partially blank graphic organizer. Used to assess sensitivity to the rhetorical structure of a passage or the ability to recognize main ideas, major ideas, and supporting details.

incomplete outline: Limited production task format in which test takers fill in empty spaces in a blank or partially outline. Used to assess sensitivity to the rhetorical structure of a passage or the ability to recognize main ideas, major ideas, and supporting details.

independent task: Test task that does not require the processing of any additional material; test takers can respond to the task based solely on the item or prompt itself. Examples of independent tasks include a grammar item that does not have any relationship to a reading or listening passage, or a speaking or writing prompt that is not based on a reading or listening passage.

indirect test: Test that attempts to assess one of the so-called "productive skills" through related tasks that do not require any speaking or writing. Instead, they rely upon tasks that will be easier and/or faster to grade; for example, an indirect test of writing might include a multiple-choice test of grammatical knowledge or error detection, and an indirect test of speaking might include a test of listening comprehension or the ability to select the response that best completes a short dialog.

integrated test: Test that requires examinees to use multiple aspects of language ability, typically to perform more life-like tasks. Examples might include taking notes over a listening passage and then writing a summary, or writing something about one or more texts read during the test. Such tests more closely resemble real-life language use tasks, and thus require more communicative language use.

internal consistency reliability: Ways of estimating reliability that only require administering a test once, and look at the extent to which different parts of the test are measuring the same thing, or the degree to which they are measuring it in the same way.

interpretive framework: The way in which a test or test score is viewed; most importantly, whether the test is norm-referenced or criterion-referenced.

inter-rater reliability: The degree of consistency across scores by different raters.

interval variables: Variables which are arranged in order, as with ordinal data, but there are equal distances between each point on the scale.

intervention study: Essentially a pre-test/post-test approach to calculating the DI in which the test is administered to one group of students twice, before and after they have received instruction in whatever material is being assessed.

intra-rater reliability: The consistency of the scores assigned by a single rater.

intuitive rating scale development: Constructing a rating scale by having one or more teachers or other experts base the scale on their expert judgment, knowledge of the teaching and testing context, and so on.

IRT: See *item response theory*.

IRT *a* parameter: Item response theory estimate of item discrimination.

IRT *b* parameter: Item response theory estimate of item difficulty.

IRT *c* parameter: Item response theory pseudo-chance parameter; typically slightly lower than the estimated likelihood of answering an item correctly by randomly guessing.

item: A test question that requires a short answer, or the selection of an appropriate response. Also commonly referred to as a test question.

item ϕ: See ϕ.

item analysis: Process of statistically identifying how well the questions did their jobs, and which ones might need improvement. It includes looking at item difficulty (primarily in NRT) and discrimination (in both NRT and CRT).

item discrimination: Estimate of how well an item separates high- and low-ability test takers (NRT) or masters and non-masters (CRT).

item facility (IF): Estimate of item difficulty. Equal to the proportion of test takers answering a question correctly. For NRT, the IF should be $\geq .30$ and $\leq .70$.

item independence: The principle that getting one item right should not depend on answering others correctly.

item response theory (IRT): Statistical approach to performing item and reliability analysis with large groups of test takers. It assumes that for an item with a given level of difficulty, the probability that a test taker will answer correctly depends on their level of ability.

item stem: The part of an item that actually poses the question. In a multiple-choice question, the stem is the portion before the options. In short-answer and true-false questions, it is the whole question.

item variance: The variance of the scores on a single item on a test; when used for calculating Cronbach's alpha, the population variance formula must be used.

Kendall's τ (tau): Correlation coefficient used for two ordinal variables. Used as an alternative to Spearman ρ.

key: The correct option on a multiple-choice or matching item.

K-R 20 (also KR-20, KR 20, and KR20): Shortcut estimate of Cronbach's alpha developed by Kuder and Richardson (1937). Requires dichotomous data, and provides the same result as alpha.

K-R 21 (also KR-21, KR 21, and KR21): Shortcut estimate of Cronbach's alpha developed by Kuder and Richardson (1937). Requires dichotomous data, and assumes all items are equally difficult.

kurtosis: A statistic that tells the degree to which a distribution is peaked or flattened.

language for specific purposes (LSP): The teaching or learning of a language with a focus on a specific professional area. The goal of LSP programs is not to improve language ability in the general sense, but rather to focus predominantly on the elements of language ability needed in that particular job or career field.

levels of data: The types of variables we are correlating (categorical/nominal, ordinal, interval, or ratio).

lexical density: The proportion of words that are lexical, or content words, as opposed to grammatical, or function words.

limited production task: Test task calling for examinees to provide a short answer, which may be as short as one word, or as long as a sentence (if written) or an utterance (if spoken).

low-stakes test: A test where the consequences for test takers and other stakeholders are generally considered less serious or important.

many-facet Rasch measurement: Use of the many-facet Rasch model.

many-facet Rasch model: Variant of a one-parameter IRT model which views item difficulty as a function of the various facets of the measurement process: differences among students, differences in rater severity, differences in task difficulty, and so on. It provides estimates of how much each facet contributes to task difficulty, and thus to task scores, and can be used to identify raters who need additional training, tasks that are too difficult or easy in comparison to others, and estimates of student ability.

matching: Selected response format in which the correct option is accompanied by a relatively large number of distractors, many of which are the correct answers to other items.

mean (M): The arithmetic average of a set of scores, equal to the total of the scores divided by the number of scores.

measurement error: The difference between a test taker's true score and observed score. Classical test theory treats all measurement error as being random error, while generalizability theory divides measurement error into random and systematic components.

measures of central tendency: Measures showing where most of the scores are in the distribution—that is, whether test takers mostly received high scores, low scores, or scores in the middle. The three measures of central tendency are the mean, median, and mode.

measures of dispersion: Measures showing how spread out a set of scores is. The four most common measures of dispersion are the standard deviation, variance, semi-interquartile range, and range.

median (Mdn): The middle score, equal to the 50th percentile. Half the scores are below this point, and half are above it.

mixed cell reference: Referring to a cell or range in a spreadsheet using a combination of relative and absolute cell referencing (relative for the rows and absolute for the columns, or vice versa).

mode (Mo): The most common score. It is the peak of the "hump" of the distribution.

model fit: In IRT, how well the actual responses of test takers match what we would expect based on the item parameters.

multiple choice: Selected response task format in which test takers select one of several (usually three to five) options.

multiple true-false: items with stems along the lines of "Choose all that apply," followed by a list of binary-choice options.

multiple-trait scoring: Using an analytic rating scale that includes features of the specific test task.

multivariate generalizability theory: Variant of generalizability theory; when a composite score is used for a test composed of several sections, it provides an overall reliability or dependability coefficient.

nominal variables: See *categorical variables*.

normal distribution: Situation in which a set of scores has skewness and kurtosis both equal to 0.0, producing a "bell-shaped" frequency distribution.

norming: See *rater norming*.

norming sample: A representative group that takes a test (usually a large-scale test) before it enters operational use, and whose scores are used for purposes such as estimating item (i.e., test question) difficulty and establishing the correspondence between test scores and percentiles. The norming sample needs to be large enough to ensure that the results are not due to chance. Not to be confused with *rater norming*.

norm-referenced test (NRT): Test on which an examinee's results are interpreted by comparing them to how well others did on the test. NRT scores are often reported in terms of test takers' percentile scores, not percentage correct.

NRT: See *norm-referenced test*.

***n*th-word deletion cloze:** See *fixed-deletion cloze*.

objective scoring for extended response tasks: Term describing a variety of problematic methods aimed at speeding up the rating process, and making it less subjective and more mechanical. Examples include asking several yes-no questions and counting the number of "yes" answers, counting the number of errors or errors per T-unit, or counting the number or proportion of error-free T-units.

objective test: A test that can be scored objectively, and therefore uses selected-response questions (particularly multiple-choice questions, but sometimes true-false or matching questions as well). Because the planning and writing of a test cannot be truly objective, this is a misnomer, and it is better to think of these as objectively *scored* tests.

observed score: The score that a person actually receives on a test. An observed score is considered to be the combination of measurement error and the test taker's true score.

one-parameter IRT model: Item response theory model that includes only item difficulty. (See *IRT* b *parameter*.)

options: The possible answers on a multiple-choice or matching task, from which the test taker must choose.

ordering tasks: Test tasks that ask examinees to arrange words, sentences, or paragraphs into the appropriate order.

ordinal variables: Variables where different levels—*ordered* categories essentially—can be observed, and put in some sort of order, or ranked. We do not assume that the distances between different levels of an ordinal variable are the same.

outliers: Test takers who do much better or worse than most, usually defined as those who score more than three standard deviations above or below the mean.

p*: See *IF**.

parallel forms reliability: The correlation between scores by the same group of examinees on two forms of a test.

parallel forms: Forms of the same test that yield the same scores; if a student takes two truly parallel forms of a test, his or her score should be the same on both forms. In actual practice, parallel forms are never *perfectly* parallel, but they should be close enough for the difference not to matter.

passage dependence: The need to comprehend a reading or listening passage in order to answer questions about it.

passage-based task: Test task that requires examinees to read or listen to material in order to perform the task, as with reading comprehension questions (see Table 2.1).

Pearson product-moment correlation coefficient (*r*): Correlation coefficient used with two interval or ratio variables. Assumes variables are normally distributed.

Pearson *r*: See *Pearson product-moment correlation coefficient*.

Pearsonian correlation coefficients: Term used for several members of a family of correlation coefficients (the Pearson *r*, ϕ, and the point-biserial). All except the Pearson *r* are special cases of the Pearson *r*.

percentile scores: The percentage of examinees who scored below someone. Used in NRT, and most commonly used in large-scale testing.

performance assessments: Assessments that require actual performances of relevant tasks, usually involving writing or speaking.

pilot testing: Giving a new test or a new test form to a sample of learners who are similar to those who will take the actual test once it becomes operational.

placement test: Test used to decide at which level in the language program a student should study.

point-biserial ($r_{p\text{-bis}}$): A correlational estimate of item discrimination for NRT, it is the correlation between item performance and total test score. Also a correlation coefficient used to correlate a dichotomous variable with an interval variable. As a rule of thumb, $r_{p\text{-bis}}$ should be $\geq$ .30 when used for item discrimination.

polytomous: Scored with more than one category, as with partial-credit scoring. Often refers to questions worth more than one point, but also includes one-point questions that can receive partial credit.

population variance: Variance, calculated for the entire population of interest, rather than for just a sample taken from that population. Used for calculating reliability of a test.

portfolios: Collections of student work from a course, useful for showing a student's development and improvement. Portfolios are most commonly associated with writing, but they can be used in the assessment of speaking as well.

practicality: Degree to which there are enough resources to develop and use the test.

predictive validity: The correlation between test scores and later performance on something, such as overall academic success. Later subsumed under criterion-related validity, but now viewed as a type of evidence (predictive utility) supporting construct validity, not as a separate type of validity in its own right.

pre-testing: See *pilot testing*.

primary trait scoring: Using a holistic rating scale that includes features of the specific test task.

proficiency test: Assesses an examinee's level of language ability, but without respect to a particular curriculum. Typically, this involves assessing more than one narrow aspect of language ability.

progress test: Test used to assess how well students are doing in terms of mastering course content and meeting course objectives. This is done from the point of view that the learning is still ongoing—that is, that students are not expected to have mastered the material yet.

prompt: Test task that asks the test taker to provide an extended response. This is the sort of task format most commonly used with speaking and writing assessments.

proportion-correct metric: The decimal equivalent of the percentage of questions that were answered correctly; for example, a proportion-correct score of .80 means that the student answered 80% of the questions correctly.

pseudo-chance parameter: See *IRT c parameter*.

***p*-value:** See *item facility (IF)*. Not to be confused with the *p* of statistical significance testing.

***Q*:** See *semi-interquartile range*.

qualities of usefulness: Characteristics that make a test more or less useful for its intended purposes (see Table 1.2). One or more will often be prioritized in a given situation, but not to the extent that the others are ignored. Test developers need to decide how important each quality is, and set minimally acceptable levels for it.

quartile: A percentile divisible by 25 (the 75th percentile, 50th percentile, or 25th percentile).

$r_{\text{item-mastery}}$: Polytomous CRT correlational item discrimination index, equivalent to item ϕ (Pearson r between a polytomous item and test mastery/non-mastery).

$r_{\text{item-total}}$: Polytomous NRT item discrimination index, equal to the correlation (a Pearson r) between the item and total score.

random deletion cloze: See *fixed-deletion cloze*.

range: (1) A group of contiguous cells in a spreadsheet. (2) Measure of dispersion equal to the highest score minus the lowest score, plus one.

Rasch model: Measurement model equivalent in its basic form to a one-parameter IRT model. See also *many-facet Rasch model*.

rater norming: When fully-trained raters review the rating scale together before using it again, and perhaps do some practice scoring, especially if it has been a long time since the last time they rated. Also refers to a group of raters meeting to review a sample of responses, and then determining how strictly or leniently they should score on that particular occasion. (Note that, strictly speaking, the sample of responses can be referred to as a *norming sample*, but that is not the normal sense of the word.)

rater standardization: See *rater norming*.

rating scale: A set of generic descriptions of test taker performance which can be used to assign scores to an individual examinee's performance in a systematic fashion.

ratio variables: Similar to interval variables, in that there is an equal distance between each pair of points on the scale, but ratio variables also include a true zero point. Somewhat rare in language learning research and testing.

rational-deletion cloze (also referred to as *gap-fill*): tasks in which words of a specific type (for example, connectors, nouns, or prepositions) are deleted.

recall protocol: Type of verbal protocol that takes place after the task of interest has been completed. The person is guided through this process by an interviewer who prompts them to recall what they thought or did during specific portions of the process, often while viewing a video recording of the task.

recall tasks: Task format in which students write as detailed a summary as they can remember after listening to or reading a passage.

relative cell reference: Referring to a cell or range in a spreadsheet in terms of how far from the active cell (to the left or right, and above or below) it is.

relative decisions: Ranking students, as in NRT.

reliability: Consistency of scoring. Estimated statistically. Strictly speaking, applies to NRT (compare *dependability*).

retrospective protocol: See *recall protocol*.

row: A horizontal line of cells in a spreadsheet.

*s***:** See *standard deviation*.

*s²***:** See *variance*.

sample variance: Variance, calculated for a sample taken from the population of interest. Not appropriate for calculating test reliability.

score bands: The levels on a rating scale, each of which has its own description of what performance looks like at that level.

score intervals: See *bins*.

score variance: Variation in scores; essentially, any differences in scores across students, across items, or across any other facet of the measurement process such as tasks, raters, occasions, test sections, etc.

scoring rubric: A set of generic descriptions of test taker performance which can be used to assign scores to an individual examinee's performance in a systematic fashion.

screening test: Proficiency test used to make selection decisions—most commonly about whether someone is sufficiently proficient in the target language to be qualified for a particular job.

scripted passages: Listening passages that are written out and then read or performed verbatim. All too frequently, however, these passages sound scripted, and may resemble written language use more than the patterns used in actual spoken language.

SD: See *standard deviation*.

selected response task: Test task requiring the examinee to choose the correct answer from among several options, where "several" can mean as few as two, or as many options as can be squeezed onto one page.

semi-direct test: Speaking test that requires the test takers to record their speech rather than talk directly to a human interlocutor. These tests are generally tape-mediated or computer-mediated. It is the lack of a live interlocutor with whom the test taker can interact reciprocally that distinguishes semi-direct from direct tests.

semi-interquartile range (*Q*): Measure of dispersion equal to half the difference between the first and third quartiles.

semi-scripted passages: A plan or outline for a listening passage, which is then improvised according to that plan. The "semiscripts" can vary from as general as the cue cards for a role-play to as specific as a turn-by-turn outline of what should be said (but without providing the actual words). Listening passages based on semiscripts tend to sound more spontaneous and authentic than fully scripted passages.

sentence writing or combining tasks: Limited production tasks in which examinees are given a set of words with which to form a sentence.

short-answer questions: Item-based limited production items that require the test taker to write (or, less commonly, to say) an answer; appropriate responses may be as short as one word, or perhaps as long as a sentence.

skewness: A statistic that tells how far off to the left or right the "hump" is in a distribution—that is, how off-center or asymmetrical the distribution is.

Spearman ρ (rho): Correlation coefficient used for ordinal data, or for badly non-normal interval variables.

Spearman rank-order correlation coefficient: See *Spearman ρ*.

Spearman-Brown prophecy formula: Formula used to estimate either (a) the effect on reliability of changing the length of the test, or (b) how many items would need to be added to achieve a particular target level of reliability.

specifications for individual test tasks: Description of each task on the test, intended to serve as directions to people writing the test. Include each task's purpose and construct definition, a description of the task and its format, the scoring method, and a sample task.

split-half reliability: Internal consistency reliability approach that divides the test questions into two halves (usually odd-even), correlates the scores on the halves, and adjusts the result using the Spearman-Brown prophecy formula.

spreadsheet: Formerly, a single large piece of paper with columns and rows of numbers used in accounting. In current usage, an electronic version of this.

squared error loss agreement indices: Approach to estimating CRT classification dependability that treats classification errors as less serious if the test taker's true score is close to the cut score, and more serious if their true score is farther away from the cut score.

standard deviation (SD, *s*): Measure of dispersion that is analogous to the average difference between individual scores and the mean.

standard error of measurement (SEM): Confidence interval for a test taker's observed score on an NRT, telling us how likely it is that their true score is within a certain range around (i.e., a certain distance from) their observed score.

standard error of the kurtosis (SEK): a statistic used in determining whether kurtosis is significant; using this is more accurate than using the rule of thumb that a kurtosis with an absolute value less than 2.0 is probably not important.

standard error of the skewness (SES): a statistic used in determining whether skewness is significant; using this is more accurate than using the rule of thumb that a skewness with an absolute value less than 2.0 is probably not important.

standard score: A way of reporting test scores that shows how far above or below the mean each examinee scored. The two most common of these are z and T scores.

stem: See *item stem*.

strong sense of language performance assessment: Concern with how well a task is performed, using real-world criteria; the level of linguistic accuracy displayed only matters to the extent that it interferes with or enables task performance. The strong sense is more likely to be relevant in vocational training than in regular language teaching and assessment.

subjective test: A test that involves human judgment to score, as in most tests of writing or speaking. Despite the name, however, it is possible to reduce the degree of subjectivity in rated tests through well-written rating scales and appropriate rater training.

subscales: In analytic rating scales, these are essentially smaller (i.e., more narrowly focused) scoring rubrics that are each concerned with a specific performance feature or portion of the overall construct.

subtractive approach to estimating discrimination: In order to estimate item discrimination, the IF of a low-scoring group is subtracted from the IF of a high-scoring group. In NRT the groups are the top and bottom 25–33% of the test takers (ID_{UL}); in CRT, they are the masters and non-masters, or passing and failing students (B-index, or DI).

summary cloze: Variant of rational-deletion cloze intended to assess reading comprehension. It involves writing a summary of a reading passage, and choosing the deletions that would be required to demonstrate comprehension of the original passage; that is, each word deleted provides information that could serve as the focus of a multiple-choice or open-ended comprehension question.

summative assessment: Test or other assessment typically given at the end of a unit, course, program, etc. that provides information about how much students learned. Closely related to achievement tests; in fact, most achievement testing is largely summative, and summative testing usually aims to assess learner achievement.

T score: A type of standard score that rescales z scores to eliminate decimals and negative numbers. A group of T scores has a mean of 50 and a standard deviation of 10.

T-unit: An independent clause and all the subordinate clauses associated with it.

target language use (TLU) domain: The contexts outside the test, whether in the real world or in the classroom, where test takers will use the language. It is these contexts to which we are hoping to generalize our score-based inferences.

task format: What a test task "looks like," in terms of what sort of input test takers must process, and how we expect them to respond (e.g. choosing an option, writing one word, or performing a role-play). Other writers have sometimes referred to this as "task type," "item format," "test method," "method," "response format," or "technique."

task specifications: See *test task specifications*.

task-centered test development: Approach to planning tests that starts with deciding which tasks from the TLU domain—typically real-world language use tasks—are of greatest interest, sampling from among those tasks, and adapting those selected tasks for use on the test.

test context and purpose specifications: Fundamental assumptions and decisions about the test that state how the test will be used, how results will be interpreted, and why the test is being given. They include the test purpose(s), construct(s), interpretive framework, TLU domain, test taker characteristics, minimum acceptable levels for the qualities of usefulness, and a resource plan (see Table 3.1).

test specifications: The plans for a test, which are used as an outline when the test is written, and as directions for the people writing the test.

test structure specifications: Description of the task format(s) to be used for assessing each construct, or for each aspect of each construct, and the number of each task (questions, passages, prompts, etc.) to be used in each section (see Table 3.4).

test task specifications: Descriptions of how each task is to be written, going beyond merely identifying the task format to be used, which is done in the test structure specifications (see Table 4.1).

test-centered continuum models: Standard setting approaches that involve expert judgments being made about the content of the test itself.

test-retest reliability: Way of estimating reliability in which examinees take the same test twice. The reliability estimate is the correlation between their two scores.

tetrachoric correlation coefficient: Correlation coefficient used with two dichotomous variables. Used as an alternative to ϕ.

think-aloud protocol: Type of verbal protocol that involves performing the task of interest while thinking out loud—that is, talking about what is going through one's mind as the task is performed.

three-parameter IRT model: Item response theory model that includes item difficulty, item discrimination, and random guessing. (See *IRT a parameter*, *IRT b parameter* and *IRT c parameter*.)

threshold loss agreement indices: Approach to estimating CRT classification dependability that treats all classification errors as being equally severe, regardless of how close or far apart a test taker's observed and true scores are.

TLU domain: See *target language use (TLU) domain*.

trialing: See *pilot testing*.

true score: the score that a test taker would receive with perfect measurement, that is, if there were no measurement error (if such a thing were possible).

true-false questions: Essentially multiple-choice items with only two answers; easier to guess correctly than ordinary multiple-choice items; difficult to write well, and often wind up becoming trick questions.

two-parameter IRT model: Item response theory model that includes both item difficulty and item discrimination. (See *IRT* a *parameter* and *IRT* b *parameter*.)

type-to-token ratio: The total number of words in a passage divided by the number of different word forms. For example, if a particular word occurs five times in a passage, it counts as five *tokens* but only one *type*.

unscripted passages: Recordings of naturally occurring speech. Their authenticity is obviously quite high, but it can be very difficult (or even impossible) to find such a recording that will be appropriate in terms of all the categories discussed here.

upper-lower item discrimination (ID_{UL}): Subtractive estimate of item discrimination for NRT, equal to the difference in item facility between high- and low-scoring groups. As a rule of thumb, ID_{UL} should be ≥ .40.

validation argument: See *validity argument*.

validity argument: Interpretive argument that presents evidence to make a case justifying the score-based inferences and the intended uses of the test.

variance (s^2): Measure of dispersion equal to the square of the standard deviation; primarily used in other formulas, not interpreted in its own right.

verbal protocol analysis (VPA): A tool for studying the processes involved in different parts of the testing process. The person whose mental processes are being studied talks through or otherwise describes what they do and think during the task being analyzed, normally in a think-aloud protocol or a retrospective or recall protocol.

vocabulary-in-context item: Type of reading comprehension question that requires examinees to identify the sense of a word that is being used in a passage, or to identify the meaning of an unfamiliar word using context clues. It does not assess *knowledge* of vocabulary.

washback: (1) The effect of a test on teaching and learning, including effects on all aspects of the curriculum, including materials and teaching approaches, as well as on what the students do to learn and to prepare for tests. (2) The effect of a test on teaching and learning.

WBT: See *web-based testing.*

weak sense of language performance assessment: Concern with the level of the language used in performing the task. The purpose of the task is to elicit a sample of language to be evaluated; performance of the task, as such, is secondary, and if task completion or fulfillment is considered in the scoring, it is typically done with reference to language. In language teaching and assessment, we are generally more concerned with the weak sense of performance assessment.

web-based testing (WBT): Administration of computer-based tests via the World-Wide Web, typically using standard web browsers.

workbook: Formerly, several related paper spreadsheets kept together (perhaps even attached or bound together); in current usage, a Microsoft Excel file.

worksheet: Formerly, a single large piece of paper with columns and rows of numbers used in accounting. A tab in an Excel file, equivalent to a single spreadsheet.

z score: A type of standard score that expresses the distance from the mean in terms of standard deviations—that is, it tells how many standard deviations above or below the mean a test taker scored. A group of *z* scores has a mean of 0 and a standard deviation of 1.

BIBLIOGRAPHY

Abedi, J., C. H. Hofstetter, and **C. Lord.** 2004. 'Assessment accommodations for English language learners: Implications for policy-based empirical research'. *Review of Educational Research* 74 (1): 1–28.

Albus, D., J. Bielinski, and **M. Thurlow.** 2005. 'Reading test performance of English-language learners using an English dictionary'. *The Journal of Educational Research* 98 (4): 245–254.

Alderson, J. C. 1983. 'A closer look at cloze: Validity and reliability' in J. W. Oller, Jr. (ed.). *Issues in Language Testing Research.* Rowley, MA: Newbury House.

Alderson, J. C. 2000. *Assessing Reading.* Cambridge: Cambridge University Press.

Alderson, J. C. 2007. 'Judging the frequency of English words'. *Applied Linguistics* 28 (3): 383–409.

Alderson, J. C., C. Clapham, and **D. Wall.** 1995. *Language Test Construction and Evaluation.* Cambridge: Cambridge University Press.

Alderson, J. C., and **A. H. Urquhart.** 1985. 'The effect of students' academic discipline on their performance on ESP reading tests'. *Language Testing* 2 (2): 192–204.

Alderson, J. C., and **A. H. Urquhart.** 1988. 'This test is unfair: I'm not an economist' in P. L. Carrell, J. Devine, and D. Eskey (eds.). *Interactive Approaches to Second-Language Reading.* Cambridge: Cambridge University Press.

Allen, M. J., and **W. M. Yen.** 1979. *Introduction to Measurement Theory.* Monterey, CA: Brooks/Cole Publishing Company.

American Council on the Teaching of Foreign Languages. 1999. *ACTFL Proficiency Guidelines—Speaking.* (revised 1999). Retrieved March 29 2008, from http://www.actfl.org/files/public/Guidelinesspeak.pdf.

American Educational Research Association, American Psychological Association, and National Council on Measurement in Education. 1999. *Standards for Educational and Psychological Testing.* Washington, DC: Author.

Association of Language Testers in Europe. 2001. *Principles of Good Practice for ALTE Examinations.* Retrieved July 10 2009, from http://www.alte.org/downloads/index.php?docid=29.

Association of Language Testers in Europe. 2007. *Minimum Standards for Establishing Quality Profiles in ALTE Examinations.* Retrieved July 10 2009, from http://www.alte.org/downloads/index.php?docid=27.

Babaii, E., and **H. Ansary.** 2001. 'The C-test: A valid operationalization of reduced redundancy principle?'. *System* 29: 209–219.

Bachman, L. F. 1985. 'How "communicative" are language proficiency tests?'. *PASAA Journal* 15 (2): 1–14.

Bachman, L. F. 1990. *Fundamental Considerations in Language Testing.* Oxford: Oxford University Press.

Bachman, L. F. 2002a. 'Alternative interpretations of alternative assessments: Some validity issues in educational performance assessments'. *Education Measurement: Issues and Practice* 21 (3): 5–18.

Bachman, L. F. 2002b. 'Some reflections on task-based language performance assessment'. *Language Testing* 19: 453–476.

Bachman, L. F. 2004. *Statistical Analyses for Language Assessment.* Cambridge: Cambridge University Press.

Bachman, L. F. 2005. 'Building and supporting a case for test use'. *Language Assessment Quarterly* 2 (1): 1–34.

Bachman, L. F. and **J. L. D. Clark.** 1987. 'The measurement of foreign/second language proficiency'. *Annals of the American Academy of Political and Social Science: Vol. 490. Foreign Language Instruction: A National Agenda,* pp. 20–33.

Bachman, L. F., B. K. Lynch, and **M. Mason.** 1995. 'Investigating variability in tasks and rater judgments in a performance test of foreign language speaking'. *Language Testing* 12 (2): 238–257.

Bachman, L. F., and **A. S. Palmer.** 1996. *Language Testing in Practice.* Oxford: Oxford University Press.

Bachman, L. F., and **A. S. Palmer.** 2010. *Language Assessment in Practice.* Oxford: Oxford University Press.

Bailey, K. M. 1998. *Learning about Language Assessment: Dilemmas, Decisions, and Directions.* Boston: Heinle and Heinle Publishers.

Barkaoui, K. 2010. 'Variability in ESL essay rating processes: The role of the rating scale and rater experience'. *Language Assessment Quarterly* 7 (1): 54–74.

Basturkmen, H., and **C. Elder.** 2004. 'The practice of LSP' in A. Davies and C. Elder (eds.). *The Handbook of Applied Linguistics.* Malden, MA: Blackwell Publishing, pp. 672–694.

Bechger, T. M., H. Kuijper, and **G. Maris.** 2009. 'Standard setting in relation to the Common European Framework of Reference for Languages: The case of the State Examination of Dutch as a Second Language'. *Language Assessment Quarterly* 6 (2): 126–150.

Berk, R. A. 1986. 'A consumer's guide to setting performance standards on criterion-referenced tests'. *Review of Educational Research* 56 (1): 137–172.

Biber, D., S. Conrad, and **R. Reppen.** 1998. *Corpus Linguistics: Investigating Language Structure and Use.* Cambridge: Cambridge University Press.

Bonk, W. J., and **G. Ockey.** 2003. 'A many-facet Rasch analysis of the second language group oral discussion task'. *Language Testing* 20 (1): 89–110.

Brantmeier, C. 2006. 'The effects of language of assessment and L2 reading performance on advanced readers' recall'. *The Reading Matrix* 6 (1): 1–17.

Brennan, R. L. 1980. 'Applications of generalizability theory' in R. A. Berk (ed.). *Criterion-Referenced Measurement: The State of the Art.* Baltimore, MD: The Johns Hopkins University Press.

Brennan, R. L. 1992. *Elements of Generalizability Theory.* Iowa City, IA: American College Testing Program.

Brennan, R. L. 2001. *Generalizability Theory.* New York: Springer Verlag.

Brown, H. D. 2007. *Teaching by Principles: An Interactive Approach to Language Pedagogy* (3rd ed.). White Plains, NY. Pearson Education.

Brown, J. D. 1980. 'Relative merits of four methods for scoring cloze tests'. *Modern Language Journal* 64: 311–317.

Brown, J. D. 1988. *Understanding Research in Second Language Learning.* Cambridge: Cambridge University Press.

Brown, J. D. 1990. 'Shortcut estimators of criterion-referenced test consistency'. *Language Testing* 7 (1): 77–97.

Brown, J. D. 1995. *The Elements of Language Curriculum: A Systematic Approach to Program Development.* Boston: Heinle and Heinle Publishers.

Brown, J. D., and **T. Hudson.** 2002. *Criterion-Referenced Language Testing.* Cambridge: Cambridge University Press.

Buck, G. 2001. *Assessing Listening.* Cambridge: Cambridge University Press.

Budescu, D. V. 1988. 'On the feasibility of multiple matching tests—variations on a theme by Gulliksen'. *Applied Psychological Measurement* 12 (1): 5–14.

Burns, A. and **H. Joyce.** 1997. *Focus on Speaking.* Sydney: National Centre for English Language Teaching and Research (NCELTR).

Cambridge ESOL Examinations. 2006a. *Key English Test: Information for Candidates.* Retrieved June 18 2010, from http://www.candidates.cambridgeesol.org/cs/digitalAssets/105327_3812_6Y05_KET_IforC_w.pdf.

Cambridge ESOL Examinations. 2006b. *Preliminary English Test: Information for Candidates.* Retrieved June 18 2010, from http://www.candidates.cambridgeesol.org/cs/digitalAssets/105331_3813_6Y05_PET_IforC_w_Eng.pdf.

Cambridge ESOL Examinations. 2007a. *Certificate of Proficiency in English: Information for Candidates.* Retrieved June 18 2010, from http://www.candidates.cambridgeesol.org/cs/digitalAssets/113322_cpe_infoforcand. pdf.

Cambridge ESOL Examinations. 2007b. *IELTS Handbook 2007.* Retrieved June 18 2010, from http://www.cambridgeesol.org/assets/pdf/resources/IELTS_Handbook.pdf.

Cambridge ESOL Examinations. 2008a. *Certificate in Advanced English: Information for Candidates for Examinations from December 2008.* Retrieved June 18 2010, from http://www.candidates.cambridgeesol.org/cs/digitalAssets/121084_cae_ infoforcand_dec08_E.pdf.

Cambridge ESOL Examinations. 2008b. *First Certificate in English: Information for Candidates for Examinations from December 2008.* Retrieved June 18 2010, from http://www.candidates.cambridgeesol.org/cs/digitalAssets/121063_fce_infoforcand_ dec08_E.pdf.

Canale, M. and **M. Swain.** 1980. 'Theoretical bases of communicative approaches to second language teaching and testing'. *Applied Linguistics* 1: 1–47.

Cangelosi, J. S. 1990. *Designing Tests for Evaluating Student Achievement.* White Plains, NY: Longman.

Carr, N. T. 2000. 'A comparison of the effects of analytic and holistic rating scale types in the context of composition tests'. *Issues in Applied Linguistics* 11 (2): 207–241.

Carr, N. T. 2004. 'A review of Lertap (Laboratory of Educational Research Test Analysis Package) 5.2'. *International Journal of Testing* 4 (2): 189–195.

Carr, N. T. 2006a. 'Computer-based testing: Prospects for innovative assessment' in L. Ducate and N. Arnold (eds.). *Calling on CALL: From Theory and Research to New Directions in Foreign Language Teaching* (CALICO Monograph Series Vol. 5). San Marcos, TX: CALICO, pp. 289–312.

Carr, N. T. 2006b. 'The factor structure of test task characteristics and examinee performance'. *Language Testing* 23 (3): 269–289.

Carr, N. T. 2008a. 'Decisions about automated scoring: What they mean for our constructs' in C. A. Chapelle, Y. R. Chung, and J. Xu (eds.). *Towards Adaptive CALL: Natural language Processing for Diagnostic Language Assessment.* Ames, IA: Iowa State University, pp. 82–101.

Carr, N. T. 2008b. 'Using Microsoft Excel to calculate descriptive statistics and create graphs'. *Language Assessment Quarterly* 5 (1): 43–62.

Carr, N. T. and **X. Xi.** 2010. 'Automated scoring of short answer reading items: Implications for constructs'. *Language Assessment Quarterly* 7 (3): 1–14.

Carr, N. T. 2010. 'Computer-automated scoring of English writing: Advantages, disadvantages, and alternatives' in M.-H. Tsai, S.-W. Chen, R.-C. Shih, T.-H. Hsin, I. F. Chung, C.-C. Lee, and S.-Y. Lin (eds.). *Proceedings of the 2010 International Conference on ELT Technological Industry and Book Fair: Computer-Scoring English Writing.* Pingtung, Taiwan: Department of Modern Languages, National Pingtung University of Science and Technology, pp. 16–28.

Carrell, P. L. 1987. Readability in ESL. *Reading in a Foreign Language* 4 (1): 21–40.

Carroll, L. 1865. *Alice's Adventures in Wonderland.* Retrieved June 11 2010, from http://www.gutenberg.org/files/19002/19002-h/19002-h.htm.

Celce-Murcia, M., D. M. Brinton, and **J. M. Goodwin.** 1996. *Teaching Pronunciation: A Reference for Teachers of English to Speakers of Other Languages.* Cambridge: Cambridge University Press.

Celce-Murcia, M. and **D. Larsen-Freeman.** 1999. *The Grammar Book: An ESL/EFL Teacher's Course* (2nd ed.). Boston: Heinle and Heinle.

Chalhoub-Deville, M. 2001. 'Language testing and technology: Past and future'. *Language Learning and Technology* 5 (2): 95–98. Retrieved July 10 2009, from http://llt.msu.edu/vol5num2/pdf/deville.pdf.

Chapelle, C. A. 1994. 'Are C-tests valid measures for L2 vocabulary research?'. *Language Testing* 10: 157–187.

Chapelle, C. A. 1998. 'Construct definition and validity inquiry in SLA research' in L. F. Bachman and A. D. Cohen (eds.). *Interfaces between Second Language Acquisition and Language Testing Research.* Cambridge: Cambridge University Press, pp. 32–70.

Chapelle, C. A. 1999. 'Validity in language assessment'. *Annual Review of Applied Linguistics* 19: 254–272.

Chapelle, C. A. and **R. G. Abraham.** 1990. 'Cloze method: What difference does it make?' *Language Testing* 7: 121–146.

Chapelle, C. A. and **P. Green.** 1992. 'Field independence/dependence in second-language acquisition research'. *Language Learning* 42: 47–83.

Clauser, B. E., M. T. Kane, and **D. B. Swanson.** 2002. 'Validity issues for performance-based tests scored with computer-automated scoring systems'. *Applied Measurement in Education* 15 (4): 413–432.

Cobb, T. 2007. 'Computing the vocabulary demands of L2 reading'. *Language Learning and Technology* 11 (3): 38–63.

Cobb, T. n. d. *Compleat Lexical Tutor* v.6.2. Retrieved June 18 2009, from http://www.lextutor.ca/.

Connor, U. and **C. Read.** 1978. 'Passage dependency in ESL reading comprehension tests'. *Language Learning* 28 (1): 149–157.

Cronbach, L. J. 1988. 'Five perspectives on validity argument' in H. Wainer and H. I. Braun (eds.). *Test Validity.* Hillsdale, NJ: Lawrence Erlbaum Associates, pp. 3–17.

Cronbach, L. J. and **P. E. Meehl.** 1955. 'Construct validity in psychological tests'. *Psychological Bulletin* 52 (4): 281–302.

Crosson, A. C. and **N. K. Lesaux.** 2010. 'Revisiting assumptions about the relationship of fluent reading to comprehension: Spanish-speakers' text-reading fluency in English'. *Reading and Writing* 23 (5): 475–494.

Davidson, F. and **B. K. Lynch.** 2002. *Testcraft: A Teacher's Guide to Writing and Using Language Test Specifications.* New Haven, CT: Yale University Press.

Davis, S. L., C. W. Buckendahl, and **B. S. Plake.** 2008. 'When adaptation is not an option: An application of multilingual standard setting'. *Journal of Educational Measurement* 45 (3): 287–304.

Deeney, T. A. 2010. 'One-minute fluency measures: Mixed messages in assessment and instruction'. *The Reading Teacher* 63 (6): 440–450.

Douglas, D. 2000. *Assessing Language for Specific Purposes.* Cambridge: Cambridge University Press.

Douglas, D. 2001. 'Language for specific purposes assessment criteria: Where do they come from?'. *Language Testing* 18 (2): 171–185.

Douglas, D. and **V. Hegelheimer.** 2007. 'Assessing language using computer technology'. *Annual Review of Applied Linguistics* 27: 115–132.

Eckes, T. and **R. Grotjahn.** 2006. 'A closer look at the construct validity of C-tests'. *Language Testing* 23: 290–325.

Educational Testing Service. 2009a. *Structure of TOEFL iBT and TOEFL PBT.* Retrieved June 20 2009, from http://www.ets.org/portal/site/ets/menuitem.1488512ecfd5b8849a77b13bc3921509/?vgnextoid=8313fd80dbbdb110VgnVCM10000022f95190RCRDandvgnextchannel=555ad898c84f4010VgnVCM10000022f95190RCRD.

Educational Testing Service. 2009b. *TOEIC: Test of English for International Communication.* Retrieved June 22, 2009, from http://www.ets.org/portal/site/ets/menuitem.fab2360b1645a1de9b3a0779f1751509/?vgnextoid=06cfd898c84f4010VgnVCM10000022f95190RCRD.

Embretson, S. E., and **S. P. Reise.** 2000. *Item Response Theory for Psychologists.* Mahwah, NJ: Lawrence Erlbaum Associates.

Enright, M. K. 2004. 'Research issues in high-stakes communicative language testing: Reflections on TOEFL's New Directions'. *TESOL Quarterly* 38 (1): 147–151.

European Association for Language Testing and Assessment. 2006. *EALTA Guidelines for Good Practice in Language Testing and Assessment.* Retrieved June 25 2010, from http://www.ealta.eu.org/guidelines.htm.

Eyring, J. E. 1998. 'What's an objective anyway?'. *TESL Canada Journal/La Revue TESL du Canada* 15 (2): 24–35.

Famularo, L. 2008. 'The effect of response format and test taking strategies on item difficulty: A comparison of stem-equivalent multiple-choice and constructed-response test items' (Doctoral dissertation, Boston College, 2008). *Dissertation Abstracts International* 68 (10): 4268A. (UMI No. AAI3283877).

Fleenor, J. W., J. W. Fleenor, and **W. F. Grossnickle.** 1996. 'Interrater reliability and agreement of performance ratings: A methodological comparison'. *Journal of Business and Psychology* 10 (3): 367–380.

Folland, D. and **D. Robertson.** 1976. 'Towards objectivity in group oral testing'. *ELT Journal* 30: 156–157.

Fouly, K. A. and **G. A. Cziko.** 1985. 'Determining the reliability, validity, and scalability of the graduated dictation test'. *Language Learning* 35 (4): 555–566.

Freedle, R. and **I. Kostin.** 1994. 'Can multiple-choice reading tests be construct-valid? A reply to Katz, Lautenschlager, Blackburn, and Harris'. *Psychological Science* 5 (2): 107–110.

Fulcher, G. 2003. *Testing Second Language Speaking.* Harlow, UK: Pearson Longman.

Fulcher, G. 1996. 'Does thick description lead to smart tests? A data-based approach to rating scale construction'. *Language Testing* 13 (2): 208–238.

Galaczi, E. D. 2008. 'Peer-peer interaction in a speaking test: The case of the First Certificate in English examination'. *Language Assessment Quarterly* 5 (2) 89–119.

Gardner, R. 2004. 'Conversation analysis' in A. Davies and C. Elder (eds.). *The Handbook of Applied Linguistics.* Malden, MA: Blackwell Publishing, pp. 262–284.

Geddes, M. and **R. White.** 1978. 'The Use of semi-scripted simulated authentic speech and listening comprehension'. *Audio-Visual Language Journal* 16 (3): 137–145.

Graddol, D. 2006. *English Next: Why Global English May Mean the End of 'English as a Foreign Language'.* Retrieved July 18 2010, from http://www.britishcouncil.org/learning-research-english-next.pdf.

Green, A. 1998. *Verbal Protocol Analysis in Language Testing Research: A Handbook.* Cambridge: University of Cambridge Local Examinations Syndicate/Cambridge University Press.

Guilford, J. P. and **B. Fruchter.** 1978. *Fundamental Statistics in Psychology and Education* (6th ed.). New York: McGraw-Hill.

Gutteridge, M. 2003. 'Assistive technology for candidates with special needs'. *Research Notes* 12, 15. Retrieved June 27 2010 from http://www.cambridgeesol.org/rs_notes/offprints/pdfs/RN12p15.pdf'

Haladyna, T. M., S. M. Downing, and **M. C. Rodriguez.** 2002. 'A review of multiple-choice item-writing guidelines for classroom assessment'. *Applied Measurement in Education* 15 (3): 309–334.

Hambleton, R. K., C. N. Mills, and **R. Simon.** 1983. 'Determining the lengths for criterion-referenced tests'. *Journal of Educational Measurement:* 20 (1): 27–38.

Hambleton, R. K. and **H. Swaminathan.** 1985. *Item Response Theory: Principles and Applications.* Boston: Kluwer-Nijhoff Publishing.

Hambleton, R. K., H. Swaminathan, and **H. J. Rogers.** 1991. *Fundamentals of Item Response Theory.* Newbury Park, CA: Sage Publications.

Hanna, G. S. and **T. R. Oaster.** 1978–1979. 'Toward a unified theory of context dependence'. *Reading Research Quarterly* 14 (2): 226–243.

Hargis, C. H. 2003. *Grades and Grading Practices: Obstacles to Improving Education and to Helping At-Risk Students* (2nd ed.). Springfield, IL: Charles C. Thomas Publisher, Ltd.

Haynie, W. J., III. 2003. 'Effects of multiple-choice and matching tests on delayed retention learning in postsecondary metals technology'. *Journal of Industrial Teacher Education* 40 (2): 7–22.

He, A. W. and **R. Young.** 1998. 'Language proficiency interviews: A discourse approach' in R. Young and A. W. He (eds.). *Talking and Testing: Discourse Approaches to the Assessment of Oral Proficiency.* Amsterdam: John Benjamins Publishing Company.

He, L. and **Y. Dai.** 2006. 'A corpus-based investigation into the validity of the CET-SET group discussion'. *Language Testing* 23 (3): 370–401.

Hopkins, K. D., G. V. Glass, and **B. R. Hopkins.** 1987. *Basic Statistics for the Behavioral Sciences* (2nd ed.). Englewood Cliffs, NJ: Prentice-Hall.

Hunt, K. W. 1965. *Grammatical Structures Written at 3 Grade Levels.* Champaign, IL: National Council of Teachers of English.

International Language Testing Association. 2000. *Code of Ethics for ILTA.* Retrieved July 10 2009, from http://www.iltaonline.com/index.php?option=com_contentandview=articleandid=57andItemid=47.

International Language Testing Association. 2007. *International Language Testing Association Guidelines for Practice.* Retrieved July 10 2009, from http://www.iltaonline.com/index.php?option=com_contentandview=articleandid=122andItemid=133.

Jacoby, S. and **T. McNamara.** 1999. 'Locating competence'. *English for Specific Purposes* 18 (3): 213–241.

Jaeger, R. M. 1989. 'Certification of student competence' in R. L. Linn (ed.), *Educational Measurement* (3rd ed.). New York: American Council on Education/ Macmillan Publishing Company, pp. 485–514.

Jaén, M. M. 2007. 'A corpus-driven design of a test for assessing the ESL collocational competence of university students'. *International Journal of English Studies* 7 (2): 127–147.

Jamieson, J. 2005. 'Trends in computer-based second language assessment'. *Annual Review of Applied Linguistics* 25: 228–242.

Johnson, J., S. Prior, and **M. Artuso.** 2000. 'Field dependence as a factor in second language communicative competence'. *Language Learning* 50: 529–567.

Kane, M. T. 1992. 'An argument-based approach to validation'. *Psychological Bulletin:* 12: 527–535.

Kane, M. T. 2001. 'Current concerns in validity theory'. *Journal of Educational Measurement 38:* (4): 319–342.

Kane, M., T. J. Crooks, and **A. S. Cohen.** 1999. 'Validating measures of performance'. *Educational Measurement: Issues and Practice* 18 (2): 5–17.

Kaplan, R. 1966. 'Cultural thought patterns in intercultural education'. *Language Learning* 16: 1–20.

Keenan, J. M., R. S. Betjeman, and **R. K. Olson.** 2008. 'Reading comprehension tests vary in the skills they assess: Differential dependence on decoding and oral comprehension'. *Scientific Studies of Reading* 12 (3): 281–300.

Kennedy, G. 1998. *An Introduction to Corpus Linguistics.* Harlow, England: Addison Wesley Longman.

Kenyon, D. 1997. 'Further research on the efficacy of rater self-training' in A. Huhta, V. Kohonen, L. Kurki-Suonio, and S. Luoma (eds.). *Current Developments and Alternatives in Language Assessment: Proceedings of LTRC '96.* Jyväskylä, Finland: University of Jyväskylä and University of Tampere.

Khalifa, H. 2005. 'Are test taker characteristics accounted for in Main Suite reading papers?'. *Research Notes* 21: 7–10. Retrieved June 27 2010, from http://www.cambridgeesol.org/rs_notes/offprints/pdfs/RN21p7-10.pdf.

Khalifa, H., and **Weir, C. J.** 2009. *Examining Reading: Research and Practice in Assessing Second Language Reading.* Cambridge: University of Cambridge Local Examinations Syndicate/Cambridge University Press.

Kim, J., Y. Chi, A. Huensch, H. Jun, H. Li, and **V. Roullion.** 2010. 'A case study on an item writing process: Use of test specifications, nature of group dynamics, and individual item writers' characteristics'. *Language Assessment Quarterly* 7 (2): 160–174.

Kirschner, M., C. Wexler, and **E. Spector-Cohen.** 1992. 'Avoiding obstacles to student comprehension of test questions'. *TESOL Quarterly* 26: 537–556.

Kopriva, R. J., J. E. Emick, C. P. Hipolito-Delgado, and **C. A. Cameron.** 2007. 'Do proper accommodation assignments make a difference? Examining the impact of improved decision making on scores for English language learners'. *Educational Measurement: Issues and Practice* 26 (3): 11–20.

Kozaki, Y. 2004. 'Using GENOVA and FACETS to set multiple standards on performance assessment for certification in medical translation from Japanese into English'. *Language Testing* 21 (1): 1–27.

Kuder, G. F. and **M. W. Richardson.** 1937. 'The theory of the estimation of test reliability'. *Psychometrika* 2 (3): 151–160.

Kunnan, A. J. 2004. 'Test fairness' in M. Milanovic and C. J. Weir (eds.). *European Language Testing in a Global Context: Proceedings of the ALTE Barcelona Conference, July 2001.* Cambridge: University of Cambridge Local Examinations Syndicate/Cambridge University Press, pp. 262–284.

Kunnan, A. J. 2008. Towards a model of test evaluation: Using the Test Fairness and Test Context Frameworks. In L. Taylor and C. J. Weir (Eds.), *Multilingualism and Assessment: Achieving Transparency, Assuring Quality, Sustaining Diversity: Proceedings of the ALTE Berlin Conference, May 2005.* Cambridge: UCLES/Cambridge University Press, (pp. 229)

Kunnan, A. J. and **N. T. Carr** (in press). 'Statistical analysis of test results' in C. Chapelle (ed.). *The Encyclopedia of Applied Linguistics.* Addison-Wiley.

Language Acquisition Resource Center at San Diego State University. 2009. CAST: *Computer Assisted Screening Tool.* Retrieved June 21 2009, from http://larc.sdsu.edu/outreach/diagnostic-assessment/.

Lantolf, J. P. and **W. Frawley.** 1985. 'Oral-proficiency testing: A critical analysis'. *The Modern Language Journal* 69 (4): 337–345.

Laufer, B. and **Z. Goldestein.** 2004. 'Testing vocabulary knowledge: Size, strength, and computer adaptiveness'. *Language Learning* 54 (3): 399–436.

Lazaraton, A. 1996. 'Interlocutor support in oral proficiency interviews: The case of CASE'. *Language Testing* 13 (2): 151–172.

Lazaraton, A. 2002. *A Qualitative Approach to the Validation of Oral Language Tests.* Cambridge: University of Cambridge Local Examinations Syndicate/Cambridge University Press.

Lazaraton, A. and **L. Davis.** 2008. 'A microanalytic perspective on discourse, proficiency, and identity in paired oral assessment'. *Language Assessment Quarterly* 5 (4): 313–335.

Lee, J. F. 1986. 'Background knowledge and L2 reading'. *The Modern Language Journal* 70 (4): 350–354.

Leeser, M. J. 2007. 'Learner-based factors in L2 reading comprehension and processing grammatical form: Topic familiarity and working memory'. *Language Learning* 57 (2): 229–270.

Leung, C. 2004. 'Developing formative teacher assessment: Knowledge, practice, and change'. *Language Assessment Quarterly* 1 (1): 19–41.

Li, L. and **L. J. MacGregor.** 2010. 'Investigating the receptive vocabulary size of university-level Chinese learners of English: How suitable is the Vocabulary Levels Test?'. *Language and Education* 24 (3): 239–249.

Linacre, J. M. 1989. *Many-facet Rasch Measurement.* Chicago, IL: MESA Press.

Livingston, S. A. 1972. 'Criterion-referenced applications of classical test theory'. *Journal of Educational Measurement* 9 (1): 13–26.

Lord, F. M. 1984. 'Standard errors of measurement at different ability levels'. *Journal of Educational Measurement* 21 (3): 239–243.

Luk, J. 2010. 'Talking to score: Impression management in L2 oral assessment and the co-construction of a test discourse genre'. *Language Assessment Quarterly* 7(1): 25–53.

Luoma, S. 2004. *Assessing Speaking.* Cambridge: Cambridge University Press.

Lynch, B. K. 2001. 'Rethinking assessment from a critical perspective'. *Language Testing* 18 (4): 351–372.

Lynch, B. K. and **T. F. McNamara.** 1998. 'Using G-theory and many-facet Rasch measurement in the development of performance assessments of the ESL speaking skills of immigrants'. *Language Testing* 15 (2): 158–180.

Malabonga, V., D. M. Kenyon, and **H. Carpenter.** 2005. 'Self-assessment, preparation and response time on a computerized oral proficiency test'. *Language Testing* 22 (1): 59–92.

Malone, M. E. 2007. *Oral Proficiency Assessment: The Use of Technology in Test Development and Rater Training* (Center for Applied Linguistics Research Digest). Retrieved June 18 2009, from http://www.cal.org/resources/digest/oralprof.html.

Marshall, H. 2006. The Cambridge ESOL item banking system. *Research Notes* 23: 3–5. Retrieved April 6 2008, from ttp://www.cambridgeesol.org/rs_notes/rs_nts23.pdf.

McKay, P. 2006. *Assessing Young Language Learners.* Cambridge: Cambridge University Press.

McNamara, T. F. 1996. *Measuring Second Language Performance.* London: Addison Wesley Longman.

McNamara, T. F. and **T. Lumley.** 1997. 'The effect of interlocutor and assessment mode variables in overseas assessments of speaking skills in occupational settings'. *Language Testing* 14 (2): 140–156.

Mendelsohn, D. J. 1994. *Learning to Listen.* Carlsbad, CA: Dominie Press.

Messick, S. 1988. 'The once and future issues of validity: Assessing the meaning and consequences of measurement' in H. Wainer and H. I. Braun (eds.). *Test Validity.* Hillsdale, NJ: Lawrence Erlbaum Associates, pp. 262–284.

Messick, S. 1989a. 'Meaning and values in test validation: The science and ethics of assessment'. *Educational Researcher* 18 (2): 5–11.

Messick, S. 1989b. 'Validity' in R. L. Linn (ed.). *Educational Measurement* (3rd ed.). New York: American Council on Education and Macmillan Publishing Company, pp. 13–103.

Messick, S. 1995. 'Validity of psychological assessment: Validation of inferences from persons' responses and performances as scientific inquiry into score meaning'. *American Psychologist* 50 (4): 741–749.

Messick, S. 1996. 'Validity and washback in language testing'. *Language Testing* 13 (3): 241–256.

Microsoft Corporation. (n. d.). *Excel 2008 Help and How-to: I Can't Find the Analysis ToolPak* [Website]. Retrieved July 21 2010, from http://www.microsoft.com/mac/help.mspx?target=71e42c24-7152-437d-ac3e-a741b1a60d881033andclr=99-1-0andparentid=91f7ac25-b074-449e-8464-7d5fa5e8309c1033andep=7andCTT=CategoryandMODE=pvandlocale=en-USandusid=1a71bc09-556f-4f18-ad00-bc31d06a7592.

Mislevy, R. J. 2007. 'Validity by design'. *Educational Researcher* 36 (8): 463–469.

Mislevy, R. J. and **G. D. Haertel.** 2006. 'Implications of evidence-centered design for educational testing'. *Educational Measurement: Issues and Practice* 25 (4): 6–20.

Mosier, C. I. 1947. 'A critical examination of the concepts of face validity'. *Educational and Psychological Measurement* 7: 191–205.

Natalicio, D. S. 1979. 'Repetition and dictation as language testing techniques'. *Modern Language Journal* 63 (4): 165–176.

Nation, P. (n. d.). *Paul Nation.* Retrieved June 18 2009, from http://www.victoria.ac.nz/lals/staff/paul-nation/nation.aspx

Nekrasova, T. M. 2009. 'English L1 and L2 speakers' knowledge of lexical bundles'. *Language Learning* 59 (3): 647–686.

Nelson, L. R. 2001. *Item Analysis for Tests and Surveys Using Lertap 5.* Retrieved June 282009, from http://assess.com/xcart/product.php?productid=235anddownload=1andnext=1andfile=Lertap5Man.zip.

Nelson, L. R. 2008. 'Lertap (Version 5)'. Retrieved July 21 2009, from http://assess.com/xcart/product.php?productid=235andcat=0andpage=1

Neter, J., M. H. Kutner, C. J. Nachtsheim, W. Wasserman. 1996. *Applied Linear Statistical Models* (4th ed.). Chicago: Richard D. Irwin.

Norris, J. M., J. D. Brown, T. Hudson, and **J. Yoshioka.** 1998. *Designing Second Language Performance Assessments* (Technical Report No. 18). Honolulu: University of Hawai'i, Second Language Teaching and Curriculum Center.

North, B. 1997. 'The development of a common framework scale of descriptors of language proficiency based on a theory of measurement' in A. Huhta, V. Kohonen, L. Kurki-Suonio, and S. Luoma (eds.). *Current Developments and Alternatives in Language Assessment: Proceedings of LTRC '96.* Jyväskylä, Finland: University of Jyväskylä and University of Tampere.

Ockey, G. J. 2009a. 'Developments and challenges in the use of computer-based testing (CBT) for assessing second language ability'. *Modern Language Journal* 93 (s1): 836–847.

Ockey, G. J. 2009b. 'The effects of a test taker's group members' personalities on the test taker's second language group oral discussion test scores'. *Language Testing* 26 (2): 161–186.

Oller, J. W. 1972. 'Dictation as a test of ESL proficiency' in H. B. Allen and R. N. Campbell (eds.). *Teaching English as a Second Language: A Book of Readings* (2nd ed., pp. 346–354.

Oller, J. W. 1979. *Language Tests at School.* New York: Longman.

O'Neill, T. R., C. W. Buckendahl, B. S. Plake, and **L. Taylor.** 2007. 'Recommending a nursing-specific passing standard for the IELTS Examination'. *Language Assessment Quarterly* 4 (4): 295–317.

O'Sullivan, B. 2002. 'Investigating variability in a test of second language writing ability'. *Research Notes* 7: 14–17. Retrieved April 6 2008, from http://www.cambridgeesol.org/rs_notes/rs_nts7.pdf.

Peck, S. 2001. 'Developing children's listening and speaking in ESL' in M. Celce-Murcia (ed.). *Teaching English as a Second or Foreign Language.* Boston: Heinle and Heinle, 3rd ed., pp. 139–149.

Perkins, J. and **B. Jones.** 1985. 'Measuring passage contribution in ESL reading comprehension'. *TESOL Quarterly* 19 (1): 137–153.

Plakans, L. 2009. 'Discourse synthesis in integrated second language writing assessment'. *Language Testing* 26 (4): 561–587.

Porter, D. 1978. 'Cloze procedure and equivalence'. *Language Learning* 28: 333–341.

Powers, D. E. and **S. T. Wilson.** 1993. *Passage Dependence of the New SAT Reading Comprehension Questions.* (ERIC Document Reproduction Service No. ED346082; College Board Report No. 93–3; Educational Testing Service Research Report No. 96–60). New York: College Entrance Examination Board.

Purpura, J. E. 2004. *Assessing Grammar.* Cambridge: Cambridge University Press.

Rahimi, M. 2007. L2 reading comprehension test in the Persian context: Language of presentation as a test method facet. *The Reading Matrix* 7 (1): 151–165.

Read, J. 2000. *Assessing Vocabulary.* Cambridge: Cambridge University Press.

Read, J. 2007. 'Second language vocabulary assessment: Current practices and new directions'. *International Journal of English Studies* 7 (2): 105–125.

Reinders, H. 2009. 'Learner uptake and acquisition in three grammar-oriented production activities'. *Language Teaching Research* 13 (2): 201–222.

Rietveld, T., R. van Hout, and **M. Ernestus.** 2004. 'Pitfalls in corpus research'. *Computers and the Humanities* 38 (4): 343¬–362.

Riley, G. L. and **J. F. Lee.** 1996. 'A comparison of recall and summary protocols as measures of second language reading comprehension'. *Language Testing* 13 (2): 173–189.

Robb, T., S. Ross, and **I. Shortreed.** 1986. 'Salience of feedback on error and its effect on EFL writing quality'. *TESOL Quarterly* 20 (1): 83–95.

Rupp, A. A., T. Ferne, and **H. Choi.** 2006. 'How assessing reading comprehension with multiple-choice questions shapes the construct: A cognitive processing perspective'. *Language Testing* 23 (4): 441–474.

Savignon, S. J. 2001. 'Communicative language teaching for the Twenty-First Century' in M. Celce-Murcia (ed.). *Teaching English as a Second or Foreign Language,* pp. 13–28.

Sawaki, Y. and **S. Nissan.** 2009. *Criterion-Related Validity of the TOEFL® iBT Listening Section.* (TOEFL iBT Research Report No. TOEFLiBT-08; ETS Research Report No. RR-09-02). Retrieved July 5 2010, from http://www.ets.org/Media/Research/pdf/RR-09-02.pdf.

Sciarone, A. G. and **J. J. Schoorl.** 1989. 'The cloze test: Or why small isn't always beautiful'. *Language Learning* 39: 415–438.

Shaha, S. H. 1982. *Reduced Anxiety and Increased Assessment Effectiveness with Matching Test Formats* (Center for the Study of Evaluation Report No. 192). Los Angeles, CA: Graduate School of Education, University of California, Los Angeles. Retrieved June 20 2009, from http://www.cse.ucla.edu/products/reports/R192.pdf.

Shaha, S. H. 1984. 'Matching-tests: Reduced anxiety and increased test effectiveness'. *Educational and Psychological Measurement* 44(4): 869–881.

Shavelson, R. J. and **N. M. Webb.** 1991. *Generalizability Theory: a Primer.* Newbury Park, CA: Sage.

Shaw, S. D. and **C. J. Weir.** 2007. *Examining Writing: Research and Practice in Assessing Second Language Writing.* Cambridge: University of Cambridge Local Examinations Syndicate/Cambridge University Press.

Sheen, Y. 2009. 'Recasts, language anxiety, modified output, and L2 learning'. *Language Learning* 58 (4): 835–874.

Shepard, L. A. 1993. 'Evaluating test validity'. *Review of Research in Education* 19: 405–450.

Sherman, J. 1997. 'The effect of question preview in listening comprehension tests'. *Language Testing* 14 (2): 185–213.

Shin, S. 2008. 'Examining the construct validity of a web-based academic listening test: An investigation of the effects of response formats'. *Spaan Fellow Working Papers in Second or Foreign Language Assessment* 6: 95–129.

Shin, S. K. 2005. 'How much is good enough? Setting and validating performance standards and cut scores for the Web-Based English as a Second Language Placement Exam at UCLA'. (Doctoral dissertation, University of California, Los Angeles, 2005). *Dissertation Abstracts International, A: The Humanities and Social Sciences* 66 (2): 575.

Schmitt, N. 1999. 'The relationship between TOEFL vocabulary items and meaning, association, collocation and word-class knowledge'. *Language Testing* 16 (2): 189–216.

Schmitt, N., and **B. Dunham.** 1999. 'Exploring native and non-native intuitions of word frequency'. *Second Language Research* 15 (4): 389–411.

Shohamy, E. 1984. 'Does the testing method make a difference? The case of reading comprehension'. *Language Testing* 1: 147–170.

Shohamy, E. 2001. *The Power Of Tests: A Critical Perspective on the Uses of Language Tests.* Harlow, England: Pearson Education Limited.

Sireci, S. G. 2007. 'On validity theory and test validation'. *Educational Researcher* 36 (8): 477–481.

Sireci, S. G., S. E. Scarpati, and **S. Li.** 2005. 'Test accommodations for students with disabilities: An analysis of the interaction hypothesis'. *Review of Educational Research* 75 (4): 457–490.

Sireci, S. G., A. Wiley, and **L. A. Keller.** 1998. *An Empirical Evaluation of Selected Multiple-Choice Item-Writing Guidelines.* Paper presented at the Annual Meeting of the Northeastern Educational Research Association, Ellenville, NY. (ERIC Document Reproduction Service No. ED428122).

Skorupski, W. P. and **R. K. Hambleton.** 2005. 'What are panelists thinking when they participate in standard-setting studies?' *Applied Measurement in Education* 18 (3): 233–256.

Stansfield, C. W. (April 27 1977). *Dictation as a Measure of Spanish Language Proficiency.* 'Paper presented at the annual convention of the Teachers of English to Speakers of Other Languages'. Miami, FL. (ERIC Document Reproduction Service No. ED139281).

Stansfield, C. W. 1985. 'A history of dictation in foreign language teaching and testing'. *The Modern Language Journal* 69 (2): 121–128.

Stevenson, D. K. 1985. 'Authenticity, validity and a tea party'. *Language Testing* 2 (1): 41–47.

Stubbs, M. 2004. 'Language corpora' in A. Davies and C. Elder (eds.). *The Handbook of Applied Linguistics.* Malden, MA: Blackwell Publishing, pp. 106–132.

Swender, E., K. E. Breiner-Sanders, L. M. Laughlin, P. Lowe, Jr., and **J. Miles.** 1999. *ACTFL Oral Proficiency Interview Tester Training Manual.* Yonkers, NY: The American Council on the Teaching of Foreign Languages.

Taylor, L. 2004. 'Testing times: Research directions and issues for Cambridge ESOL Examinations'. *TESOL Quarterly* 38 (1): 141–146.

Taylor, L. 2008. 'Language varieties and their implications for testing and assessment' in L. Taylor and C. J. Weir (eds.). *Multilingualism and Assessment: Achieving Transparency, Assuring Quality, Sustaining Diversity.* Cambridge: University of Cambridge Local Examinations Syndicate/Cambridge University Press.

Taylor, L. and **F. Barker.** 2008. 'Using corpora for language assessment' in E. Shohamy and N. H. Hornberger (eds.). *Encyclopedia of Language and Education* (2nd ed.). Heidelberg, Germany: Springer Science + Business Media, pp. 1–14.

Taylor, L. and **M. Gutteridge.** 2003. 'Responding to diversity: Providing tests for language learners with disabilities'. *Research Notes* 11: 2–4. Retrieved June 27 2010, from http://www.cambridgeesol.org/rs_notes/offprints/pdfs/RN11p2-4.pdf.

Thorndike, R. L., and **E. Hagen.** 1969. *Measurement and Evaluation in Psychology and Education* (3rd ed.). New York: John Wiley and Sons.

Toulmin, S. E. 2003. *The Uses of Argument.* Cambridge: Cambridge University Press.

Trappes-Lomax, H. 2004. 'Discourse analysis' in A. Davies and C. Elder (eds.). *The Handbook of Applied Linguistics.* Malden, MA: Blackwell Publishing, pp. 133–164.

Tuinman, J. J. 1973–1974. 'Determining the passage dependency of comprehension questions in 5 major tests'. *Reading Research Quarterly* 9 (2): 206–223.

University of Cambridge ESOL Examinations. 2008. *Exams.* Retrieved March 29 2008, from http://www.cambridgeesol.org/exams/index.html.

University of Cambridge ESOL Examinations. 2009. *Information for Candidates.* Retrieved June 6 2010, from http://www.ielts.org/PDF/Information_for_Candidates_2009.pdf.

van Lier, L. 1989. 'Reeling, writhing, drawling, stretching, and fainting in coils: Oral proficiency interviews as conversation'. *TESOL Quarterly* 23: 489–508.

Van Moere, A. 2006. 'Validity evidence in a university group oral test'. *Language Testing* 23 (4): 411–440.

Vongpumivitch, V. 2004. 'Measuring the knowledge of text structure in academic English as a second language (ESL)' (Doctoral dissertation, University of California, Los Angeles, 2004). *Dissertation Abstracts International* 65 (9): 3314A–3315A. (UMI No. DA3147737).

Wainer, H. and **D. Thissen.** 2001. 'True score theory: The traditional method' in D. Thissen and H. Wainer (eds.). *Test Scoring.* Mahwah, NJ: Lawrence Erlbaum Associates.

Wanzek, J., G. Roberts, S. Linan-Thompson, S. Vaughn, A. Woodruff, and **C. Murray.** 2010. 'Differences in the relationship of oral reading fluency and high-stakes measures of reading comprehension'. *Assessment for Effective Intervention* 35 (2): 67–77.

Weigle, S. C. 1994. 'Effects of training on raters of ESL compositions'. *Language Testing* 11 (2): 197–223.

Weigle, S. C. 1998. 'Using FACETS to model rater training effects'. *Language Testing* 15 (2): 263–287.

Weigle, S. C. 2002. *Assessing Writing.* Cambridge: Cambridge University Press.

van Weijan, D., H. van den Bergh, G. Rijlaarsdam, and **T. Sanders.** 2009. 'L1 use during L2 writing: An empirical study of a complex phenomenon'. *Journal of Second Language Writing* 18 (4): 235–250.

Wigglesworth, G. and **C. Elder.** 2010. 'An investigation of the effectiveness and validity of planning time in speaking test tasks'. *Language Assessment Quarterly* 7 (1): 1–24.

Wolf, D. F. 1993. 'A comparison of assessment tasks used to measure FL reading comprehension'. *The Modern Language Journal* 77: 473–489.

Xi, X. 2005. 'Do visual chunks and planning impact performance on the graph description task in the SPEAK exam?' *Language Testing* 22: 463–508.

Xi, X. 2007. 'Validating TOEFL® iBT Speaking and setting score requirements for ITA screening'. *Language Assessment Quarterly* 4 (4): 318–351.

Xi, X. 2008. 'What and how much evidence do we need? Critical considerations in validating an automated scoring system' in C. A. Chapelle, Y. R. Chung, and J. Xu (eds.). *Towards Adaptive CALL: Natural Language Processing for Diagnostic Language Assessment.* Ames, IA: Iowa State University, pp. 102–114.

Yang, Y., C. W. Buckendahl, P. J. Juszkeiwicz, and **D. S. Bhola.** 2002. 'A review of strategies for validating computer-automated scoring'. *Applied Measurement in Education* 15 (4): 391–412.

Young, D. J. 1987. 'The relationship between a communicative competence oriented dictation and ACTFL's Oral Proficiency Interview'. *Hispania* 70 (3): 643–649.

Zimmerman, D. W., R. H. Williams, and **D. L. Symons.** 1984. 'Empirical estimates of the comparative reliability of matching tests and multiple-choice tests'. *Journal of Experimental Education* 52 (3): 179–182.

INDEX

CD-ROM LIST OF CONTENTS

Video Tutorials to accompany Worksheets within Chapters 11–19

The following video tutorials demonstrate how to complete most of the worksheets in *Designing and Analyzing Language Tests*.

Please note: There is no video tutorial to accompany either of Worksheets 18.2 and 19.1.